CROSS
and
SWORD

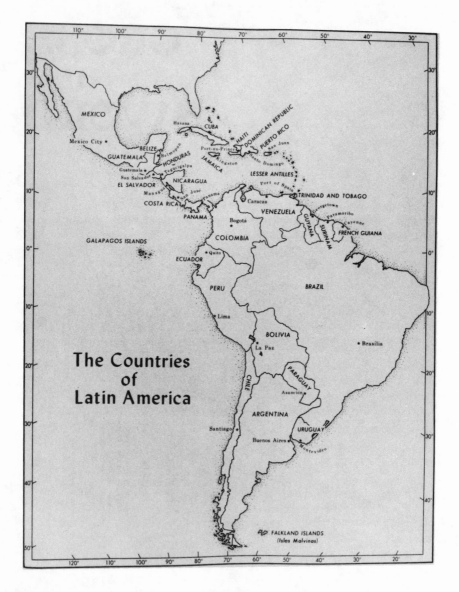

The Countries of Latin America

CROSS and SWORD

*An Eyewitness History
of Christianity in Latin America*

**H. McKennie Goodpasture,
Editor**

ORBIS BOOKS

Maryknoll, New York 10545

The cover design by Patricia Curran was based on drawings by an Aztec artist of the sixteenth century

Library of Congress Cataloging in Publication Data

Cross and sword: an eyewitness history of Christianity in Latin
  America/H. McKennie Goodpasture. editor.
      p. cm.
    Includes bibliographical references.
    ISBN 0-88344-590-5. — ISBN 0-88344-591-3 (pbk.)
    1. Latin America — Church history — Sources. I. Goodpasture, H.
  McKennie.
  BR600.C765 1989
  278 — dc20
                                                            89-36324
                                                              CIP

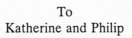

To
Katherine and Philip

Contents

Illustrations

Preface

"Latin America is in the process of upheaval," wrote Herbert L. Matthews thirty years ago. "It is one of the most dramatic and explosive movements in all history. ... [D]ynamic forces are creating a situation comparable in its way, and in the impact it is going to have on the Western World, to the European Renaissance."[1] That process of transformation has now been under way for several decades. A surprising factor in it has been the changing role of the Catholic Church and its corollaries within the Protestant churches. In both of these traditions, unprecedented debate and renewal are under way.

Without some acquaintance with the history of the churches, today's currents may be difficult to understand, and the astonishing newness and urgency in some of them may be missed. Furthermore, since 1992 is at hand and will be such a notable date—the 500th anniversary of the landing of Christopher Columbus and of the first Catholic mass in the New World—this is a convenient time to review the record. A year later, Columbus's second expedition left on the island of Hispaniola a continuing Spanish settlement and a church.

Over the intervening years, the story of Christianity in the Caribbean and throughout Latin America has been intriguing. In the pages of this book, it is my purpose to let observers who were on the scene in each period tell that story. Since history is a tapestry of many colors and designs, it is appropriate that in what follows no less than one hundred and eighteen people are called in as witnesses to what happened. Their writings are not official documents, such as those produced at a distance by popes, councils, or mission boards. Rather they are first-hand, vivid descriptions by interested individuals who were participants in what they described. This, then, is a history through letters, diaries, and travel reports written by men and women and at least one child who were eyewitnesses and often deeply engaged in the life of the churches and the missions. I have tried to select readings that are fresh, informative, and interesting, so that through them readers may enter into dialogue with the past and gain insights into the present.

The readings are placed within a three-part periodization that I developed from the published papers of a group of prominent Latin American and Caribbean historians. The group includes Catholics and Protestants and is called CEHILA, an acronym for The Commission of Studies for Latin American Church History. The dates that I have selected to mark off the major periods have both political and ecclesiastical importance. In the first period, 1492–1808, we have the church's life during the colonial era, "Hispanic Christendom." The second period, 1808–1962, covers the break-up of Christendom, the old church-state synthesis, and the emergence of religious diversity with the coming of the Protestants. The third period, 1960–1985, features the region-wide struggle for liberation and contains the most dramatic shifts in the life of the churches. These changes were stimulated by numerous cooperative and ecumenical efforts, by Vatican Council II, and by the increasing confrontation of the churches with poverty and injustice.

Each of the three major eras and each of their subdividing chapters are introduced with a brief summary of their prominent events. Within these chapters come the eyewitness accounts, and over each one is a headnote to identify the writer, the date and context. Thus anyone reading through the whole or a part of the work will have the freshness of the individual accounts and also a connected story.

My inspiration for this work came from reading the fascinating and comprehensive anthology *Latin American Civilization,* edited by Benjamin Keen (2 vols., 3rd. ed. [Boston: Houghton Mifflin, Co., 1974]). Those readings, many of which I was using in my classes, challenged me to make a similar collection focusing on the churches. In the middle 1970s, when I first envisioned this work, I visited Professor Keen at Northern Illinois University at De Kalb and was pleased by his welcome and encouragement.

My research was greatly helped by having close at hand the resources of the Library of Congress, where Everette E. Larson, Reference Librarian in the Hispanic Division, was an untiring source of information, help, and friendship. The Library at Union Theological Seminary in Virginia has considerable holdings in Latin American religious studies, and the library staff continually supplemented their holdings for me through inter-library loans. To the librarian, John B. Trotti; associate librarian, Martha B. Aycock; assistant reference librarians, Cecilia Clark, Nancy Gladden, and Elaine Christensen; catalogist, Dottie G. Thomason; and acquisitions librarian, Hobbie Bryant, I owe a large debt of gratitude. In addition, three other libraries have been helpful during my repeated visits: the Virginia State Library, the Library of the Virginia Commonwealth University, and the Royal Library at Copenhagen, Denmark.

While this book was in manuscript form, several people kindly read it: Richard Foulkes, Alan Neely, John H. Sinclair, and the late Orlando E. Costas. Their interest and suggestions were invaluable. My thanks also go to Sally Hicks of the staff of Union Seminary, who typed the manuscript and saw it through many revisions before it went to the publisher.

To Robert Ellsberg, editor-in-chief of Orbis Books, and Eve Drogin, the senior editor, I am especially indebted. Their good judgment and eagle eye were a great help in clarifying the text and reducing the number of inevitable errors.

Special appreciation goes to my wife. Her youth in Venezuela, working years with me in Portugal, companionship on various travel-studies in Latin America, keen interest in the literature of the region, and consistent enthusiasm for this project made her suggestions invaluable.

H. McKennie Goodpasture
Richmond, Virginia

CROSS
and
SWORD

Part 1

Hispanic Christendom
of the Indies

1492-1808

When the Spanish ships first arrived in the Caribbean in 1492, no one realized how widespread European rule would become over the next three hundred years. Over that period, the church would be an intimate co-partner with colonial power and privilege. It would also be deeply engaged with the lives of ordinary people.

The story was one of conquest and colonization, and along with both went the church. The enterprise began around the Caribbean basin, and from there spread outward to the surrounding mainlands. Within a few decades the conquerors even crossed the Isthmus of Panama to connect with Peru. Fueling the enterprise was an annual cycle of ships coming from Spain. Each one brought soldiers, merchants, priests, and missionaries and took home silver, gold, other produce, and passengers going the opposite direction. Each spring, the galleons would sail south from Spain to the Canary Islands on Africa's northwest coast, then ride the east winds across to the ports of the Caribbean islands and the mainland. After a summer of trade, the ships would reassemble in Havana; and, fending off the French and English pirates, they would ride the Gulf Stream to the coast of North Carolina, and catch the west winds back home.

The church that came on those ships was a part of Spanish and later Portuguese Christendom; it was not a separate, voluntary body of believers but included everyone on shipboard. The church was part and parcel of the state. Queen Isabella and King Ferdinand were faithful Catholics; they and their subjects considered Christianity to be of the essence of Spanish life. Bishops, priests, and religious orders were agents for maintaining civilization. Such intimacy between throne and altar was not unique to Iberia; it had been the tradition in medieval Europe since Charlemagne. Nevertheless, it assumed a renewed intensity in Iberia around 1500. The reason was not hard to find.

In the Crusades against the Muslims and Jews of the twelfth and thirteenth centuries, most of the European Christian armies, in order to fight the "infidels," had to leave their own countries. However, this was not the case in Spain and Portugal. Since the Muslims of north Africa had invaded their peninsula in the eighth century and had remained in control of most of it, the Spanish and Portuguese perceived the Crusades in Iberia as a reconquest of their own territory. Finding their unity in Christianity, the small rival kingdoms in the north of Spain and Portugal crusaded in the name of Christ and pushed the Muslims down the peninsula to Granada in the south of Spain. A consequence of that victory on home soil was the embedding in Iberian self-identity and in their church of a spirit of triumphalism.

This enthusiasm for crusading should have faded into the distant past by the end of the fifteenth century, but quite the opposite happened. In the 1470s–1490s, when Isabella and Ferdinand sought unity and renewal for their realm, they activated the Inquisition, set about reforming the religious orders, and sent their armies to oust the remaining Muslims in the south. In the process, they also expelled the Jews; so the Crusades had clearly returned. Furthermore, these conquests at home were contemporaneous with amazing discoveries abroad. On the wider Catholic scene, the Iberian successes appeared to be a divine answer to the new threat of the Muslims on the east flank of Europe, where the Turks had shocked the Christians, East and West, by capturing Constantinople in 1453. In gratitude to Spain and Portugal and in hope of their continuing victories, the popes issued a series of bulls granting these countries the lands and peoples that they were discovering. The colonizers were also commissioned to Christianize the new areas. Thus, the Iberian crowns were the patrons of evangelization, and in turn the church was an agency of the state's civilizing and governing. The medieval synthesis was now being exported to the New World.

When the Europeans arrived in the Indies, they met a race of people who were already there, the native Americans. The ancestors of these people had probably migrated from Asia by way of the Bering Strait thousands of years earlier. Slowly, they had diffused across the two continents and the Caribbean. Those who had settled in the highlands of Mexico and Peru and in parts of southern Mexico and Guatemala had attained the highest cultural development. Their science and social order were impressive, but their military capacities were no match for the weapons, horses, and fighting skills of the Iberians.

The Europeans quickly dominated every area they entered. With the help of missionary friars, the conquerors pacified and evangelized the Indians, and also extracted their labor. The methods employed occasionally disturbed the European conscience. When protests arose, they usually came from the missionary orders. This was not surprising, for when the church was planted among the Indians, the process had involved not only coercion but also genuine pastoral care. Sensitive missionaries could see the destructive impact of forced labor. The few prophets among them, however, could not stop the slavery. During the three centuries which followed, the impact of colonial rule proved to be devastating to the indigenous populations and to the growing numbers of mixed bloods. The highland Indians survived better than those in the lowlands, who were less sophisticated. Perhaps this was because the highlanders, long accustomed to hierarchical structures, were better able to adjust to the imposition of yet another one.

The "Christendom" reality, the interlacing and blending of church and state, continued without serious challenge throughout the colonial era. By the late eighteenth century, however, ideas from the Enlightenment seeped into the colonies and combined with local factors for change; the mix eventually broke up the old synthesis. When that happened in the nineteenth century, church leadership was not prepared.

Bartholomé de Las Casas (1474-1566), Dominican missionary, historian, and defender of the Indians.

1 ✠ First Steps of the Church in the New World

1492-1519

When Columbus returned to Spain in 1493 after the first voyage to the Indies, his reports caused excitement in many parts of society. Spanish religious life was as stirred and hopeful as any other. Reports of fruitful lands and simple, friendly people stimulated a thirst for souls as well as for wealth. Before the second voyage, Queen Isabella wrote Columbus that her first concern was the conversion of the natives in the new land, and Pope Alexander VI gave his full support. When he granted the western isles to Spain in a papal bull in 1493, he commissioned the crown to "bring to the worship of our Redeemer and the profession of the Catholic faith their residents and inhabitants, . . ."

On his second crossing, Columbus took a large fleet and included among the passengers twelve Franciscan friars. When he arrived in the Caribbean, he installed them with a group of other passengers on the island of Hispaniola (Dominican Republic and Haiti). For the next twenty-five years, this island was to be the center of the Spanish conquests and church life, and from it would radiate all Spanish administration and expansion.

When the Spaniards arrived in the Indies, a large population of native people, or Caribs, were there, but they would not last long. The conquerors did not consider themselves laborers, and had not come to settle but to get rich quickly and return. In the end, this meant that the hope of evangelizing the Indians and even the continued existence of the Indians would be in jeopardy.

During their first years on Hispaniola, the Spanish were poorly organized, and Indian revolts, hunger and disease were common. Ships returned to Spain with sad stories and with more disillusionment than riches. But a new start came in 1501 when the queen sent Governor Nicolás de Ovando, a capable administrator who stopped the anarchy, organized the search for gold, and attracted more Spanish adventurers. By 1504, a number of clergy and churches had appeared on Hispaniola and also on neighboring Puerto Rico. In the same year, the queen assumed royal patronage over the church in the new area, as she had in Spain, and appointed three bishops for it. In 1508, Pope Julius II confirmed her move by conceding to the crown authorization to name and place all the bishops and other personnel, and also to map out the dioceses and determine the location of all churches and church-related structures. In return for these powers, the crown agreed to pay all the church's expenses.

As for evangelization, Isabella combined it with her labor policy, and decreed that the islanders were to submit to the teaching of the church and be obliged to work, but they were not to be enslaved. This was the official position; nevertheless, the conquerors soon found that the comfortable life that they desired and the riches that the crown wanted required an obligatory labor system. As a consequence, any work of evangelization was virtually nullified.

While the Spanish worked the Caribbean, the Portuguese were circling Africa and developing a lucrative spice trade in southern Asia. To them, the lands on the west side of the Atlantic were less important. Nevertheless, in 1500, while Pedro Álvares Cabral was leading a Portuguese expedition to India and sailed off course, he sighted an "island" that turned out to be the northeast coast of Brazil. On April 26, his expedition christened it "the land of the true cross," and planted the Portuguese flag, calling on his priests to celebrate mass. Thus they claimed the land, but no colony or church was established until the first group of settlers arrived in 1532, a generation later.

MISSION OF COLUMBUS

"Your Highnesses . . . propagators of the Christian faith, . . ."

In an excerpt from the journal of Christopher Columbus, we find the evangelistic motivation behind the Spanish venture to the West. The way he expressed it recalls the spirit of the old Crusades, which had been reignited in 1492 by Spain's victory over the Muslim kingdom of Granada in the south of the peninsula. Later that year, Columbus sailed and wrote these lines to the King and Queen.[1]

✠ In the name of the Lord Jesus Christ, the Most Christian, the most high, the most excellent and most powerful princes, King and Queen of the Spains. . . . In this present year 1492, after Your Highnesses had brought to an end the war against the Moors who reigned in Europe, and after Your Highnesses had terminated this war in the very great city of Granada, where, in this present year, on the 2nd of the month of January, I saw, by force of arms, the royal banners of Your Highnesses planted on the towers of the Alhambra, the citadel of the said city, and where I saw the Moorish king come out of his gates and kiss the royal hands of Your Highnesses;

And immediately afterwards, in this same month, in consequence of information which I had given Your Highnesses on the subject of India, and of the Prince who is called the 'Great Khan,' which, in our Roman, means 'the King of Kings'—namely, that many times he and his predecessors had sent ambassadors to Rome to seek doctors of our holy faith, to the end that they should teach it in India, and that never has the Holy Father been able so to do, so that accordingly so many peoples were being lost, through falling into idolatry and receiving sects of perdition among them;

Your Highnesses, as good Christian and Catholic princes, devout and propagators of the Christian faith, as well as enemies of the sect of Mahomet and of all idolatries and heresies, conceived the plan of sending me, Christopher Columbus, to this country of the Indies, there to see the princes, the peoples, the territory, their disposition and all things else, and the way in which one might proceed to convert these regions to our holy faith.

And Your Highnesses have ordered that I should go, not by land, towards the East, which is the accustomed route, but by way of the West, whereby hitherto nobody to our knowledge has ever been. And so, after having expelled all the Jews from all your kingdoms and lordships, in this same month of January, Your Highnesses ordered me to set out, with a sufficient fleet, for the said country of India, and, to this end, Your Highnesses have shown me great favour. . . .

A LABOR POLICY

" . . . force the . . . Indians to associate with the Christians . . ."

From the beginning of the Spanish conquest, there arose a conflict between the desire to evangelize the Indians on the one hand and the demand for massive amounts of Indian labor on the other. In 1503, Isabella wrote to her governor on Hispaniola that she wanted both these desires fulfilled. She aimed toward a policy that would provide workers and also teach the faith. Her instructions became the basis for the encomienda system that persisted through the whole colonial period. [2]

✠ Medina del Campo, Dec. 20, 1503. Isabella, by the Grace of God, Queen of Castile, etc. In as much as the King, my Lord, and I, in the instruction we commanded given to Don Fray Nicholas de Ovando, Comendador mayor of Alcantara, at the time when he went to the islands and mainland of the Ocean Sea, decreed that the Indian inhabitants and residents of the island of Española, are free and not subject . . . and as now we are informed that because of the excessive liberty enjoyed by the said Indians they avoid contact and community with the Spaniards to such an extent that they will not even work for wages, but wander about idle, and cannot be had by the Christians to convert to the Holy Catholic Faith; and in order that the Christians of the said island . . . may not lack people to work their holdings for their maintenance, and may be able to take out what gold there is on the island . . . and because we desire that the said Indians be converted to our Holy Catholic Faith and taught in its doctrines; and because this can better be done by having the Indians living in community with the Christians of the island, and by having them go among them and associate with them, by which means they will help each other to cultivate and settle and increase the fruits of the island and take the gold which may be there and bring profit to my kingdom and subjects.

I have commanded this my letter to be issued on the matter, in which I command you, our said Governor, that beginning from the day you receive my letter you will compel and force the said Indians to associate with the Christians of the island and to work on their buildings, and to gather and mine the gold and other metals, and to till the fields and produce food for the Christian inhabitants and dwellers of the said island; and you are to have each one paid on the day he works the wage and maintenance which you think he should have . . . and you are to order each cacique [chief] to take charge of a certain number of the said Indians so that you may make them work wherever necessary, and so that on feast days and such days as you think proper they may be gathered to hear and be taught in matters of the Faith. . . . This the Indians shall perform as free people, which they are, and not as slaves. And see to it that the said Indians are well treated, those who become Christians better than the others, and do not consent or allow that any person do them any harm or oppress them.

I, THE QUEEN

A ROYAL DECREE GOES AWRY

" . . . in those eight years 90 per cent had perished."

The queen's intentions for the native islanders were not carried out through the conquerors' behavior toward them. An eyewitness was Bartolomé de Las Casas, a diocesan priest who came to Hispaniola with Governor Ovando in 1501. Las Casas did some parish work, but spent most of his first ten years as an enforcer of the labor system and as a plantation owner who received allotments of Indian workers from the government. When his change of heart came in 1514, he sold his properties, joined the Dominican order, and dedicated his life to defending the Indians. When he later completed his History of the Indies *(about 1540), he contrasted the points he saw in Isabella's decree of 1503 with the destruction he saw happening in the decade that followed.*[3]

✠ That was the substance of Queen Isabella's warrant; now it is well to mention how the comendador mayor [supreme commander] executed the eight points it contained.

1. I have already said and I repeat, the truth is that in the nine years the comendador governed the island, no measures were taken for the conversion of Indians and no more was done about the matter nor any more thought given to it than if the Indians were sticks, stones, cats or dogs. This applies not only to the comendador and those who owned Indians but also to the Franciscan friars who had come with him. These were good people but they lived religiously in their houses here and in La Vega and had no other aspiration. One thing they did was brought to my knowledge: they asked permission to have the sons of some caciques (few of them to be sure), perhaps four, and taught them to read and write and I suppose their good example taught Christian doctrine, for they were good and lived virtuously.

2. He disrupted villages and distributed Indians at his pleasure, giving fifty to one and a hundred to another, according to his preferences, and these numbers included children, old people, pregnant women and nursing mothers, families of high rank as well as common people. They called this system "Indian grants" (*repartimientos*) and the King had his grant and his manager in each town who worked his land and mined his part of the gold. The wording of the comendador's Indian grants read like this: "Mr. X, I grant you fifty or a hundred Indians under the cacique X so that you may avail yourself of their services and teach them our holy Catholic Faith," by which was meant, "Mr. X, I grant you fifty or a hundred Indians together with the person of the cacique X, so that you may use them in your lands and your mines and teach them our holy Catholic Faith." And this was the same as to condemn them all to an absolute servitude which killed them in the end, as we shall see. This, then, was the nature of their freedom.

3. The men were sent out to the mines as far as eighty leagues away while their wives remained to work the soil, not with hoes or plowshares drawn by oxen, but with their own sweat and sharpened poles that were far from equaling the equipment used for similar work in Castile. . . . Thus husbands and wives were together only once every eight or ten months and when they met they were so exhausted and depressed on both sides that they had no mind for marital communication and in this way they ceased to procreate. As for the newly born, they died early because their mothers, overworked and famished, had no milk to nurse them, and for this reason, while I was in Cuba, 7,000 children died in three months. Some mothers even drowned their babies from sheer desperation, while others caused themselves to abort with certain herbs that produced stillborn children. . . .

4. The comendador provided continuous work for them. If he imposed

a limitation later I do not remember it, but this is certain, he gave them little rest and most of them worked ceaselessly. He allowed cruel Spanish brutes to supervise Indians: they were called *mineros* if the work was done in the mines and *estancieros* if it was done on plantations. They treated the Indians with such rigor and inhumanity that they seemed the very ministers of Hell, driving them day and night with beatings, kicks, lashes and blows and calling them no sweeter name than dogs. The Spaniards then created a special police to hunt them back because mistreatment and intolerable labor led to nothing but death and the Indians, seeing their companions die, began escaping into the woods. . . . Our own eyes have seen such inhuman conduct several times and God is witness that whatever is said of it falls short of reality.

5. "Moderate labor" turned into labor fit only for iron men: mountains are stripped from top to bottom and bottom to top a thousand times, they dig, split rocks, move stones and carry dirt on their backs to wash it in rivers, while those who wash gold stay in the water all the time with their backs bent so constantly it breaks them; and when water invades the mines, the most arduous task of all is to dry the mines by scooping up pansful of water and throwing it up outside. . . .

6. The comendador arranged to have wages paid as follows, which I swear is the truth: in exchange for his life of services, an Indian received 3 *maravedis* every two days, less one-half a *maravedi* in order not to exceed the yearly half gold peso, that is, 225 *maravedis*, paid them once a year as pin money or *cacona*, as Indians call it, which means bonus or reward. This sum bought a comb, a small mirror and a string of green or blue glass beads, and many did without that consolation for they were paid much less and had no way of mitigating their misery, although in truth, they offered their labor up for nothing, caring only to fill their stomachs to appease their raging hunger and find ways to escape from their desperate lives. . . .

7. I believe the above clearly demonstrates that the Indians were totally deprived of their freedom and were put in the harshest, fiercest, most horrible servitude and captivity which no one who has not seen it can understand. Even beasts enjoy more freedom when they are allowed to graze in the fields. . . .

8. This order was difficult or impossible and not designed to bring Indians to the Faith; indeed, it was pernicious and deadly and designed to destroy all Indians. Obviously, the Queen had not intended the destruction but the edification of the Indians, and the comendador would have done well to consider this, as well as the fact that, had the Queen been alive to see the results of her order, she would have revoked and abominated it. It is amazing how this prudent man did not realize what a deadly pestilence his order was when, at the end of each shift, he found out how many Indians were missing and how the rest suffered. . . . As I said, the Queen died shortly after sending her warrant and therefore never found out about this cruel decimation. Philip and Juana succeeded her, but Philip died before

he could appraise the situation in the Indies and Castile was two years without the presence of a King. Thus, the decimation of these poor Indians had begun and could be kept silent, and when King Hernando came to rule Castile they kept it from him too. About eight years passed under the comendador's rule and this disorder had time to grow; no one gave it a thought and the multitude of people who originally lived on this island, which, according to the admiral, was infinite, as we said in Book I, was consumed at such a rate that in those eight years 90 per cent had perished. From here this sweeping plague went to San Juan, Jamaica, Cuba and the continent, spreading destruction over the whole hemisphere. . . .

FIRST PUBLIC PROTEST

". . . you are all in mortal sin . . ."

The first voices to be heard in public on behalf of the Indians came from some Dominican friars on Hispaniola in 1511. Living ascetically in their primitive chapter house, they served as preachers at the cathedral church where the leading citizens, such as the governor and other colonial authorities, attended mass. As the friars performed their pastoral duties on the island, they were dismayed by the harsh treatment of the Indians and decided to attack the problem in a Sunday sermon. Choosing their best preacher, António Montesinos, they set a Sunday before Christmas for its presentation. The shocked audience demanded a retraction, but on the following Sunday, Montesinos reiterated the charges even more eloquently. Las Casas describes what happened.[4]

✠ Sunday having arrived, and the time for preaching, Father António Montesino rose in the pulpit, and took for the text of his sermon, which was written down and signed by the other friars, "I am the voice of one crying in the wilderness." Having made his introduction and said something about the Advent season, he began to speak of the sterile desert of the consciences of the Spaniards on this isle, and of the blindness in which they lived, going about in great danger of damnation and utterly heedless of the grave sins in which they lived and died.

Then he returned to his theme, saying: "In order to make your sins known to you I have mounted this pulpit, I who am the voice of Christ crying in the wilderness of this island; and therefore it behooves you to listen to me, not with indifference but with all your heart and senses; for this voice will be the strangest, the harshest and hardest, the most terrifying that you ever heard or expected to hear."

He went on in this vein for a good while, using cutting words that made his hearers' flesh creep and made them feel that they were already experiencing the divine judgment. . . . He went on to state the contents of his message.

"This voice," said he, "declares that you are in mortal sin, and live and die therein by reason of the cruelty and tyranny that you practice on these innocent people. Tell me, by what right or justice do you hold these Indians in such cruel and horrible slavery? By what right do you wage such detestable wars on these people who lived mildly and peacefully in their own lands, where you have consumed infinite numbers of them with unheard-of murders and desolations? Why do you so greatly oppress and fatigue them, not giving them enough to eat or caring for them when they fall ill from excessive labors, so that they die or rather are slain by you, so that you may extract and acquire gold every day? And what care do you take that they receive religious instruction and come to know their God and creator, or that they be baptized, hear mass, or observe holidays and Sundays?

"Are they not men? Do they not have rational souls? Are you not bound to love them as you love yourselves? How can you lie in such profound and lethargic slumber? Be sure that in your present state you can no more be saved than the Moors or Turks who do not have and do not want the faith of Jesus Christ.

Thus he delivered the message he had promised, leaving his hearers astounded. Many were stunned, others appeared more callous than before, and a few were somewhat moved; but not one, from what I could later learn, was converted.

When he had concluded his sermon he descended from the pulpit, his head held high, for he was not a man to show fear, of which indeed he was totally free; nor did he care about the displeasure of his listeners, and instead did and said what seemed best according to God. With his companion he went to their straw-thatched house, where, very likely, their entire dinner was cabbage soup, unflavored with olive oil. . . . After he had left, the church was so full of murmurs that . . . they could hardly complete the celebration of the mass.

NATIVE BRAZILIANS

". . . Our Lord gave them fine bodies . . ."

When the India-bound ships of the Portuguese explorer Pedro Álvares Cabral detoured in April of 1500, they unexpectedly reached the coast of Brazil. The native people seemed to the Portuguese to be children of nature, similar to Adam and Eve in the garden before the fall. A member of the expedition, Pedro Vaz de Caminha, wrote that same year for King

Manuel an account of what he saw. The religious values and the feelings
of a sailor, perhaps one too long at sea, are revealed in his description.[5]

✠ They seem to me to be people of such innocence that, if we could
understand them and they us, they would soon become Christians, because
they do not seem to have or to understand any form of religion. . . . For it
is certain that this people is good and of pure simplicity, and there can
easily be stamped upon them whatever belief we wish to give them. And
furthermore, Our Lord gave them fine bodies and good faces as to good
men, and He who brought us here, I believe, did not do so without purpose . . . there were among them three or four girls, very young and very
pretty, with very dark hair, long over the shoulders, and their privy parts
so high, so closed and so free from hair that we felt no shame in looking
hard at them . . . one of the girls was all painted from head to foot with
that [bluish-black] paint, and she was so well built and so rounded, and her
lack of shame was so charming, that many women of our own land seeing
such attractions, would be ashamed that theirs were not like hers.

2 ✠ Missions in New Spain, Peru and Brazil

1519–1551

Hernán Cortés and six hundred soldiers landed in Mexico on Good Friday of 1519. As the Spaniards knelt on the beach in prayer, any Indians who saw them could not have dreamed what they were about to confront. It was not the desire of the Spaniards that the native Mexicans die off, for they wanted Indian laborers and also wished to evangelize them. Nevertheless, over the next seventy-five years, about seventeen million Indians in central Mexico would diminish to about one million. After a rapid conquest, Cortés became the governor of New Spain, and granted to the officers of his army parcels of land and allotments of Indian laborers (*encomiendas*). The crown in Spain controlled the colonial enterprise through the Council of the Indies, established in Seville in 1524. The Council ruled through an administrative court, the *Audiencia*, established in Mexico City in 1527 and later strengthened with a viceroy as its president.

The evangelization of the Indians was a genuine interest of Cortés; he even pleaded with King Charles in 1524 to send Franciscan missionaries. Working together, the missionaries and government officials obliged the scattered Indians to abandon the mountains and settle in concentrated mission villages, called "reductions," where families would be easier to control, educate, and Christianize. Of course, the Indians were also more accessible for labor services. By mid-century, there were hundreds of these "reductions," and wherever the Indians were recalcitrant, the military were at hand to enforce submission. The friars administered these villages, using the farming skills of the Indians and introducing European livestock and horticulture. In the heart of each village was a convent with its church attached. By the 1540s, these had become solid, impressive structures that served for worship and teaching and also as fortresses in the event of Indian uprisings. Also by mid-century, convents for female orders began to appear in Mexico City.

Soon after the conquest of Mexico came the one in Peru. An expedition, led by Francisco Pizarro, set out in 1530 with about 180 men and 27 horses. In 1533, they took the Inca stronghold of Cuzco, looted its wealth, and destroyed its temples. Six of the conquerors were Dominican friars. Later,

Cloister of Augustinian convent at Acolmán, near Mexico City, 1550-60. Such convents served as stations for evangelism and pastoral care of people in the area.

other missionaries and more military recruits and fortune seekers joined the initial group. Vincente de Valverde, the Dominican counselor to Pizarro, became the first bishop and was assigned to Cuzco.

Across the continent, the Portuguese had laid claim to Brazil, but they had neglected their responsibilities. Only in 1532 did King John III finally send out colonists. His plan for the territory was similar to that followed by the Spanish. Large blocks of coastal land, "captaincies," were granted to Portuguese concessionaires, with privileges and duties similar to those of the Spanish *encomenderos*. With the first colonists came priests who dispensed the sacraments to their own people, but who made little effort to reach the native Brazilians. In 1549, the king resolved to establish a capital at Bahía and centralize his control. He sent Tomé de Souza with a large group of colonists, including six of the newly founded Society of Jesus and their Superior, Father Manoel de Nóbrega. The two leaders, Souza and Nóbrega, found the colony to be in social and moral disarray and collaborated to guide its development. As in the case of the Spanish colonies, all the financing and ultimate authority remained with the king in Lisbon.

CORTÉS AS EVANGELIST

". . . the Spaniards baptized a great multitude . . ."

In the Spanish conquest, the figure of Hernán Cortés illustrates the two drives for gold and souls. He was a cunning and ruthless fighter, yet religion played a part in his character. In 1519, as he and his expedition pushed toward Tenochtitlan, present day Mexico City, they passed through a community of people who had long resented Aztec domination, the Tezcoco. As Cortés entered, their prince, Ixtlilxochitl, went to meet him and proposed friendship. That meeting included an example of evangelization, which an anonymous Indian observer described.[6]

✠ At the request of Ixtlilxochitl, Cortes and his men ate the gifts of food that had been brought out from Tezcoco. Then they walked to the city with their new friends, and all the people came out to cheer and welcome them. The Indians knelt down and adored them as sons of the Sun, their gods, believing that the time had come of which their dear king Nezahualpilli had so often spoken. The Spaniards entered the city and were lodged in the royal palace.

Word of these events was brought to the king, Motecuhzoma, who was pleased by the reception his nephews had given Cortes. He was also pleased by what Cohuamacotzin and Ixtlilxochitl had said to the Captain, because he believed that Ixtlilxochitl would call in the garrisons stationed on the frontiers. But God ordered it otherwise.

Cortes was very grateful for the attentions shown him by Ixtlilxochitl and his brothers; he wished to repay their kindness by teaching them the law of God, with the help of his interpreter Aguilar. The brothers and a number of the other lords gathered to hear him, and he told them that the emperor of the Christians had sent him here, so far away, in order that he might instruct them in the law of Christ. He explained the mystery of the Creation and the Fall, the mystery of the Trinity and the Incarnation and the mystery of the Passion and the Resurrection. Then he drew out a crucifix and held it up. The Christians all knelt, and Ixtlilxochitl and the other lords knelt with them.

Cortes also explained the mystery of Baptism. He concluded the lesson by telling them how the Emperor Charles grieved that they were not in God's grace, and how the emperor had sent him among them only to save their souls. He begged them to become willing vassals of the emperor, because that was the will of the pope, in whose name he spoke.

When Cortes asked for their reply, Ixtlilxochitl burst into tears and answered that he and his brothers understood the mysteries very well. Giving thanks to God that his soul had been illumined, he said that he wished to become a Christian and to serve the emperor. He begged for the crucifix, so that he and his brothers might worship it, and the Spaniards wept with joy to see their devotion.

The princes then asked to be baptized. Cortes and the priest accompanying him said that first they must learn more of the Christian religion, but that persons would be sent to instruct them. Ixtlilxochitl expressed his gratitude, but begged to receive the sacrament at once because he now hated all idolatry and revered the mysteries of the true faith.

Although a few of the Spaniards objected, Cortes decided that Ixtlilxochitl should be baptized immediately. Cortes himself served as godfather, and the prince was given the name Hernando, because that was his sponsor's name. His brother Cohuamacotzin was named Pedro because his godfather was Pedro de Alvarado, and Tecocoltzin was named Fernando, with Cortes sponsoring him also. The other Christians became godfathers to the other princes, and the baptisms were performed with the greatest solemnity. If it had been possible, more than twenty thousand persons would have been baptized that very day, and a great number of them did receive the sacrament.

Ixtlilxochitl went to his mother, Yacotzin, to tell her what had happened and to bring her out to be baptized. She replied that he must have lost his mind to let himself be won over so easily by that handful of barbarians, the conquistadors. Don Hernando said that if she were not his mother, he would answer her by cutting off her head. He told her that she would receive the sacrament, even against her will, because nothing was important except the life of the soul.

Yacotzin asked her son to leave her alone for the time being. She said she would think about what he had told her and make her decision the next day. He left the palace and ordered her rooms to be set on fire (though others say that he found her in a temple of idolatry).

Finally she came out, saying that she wanted to become a Christian. She went to Cortes and was baptized with a great many others. Cortes himself was her godfather, naming her Dona Maria because she was the first woman in Tezcoco to become a Christian. Her four daughters, the princesses, were also baptized, along with many other women. And during the three or four days they were in the city, the Spaniards baptized a great multitude of people.

DESTROYING AZTEC SYMBOLS

"Shall we not do something for God?"

The Spanish conquerors and most of the clergy totally rejected the Aztec religion. By the middle 1500s, however, a few missionary friars, like Bernardino de Sahagún and Toribio de Motolinía were seriously studying it. Their bishops considered such inquiries to represent dangerous sympathies for the pagans; consequently, the friars' manuscripts were sequestered. The works were not published until the nineteenth century. In the account that follows, Andrés de Tápia, one of Cortés' officers, describes his commander's encounter in 1520 with Aztec religious images in Tenochtitlan, Mexico City.[7]

✠ Walking in the court of the idols, the marquis said to me, "Climb up that Tower and see what there is in it." So I went up with some of the native priests and came to a thickly-woven veil on which were hung many small bells. When I moved it to enter, it made such a sound that I thought the house was falling about me. The marquis, to pass the time, climbed up also with eight or ten Spaniards, and because this veil made the room so dark, with our swords we cut it down and the room became quite light. . . . About the walls were images of their gods. . . . The marquis, at the sight of the blood of sacrifice, sighed and cried out, "Oh God, why dost thou permit the devil to be so greatly honored in this land? Lord, let it appear good to thee that we serve thee!"

Calling his interpreters, he began to speak to the people, for at the sound of the bells many priests had surrounded them. "God, who made the heavens and the earth, made you and us and everybody and gives that which you need. If we are good he will take us to heaven; if we are evil we will go to hell, as we shall explain further when we understand each other better. I desire that here where these idols stand there shall be placed the image of God and his Holy Mother, and that you bring water and wash these walls and take all these things away." The people laughed, as if such a thing could not be done and said, "Not only this city but the whole world have these for gods; and the people esteem their fathers, mothers, sons, or daughters as nothing in comparison with these, and they will die sooner than do so. Already they have taken up their arms and will die for their gods."

The marquis at once despatched a soldier to the palace with orders to guard Montezuma carefully, and to send thirty or forty soldiers. To the priests he replied: "Well pleased am I to fight for my God against your gods which are nothing"; and before the Spaniards arrived, angered at certain words which he heard, he seized an iron bar and began to strike the idols of stone. I swear by my faith as a gentleman and before God it is the truth, it seemed to me that the marquis with a marvelous leap threw himself upon the idol and with the iron bar struck at the eyes of the figure, breaking away thus the golden mask it wore, crying, "Shall we not do something for God?"

The people sent word to the emperor who besought Cortés to allow him to come thither and that meanwhile he should do nothing to the idols. The marquis sent to bring him under heavy guard, and on his arrival, he told us to put up our images on one side, leaving the other to the pagan gods. The marquis was unwilling. Then Montezuma said, "Well, then, I will try to have done that which you wish, but you must give us the idols that we may carry them to any other place we desire." So the marquis consented saying, "See, they are but stone; believe in God who made heaven and earth; and by His works, know the Master." The idols were then taken with great skill and care, and they washed the walls of the rooms. . . . The marquis set up two altars.

MISSIONARY MOTIVATION

". . . God so loved the world . . ."

In 1523, the minister general of the Franciscan order in Spain sent twelve of his friars as missionaries to New Spain and named Fr. Martin de Valencia to be their superior. The instructions he sent along with Fr. Martin give us a remarkable account of the theology that motivated much of the "spiritual conquest" of Mexico in the first half of the sixteenth century.[8]

✠ Fr. Francisco de los Angeles, minister general and servant of the whole Order of the Friars Minor. To the venerable and devoted father, Fr. Martin de Valencia, Custos of the Custody of the Holy Gospel in New Spain and land of Yucatan, and to the other Religious sent by me to the said land, peace and paternal blessing. As long as the hand of the Most High is not shortened in doing mercy toward His creatures, that sovereign Father of families, [our] God and Creator, does not cease to enlist good-will in the vineyard of His Church, so as to gather from it the fruit which His precious Son merited on the Cross. Nor shall He desist onto [sic] the end sending new laborers to His Church. And because in this land of New Spain already mentioned, since its vintage is being gathered by the devil and the flesh, Christ does not enjoy the possession of the souls which He purchased with His Blood, it seems to me that, if Christ lacks for no insults there, neither was there reason for me to lack any feeling concerning them; for I have as great, and even greater reason, than the prophet David to feel and say with him: *zelus domus tuae comedit me, et opprobia exprobrantium ceciderunt super me*. ["The zeal of thy house has eaten me up; and the reproaches of them that reproached thee are fallen upon me," Ps. 68:10.]

And feeling this, and following in the footsteps of our father St. Francis who used to send friars to the places of the infidels, I thought of sending you, father, with twelve companions assigned by me, to those places already mentioned, commanding you and them by virtue of holy obedience to accept this laborious pilgrimage in behalf of the one which Christ the Son of God undertook for us, reminding you that God so loved the world that, to restore it, He sent His only begotten son from heaven to earth, who walked and conversed among men thirty-three years, seeking the honor of God His Father and the salvation of wandering souls, and for these two things lived through many hardships and poverty, humbling Himself even onto death, and death by means of the cross. And on a day before He died He said to His apostles: An example I leave you, that as I have conducted Myself with you, so you also conduct yourselves with one another. This [example] the apostles afterwards showed us by deed and word, by faring through the world preaching the faith with much poverty and hardships, by raising aloft the banner of the cross in foreign parts, to which enterprise they lost their lives with great joy for the love of God and neighbor; knowing that in these two commandments are enclosed the whole law and the prophets. And the saints who came later ever seeking to follow this way of action, and aflame with these two loves of God and neighbor, ran throughout the world as it were with two feet, seeking not their honor but that of God, not their ease but that of their neighbor. . . .

Because even if you do not convert the infidel, but should you drown instead in the sea, or should men kill you, or should the wild beasts devour you, you have done your duty, and God will do His. These few plain and simple words (dear brothers) I have wanted to tell you, more to comply with my duty than to supply your good will. In which I confide more than in mine. . . .

And because I entrust this and all the rest to your superior, I say no more. And other particulars that should be set down, regarding mutual conduct and the conversion of the infidels, I refrain from setting down now, until, when the general chapter comes (if it please our Lord), you give an opinion of what is to be done from the experience you shall have had. And meanwhile I place myself at your discretion, confiding in the grace which our Lord will communicate to you. May He hold you in His keeping.

Datis in the Province of Los Angeles in the friary of Santa Maria de los Angeles, the feast day [Oct. 4] of our father St. Francis, of the year fifteen hundred and twenty-three. Signed by my hand and sealed with the major seal of my office.

Frater Francisco Angelorum, generalis minister et servus.

A FRANCISCAN MISSIONARY

"... teaching boys ... to read, write, preach, and sing; ..."

The evangelistic methods of the Franciscans in New Spain were similar to those used in the early Middle Ages by the Benedictine monks in Britain and western Europe—preaching, teaching, worshiping, and providing practical human services. A major difference was that within the Spanish colonial context the Indian was usually under duress. Peter of Ghent, a Franciscan missionary from Belgium, worked in central Mexico for nearly fifty years, from 1523 until his death in 1572. Here we have an excerpt from his engaging letter to King Charles I, describing his pastoral activities in 1532 and seeking financial support. [9]

✠ Sacred Catholic Caesarean Majesty: ...

Your majesty, I am a lay brother, companion of fray Juan de Tecto, who was father guardian in Ghent when your majesty sent him, along with another friar and myself, to these shores nine years ago, as your majesty may already be aware. Fray Juan de Tecto and the other friar went with the Marques del Valle don Hernando Cortés to the cape of Honduras, and died on the way back, from the storms and hardships of the journey. In the time since we entered this land, through the work of the Lord I have labored middlingly, as a useless servant, at the conversion and instruction of the natives. My task has been and is to teach them Christian doctrine generally, conveying it to them in their language, at first in Texcoco and Tlaxcala, and for the last six years in Mexico City and the surrounding towns, and other towns farther away, making tours and seeking to destroy the idols and idolatries.

Aside from this and other tasks of different kinds relating to conversion, which would be too long to tell, I have had and have charge of teaching boys of different ages to read, write, preach and sing; since I am not or-dained, I have had more time and opportunity for all this. Because of that, and because there is a reasonable ability for these things in the people, fair progress has been made; without falsifying I can say that there are very good scribes, and preachers or speakers of great fervor, and singers who could sing in your majesty's chapel choir, so good that perhaps if it is not seen it will not be believed. To teach and indoctrinate these boys, a school or chapel has been made within the site or enclosures of our house, where continually every day five or six hundred boys are taught.

Next to our monastery we have built an infirmary for the sick among the natives, where besides those who are being taught in the house, others come for treatment, which is a great comfort for the poor and needy, and aid in their conversion, because they come to know the charity that is practiced among Christians, and are attracted to the faith and to liking us well and conversing with us.

For all these things I always try to seek what alms I can, but they are hard to obtain, since most of the natives are poor. The Spaniards, though they perform charities, have other necessities of their own which they are more obliged to meet. If your majesty would order that this work be entirely yours, you could grant us alms that would relieve us of hardship and satisfy all the necessities of your new subjects and vassals; it would be a great augmentation of our holy faith and very much in the service of God our Lord and in earnest of your majesty's salvation. If your majesty would grant three or four thousand bushels of maize each year, a thousand five hundred for the school and the rest for the infirmary and the patients, that or whatever your majesty should grant would be just and very good and a great example so that the natives will believe that your majesty loves them and considers them your children; and indeed they are recognizing it more every day by the rectitude which they see that now, more than in other times, is being maintained in matters of justice, and they are more favored on your majesty's part and by your command, for these people know how to distinguish the good from the bad, and thus they would wish to be subjects of your majesty alone rather than being distributed among the Spaniards.

Our God preserve your Sacred Catholic Caesarean Majesty in your imperial estate and increase your life and illumine you always to do His holy will. Amen. From Mexico City here in New Spain, the eve of All Saints, year of our Lord 1532.

> Chaplain and least vassal of your majesty,
> Fray Pedro de Gant

In the infirmary that I mentioned there are always many patients, at times three or four hundred.

NATURE OF THE INDIANS

"no leaven of goodness"? or "meek as lambs"?

A recurrent debate in the Indies and in Spain was about the basic nature of the native people. Were they fully human? Were they capable of rational thought? Did they have a capacity for the knowledge of God? Among the accounts from firsthand observers were testimonies on both sides. A negative assessment was widely held, and thus Indians were usually barred from the sacrament of Holy Communion. This attitude also helped justify the continued use of forced labor. A bull of Pope Paul III in 1536 declared that the native inhabitants were, indeed, fully human and not to be barred from the eucharist. Nevertheless, the debate continued. The following are two examples of these reflections. The first is from Fray Tomás Ortiz, a Dominican monk in Santa Marta, on the northern coast of Colombia, in 1524.[10] The second is from Toribio de Motolinía, a Franciscan missionary on the central plateau of Mexico, writing about 1540.[11]

I

✠ The men on the mainland of the Indies eat human flesh and are more sodomistic than any generation. There is no justice among them, they go about naked, they feel neither love nor shame, they are asses, stupid, mad, insane; to kill or be killed is all the same to them; they have no truth in them unless it be to their advantage; they are inconstant; they do not know what counsel is; they are ingrates and fond of novelties; they boast of their drunkenness; they distill wine from various herbs, fruits, roots, and grain; they also get drunk on smoke and on certain herbs that steal away their brains; they are bestial in their vices; neither obedience nor courtesy do the young boys show to the old, nor sons to their father; nor are they capable of learning from doctrine and punishment; they are treacherous, cruel, vengeful, for they never forgive; extremely inimical toward religion, idlers, thieves, liars, and poor and mean in judgment; they keep neither faith nor order; men do not stay faithful to their wives, nor wives to their husbands; they are sorcerers, soothsayers, and necromancers; they are as cowardly as rabbits, as dirty as pigs; they eat lice, spiders, and raw worms wherever they find them; they have neither the art nor the dexterity of men; when they forget the matters of faith they have learned, they say that such things are for Castile and not for them, and they wish not to change customs or gods; they are beardless, and if some beard hairs sprout, they pull them out; they treat the sick with no pity at all; even though they be neighbors and kinsmen they leave them helpless at the moment of death; or else they carry them into the wilderness to die with a sup of bread and water; the older they grow the worse they are; up to the age of ten or twelve years, it seems to me they come forth with some breeding or virtue; from then on they become as brute beasts. In short, I say that God never created people so steeped in vices and bestiality, with no leaven of goodness or politeness.

II

✠ There is hardly anything to hinder the Indians from reaching heaven, nothing like the obstacles which hinder us Spaniards and which submerge us. The Indians live in contentment, though what they possess is so little that they have hardly enough to clothe and nourish themselves. Their meal is extremely poor and the same is true of their clothing; for sleep the majority of them have not even a whole mat. They lose no sleep over acquiring and guarding riches, nor do they kill themselves trying to obtain ranks and dignities. They go to bed in their poor blanket and on awakening are immediately ready to serve God; and if they wish to take the discipline, they are neither troubled nor embarrassed with dressing and undressing. They are patient, exceedingly long-suffering, meek as lambs. I do not recall having ever seen them nurturing an injury. They are humble, obedient to all, either of necessity or voluntarily; all they know is to serve and work. They all know how to build a wall and erect a dwelling, to twist a rope, and to engage in such crafts as do not require much skill. Great is their patience and endurance in time of sickness. Their mattress is the hard and bare ground. At most, they have only a ragged mat to sleep on and for a pillow a piece of wood, while some have no other pillow than the bare earth. Their dwellings are very small, some with a very low roof, and others with a roof of straw, while some dwellings resemble the cell of that holy abbot Hilarion, looking more like a grave than a dwelling. The riches that suffice to fill such dwellings show what treasures the Indians have! These Indians live in their little houses—the parents, the children, and the grand-children. They eat and drink without much noise and talking. They spend their days peacefully and amicably. They seek only what is necessary to sustain life.

SPREAD OF THE MISSIONS

"... children ... come every day to be baptized ..."

> *The Franciscans sent the largest number of friars to New Spain. One of their number, Toribio de Motolinía, reviewed the patterns and results of their work as of 1536 and 1540. He evidently combined some manuscripts that he prepared at different times. Even if he exaggerated his report, the initial "spiritual conquest" was remarkably rapid.*[12]

✠ When the land had been conquered and allotted by the Spaniards, the friars of Saint Francis who were there at the time began to go about among the Indians and converse with them, at first only in the places where they had a house of the Order, as was the case in Mexico, Tetzcoco, Tlaxcallan, and Huexotzinco, for the few friars who were there at first were divided among those provinces. In each of these and in those in which the Order later had houses (there are nearly forty in this year of 1540) there was so much to tell that not all the paper in New Spain would suffice....

The town in which the friars first went out to teach was Cuautitlán, four leagues from Mexico. They went also to Tepotzotlán. This they did because there was much disturbance in Mexico, and because among the sons of lords who were being taught in the House of God there were the young lords of these two towns, nephews or grandsons of Moteuczuma and among the most important members of the school. Out of deference to them the friars began to teach in these two towns, and to baptize the children. . . .

The first two years the friars did not go out very much from the town where they had their residence, both because they knew very little of the country and of the language, and because they had plenty to attend to where they lived. The third year the people in Tetzcoco began to assemble daily to learn the catechism, and a great many also came to be baptized; as the province of Tetzcoco is very populous, the friars, both inside and outside of the monastery, were unable to keep up with the work or to help others, for many people were baptized from Tetzcoco, Huetotzinco, Coatlichan, and Coatepec. Here in Coatepec they began to build a church and made great haste to finish it because it was the first church outside of the monasteries. . . .

It is very striking now to see the children that come every day to be baptized, especially here in Tlaxcallan. There are days when we have to perform the baptismal service four or five times. Counting those who come on Sundays, there are weeks when we baptize three hundred children, and sometimes we baptize four or five hundred, taking in the children within the radius of a league. And if ever, out of carelessness or because of some obstacle, we fail to visit the towns two or three leagues away, there are so many to be baptized later that it is a marvel.

Also many have come, and still do come, from a distance to be baptized, bringing their wives and children, the sick and the well, the lame, the blind and the deaf, dragging along and suffering great hardships and hunger, for these people are very poor.

CROSSING THE ATLANTIC

". . . death constantly staring you in the face; . . ."

In the sixteenth century, thousands of soldiers, adventurers, and clergy crossed the perilous Atlantic in Spanish galleons. The precarious conditions of health and life on board usually made those voyages unpleasant and dangerous. Starting from the southwest of Spain at Seville, the ships maneuvered down the Guadalquivir River to the Atlantic, then sailed south to the Canary Islands, where they caught the east winds across to the Caribbean. Fr. Tomás de la Torre, a Dominican friar, accompanied

Bishop Bartolomé de las Casas on his way to Mexico in 1544. He describes the trials of crossing the Atlantic before the days of luxury liners.[13]

✠ After boarding our ship we passed the day there, exposed to a burning sun. On the following day (July 10) we hoisted sail with a very feeble wind, because the sailors said that once on the high seas we could navigate with any kind of wind. That day all the other ships got off that difficult and dangerous sandbar at San Lucar. Only ours remained in the middle of the bar and its dangers. They put the blame on the land pilot; but it was really the fault of our sailors, who had ballasted the ship badly, . . .

The following day, which was Friday, July 11, we raised sails and with perfectly dry eyes lost sight of our Spain. The wind was good but weak. The sea quickly gave us to understand that it was not meant to be the habitation of men, and we all became so deathly sick that nothing in the world could move us from where we lay. Only the Father Vicar and three others managed to keep their feet, but these three were so ill that they could do nothing for us; the Father Vicar alone served us all, placing basins and bowls before us so that we could bring up our scanty meals, which did us no good at all. There were four or five neophytes in our company, on their way to serve God in the Indies, who usually took care of us, but they also became sick and had to be nursed themselves. We could not swallow a mouthful of food, although we were quite faint, but our thirst was intense.

One could not imagine a dirtier hospital, or one that resounded with more lamentations, than ours. Some men went below deck, where they were cooked alive; others roasted in the sun on deck, where they lay about, trampled upon, humiliated, and indescribably filthy; and although after several days some of them had recovered, they were not well enough to serve those who were still sick. His Lordship the Bishop donated his own hens to the sick, for we had not brought any, and a priest who was going as a schoolteacher to Chiapa helped the Father Vicar. . . . We were a pitiful sight indeed, and there was no one to console us, since nearly everyone was in the same condition.

When we left Spain the war with France was at its height, so we departed in great fear of the enemy. On the afternoon of that day those who could raise their heads saw sixteen sails. They feared that they were Frenchmen, and all that night the fleet was much alarmed, although the enemy had greater reason to fear us, because of our superior numbers. But in the morning nothing could be seen, so we decided it was a fleet coming from the Indies. . . . In the evening our stomachs quieted down and we did not vomit, but the heat, especially below deck, was intolerable.

Saturday morning we saw a large boat, and, thinking that it was a French spy, a ship went after it. The bark began to escape, when the ship fired a shot, whereupon the bark lowered its sails, was recognized as Spanish, and was permitted to go in peace. The crews of the vessels that heard the shot thought that we had run into Frenchmen and that the ships were firing at each other. When we below deck heard the noise of arms being got ready, we were alarmed and suddenly recovered enough to say a litany; some even confessed themselves. Others made a joke of the whole affair. When we learned it was nothing at all, we returned to our former supine misery. After this there was no more disturbance.

So that those who do not know the sea may understand the suffering one endures there, especially at the beginning of a voyage, I shall describe some things that are well known to anyone who has sailed on it. First, a ship is a secure prison, from which no one may escape, even though he wears neither shackles nor irons; so cruel is this prison that it makes no distinctions among its inmates but makes them all suffer alike. The heat, the stuffiness, and the sense of confinement are sometimes overpowering. The bed is ordinarily the floor. Some bring a few small mattresses; ours were very poor, small, and hard, stuffed with dog hairs; to cover us we had some extremely poor blankets of goat's wool. Add to this the general nausea and poor health; most passengers go about as if out of their minds and in great torment—some longer than others, and a few for the entire voyage. There is very little desire to eat, and sweet things do not go down well; there is an incredible thirst, sharpened by a diet of hardtack and salt beef. The water ration is half an *azumbre* [1 azumbre = 2 quarts] daily; if you want wine you must bring your own. There are infinite numbers of lice, which eat men alive, and you cannot wash clothing because the sea water shrinks it. There is an evil stink, especially below deck, that becomes intolerable throughout the ship when the pump is working—and it is going more or less constantly, depending on how the ship sails. On a good day the pump runs four or five times, to drain the foul-smelling bilge water.

These and other hardships are common on board ship, but we felt them more because they were so foreign to our usual way of living. Furthermore, even when you are enjoying good health there is no place where you can study or withdraw for a little while, and you have to sit all the time, because there is no room to walk about. . . . The most disturbing thing of all is to have death constantly staring you in the face; you are separated from it by only the thickness of one board joined to another with pitch.

3 ✠ Strengthening and Organizing the Church

1551–1620

Philip II ruled Spanish America from 1556 to 1592. Both he and the church, after the Council of Trent (1545–1563) wished to centralize the political organization and to strengthen the role of the bishops. From the first provincial council of bishops in Lima in 1551, until new dioceses were established to the far north and far south in 1620, the central role of the earlier missionaries and pioneer clergy faded before the increasing power of the church administrators and the Inquisitors. Along with that shift, some of the zeal and higher religious motivation of the first half of the century were lost.

Missionary efforts slowed, and emphasis shifted to the building of impressive churches, convents, and charitable institutions. The church benefited from the *encomiendas* (allotments of Indians for labor) and slave labor, and profit from these and rental properties in the cities financed building programs on a grand scale. The church was the major patron of education and also of the arts; most of the work of the painters, sculptors, and musicians was dedicated to religious themes. Over the morals and orthodoxy of the people, the Inquisition kept a threatening vigil. This duty was exercised by the bishops in the first generations of the conquest, but in 1570 Philip II wished for firmer control and established a tribunal in Mexico City.

With regard to the priesthood, an early decision of the church came to have enormous consequences. The bishops ruled that no native Mexicans were to be prepared for ordination. The Indians could be interpreters, acolytes, and even teachers (*doctrineros*), but they were not allowed to be priests or to become members of the religious orders, male or female. Since the white population, both lay and clergy, was such a small minority among the native peoples and enjoyed such high privileges, and since the office of priest exerted considerable influence, the colonists felt more secure when native people were excluded from it.

The viceroyalty of Lima, Peru, in this period, 1551–1620, embraced all of Spanish South America, except for the coast of Venezuela. Along all of the western coastline, the conquerors had carved out their holdings, and

Baptism of a child in Peru, late 1500s.

were constantly pushing farther into the interior. The driving force behind them was the pursuit of gold and silver. The fabulous silver deposits at Potosí, discovered in 1545, made upper Peru (Bolivia) the center of concentration. Over the next hundred years, the Potosí mine was to become a bleak graveyard for countless Indian laborers and a mint for Spain and the colonists.

Meanwhile, the church in Peru was in dire need of organization and reform. The colonists had come for quick wealth, and church leaders were infected by the same disease. When Francisco de Toledo, the viceroy from 1569 to 1581, first arrived, he wrote to the king that he was appalled at the wretched condition of the church. The rush for gold and silver, he said, had attracted many unscrupulous clergy and distracted the rest.

A tribunal of the Inquisition was opened in Lima in 1570, and their jurisdiction reached throughout the viceroyalty. As in Mexico, the system of enforced labor was the reigning policy, and all the Europeans depended upon it. In the same spirit of European control, the ecclesiastical hierarchy in Peru ruled out the possibility of raising Indians and Mestizos to the priesthood and the religious orders. Only "purebloods," the Spanish-born and the Creoles, were accepted.

In Brazil, colonizing and Christianizing went along together. Church activities sought to express both spiritual concern and political pacification. Under the special patronage of the Portuguese crown, the Jesuits became the leaders in mission and in all of early Brazilian culture. The major economic and social entities were the sugar plantations, all based on the slave labor of Indians and Africans. On these *fazendas* (plantations or ranches) lived ninety percent of the colonists, so that a plantation Christianity arose where the plantation owners exercised more control than did bishops. Otherwise, church life in Brazil was similar to that in the Spanish colonies. A significant additional contrast was that the Portuguese crowns allowed no nunneries until late in the seventeenth century. Their argument was that women were scarce in the colony and were needed for families.

RIVAL MISSIONS

". . . they prevent the entry of other friars; . . ."

The Franciscans, the first missionary order at work in Mexico, emphasized preaching, baptizing, and building. When other orders arrived, the scene became complicated. Later arrivals often found the Franciscans to be uncooperative. Furthermore, when the Dominicans emphasized education and indoctrination, tensions between the two orders were inevitable. A letter from Mexico City in 1554 by Fray Andrés de Moguer, a Dominican friar, illustrates this. He wrote to the Council of the Indies in Seville and complained about the monopoly of the Franciscans. The "one language" that he criticized them for using was Nahuatl, which, indeed, was the lingua franca in much of central Mexico.[14]

✠ Very powerful lords:

To the glory of our God and Lord and His honor and with royal favor, we have here in New Spain nineteen houses of friars in Indian towns, with four to six friars in each one, and even in the smallest one two friars, not counting three other houses that we have in the Spanish towns, which are here in Mexico City, in Puebla and in Oaxaca; in these three houses the friars are numerous and there is higher instruction in the necessary sciences, and we teach the faith and good customs that are necessary to instruct and indoctrinate the natives. In these houses we also treat the friars who fall ill in the Indian towns, and punish those who are delinquent because, with our weaknesses, everything is necessary.

Following the counsel of the oldest and wisest, that those who have taken the habit in this country should be taught before they teach, it has been necessary to occupy ourselves in that effort for some time, and during that time the very reverend Franciscan fathers, imitating the holy apostles, have taken and occupied three fourths of the country, though they do not have enough friars for it, because in towns where ten or twelve ministers are needed they content themselves with having one or two. In most places they are content to say a mass once a year; consider what sort of indoctrination they can give them! His lordship the archbishop, wishing as pastor to remedy the situation and give ministers to his flock, has given some towns to others, but the natives have not been willing to obey them or give them food, on the advice, it is said, of a fray Pedro de Gante, lay brother of the order of St. Francis, and the archbishop in annoyance had four or five of them given a lashing in jail, but even then they will not obey him.

We wish you to know that existing, as indeed there exist such high abilities in the order of Saint Augustine, and in ours of Saint Dominic, and desire to learn these languages, the friars of Saint Francis have occupied a land as large as the Mexican using only one language, where more than two hundred languages are necessary, and they prevent the entry of other friars; this is clear, because the Indians say they want no others than the fathers of Saint Francis, and will not feed those whom the archbishop sends. As it concerns the royal conscience, they should be ordered not to intrude in more than they can accomplish, since we all preach one God and one faith, and not to permit so many souls to go to perdition because they cannot give them sufficient instruction, and to obey his lordship the archbishop as prelate and pastor that he is of all, and for the ministers his lordship assigns to be received, since he was given their governance. And you should write to the provincial superior of Saint Francis who resides here in New Spain, giving him these orders. From Mexico City, 10th of December, 1554.

Your highness' servant and chaplain,
Fray Andrés de Moguer

MISSION FERVOR DECLINES

"... it would require some new theology to believe ... these adults are saved."

Reports of missionary work in the first decades in New Spain described thousands of baptisms and much religious fervor among the friars. By the second half of the century, evaluations of their work were sobering. Here are two assessments. The first (1) is by the Archbishop of Mexico to the royal Council of the Indies in Seville in 1556.[15] He wanted to transfer the work of the missions to the secular priests and exact the tithes from the Indians, so he may have overstressed the failures of the missionaries. Yet the second reflection (2) by Gerónimo de Mendieta, a Spanish Franciscan missionary and historian living in Mexico, supports the bishop. Mendieta wrote in 1562 to the Commissary General of his own order about the declining morale in their missions.[16]

I

✠ The state of the church is this. In some parts there are monasteries of two or three friars, more frequently two, who live in one center and visit the country within a radius of two to thirty or more leagues around. One priest remains in the monastery while the other visits sometimes twenty or more head towns to which still others are subordinate. So the two friars frequently have charge of over one hundred thousand souls. The towns are visited anywhere from once in two weeks to once in six months and in some cases not more than two or three times in five years; moreover, the visits are of necessity hurried. The priest arrives late, baptizes and marries those who are waiting, says mass and passes on. The people come in at times to the center of the circuit for mass and the sacraments....

The friars do not like to go out of the monastery to confess the sick. They say it is not the practice of their Order and they only do it of their own free will and as an act of charity....

Here in Mexico City we would not think it a small matter if as many as three or four thousand, out of the fifty or sixty thousand who are accustomed to confess at all, should make confession in a single year. The rest of the Indians never confess. . . . There are some who have not confessed in four, ten, or even twenty years, and others in their whole lives have not done so; yet in the number of priests this is the best provided for of all the provinces, and the best Christians are here. If it is thus here, what is the case in other places where only once in a long time do they ever see a priest?

Herein is the great need for ministers. . . . Nearly all the people die without confession or other sacrament than baptism. . . .

There is great rivalry among the Orders. Even though there be but one monastery and two friars in an area where not even a dozen would suffice, one Order is unwilling that another comes in to help. Each defends its territory as if the villages were its own property. There has been and is great feeling between the Orders, not about which can best care for the flock, but which can have the greatest number of places and provinces in its hands; and so they go, occupying the best centers, building monasteries close together (a league and a half apart) not wishing to live in the difficult and needy places. If we assign a priest to help them, they cause the Indians not to admit him. . . . So great is the fear which the Indians have of the friars because of the severe punishment they practice upon them that they do not dare to complain. And if this is true in the province of Mexico, what of the mountains?

Things being as I have described, and no priest will deny it, very little fruit, it may be suspected, has come of the gospel among the people. Taking out the children, how very few adults have been saved or will be saved? From what has been said and will be said you can easily conjecture. . . .

If the gospel consisted only of holy baptism, we might believe in the salvation of the majority of the people, but since it is true that it is necessary, besides being baptized, to believe and do and perform penance for sins, it would require some new theology to believe and say that some of these adults are saved.

With regard to belief, the fault which we find is that they do not believe those things which are commonly thought by theologians to be necessary, such as the articles of faith and the mysteries which the church celebrates. Many of the people know the articles of faith and the prayers of the church fairly well, though many do not know them, and, of those who do know them, many say them like parrots, without knowing what they mean.

With regard to words and penance, this people is much inclined to vices and carnal practices. Rare are the women who are chaste. They are inclined to drunkenness, stealing, lying, and taking usury. . . . There are few vices they will not commit, and so great is their lack of firmness in the faith that if any other great power, greater than the gospel should come along it would sweep them off their feet.

II

✠ From what we see and hear in our congregations, everywhere the superiors are resigning. In visiting the convents one hardly finds a single monk who is content and happy. Discontent is manifest everywhere; many are seeking leave to return to Spain. It is a miracle to find a friar who is seriously trying to learn the language, for those who know it use it with so little satisfaction and profit. . . . The old fervor and enthusiasm for the salvation of souls seems to have disappeared. The primitive spirit is dead. The newly converted Indians no longer throng the churches to hear the word, confess or receive the sacraments, . . .

THE CROWN CONTROLS THE CHURCH

". . . no . . . parish church . . . created . . . without our express consent . . ."

The church in New Spain was under strict control of the Spanish monarchs. In a letter from the king in Madrid to his viceroy in 1574, we can see what "royal patronage" meant. The writer was Philip II, who reigned from 1556 to 1592, during the era of Spain's greatest power and influence. Philip was devotedly religious and respected the position of the pope, but when it came to appointing bishops, priests, and leaders of the church both at home and in the Indies, he kept the reins in his own hands. [17]

✠ The King. To our viceroy of Nueva España, or the person or persons who shall, for the time being, be exercising the government of that country: As you know, the right of the ecclesiastical patronage belongs to us throughout the realm of the Yndias—both because of having discovered and acquired that new world, and erected there and endowed the churches and monasteries at our own cost, or at the cost of our ancestors, the Catholic Sovereigns; and because it was conceded to us by bulls of the most holy pontiffs, conceded of their own accord. For its conservation, and that of the right that we have to it, we order and command that the said right of patronage be always preserved for us and our royal crown, singly and *in solidum*, throughout all the realm of the Yndias, without any derogation therefrom, either in whole or in part; and that we shall not concede the right of patronage by any favor or reward that we or the kings our successors may confer. . . . We desire and order that no cathedral church, parish church, monastery, hospital, votive church, or any other pious or religious establishment be erected, founded, or constructed, without our express consent for it, or that of the person who shall exercise our authority; and further; that no archbishopric, dignidad, canonry, racion, media-racion, rectorial or simple benefice, or any other ecclesiastical or religious benefice or office, be instituted, or appointment to it be made, without our consent or presentation, or that of the person who shall exercise our authority, and such presentation or consent shall be in writing, in the ordinary manner.

The archbishoprics and bishoprics shall be appointed by our presentation, made to our very holy father [*i.e.*, the Roman pontiff] who shall be at that time, as has been done hitherto.

The dignidades, canonries, racions and media-racions of all the cathedral churches of the Indias shall be filled by presentation made by our royal warrant, given by our royal Council of the Indias, and signed by our name. . . .

The provincials of all the orders who are established in the Yndias, each one of them, shall always keep a list ready of all the monasteries and chief residences [maintained there by his orders] and of the members [resident in each] that fall in his province, and of all the religious in the province—noting each one of them by name, together with a report of his age and qualifications, and the office or ministry in which each one is occupied. He shall give that annually to our viceroy, Audiencia, or governor, or the person who shall have charge of the supreme government in the province, adding to or removing from the list the religious who shall be superfluous and those who shall be needed. Our viceroy, Audiencia, or governor, shall keep those general lists which shall thus be given, for himself, and in order that he may inform us by report of the religious that there are, and those of whom there is need of provision, by each fleet sent out. . . . Therefore we strictly charge the diocesan prelates, and those superiors of the religious orders, and we order our viceroys, presidents, audiencias, and governors, that in the nominations, presentations, and appointments that they shall have to make there, as is said, in conformity [with this decree], they shall always prefer, in the first place, those who shall have been occupied, by life and example, in the conversion of the Indians, and in instruction and in administering the sacraments, and those who shall know the language of the Indians whom they have to instruct; and, in the second place, those who shall be the sons of Spaniards and who shall have served us in those regions. . . . Accordingly we request and charge the very reverend father in Christ, the archbishop of that city, and member of our Council, and the reverend fathers in Christ, the archbishop of Nueva España, the venerable deans and cabildo of the cathedral churches of that country, and all the curas, beneficiaries, and other ecclesiastical persons, the venerable and devout fathers provincial, guardians, priors, and other religious of the orders of St. Dominic, St. Augustine, St. Francis, and of all the other orders, that in what pertains to, and is incumbent on them, they observe and obey this decree, acting in harmony with you, for all that shall be advisable. Given in San Lorenzo el Real, June first, one thousand five hundred and seventy-four.

I, THE KING

By order of his Majesty:

ANTONIO DE ERASO

THE INQUISITION

"... English dogs, Lutherans, enemies to God, ..."

Some English sailors were among the victims of the Inquisition in Mexico. In 1569, when the ships of Sir John Hawkins had barely survived a fight with the Spanish in the harbor of Vera Cruz, some of his sailors requested to be left on the Mexican shore. The little group of Englishmen lived in New Spain for six years and received decent treatment from the colonists until the Tribunal of the Inquisition arrested them and brought them to Mexico City. The English were punished in a public judgment, Auto da fé, on Good Friday of 1575. Miles Philips survived the ordeal, returned to England, and described what happened to the "heretics."[18]

✠ Now after that six years were fully expired after our first coming into the Indies, in which time we had been imprisoned and served in the said countries as is before truly declared, in the year of our Lord one thousand five hundred seventy four, the Inquisition began to be established in the Indies very much against the minds of the Spaniards themselves. For never until this time since their first conquering and planting in the Indies, were they subject to that bloody and cruel Inquisition.

The chief Inquisitor was named Don Pedro Moya de Contreras, and John de Bovilla his companion, and John Sanchez the fiscal, and Pedro de los Rios, the secretary. They being come and settled, and placed in a very fair house near unto the white friars, considering with themselves that they must make an entrance and beginning of that their most detestable Inquisition here in Mexico, to the terror of the whole country, thought it best to call us that were Englishmen first in question, and so much the rather, for that they had perfect knowledge and intelligence that many of us were become very rich, as has been already declared, and therefore we were a very good booty and prey to the Inquisitors.

So that now again began our sorrows afresh, for we were sent for, and sought out in all places of the country, and proclamation made upon pain of losing of goods and excommunication, that no man should hide or keep secret any Englishman or any part of their goods. By means whereof we were all soon apprehended in all places, and all our goods seized and taken

for the Inquisitor's use, and so from all parts of the country we were conveyed and sent as prisoners to the city of Mexico, and there committed to
prison in sundry dark dungeons, where we could not see but by candle light,
and were never past two together in one place, so that we saw not one
another, neither could one of us tell what was become of another.

Thus we remained close imprisoned for the space of a year and a half,
and others for some less time, for they came to prison ever as they were
apprehended. During which time of our imprisonment, at the first beginning
we were often called before the Inquisitors alone, and there severely examined of our faith, and commanded to say the Pater Noster, the Ave
Maria, and the Creed in Latin, which God knows a great number of us
could not say, otherwise than in the English tongue. And having the said
Robert Sweeting who was our friend at Tescuco always present with them
for an interpreter, he made report for us, that in our own country speech
we could say them perfectly, although not word for word as they were in
Latin.

Then did they proceed to demand of us upon our oaths what we did and
believe of the Sacrament, and whether there did remain any bread or wine
after the words of consecration, yea or no, and whether we did not believe
that the host of bread which the priest did hold up over his head, and the
wine that was in his chalice, was the very true and perfect body and blood
of our Savior Christ, yea or no. To which if we answered not yea, then was
there no way but death. Then they would demand of us what we did remember of ourselves, what opinions we had held, or had been taught to
hold contrary to the same while we were in England. To which we for the
safety of our lives were constrained to say, that never we did believe, nor
had been taught otherwise than . . . before we had said.

Then would they charge us that we did not tell them the truth, that they
knew the contrary, and therefore we should call ourselves to remembrance,
and make them a better answer at the next time, or else we should be
racked, and made to confess the truth whether we would or no. And so
coming again before them the next time, we were still demanded of our
belief while we were in England, and how we had been taught, and also
what we thought or did know of such our own company as they did name
unto us, so that we could never be free from such demands, and at other
times they would promise us, that if we would tell them truth, then we
should have favor and be set at liberty, although we very well knew their
fair speeches were but means to entrap us to the hazard and loss of our
lives.

Howbeit God so mercifully wrought for us by a secret means that we
had, that we kept us still to our first answer, and would still say that we
had told the truth unto them, and knew no more by ourselves nor any other
of our fellows than as we had declared, and that for our sins and offenses
in England against God and our Lady, or any of his blessed Saints, we were
heartily sorry for the same, and did cry God mercy, and besought the

Inquisitors for God's sake, considering that we came into those countries by force of weather, and against our wills, and that never in our lives we had either spoken or done anything contrary to their laws, and therefore they would have mercy upon us.

Yet all this would not serve; for still from time to time we were called upon to confess, and about the space of three months before they proceeded to their severe judgment, we were all racked, and some enforced to utter that against themselves, which afterwards cost them their lives. And thus having gotten from our own mouths matter sufficient for them to proceed in judgment against us, they caused a large scaffold to be made in the middle of the market place in Mexico right over against the head church, and fourteen or fifteen days before the day of their judgment, with the sound of a trumpet, and the noise of their *atabales*, which are a kind of drums, they did assemble the people in all parts of the city. Before whom it was then solemnly proclaimed, that whosoever would upon such a day repair to the market place, they should hear the sentence of the holy Inquisition against the English heretics, Lutherans, and also see the same put in execution.

Which being done, and the time approaching of this cruel judgment, the night before they came to the prison where we were, with certain officers of that holy hellish house, bringing with them certain fool's coats which they had prepared for us, being called in their language San Benitos, which coats were made of yellow cotton and red crosses upon them, both before and behind. They were so busied in putting on their coats about us, and bringing us out into a large yard, and placing and pointing us in what order we should go to the scaffold or place of judgment upon the morrow, that they did not once suffer us to sleep all that night long.

The next morning being come, there was given to every one of us for our breakfast a cup of wine, and a slice of bread fried in honey and so about eight of the clock in the morning, we set forth of the prison, every man alone in his yellow coat, and a rope about his neck, and a great green wax candle in his hand unlighted, having a Spaniard appointed to go upon either side of every one of us. And so marching in this order and manner toward the scaffold in the market place, which was a bow shoot distant or thereabouts, we found a great assembly of people all the way, and such a throng, that certain of the Inquisitors' officers on horseback were constrained to make way, and so coming to the scaffold, we went up by a pair of stairs, and found seats ready made and prepared for us to sit down on, every man in order as he should be called to receive his judgment.

We being thus set down as we were appointed, presently the Inquisitors came up another pair of stairs, and the viceroy and all the chief justices with them. When they were set down and placed under the cloth of estate agreeing to their degrees and calling, then came up also a great number of friars, white, black, and gray, about the number of 300 persons, they being set in the places for them appointed. Then was there a solemn Oyes made, and silence commanded, and then presently began their severe and cruel judgment.

The first man that was called was one Roger the chief armorer of the *Jesus*, and he had judgment to have three hundred stripes on horseback, and after condemned to the galleys as a slave for ten years.

After him were called John Gray, John Brown, John Rider, John Moon, James Collier, and one Thomas Brown. These were adjudged to have 200 stripes on horseback, and after to be committed to the galleys for the space of eight years.

Then was called John Keyes, and was adjudged to have 100 stripes on horseback, and condemned to serve in the galleys for the space of six years.

Then were severally called the number of fifty-three one after another, and every man had his several judgment, some to have 200 stripes on horseback, and some 100, and condemned for slaves to the galleys, some for six years, some for eight and some for ten.

And then was I Miles Philips called, and was adjudged to serve in a monastery for five years, without any stripes, and to wear a fool's coat, or San Benito, during all that time.

Then were called John Storie, Richard Williams, Robert Cook, Paul Horsewell and Thomas Hull. The six were condemned to serve in monasteries without stripes, some for three years and some for four, and to wear the San Benito during all the said time. Which being done, and it now drawing toward night, George Rively, Peter Momfrie, and Cornelius the Irishman were called and had their judgment to be burned to ashes, and so were presently sent away to the place of execution in the market place but a little from the scaffold, where they were quickly burned and consumed. And as for us that had received our judgment, being sixty-eight in number; we were carried back that night to prison again.

And the next day in the morning being Good Friday, the year of our Lord 1575, we were all brought into a court of the Inquisitors' palace, where we found a horse in a readiness for everyone of our men which were condemned to have stripes, and to be committed to the galleys, which were in number sixty and so they being enforced to mount up on horseback naked from the middle upward, were carried to be showed as a spectacle for all the people to behold throughout the chief and principal streets of the city, and had the number of stripes to everyone of them appointed, most cruelly laid upon their naked bodies with long whips by sundry men appointed to be the executioners thereof. And before our men there went a couple of criers which cried as they went: "Behold these English dogs, Lutherans, enemies to God," and all the way as they went there were some of the Inquisitors themselves, and of the familiars of that rakehell order, that cried to the executioners, "Strike, lay on those English heretics, Lutherans, God's enemies."

And so this horrible spectacle being showed round about the city, they returned to the Inquisitors' house, with their backs all gore blood, and swollen with great bumps, and were then taken from their horses, and carried again to prison, where they remained until they were sent into Spain to the galleys, there to receive the rest of their martyrdom. And I and the six other with me which had judgment, and were condemned amongst the rest to serve an apprenticeship in the monastery, were taken presently and sent to certain religious houses appointed for the purpose.

AN AMBITIOUS CLERIC IN POTOSÍ

". . . priests and friars who have a nephew whom they can trust are very rich, . . ."

Whether they were secular or religious, the priests often engaged in auxiliary businesses to increase their income. Amid Peru's wealth, the opportunities were multiplied. Here, Bachelor Francisco de la Calzada, a priest assigned to teach groups of Indians in Potosí, writes to his sister back in Spain and pleads that she send her son to help his uncle set up a silver refining business. The letter was dated 1577.[19]

✠ Dear Sister:

Since I have been in this realm of Peru I have written many letters, over fifteen of them, to you and to my nephew Próspero de Viso. And I have received only two from you, and one from my nephew, which I so prize and guard that they will accompany me when I return to Spain, if God permits.

I have always begged you to get my nephew Pedro de la Calzado started on his way here, since it would be greatly to my advantage and his. He has been so missed that if he had come I wouldn't be surprised to see us on the road to Spain within two years, because Potosí is more prosperous now than it has been since the world began. With this new invention of mercury, there are many men I know who less than three years ago were penniless and 3,000 or 4,000 pesos in debt, and now some of them have 50,000 pesos, others 40,000 and others who came only two years ago have 10,000 or 12,000 pesos.

The priests and friars who have a nephew whom they can trust are very rich, both groups of them. And those of us who have no one to trust have nothing but our parish salaries; there we spend more than we earn. This viceroy has done us a bad turn by reducing our salaries and removing our rations, all of which was worth over 2,000 pesos, and allowing us only 600 pesos of assayed silver, which is not enough for drinking water. If we don't devise other businesses or dealings, we can't outfit ourselves to go to Spain; but anyone who has someone to help him can leave very quickly. If my nephew had come, I would have bought him a mercury mill, that is, where silver is extracted through mercury, and with that, in less than two years we could leave with 6,000 or 7,000 pesos each. As it is, I don't know when I will be able to leave, because I am involved in spending so much in this and that endeavor that though I wish to cut down, I can't.

I was about to send three or four bars of silver, worth 1,500 ducats there, but here we have heard such bad news of everything in Seville being taken for the king, that I decided not to. And many who were about to leave for Spain are staying for the same reason. Also some tell of such misfortunes of wars and successions and many other troubles, that it clips the wings of men who want to go to Spain. Many buy properties and possessions and marry here, intending not to see Spain again. I don't know what I will do. Surely my desire is to die not here, but where I was born. If I am to go, it will be within three years, even if I take only 4,000 or 5,000 pesos with me. If I decide to stay, I will buy a very good farm or *chacara*, with a vineyard of 10,000 or 12,000 stocks and many trees, Castilian and local, that will support me when I want to retire and rest, and not go about instructing Indians, which is surely a great travail. But, as I said, if I can I would rather go to Spain, because I am very gray and fat, and this life is hard on me.

I beg you always to write me and advise me of the health of yourself and all your household, of my nieces and nephews, and all the news you get about things there and about our relatives. Here I have been told that Rodrigo de la Calzada's wife is dead, and also his son, the oldest, António de la Calzada. I was greatly grieved that we are diminishing this way. I have heard nothing of our relatives the canons of Leon and Astorga. Keep me posted on everything.

I stay well, praise our Lord. Luis Alvarez, son-in-law of Luis del Cerro, is here in Potosí, and is applying himself to earning a living from mercury. Licentiate Gómez Hernández, brother-in-law of Licentiate Flores, is corregidor [governor of a district] here. He is a citizen of Arequipa, and is very rich. He would like to know of his nephews, and whether Licentiate Flores is alive. Nothing else presents itself. Our Lord, etc. From Potosí, 15th of January, 1577.

> Milady sister, your least brother kisses your hands,
> Bachelor Francisco de la Calzada

CONVENTS, NUNNERIES, AND HOSPITALS

"... 16 very strict nunneries, of great virtue ..."

The late sixteenth and early seventeenth centuries were times of much construction related to the church. Most conspicuous were those in the urban centers such as Vera Cruz, Puebla, Mexico City, Guadalajara, and other towns, but they were numerous in almost all inhabited areas. A

Carmelite friar, Fray António Vazquez de Espinosa, traveled through New Spain, including present-day Central America and Peru, in the years 1610–1620 and published a description of the places, people, and activities that he saw. The selections that follow are from his account of Mexico City. His book contains many descriptions of similar churches and institutions found in scores of other towns and provinces. He was an uncritical observer, but gives evidence of the phenomenal physical and cultural development of the church in its first century in the New World.[20]

✠ There are in Mexico City splendid and famous convents of friars, with sumptuous temples, richly and perfectly appointed, with large incomes and charitable contributions which support them. All of them maintain schools of Arts and Theology; the chief one, Santo Domingo, is one of the best and richest to be found in the Indies, and I doubt whether there be its equal in Spain. It has over 200 friars, many of whom are highly educated and great preachers. In this splendid convent they teach Arts and Theology; the church has become a glowing coal of gold, with great majesty of chapels along its sides. Although the foundations have sunk more than 5 feet below ground level, the convent is an excellent one, with large cloisters and dormitories, well designed and carried out. . . .

Of the Seraphic Order of St. Francis there are six convents, the largest with about 200 (or 300) friars and a school of Arts and Theology; the church is one of the largest and finest in all the Indies, with many handsome chapels and extensive cloisters and dormitories, all beautifully done, with remarkable paintings; the Seraphic Patriarch having founded his order in poverty, it has been enriched with virtue, membership, and buildings. The convent of St. Joseph is connected with the large one; there is a local superior there and friars with pastoral circuits and Indians under instruction, in which they administer the Holy Sacraments and teach them the facts of our Holy Faith and virtue. . . .

Of the Order of the Glorious Doctor and Patriarch St. Augustine there are four convents; the chief one contains over 150 friars; they teach Arts and Theology; the church is one of the largest and best designed and carried out, to be seen in Mexico; it is all one cluster of gold, with famous cloisters and dormitories and a great refectory. This splendid convent receives every year from its income and church contributions, not counting other alms, over 100,000 pesos. The College of San Pablo of the same Augustinian Order has about 100 friars; there they teach Arts and Theology with great diligence and exactitude, and education flourishes; from this distinguished order have risen such remarkable men as Master Fray Juan Zapata, Bishop of Guatemala, Master Fray Gabriel de Ribera, a son of that splendid convent, and many others whom I do not mention because their virtue and learning are well known in that kingdom and they have accomplished much there. The convent of San Sebastian will have some 12 friars busied with pastoral visits and catechizing the Indians, and in administering the Holy

Sacraments; these belonged to the friars of the Barefoot Carmelite Order. The Augustinians have another convent with some 8 friars, called Santa Cruz. . . .

There are in this royal city 16 very strict nunneries, of great virtue and sanctity; among them there are many handmaids of God who lead holy lives. The nunnery of Santa Ines ranks among the strictest and finest of all Christendom. This was founded by Diego Caballero with 33 nuns, in pious imitation of the number of years our Lord passed on earth; there may be neither more nor less, except that when one dies, another enters in her place, to keep the number full. They enter without dowry, for this noble knight, to whom God had given much wealth, and who had no heirs, established this nunnery with a total of 33 nuns and for their support he left an annual income of 33,000 pesos, together with 2,000 pesos of income for the patron or patroness of his family. They have excellent music in this nunnery.

Mexico contains the nunneries of La Concepción, San Lorenzo, Santa Catalina de Sena, La Encarnación, Santa Clara, Santa Teresa, Jesús María, Regina Celi, San Jerónimo; Santa Mónica, with an annex where they bring up children under instruction; Santa Isabel, of Franciscan barefoot nuns; Santa María de Gracia, which consists of two separate convents with one church and a boarding school for girls already novitiates; the nunnery of Las Recogidas is very wealthy; San Juan de Letrán is a boarding school in which they bring up orphan children.

In this great city there are nine famous hospitals, in which they care for the indigent sick of various nationalities, and with different diseases. These are: The general hospital for the Indians, called the Royal Hospital, whose patron is His Majesty. This receives large revenues and charitable contributions; and the sainted Count of Monterrey when Viceroy of that kingdom gave it his favor and assistance by establishing a theatrical playhouse (corral de comedias) all the income from which he turned over to it for the care, maintenance, and comfort of the poor among the Indians.

The Hospital of Los Desamparados (The Destitute) is run by the friars and brethren of the blessed San Juan de Diós; it is rich and sumptuous. It has a revolving dumbwaiter into which foundlings are dropped or put — they commonly call them children of the church door — and these friars care for these orphaned children and find women to nurse them and pay them out of the hospital's revenues and the large daily charitable contributions which they get from the city's various wards every day.

AN INDIAN CRITIQUE OF CLERGY IN PERU

". . . I have set down both the good and the evil of life in my country, . . ."

By the early seventeenth century, the institution of the church had become a disproportionately strong part of society. The population of Lima in

1611 was said to be 26,500, and a census revealed that ten percent of the inhabitants were priests, canons, friars, and nuns.[21] An invaluable eye-witness account of Peruvian life at the time was written by Felipe Huamán Poma de Ayala, a descendant of an Incan chief. Poma's dates were approximately 1532–1615. He and his father accepted Christian faith, cooperated with the Spanish, and served as interpreters for colonial officials. Out of these experiences, this native Peruvian wrote to King Philip III in 1613–1615, pleading for colonial officials of better quality and for humane treatment toward his fellow Indians. His "letter" of 1200 pages, with 400 vivid line drawings, provides a gold mine of information about indigenous Peruvian society and Spanish colonial life. His descriptions of the clergy and church in the period 1585 – 1615 reveal his ideals and also his concern over abuses.[22]

✠ The Fathers

The priesthood began with Jesus Christ and his Apostles, but their successors in the various religious orders established in Peru do not follow this holy example. On the contrary, they show an unholy greed for worldly wealth and the sins of the flesh and a good example would be set to everyone if they were punished by the Holy Inquisition.

These priests are irascible and arrogant. They wield considerable power and usually act with great severity towards their parishioners, as if they had forgotten that Our Lord was poor and humble and the friend of sinners. Their own intimate circle is restricted to their relations and dependants, who are either Spanish or half-caste.

They readily engage in business, either on their own or other people's account, and employ a great deal of labour without adequate payment. Often they say that the work is for ecclesiastical vestments, when really it is for the sale of ordinary clothing. . . .

The usual practice is for a priest to have a man and two girls in the kitchen, a groom, a gardener, a porter, and others to carry wood and look after the animals.

Sometimes there are as many as ten mules in the stables, not counting the beasts belonging to neighbours, and they all have to be sustained at the Indians' expense. Herds of 1,000 cattle, goats, pigs or sheep are a commonplace and there are often hundreds of capons, chickens and rabbits, all requiring their own special arrangements, as well as market gardens. If a single animal is lost, the Indian held responsible has to pay for it in full. . . .

A favourite source of income of the priesthood consists in organising the porterage of wine, chillies, coca and maize. These wares are carried on the backs of Indians and llamas and in some cases need to be brought down from high altitudes. The descent often results in death for the Indians, who catch a fever when they arrive in a warm climate. Any damage to their loads during the journey has to be made good at their own expense.

The priests make a practice of confiscating property which really belongs to a church, a society or a hospital and putting it to their own uses. In the same way they often overcharge for Masses for the dead. For a sung Mass they charge 6 reales [1 real = 25¢] instead of 3; and for spoken Mass 4 reales instead of 1. . . . When a priest officiates at a wedding, he wants 5 pesos to cover the earnest-money, the candles and the collection. Similarly the usual rate for a baptism is 4 pesos. It never seems to occur to the priest that he is paid his salary for performing these offices. . . .

When these holy fathers are living as husband and wife with Indian girls and begetting children, they always refer to the half-castes as their nephews. With the aid of a little hypocrisy they make sin seem more attractive, so that it spreads and corrupts one girl after another. . . .

Many of the priests live as grandly as our former rulers, offering banquets to their friends and wasting the substance of the people on these entertainments. If they have money to spare, it ought to be spent on the local hospital or church. At present, the church is often kept in worse condition than a stable for horses.

Our clergy, being obliged to provide wax candles, incense and soap, get the Indians to pay by confiscating the silver subscribed for charity. It would be more honest to use the fees from burials, weddings and baptisms, or the money left at the foot of the altars on holy days, to provide these stores. . . .

When they occasionally travel abroad, the priests insist on being welcomed home with a peal of bells. The villagers have to come out in procession with crosses and banners, just as if these clerics were Bishops, when in reality they are no better than the rest of humanity.

In setting down truthfully this account of the way of life of the priests, the goods which they possess and the evil which they do, I am hoping to bring it to the attention of Your Majesty and other important persons. Although I feel exhausted by the effort, I propose to continue with my task. . . .

It is true that many clerics begin as men of considerable learning, but pride is usually their downfall.

Among the few kind and charitable priests I have known were Father Benavides, Francisco de Padilla and Father Ynigo. These ones at least did not run after girls or beget bastards, and they treated people of all sorts with respect. . . .

The Church

Mass should be announced by ten peals of the big or little bells, followed by a single bell ringing for quarter of an hour. By this means all the people of consequence, as well as the old and sick who are only able to walk with difficulty, would get ample warning. It would also remove the necessity of town-criers and others to make a personal tour of the parishioners' houses, in the course of which they often find opportunities for theft and lechery. One way of punishing these offenders would be to get all the parishioners together in church, while a special party would lie in wait for clandestine prowlers and make them captive. These culprits might be allowed to get off with a caution the first time, but the second time they should be whipped behind the church. The same treatment would be appropriate for magicians who throw eggs at the church door. The surviving old people from Inca times are reaching the end of their lives and their children are all baptised Christians, so the whole population ought to respond to a summons to church.

Clerks and sacristans are inclined to exploit the Indians and particularly the girls. One of their tricks is to arrange services on Wednesday and Friday evenings when the priest is away, so as to arouse the interest of those young creatures and seduce them afterwards. When their priest leaves them in charge of the parish, they pay much less attention to matters such as ringing the bells for the prayer, helping the sick to die well and burying the dead. . . .

Visitors

Cristóbal de Albornoz, who held the office of Visitor-General, was fearless in his judgements and a stern opponent of arrogance on the part of the priests. He never accepted bribes or used physical violence. . . .

One of the Visitor's duties is to confiscate any arms carried by the priests, whether for self-defence or for aggressive purposes. Not only are such arms terrifying to the Indians, but they are unsuitable in the hands of men anointed and consecrated to the service of God, who should be performing works of compassion. . . .

In the year 1611, a Visitor-General was sent out by the Bishop of Cuzco to correct the arrogance of the clergy and it is worth relating what occurred as a lesson for the future. He punished some of the priests, but others he let off because he had become good friends with them. In contempt of his orders, he himself confiscated property and provisions from the Indians, insisted on unpaid service and assumed privileges which he was in no way entitled to. Over and above this he treated the Indians with manifest hatred, going to the limits of what the law permits. . . .

It is the Visitor's job to look out for any misdemeanour or oversight on the part of the priests; visit the church buildings and see that they are properly painted, check that the doors are provided with locks, notice whether the holy images have been treated with respect and whether the bells are in order, and inspect the stocks of wax, incense, soap and oil. The high cross for processions and the vestments of the sacristans and choirboys need to be inspected. The priest's house also deserves attention. Is it clean and proper, or is it full of women? Is the priest in the habit of roaming around at night, or visiting wine-shops during the day? Does he hoard food, own property or embezzle the funds encharged to him? If he has a pillar for flogging Indians in his back yard he is nothing but an executioner, and if his barns are stuffed with loot he is a thief. A large number of dependants and servants is bound to tell against him. . . .

Some Good Examples

Among the good Christians whom I have known in Peru were the following:

Don Pedro de Córdoba y Guzmán of the Order of St. James, Captain of Cavalry, was the principal landowner and employer of our Indians in Lucanas. Neither he nor his family visited the villages or sent stewards to them as a rule, but lived all the time in Lima. He left half the tribute due to him in the hands of the Indians. The administration was conducted for him by an Indian named Diego Chachapoya and no Spaniards were employed on the estate. Once, when complaints were made against his son Rodrigo, he sent the young man to Chile as a ship's Captain. He also opposed any exploitation by administrators, priests and others. He was charitable and never abusive, an honest man who did not engage in business himself or demand presents in the customary style. If any of the Indians ever brought him a gift, he returned it eightfold, for he was really sorry for their laborious life. It is a pleasure for me to record the good example which he set during his term of office.

The royal administrator of the province of Lucanas, Don Gregorio Lopez de Puga, was a genuinely learned man whose influence was always exerted on the side of justice. He liked to travel alone, not even taking a clerk with him, and to judge cases and disputes on his own. Often his judgements reflected a sympathy with the native rulers and a distaste for vagabonds. On one occasion he sentenced two Spaniards, who held important positions, saying that Your Majesty had sent him to do justice and not to condone robbery and inhumanity. Such a person, mature and considerate, deserves to remain a long time in office. . . .

In this book I have set down both the good and the evil of life in my country, so that the next Government may be correspondingly improved. My hope is that my work will be preserved in the archives of the Cathedral in Rome.

Ordinary Christian Indians

The Indians in our country are just as gifted as Castilians in their artistry and workmanship. Some of them are excellent singers and musicians. They make themselves masters of the organ, fiddle, flute, clarinet, trumpet and horn without any difficulty. They also become capable municipal clerks. It is quite usual for them to deputise for royal administrators and mayors and they sometimes perform the duties of constables and accountants. They can use a gun, a sword or a halberd as well as any Spaniard. Often they are first-rate horsemen and trainers of animals, with a special aptitude with bulls. Some of them know Latin and study literature. If they were allowed to, they could perfectly well be ordained as priests. Above all they are loyal and admirable servants of the Crown, with no taste for rebellion.

Indians are skilful at all the decorative arts such as painting, engraving, carving, gilding, metalwork and embroidery. They make good tailors, cobblers, carpenters, masons and potters. Also, by simply watching the Spaniards, they have learnt how to do well in trade.

In the same way the Indian girls learn reading, writing, music and needlework at the convents which they attend. They are just as clever and accomplished as Spanish girls at the domestic skills.

The clever ones among the Indians get themselves jobs with the Church, either as singers or clerks. Because of the incompetence or absence of the priests they soon find themselves burying the dead with all the proper prayers and responses. They take vespers and look after the music and singing, as well as intoning the prayers. On Sundays and holy days they conduct the ceremonies as well as any Spaniard. In default of a priest they baptise the babies with holy water, reciting the proper form of words, and this is allowed by the authorities in order to avoid any of the small creatures going to limbo for lack of baptism. On Wednesdays and Fridays Indians conduct the early morning service, these being the obligatory days, and they say the prayers for the dead. However, they get nothing but interference from the priests themselves, who usually refer to them dismissively as 'clever children. . . .'

THE UNIVERSITY OF LIMA

". . . unusual intellects in subtlety and facility, . . ."

The earliest universities began in the sixteenth century in Mexico City and in Lima, Peru. Modeled after similar institutions in Spain, they taught law and theology in the medieval traditions. Respect for authority and memorization were more valued than analysis and critique. When the Spanish Carmelite friar António Vazquez de Espinosa visited the University of Lima around 1620 and wrote the report, excerpted below, most of the professors were Creoles. Though they were born in the New World, their standards for what was academically appropriate came from Salamanca back in Spain.[23]

✠ The university and Royal Schools are so distinguished that they need envy no other in the world, since they were established by the Emperor Charles V, and later by Philip II, both of glorious memory; they enlarged, ennobled and enriched them, with the same privileges as the University of Salamanca; they endowed the professorial chairs of Prime with 1,000 assay pesos, and those of Vespers with 600, per annum. The Prime chairs are in Theology, Scholastics, Scripture, Law, and Canons; the Vespers, in the Institutes, the Code, the Decretals, three in Philosophy, one in the Indian language for the training of the priests who are to be parish priests or doctrineros [teachers of Indians]; before they are commissioned, they have to be examined and certificated by the Professor of the language.

The Professors are in major part natives of the Indies and especially of this city, where it would appear that the skies, as usually in the Indies, train outstanding and unusual intellects in subtlety and facility, so that in general they are very able and keen witted; this is obvious from the professorial positions which they occupy and the pulpits, where remarkable men distinguish themselves in their mastery of science and oratory; but they are unfortunate in living far from the eyes of His Majesty. For after all their labors, since there are so few professorial chairs and so many candidates, and there cannot be many lawyers, after having drudged and done brilliantly, and having spent in attaining the degrees of Licentiate and Doctor, 3,500 pesos, they lose heart, unless they have private means, at seeing themselves unrewarded; so the clerics take benefices and Indian curacies in order to live, and many abandon their books and studies, and never take their degrees.

This University's faculty is important, for it comprises more than 80 Doctors and Masters; the members of the Circuit Court join them, for at the end of the year the fees amount to many ducats. The lecture halls in the schools are excellent, and the chapel very fine, but the most remarkable feature is the amphitheater, where [are held] the public functions and commencements; it is very large and imposing; the display at the granting of whatever degrees are given, is also imposing. They [the faculty] invite the city's nobility as an escort, and meet at the house of the Doctor-to-be in a blare of trumpets, flageolets, and bugles, with a banner which hangs from a window of the house over a canopy on crimson velvet cushions and has the arms of the University and of the graduating Doctor; these are likewise set up in the theater erected in the Cathedral under the royal arms; they remind and notify the invited guests and doctors, who form an escort the evening before; the nobility follow the banner, then the Beadles with their silver maces, then the Masters and Doctors with their insignia, in order of age, closing with the Dean of the faculty and the graduating Doctor; and in this order they repair to the Rector's house, where the members of the Circuit Court await them; with the Rector in their center, they continue in the procession, in order of age. And in this same order the following day they parade till they arrive at the Cathedral, where the theater and the stage have been decorated and provided with seats; Mass is said for them, and at its close after leaving the Cathedral, the newest

Doctor of the faculty delivers his burlesque invective, and the Chancellor gives him his degree, just as is done at Salamanca.

NATIVE BRAZILIANS IN MISSION SETTLEMENTS

". . . losing their habit of eating human flesh; . . ."

To Christianize the native Brazilians and transform them into obedient colonial subjects, the Portuguese authorities and the Jesuit fathers often rounded them up from the interior, brought them to the coastal region, and concentrated them in mission villages. Excerpts from a letter written by an anonymous Jesuit describe this work in ideal terms as it was being carried on in 1558 within a few miles of Bahía, the colonial capital.[24]

✠ Since the letter written on July 10, 1558, from Bahía, the Governor has continued zealously in his efforts and Our Lord has given him rewards for his efforts.

He continued to punish the wrongdoers with such prudence and temperance that he builds up the community and does not destroy it, and for that reason he has been able to subjugate all to the law and servitude whom he wanted.

Thus, from far away they [the Indians] send requests for priests to indoctrinate them because they want friendship with Christians and to change their habits for ours. In this way four large settlements are already constructed for them, but for the present only two of us reside among them in the newly constructed churches, because there are only three of us in this Captaincy who can say mass and we are scattered in the following three areas: in the College of Bahía resides João Gonçalves with a few Brothers, Father Nóbrega is in São Paulo, and António Pires is in São João. The other two settlements are awaiting aid.

Besides these, other settlements are being prepared in more remote parts where the Christians never imagined it possible to enter and subjugate, and we are taking care of this slowly until there are enough Fathers to reap the great harvest there. It is certain that if there were enough people to teach and to maintain them, we could easily establish twenty or thirty churches around which we could settle all the Indians from an area many leagues square.

All these are losing their habit of eating human flesh; and if we learn that some are about to eat flesh, we order them to send it to us. They send it, as they did several days ago, and they bring it to us from a long distance so that we can bury or burn it. In this way they all tremble with fear of the Governor, a fear which, although it may not last a lifetime, is enough so that we can teach them; it serves us so that we can tell them of Christ, and the kindness which Our Lord will show them will cause all human fear to flee so that they will remain a strong and stable people. . . .

With much diligence the children are being taught good habits, reading, and writing, and there are some very intelligent ones among them. From these we hope to have some good students, because, since they can no longer wander around and now remain among us, they will not be able to forget what they have learned. Those of São Paulo, the first settlement built, are all Christians, that is the children up to fourteen years of age, and every day more are baptized because those who are born again bring others for baptism and there are more than two hundred of these. . . .

Now there is nothing else to write except to ask your blessing for all these who are yours and your prayers for us to Jesus Christ Our Lord.

HARSH LABOR AND THE VANISHING INDIANS

". . . who would think that so many people could be destroyed in so short a time?"

The sugar plantations in the Brazilian northeast depended upon a regular supply of cheap labor. In the first decades of the colony, Indians were the main source of workers, but by 1550, conditions led to large numbers of them dying or running away, and the plantation owners began buying African slaves. In addition, Portuguese slavehunters continued to raid Indian villages in the interior for human workers to sell to the plantations. By 1600, there were said to be about 40,000 Europeans (Portuguese) in Brazil; 30,000 Indians related to the plantations; and 30,000 Africans. The protests against continued Indian slavery came mainly from the Jesuit missionaries. One example, thought to be Padre José de Anchieta, 1534–1597, described the inhuman practice in the latter part of the sixteenth century.[25]

✠ The number of Indians that have been destroyed in this captaincy of Baía in the past twenty years passes belief; who would think that so many people could be destroyed in so short a time? In the fourteen churches maintained by the Fathers they had brought together 40,000 souls, by count, and even more, counting those who came after—yet today it is doubtful whether the three churches that remain have 3,500 souls together. Six years ago an honored citizen of this city, a man of good conscience and a city official at the time, said that in the two preceding years 20,000 souls, by count, had been brought from the back country of Arabó and that all of them went to the Portuguese plantations. These 20,000, added to the 40,000 of the churches, come to 60,000. Now for the past six years the Portuguese have been bringing Indians for their plantations, one bringing 2,000, another 3,000, some more, others less; in six years this must come to 80,000 souls or more. Now look at the sugar-mills and plantations of Baía, and you will find them full of Guinea Negroes but very few natives; if you ask what happened to all those people, they will tell you that they died.

In this way God has severely punished the Portuguese for the many offenses that they committed and still commit against these Indians, for they go into the interior and deceive these people, inviting them to go to the coast, where, they say, they would live in their villages as they did in their lands, and the Portuguese would be their neighbors. The Indians, believing this, go with them, and for fear they will change their minds the Portuguese army destroy their gardens. On arrival at the coast they divide the Indians among themselves, some taking the women, others their husbands, and still others the children, and they sell them. Other Portuguese go into the interior and entice the Indians by saying that they will take them to the churches of the Fathers, and by this means they seduce them from their lands, for it is common knowledge in the backlands that only the Indians in the churches where the Fathers reside enjoy liberty and all the rest are captives. Matters reached such a point that a certain Portuguese, going into the back country in search of Indians, shaved his head like a priest, saying that he was a Father seeking Indians for the churches. This happened at a time when Father Gaspar Lourenço was bound for the interior, and he found these people on the road. When they heard that the Father was going into the backlands they said: "How can that be, when he who brings us says that he is a Father, and that is why we go with him?" And the Portuguese with the shaven head hid himself, not wanting the priest to see him.

The Portuguese travel 250 and 300 leagues to find the Indians, for the nearest ones are by now a great distance away, and since the land is now depopulated most of them die on the road from hunger. There have been Portuguese who seized on the road certain Indians who were enemies of the ones they were bringing, killed them, and gave their flesh to their captives to eat. And when all these people arrive at the coast, seeing that the Portuguese do not keep the promises they made in the interior but separate them from each other, some flee into the forests, never to emerge again, and others die from grief and chagrin that they, who had been free men, should be made slaves.

4 ✠ Missionary Church and Hispanic Civilization in Conflict

1620-1700

As the seventeenth century began, Spain was exhausted. The English had destroyed its Armada in 1588, so its ships no longer ruled the ocean, and, to the neglect of its own economy, Spain's profits from the colonies had long been going to other parts of Europe to pay for imported goods. Nevertheless, in the colonies, the mines continued to yield their riches of silver. One fifth was dutifully sent as tax to Seville, and the rest was kept by the white colonists for themselves, for servants, imported finery, large homes, and a growing baroque culture.

The social pyramid in the colonies was stratified by race, with the whites at the top. The ones born in Spain, the *peninsulares*, held the highest positions in the government, commerce, and church. Beneath them were the Creoles, wealthy whites who were born in the Indies, owners of lands and mines, lawyers and physicians, and holders of secondary posts in government and church. The lower classes were the *Mestizos*, the Indians, and African slaves. The former lived by their wits on small ranches and in petty commerce. The Indians were the main source of labor, and though legislation to protect them from abuse was still on the books, it was widely ignored. Black slaves, in the areas where they were used, occupied the lowest status of all.

Church life was quite visible. Most of the population was nominally Christian, and churches and monasteries abounded. On the *haciendas* and smaller ranches, chapels and the sacraments were nearly always present. In the Indian villages, the traditional religion of the people remained vigorous, but one could see evidences of changes brought by Christianity.

Meanwhile, Brazil was a small group of towns along the coast amid the large agricultural estates. The plantations were increasingly dependent on African slaves, with about 600,000 being imported during this period. The plantations had their own churches and chapels. The resident clergy were generally seculars, dominated by the owner of the plantation. The *padre* was a dispenser of the sacraments; and, as schoolteacher for the owner's sons, he represented the larger world of Latin, the classics, Europe, and

Sister Juana Inéz de la Cruz (1658-95). Poet, scholar, and nun; a member of Hieronimite Convent of San Geronimo, Mexico City.

the church. Beyond his duties at the "big house," he helped evangelize and assimilate the Indian and African slaves.

In 1630, the Dutch wrested control of Pernambuco in the northeast of Brazil and planted a vigorous Protestant colony in the heart of the sugar cane area, thereby provoking a crisis in the existence of both Brazil and Portugal. King John IV of Portugal had become dependent upon the colony, which he candidly called his "milk cow" in the Atlantic. In the campaign, 1641–1654, to reconquer the area from the Calvinist heretics, the Catholic church took an active role. The effort solidified the colony's "Brazilian" identity and gained greater recognition for the role of the Catholic church within it.

Portuguese expansion inward from the coast began in the seventeenth century, and the mixed bloods, part Indian and part white, took the lead. These *bandeirantes*, as they were called, traveling by mules and canoes, blazed trails between the coastal towns, explored and claimed for Portugal the vast interior, and usually brought back quantities of Indian slaves. Sometimes missionaries accompanied such trips; other times their missions were targets of the slave raids.

Through the century, the missionary friars continued to establish mission villages in the coastal region and in some other places. For example, the Jesuits were beginning their missions, "reductions," in the regions around present-day Paraguay. The San Francisco River system, however, with its mouth just south of Recife, was the main mission area at mid-century. The river was a highway into the interior, and missionaries from various orders used it when they set up their stations. Sometimes they were in conflict with the *bandeirantes* and the slave-hungry plantation owners. In 1680, an Indian uprising along the river led to repression by the planters. By 1700, death, disease, and flight had put an end to the San Francisco missions, and virtually eliminated the aboriginal people in the coastal area outside the plantation system.

Though not as frequently as in the Spanish colonies, the Portuguese bishops and religious orders built imposing churches and convents along the eastern coast. The first convent for women, St. Clare, was founded in Bahía in 1669.

URBAN CLOISTERS

". . . hearing their music, feeding on their sweetmeats, . . ."

The well-to-do colonists often dressed in fine apparel, lived in ornate houses, and supported the arts. Some of the religious convents in the major cities enjoyed a similar style of life. Thomas Gage, an English Dominican priest, traveled and worked in Mexico and Central America for twelve

*years, 1625–1637. Later back in England in 1641, he wrote a vivid ac-
count of his experiences in the new world. He had become Protestant;
and the following descriptions of upper-class religious life in Mexico City
in 1625–1626 reveal some Protestant and English loyalties, but these sympathies do not obscure much realism in his account.*[26]

✠ There are not above fifty churches and chapels, cloisters and nunneries,
and parish churches in that city, but those that are there are the fairest
that ever my eyes beheld. The roofs and beams are in many of them all
daubed with gold. Many altars have sundry marble pillars, and others are
decorated with brazil-wood stays standing one above another with tabernacles for several saints richly wrought with golden colors, so that twenty
thousand ducats [Viennese gold weight equivalent to 53.873 grains] is a
common price of many of them. These cause admiration in the common
sort of people, and admiration brings on daily adoration in them to those
glorious spectacles and images of saints.

Besides these beautiful buildings, the inward riches belonging to the
altars are infinite in price and value. All the copes, canopies, hangings, altar
cloths, candlesticks, jewels belonging to the saints, and crowns of gold and
silver, and tabernacles of gold and crystal to carry about their sacrament
in procession would mount to the worth of a reasonable mine of silver, and
would be a rich prey for any nation that could make better use of wealth
and riches. I will not speak much of the lives of the friars and nuns of that
city, but only that there they enjoy more liberty than in the parts of Europe
(where yet they have too much) and that surely the scandals committed by
them do cry up to Heaven for vengeance, judgment, and destruction.

In my time in the cloister of the Mercedarian friars which is entitled for
the Redemption of Captives, there chanced to be an election of a Provincial
to rule over them, to the which all the priors and heads of the cloisters
about the country had resorted. Such were their various and factious differences that upon the sudden all the convent was in an uproar, their
canonical election was turned to mutiny and strife, knives were drawn, and
many wounded. The scandal and danger of murder was so great, that the
Viceroy was fain to interpose his authority and to sit amongst them and
guard the cloister until their Provincial was elected.

It is ordinary for the friars to visit the devoted nuns, and to spend whole
days with them, hearing their music, feeding on their sweetmeats, and for
this purpose they have many chambers which they call *locutorios*, to talk in,
with wooden bars between the nuns and them, and in these chambers are
tables for the friars to dine at, and while they dine the nuns recreate them
with their voices. Gentlemen and citizens give their daughters to be brought
up in these nunneries, where they are taught to make all sorts of conserves
and preserves, all sorts of needlework, all sorts of music, which is so exquisite in that city that I dare be bold to say that the people are drawn to their
churches more for the delight of the music than for any delight in the service

of God. More, they teach these young children to act like players; and to entice the people to their churches, they make these children act short dialogues in their choirs, richly attiring them with men's and women's apparel, especially upon Midsummer Day, and the eight days before their Christmas. These are so gallantly performed that there have been many factious strifes and single combats—some were in my time—for defending which of these nunneries most excelled in music and in the training up of children. No delights are wanting in that city abroad in the world, nor in their churches, which should be the house of God, and the soul's, not the senses' delight.

MISSION IN NEW MEXICO

". . . porters, sextons, cooks, bell-ringers, gardeners, refectioners, . . ."

Although some clergy lived in comfortable surroundings, others lived very simply. Fray Alonso de Benavides, head of the Franciscan Mission in New Mexico, 1623–1629, prepared reports about the missions for the king and pope. His composite picture of the schedule and duties of a friar in an Indian village in northern Mexico is idealized, yet it helps one visualize the daily round of a missionary priest.[27]

✠ Since the land is very remote and isolated and the difficulties of the long journeys require more than a year of travel, the friars, although there are many who wish to dedicate themselves to those conversions, find themselves unable to do so because of their poverty. Hence only those go there who are sent by the Catholic king at his own expense, for the cost is so excessive that only his royal zeal can afford it. This is the reason that there are so few friars over there and that most of the convents have only one religious each, and he ministers to four, six, or more neighboring pueblos, in the midst of which he stands as a lighted torch to guide them in spiritual as well as temporal affairs. More than twenty Indians devoted to the service of the church, live with him in the convent. They take turns in relieving one another as porters, sextons, cooks, bell-ringers, gardeners, refectioners, and in other tasks. They perform their duties with as much circumspection and care as if they were friars. At eventide they say their prayers together, with much devotion in front of some image.

In every pueblo where a friar resides, he has schools for the teaching of praying, singing, playing musical instruments and other interesting things. Promptly at dawn, one of the Indian singers, whose turn it is that week, goes to ring the bell for Prime, at the sound of which those who go to school assemble and sweep the rooms thoroughly. The singers chant Prime in the choir. The friar must be present at all of this and takes note of those who have failed to perform this duty, in order to reprimand them later. When everything is neat and clean, they again ring the bell and each one goes to learn his particular specialty; the friar oversees it all. . . . After they have been occupied in this manner for an hour and a half, the bell is rung for mass. All go into the church, and the friar says mass and administers the sacraments. . . . Mass over. . . . all kneel down by the church door and sing the *Salve* in their own tongue. . . .

At mealtime, the poor people in the pueblo who are not ill come to the porter's lodge, where the cooks of the convent have sufficient food ready which is served to them by the friar; food for the sick is sent to their homes. After mealtime, it always happens that the friar has to go to some neighboring pueblo to hear a confession or to see if they are careless in the boys' school, where they learn to pray and assist at mass, for this is the responsibility of the sextons and it is their duty always to have a dozen boys for the service of the sanctuary and to teach them how to help at mass and how to pray.

In the evening they toll the bell for vespers, which are chanted by the singers who are on duty for the week, and according to the importance of the feast they celebrate it with organ chants as they do for mass. . . .

One of the weekdays which is not so busy is devoted to baptism, and all those who are to be baptized come to the church on that day, unless some urgent matter should interfere; in that case, it is performed at any time. With great care, their names are inscribed in a book; in another, those who are married; and in another, the dead.

One of the greatest tasks of the friars is to adjust the disputes of the Indians among themselves, for, since they look upon him as a father, they come to him with all their troubles, and he has to take pains to harmonize them. If it is a question of land and property, he must go with them and mark their boundaries, and thus pacify them.

For the support of all the poor of the pueblo, the friar makes them sow some grain and raise some cattle, because if he left it to their discretion, they would not do anything. Therefore the friar requires them to do so and trains them so well, that, with the meat, he feeds all the poor and pays the various workmen who come to build the churches. With the wool he clothes all the poor, and the friar himself also gets his clothing and food from this source. All the wheels of this clock must be kept in good order by the friar, without neglecting any detail, otherwise all would be totally lost. . . .

This, Most Holy Father, is the state of that new and primitive church which the seraphic sons of Saint Francis, its only workers, have founded and watered with the blood and lives of ten of their brethren. . . .

LABOR PRACTICES ON A JESUIT FARM

"The garbage that comes from the tannery flows into the river . . ."

The Jesuit estates near Quito, in present day Ecuador, were large operations requiring many laborers and even producing industrial wastes that had to be dumped somewhere. The neighbors considered the practices of the fathers in these matters to be harmful. To seek relief from alleged damages, a group of local Indian rulers, caciques, wrote to the king in 1623. Their letter reveals their perception of the Jesuit enterprise.[28]

✠ Lord. By this memorial you will learn of the harmful treatment and extortions that the Indians of the town of Sangolquí receive from the fathers of the Society of Jesus. The said fathers own in the Valley of Chillo, a quarter of a league from Sangolquí, an estate where they sow 400 fanegas [each fanega = 55.5 litres] of wheat and harvest 5,000 or 6,000 fanegas. To work this farm the said fathers have 25 gañanes [perhaps West African slaves, from old "Ghana"] a year and because these 25 cannot do all the work of plowing, the fathers ask for replacements and additional laborers and two work for one month. Thus, ordinarily 50 Indians are employed and because of this we principales [chiefs] cannot comply with other requests for laborers. Also, supplies are diminishing, and a fanega of wheat and corn becomes dearer each year because the said fathers are the only ones who have a storehouse to keep the wheat. . . . So on their own authority, at times of plowing and harvest, the fathers, with their majordomos, lay brothers, and four or five blacks and mulattoes, come to the town and distribute silver to entice workers. And the Indian who does not want to go, because he must work on other farms, is carried by the said lay brothers and mulattoes, tied up, and placed in jail at night and made to work by day, being beaten, incarcerated, and the object of other wicked treatment.

Also the fathers have a church, with cross outside and bell; and the whole town [of Pintag] is gradually moving to the estate of the Jesuits, leaving the town empty; and for this reason we the caciques cannot fulfill our other obligations of supplying laborers.

Also, the said fathers have a tannery on the estate, where they cut and cure hides and leather. The garbage that comes from the tannery flows into the river near the town and this river supplies the town's drinking water. Thus, much sickness has been caused by this dumping.

In order to remedy those things we ask your Lordship to study this memorial and favor us with justice by sending someone, whoever he might be, to investigate the charges we here make for, after God, you are our source of help, and in all we ask justice.

Also, the said fathers keep a gate shut on the Camino Real that passes through their estate, and guarding the gate continually are ferocious dogs, and this so that no one will use the said Camino Real. Don García Zangolquí. Don Domingo Humaná. Don Felipe Juali Zidemon, Don Felipe Sangolquí. Don Juan Zunno. Don Francisco Gualizanmi. Don Domingo Zangolquí. [Countersigned] Don Antonio de Morga.

A PRIEST'S DUTIES IN A GUATEMALAN MISSION

"Every christening brought two reals, every marriage two crowns; . . ."

The duties of a village priest included a variety of activities. Some of them can be seen in a description by Thomas Gage of the sources of his income. He was a Dominican and was priest in two Indian villages of Guatemala from 1630 to 1635. He writes this account about ten years later in England, where he had become a Protestant. His descriptions are valuable for understanding the rounds of a priest in an isolated parish. When he speaks of the "sodalities," he is referring to voluntary societies founded by the villagers for the mutual help of the members and for honoring a local patron saint.[29]

✠ With this subordination therefore unto the Prior and cloister of Guatemala, was I sent to preach unto the Indians of Mixco and Pinola, to replace an old friar of almost fourscore years of age, who was no longer able to perform the charge which lay upon him of two towns, three leagues distant one from another. The settled means for maintenance which I enjoyed in these towns, and the common offerings and duties which I received from the Indians was this. In Mixco I was allowed every month twenty crowns [pesos], and in Pinola fifteen, which were punctually paid by the *alcaldes* and *regidores*, mayors and jurats [councilmen], before the end of the month. To meet this payment the towns sowed a common piece of land with wheat or maize, and kept their book of accounts, wherein they set down what crops they yearly received, what moneys they took in for the sale of their corn, and in the same book I wrote down what every month I received from them. At the end of the year they presented this book to be examined by some officer appointed thereunto by the court of Guatemala. Besides this monthly allowance, I had from the sodalities of the souls in purgatory every week in each town two crowns for a Mass; every month two crowns in Pinola upon the first Sunday of the month from the sodality of the Rosary, and in Mixco likewise every month two crowns apiece from three sodalities of the Rosary of the Virgin Mary, belonging to the Indians, the Spaniards, and the Blackamoors. . . . In addition, there were offerings of either money, fowls or candles upon those days whereon these Masses were sung. All this amounted to threescore and nine crowns a month, which was surely settled and paid before the end of the month. . . .

The Christmas offerings in both those two towns were worth to me when I lived there at least forty crowns. [Maundy] Thursday and [Good] Friday offerings were about a hundred crowns; All Souls' Day offerings commonly worth fourscore crowns; and Candlemas Day [February 2] offerings commonly forty more. . . . The communicants, every one giving a real, might make up in both towns at least a thousand reals; and the confessions in

Lent at least a thousand more, besides other offerings of eggs, honey, cacao, fowls, and fruits. Every christening brought two reals, every marriage two crowns; every death two crowns more at least, and some in my time died who would leave ten or twelve crowns for five or six Masses to be sung for their souls.

Those two towns of Mixco and Pinola were far inferior yet to Petapa and Amatitlán in the same valley, and not to be compared in offerings and other church duties to many other towns about that country. Yet they yielded me with the offerings cast into the chests which stood in the churches for the souls of Purgatory, and with what the Indians offered when they came to speak unto me (for they never visit the priest with empty hands) and with what other Mass stipends did casually come in, the sum of at least two thousand crowns of Spanish money, which might yearly amount to five hundred English pounds. . . .

After I was once settled in my two towns, my first care was to provide myself with a good mule, to carry me easily and as often as occasion called from the one town to the other. I soon found one, which cost me fourscore crowns, and served my turn very well, to ride speedily the nine miles across the valley between the two towns. Though my chief study here was to perfect myself in the Indian tongue, that I might the better preach unto them and be well understood, yet I omitted not to search out the Scriptures daily, and to addict myself unto the Word of God, which I knew would profit me more than all those riches and pleasures of Egypt, which for a while I saw I must enjoy till my ten years were fully expired, and licence from Rome or Spain granted for me to return to England.

A MULATTO WOMAN IN PERU

". . . daughter of a black woman called Isabel . . ."

Black women, or women of mixed blood, were rarely allowed to be professed members of the religious orders. They sometimes lived in the convents as servants or slaves of the nuns of wealthy families, but another century had to pass before they could be full members of the orders. In the face of such barriers, black and mixed-race women who felt a religious calling had several alternatives. They could join the confraternities or sodalities that honored a particular patron saint; these were organized strictly according to social class, but within each class they were open to all. There were also retreat houses for women, beaterios or recogimientos, where routines of seclusion and devotion were followed under the guidance of a priest. Other alternatives were the lay branches of the regular orders, called the Third Orders, in which women would take simple vows and continue in their normal daily life. In the following account, probably

*written to provide an ideal for others, the spirituality of a Mulatto woman
of the Third Order of the Franciscans is described by one who knew her
and who wrote about her in the late 1640s.*[30]

✠ Sister Estefanía de San Joseph was a native of Cuzco, daughter of a
black woman called Isabel the Portuguese (because she was born in Portugal), slave of Captain Maldonado, the rich. After his death, as he had
set her free, she entered the convent of Saint Clare of that city as a *donada*
(lay sister). There I met her and talked to her many times. She professed
and died with a saintly reputation around 1580. This was, then, her mother.
Her father was a Spaniard. Estefanía remained in the house and with the
family of her master. She was a good looking girl, and in his last will her
master set her free. However, his heirs tried to retain her as a slave, which
obliged her to flee Cuzco for Lima to defend legally the cause of her
freedom. And God was served that she succeeded in gaining it from the
Royal Audiencia. Our Lord was thus disposed that she should achieve her
salvation, and free her soul, as He had freed her body. . . .

She was very compassionate, and out of charity she raised four poor
Spanish children, two boys and two girls, who, with such good breeding,
indoctrination and example, became members of the Church. One boy became a priest and the other a Jesuit. The girls went to the cloisters to serve
God as nuns. One professed in the monastery of La Encarnación, of Augustinian nuns, and the other in the Dominican convent of Saint Catherine.

She was very devoted to the Seraphic Father Saint Francis. She professed
in his Third Order, and was among those who fulfilled her obligations with
the greatest fervor and observance. She helped the abbesses in the administration; collected alms for masses and the saints' feasts. She lived from
the work of her hands, making mattresses for four reales, and with this and
some alms, she sustained herself in her poverty.

. . . She visited the sick, especially those of her Order, and with great
charity cared for them, giving them the remedies they required. She collected old linen rags, and after having them washed clean, she made band-
ages. These she took to the hospitals, to minister to the sick, whom she
continuously visited with the greatest charity.

. . . She exercised herself in all kinds of penitences and asperities, *cilicios*,
and disciplines. She fasted on Mondays, Wednesdays, Fridays and Saturdays of every week with rigor and abstinence, and especially on Advent and
Lent. She showed no anger for any offense. She was always peaceful and
patient. . . .

And as this blessed woman loved and feared God so much, she strove
by all means feasible to her person and humbleness to attract all whom she
could, to the exercise of virtues. She was happy, affable, humble, gracious,
and these qualities paved her way into the homes of the principal and
richest ladies of the city. . . .

She had several grave diseases, and the last, which was very grievous, with fever and acute pains, she endured with much patience and good example. She asked to be taken to the Hospital of Charity, a very well served women's hospital. . . .

One day, when the Most Excellent Don Pedro Toledo, Marquis of Mancera, Viceroy of these kingdoms, was visiting the sick of the hospital with My Lady the Marchioness, as they often did, they both came to Estefanía's bed, and talked to her with great love, and asked her to commend them to God. Estefanía, who was already very weak, became animated and answered: "My Lord, is not Your Excellency the Viceroy? Why are you visiting a poor mulatto, as myself?" She made them pray a prayer on their knees, and asked them to give alms to the poor, and bid them good-by, begging God to confer His grace on them. The Marquis asked for her hand, and she stretched it, and they both kissed it, and asked her for blessing. And the poor woman gave it to them, making the sign of the cross over their Excellencies. All those present, and I among them, were very edified by the strength of the virtue which made possible such actions; giving valor to a humble woman, a former slave, to talk to such high persons, who, recognizing the sanctity of the sick woman, would kiss her hand and ask for her blessing.

. . . On the following day, having received the Extreme Unction, she gave her soul to God at three o'clock in the morning of 9 May, 1645, at age 84. . . .

VIRGIN OF GUADALUPE

"Her beautiful countenance is grave and noble, and rather dark."

The story of the appearance of the Virgin Mary to Juan Diego, a poor Indian lad, strongly encouraged native Mexicans to identify with the Catholic church. The image of the Virgin, which was said to have miraculously appeared in 1531 on Juan Diego's blanket, was not the picture of a European white Mary, but a dark Indian Mary. So the story became a sign of God's special protection of the native Mexicans. As such, the legend played a leading role in the formation of the Mexican national consciousness. Luis Lasso de La Vega was the first to publish the story. He wrote about 1649, while he was priest in charge of the Shrine of Our Lady of Guadalupe. The excerpts below provide the essential skeleton of La Vega's longer narrative. [31]

✠ Ten years after the capture of the city of Mexico, the wars came to an end, and there was peace in the land, and the faith began to spread, the knowledge of the true God in whom we live. About this time, in the year 1531, early in the month of December, there was a poor Indian, called Juan

Diego, so it is said, a native of Cuautitlán. It was a Saturday, very early in the morning, and he was on his way to church and to do some errands. When he reached the hill known as Tepeyacac, day was breaking, and he heard the sound of singing on the hill; . . . Juan Diego stopped to look, and said to himself, "Am I hearing right? Perhaps I am still asleep? . . . Or could I be in heaven?" He was looking eastward, . . . and he heard something calling to him from the summit of the hill and saying, *"Juanito, Juan Die-guito."* . . . And he climbed the hill to see who was calling him. When he reached the top he saw a lady standing there, who told him to come near her. . . . her raiment was resplendent, like the sun: . . . He bent low before her and heard her speak, . . ."Juanito, littlest of my sons, where are you going?" He answered: "Lady, and *Niña mia*, I am on my way to your house in Mexico Tlatilolco to follow the divine teachings." . . . She said to him: "Know the Mother of the True God in whom we live, . . . I greatly desire that a temple be built me here, that in it I may manifest and give to all my love, pity, help, and defense, for I am your mother, yours and all the dwellers in this land and the others who love me and call upon me and trust in me; . . . go to the palace of the bishop of Mexico and tell him that I have sent you . . . that here on this spot a temple be erected to me. . . ."

When he reached the city, he went . . . straight to the palace of the bishop, . . . Fray Juan de Zumarraga, . . . After listening to all he had to say, the bishop seemed skeptical, and answered him: "Come again some other time, son, and we'll talk this over more slowly;" . . . Juan Diego departed sadly. . . .

He went back the same day and climbed to the summit of the hill, where he came upon the Lady of Heaven, who was waiting for him. . . . "Lady, . . . I gave him your message . . . he received me kindly . . . but . . . he did not believe me; . . . I beg you, Lady, and *Niña mia*, to pick out some important person . . . to carry your message . . . so they will believe him. . . ." The Blessed Virgin answered: "Listen, oh littlest of my sons, . . . it is absolutely necessary that you, and you alone, solicit what I wish, . . . So I beg you, . . . and I order you to go again tomorrow to see the bishop. . . . He must erect the temple I have requested. . . ."

The next day, which was Sunday, . . . he left his house and went straight to Tlatilolco to hear the divine teachings, and to be there when they took the roll, and see the bishop afterwards. At about ten o'clock, after mass . . . Juan Diego went to the palace of the bishop. . . . He knelt at his feet, and grew sad and wept as he told him of the command of the Lady of Heaven, . . . The bishop, to certify himself, asked him many things, where he had seen her, what she was like; . . . Nevertheless the bishop did not believe him, and told him that . . . he would have to have some sign to show that he was sent by the Queen of Heaven. . . .

Juan Diego was [again] with the Blessed Virgin, . . . she said: "It is well, my son. Tomorrow you will return here and take the bishop the sign he has asked for; . . . And know, my son, that I will repay your diligence. . . ."

The next day, Monday, when Juan Diego was to have brought the sign to prove his words, he did not return, because when he reached his house, an uncle of his, Juan Bernardino, had fallen mortally ill. He went at once for a doctor, but it was too late, ...

Early Tuesday morning Juan Diego set out for Tlatilolco to bring the priest. As he was coming to the road that skirts the slope of the hill of Tepeyacac, to the west, which he was in the habit of taking, he said to himself: "I'd better keep right on, in case the Lady may see me, and stop me, ... Now I must hurry and bring the priest, for my poor uncle is anxiously waiting for him." ... [Yet] he saw her come down from the top of the hill toward him, and she said to him: "How are you, littlest of my sons? And where are you going?" ... "My uncle is very sick. He has caught the plague, and he is dying. I am now hurrying to your dwelling in Mexico to call one of the priests beloved of Our Lord to shrive him and give him the last rites, ... But be assured that I will come back ..." After the merciful Virgin had heard Juan Diego's words, she replied: "Listen, ... littlest of my sons. This that frightens and distresses you is nothing. ... have no concern for the illness of your uncle, ... Know that he is already cured." ... When Juan Diego heard these words ... he was much comforted. ... [and] begged her to send him as soon as possible to see the bishop, and take him a sign and token so he would believe him. ... She said to him: "Go up, littlest of my sons, to the top of the hill; there where you saw me and I gave you my orders, you will find many flowers. Cut them, gather them up, and then come back. ..." Juan Diego immediately climbed the hill, and ... was amazed to see that many different roses of Castile had bloomed there before the season for them, because it was bitter cold at the time. ... He at once began to cut them and gathered them together in his lap. ... He descended quickly and brought the Lady of Heaven the different kinds of roses he had cut. ... "Littlest of my sons, these roses are the proof and token you will take to the bishop. ... You are my ambassador, ... I strictly order you not to open your blanket and reveal its contents to anyone but the bishop. Tell everything as it happened, ... so as to persuade the bishop to give you his aid to erect and build the temple I have asked." ...

When he reached the bishop's palace, ... He said: "Sir, I did as you ordered me, which was to tell my mistress, the Lady of Heaven, ... that you had asked for a sign. She graciously acceded to your request. ... She sent me to the summit of the hill, where I had first seen her, to cut different roses of Castile. Although I knew well that the summit of the hill is not a place where flowers bloom, for it is all rocks, ... As I came near the top of the hill, I thought I was in Paradise. There growing all together were the most varied and exquisite roses of Castile, ... She told me why I was to give them to you. ... Here they are; receive them." Then he unfolded his white blanket ... And as the different roses of Castile poured out on the floor, on the blanket there suddenly appeared the precious image of the ever Virgin Blessed Mary, Mother of God, as it is preserved today in her temple of Tepeyacac, which is called Guadalupe. When the bishop saw it, he and all those present knelt down; they marveled greatly at it; . . . The bishop, with tears in his eyes, prayed and begged her forgiveness, . . . When he got to his feet, he untied from Juan Diego's neck the blanket in which the image of the Lady of Heaven had appeared, and carried it into his oratory. . . . The next day . . . [the bishop] said to him: "Come, show us where it is the will of the Lady of Heaven that we build her temple." And he invited the others to join them. As soon as Juan Diego had pointed out where the Lady of Heaven wanted her temple, he asked permission to leave. He wanted to go home to see his uncle Juan Bernardino who had been very sick . . . They did not permit him to go alone, but accompanied him to his house. When he arrived, they saw his uncle, who was very happy and in no wise ailing. . . . His uncle stated that it was true that he had recovered, and that he had seen [the Virgin] in the same way she had appeared to his nephew, . . . At the same time the Lady told him that when he saw the bishop he was to reveal to him what he had seen and the miraculous way she had cured him, and that he was to call her, as her blessed image was to be known, the ever Virgin Blessed Mary of Guadalupe. . . . The bishop took the blessed image of the Queen of Heaven out of the oratory of his palace, carried it to the cathedral that all the people might see and admire . . . The blanket on which the image of the Lady of Heaven appeared was the cloak of Juan Diego. It was of *ayate* [a cloth made from the fibers of the maguey, or century plant], somewhat stiff and of good weave. . . . The Blessed Image, from her feet to the crown of her head, is six handspans, and one woman's handspan high. Her beautiful countenance is grave and noble, and rather dark. . . .

TRADITIONAL RELIGION BEHIND CHRISTIAN SYMBOLS

". . . horrendous idolatries and sacrifices to the Devil."

In spite of the widespread evangelization and teaching for 125 years after the Conquest, many native Mexicans continued to mix their Christian devotion with the former traditional religion. A description of this phenomenon is found in a report written in 1654 by Fr. Gonzalo de Balsalobre, a priest who had the special task of teaching Christian doctrine south of Mexico City in a Zapotec Indian town in Oaxaca. He admitted using inquisitorial methods to collect this information, yet confessed that his earlier punishments did not remove the problem.[32]

✠ Most Illustrious and Reverend Sir:

Moved by the zeal of reverence for God Our Lord, and zealously concerned by the slight satisfaction which the natives of this kingdom give generally in things of the Faith, and to fulfill the obligations of my office, I have for some time had strong doubts regarding my parishioners and many of the natives of this bishopric. Although in public, whether forced by Ministers of the Doctrine, whether from habit, or whether to palliate the disobedience of their repeated and perfidious idolatries and superstitions that have continued from heathen times until now. . . . they perform acts suggestive of true faith, and pretend to appear as true Christians.

And by the experience that I have acquired from communication with them during *twenty-two* years as Minister of the Doctrine, desiring with tireless care by all roads to set them upon that of the State of Blessedness, I have always found them inwardly very far removed from it, although outwardly they show the contrary. And living among them with this sorrow and affliction, motivated by the causes referred to, Our Lord permitted that the falsity of their simulated faith commence to show itself in a case of relapse that I prosecuted on the twenty-third of December of the past year, fifty-three, against Diego Luis, elder and teacher of these same natives, and himself a native of a barrio under the jurisdiction of my aforementioned district, whom a little more than nineteen years ago I punished for these same transgressions.

This and other teachers who are there, and who are called in the common language "wise men" and "teachers," have continually taught those same errors that they held during their heathenism, for which purpose they have had books and handwritten notebooks of which they avail themselves for this doctrine; and in them [are prescribed] the customs of and the teaching about thirteen gods, with names of men and women, to whom they attribute various effects, ...

From these [books], with sorceries, they take their different magical answers and prognostications; such as for all kinds of hunting, and for any fishing; for the harvest of maize, chile, and cochineal; for any sickness and for the superstitious medicine with which cures must be effected; and in order to ward off hardship and death, that these will not come to their houses; . . . .

Finally, for any thing which they need they apply to one of these wise men or teachers, who, casting lots with thirteen grains of maize in honor of the aforementioned thirteen gods, teaches them to make horrendous idolatries and sacrifices to the Devil, ...

And I specify this particularly: on collecting the first ears of green maize from their fields, on the day indicated by the teacher of these rites, they sacrifice a black native hen, sprinkling with its blood thirteen pieces of copal [a hard, lustrous resin] in memory of their thirteen gods, and burning this copal, and with the rest of the blood sprinkling the patio of the house.

This they offer to the god of maize and all food, called in their language *Locucuy*, in thanksgiving for the good harvest that they have had; and on offering it they say certain words in a very low voice as when they pray. And they do the same on cutting the first chile [red peppers], offering the sacrifice to the god of lightning called *Lociyo*, in the manner described above. . . .

For the same purpose [they sacrifice] to *Nocana*, [god] of their ancestors. In pregnancies and childbirths [they sacrifice] to the goddess *Nohuichana*, and to this same [goddess] on fishing for trout; to her they burn copal and light wax candles at the edge of the fishing hole at the river, for success in fishing. . . .

For offering alms in the church, they have good and bad days; and these are indicated to them by some counselor who judges of that, according to his computation from the book of their doctrine. If the day is good, although it be during the week, all or many of them come together to light candles or to bring other offerings, which, it is evident by their own declaration, they do in reverence of their thirteen gods.

For example: if such a day is good for offering, and the counselor told them to perform it at the altar of the Virgin offering or lighting so many candles, they do it; and they offer them in reverence of the goddess *Nohuichana*; and if at all of the altars they perform this sacrifice, it is done in reverence of all the thirteen gods; and the other offerings are made in the same respect.

They are accustomed to perform many other ceremonies and rites on burying the dead, upon getting married, on copulating with their wives, on building their houses, on sowing, and on gathering their harvests; and finally, all that they do in general is superstitious and so varied that only with difficulty can it be reduced to number and form.

Everything contained in this account is verified by a large number of witnesses, judicial confessions of many of the prisoners, and statements of others. Either induced by fear of punishment or by the repentance which they claim to feel, they have accused themselves, asking for mercy and planning to make amends.

A NUN STRUGGLES FOR INTELLECTUAL FREEDOM

". . . I looked at and wondered about everything, . . ."

Colonial institutions did not encourage a literary or intellectual life. Creativity was dampened by isolation, censorship, and hierarchical intimidation. Women faced even more obstacles than men experienced. Tradition restricted their education to piety, devotion, and training in the domestic arts. However, many women from the colonial elite spent part of their lives in the seclusion of the convents, and there found a special life of their own, with a certain degree of personal independence and security. Perhaps the best writer and poet in the Spanish colonial times was Sor. Juana Inés de la Cruz (1658–1695). Most of her life was spent in Mexico

City in the Hieronimite Convent of San Gerónimo. In the late seventeenth century, the bishop of Puebla, writing under the pen name of Sor. Filotea, sought to restrain her intellectual pursuits. Sor. Juana wrote a famous reply that revealed much about her life and her inquiring mind.[33]

✠ I was less than three years old when my mother sent an older sister to be taught reading at a school for small children, of the kind called *Amigas*. Moved by sisterly affection and by a mischievous spirit, I followed her; and seeing her receive instruction, I formed such a strong desire to learn to read that I tried to deceive the schoolmistress, telling her that *my mother wanted her to give me lessons.* She did not believe me, since it was incredible; but to humor me she acquiesced. I continued to come and she to teach me, no longer in jest but in earnest; and I learned so quickly that I already knew how to read by the time my mother heard about the lessons from the teacher, who had kept them secret in order to break the pleasant news to her and receive her reward all at once. I had concealed it from my mother for fear that I would be whipped for acting without permission. . . . Later, at the age of six or seven, when I already knew how to read and write, as well as to sew and do other women's tasks, I heard that in Mexico City there was a university, and schools where the sciences were taught. No sooner had I heard this than I began to badger my mother with pleas that she let me put on men's clothing and go to Mexico City, where I could live with some relatives and attend the university. She would not do it, and quite rightly, too, but I satisfied my desire by reading in a large number of books that belonged to my grandfather, and neither punishments nor rebukes could stop me. . . .

I began to study Latin, in which I had barely twenty lessons; and so intense was my application that although women (especially in the flower of their youth) naturally cherish the adornment of their hair, I would cut it off four or six fingers' length, making it a rule that if I had not mastered a certain subject by the time it grew back, I would cut it off again, . . . for it did not seem right to me that a head so empty of knowledge, which is the most desirable adornment of all, should be crowned with hair. I became a nun, for although I knew that the religious state imposed obligations (I speak of incidentals and not of the fundamentals) most repugnant to my temperament, nevertheless, in view of my total disinclination to marriage, it was the most becoming and proper condition that I could choose to ensure my salvation. . . . I thought that I had fled from myself, but — wretched me! — I brought myself with me and so brought my greatest enemy, that thirst for learning which Heaven gave me — I know not whether as a favor or chastisement, for repress it as I might with all the exercise that the conventual state offers, it would burst forth like gunpowder; and it was verified in me that *privatio est causa appetitus* [deprivation is the cause of appetite]. . . .

At one time my enemies persuaded a very saintly and guileless prelate, who believed that study was a matter for the Inquisition, to forbid me to study. I obeyed her (for the three months or so that she had power over me) in what concerned my reading, but as for the absolute ban on study, this was not in my power to obey, for although I did not study in books, I studied everything that God created, and all this universal machine served me as a textbook. I saw nothing without reflecting upon it; everything I heard moved me to thought. This was true of the smallest and most material things, for since there is no creature, however lowly, in which one does not recognize the *me fecit Deus* [God made me], so there is no object that will not arouse thought, if one considers it as one should. Thus I looked at and wondered about everything, so that even the people I spoke to, and what they said to me, aroused a thousand speculations in me. How did such a variety of temperaments and intellects come about, since we are all of the same species? What could be the hidden qualities and traits that caused these differences? If I saw a figure I would consider the proportion of its lines and measure it in my mind and reduce it to other figures. Sometimes I would walk about in the front part of a dormitory of ours (a very spacious room); I noticed that although the lines of its two sides were parallel and the ceiling was level, the lines seemed to run toward each other and the ceiling seemed to be lower at a distance than it was close by—from which I inferred that visual lines run straight but not parallel, forming a pyramidal figure. And I speculated whether this could be the reason that caused the ancients to wonder whether the world was a sphere or not. Because although it appeared spherical, this might be an optical illusion, presenting concavities where they perhaps did not exist....

This habit is so strong in me that I see nothing without reflecting upon it. I noticed two little girls playing with a top, and I had hardly seen the movement and the object when I began, with my usual madness, to consider the easy motion of the spherical form—and how the impulse, once given, continued independently of its cause, for there was the top dancing at a distance from the girl's hand—the motive cause. Not content with this, I had some flour brought and strewn on the floor, in order to learn whether the top's motion described perfect circles or not; and I discovered that they were only spiral lines that gradually lost their circular character as the impulse diminished....

But what shall I say, my lady, of the secrets of nature that I have discovered while cooking? I observe that an egg coheres and fries in butter or oil, but breaks up in sugar syrup; that to keep sugar fluid it is sufficient to pour on it a little water containing a quince or some other sour fruit; that the yolk and white of an egg are so opposed that each one separately will mix with sugar, but not both together. I shall not weary you with such trifles, which I mention only to give you an adequate notion of my character and which, I am sure, will make you laugh; but, my lady, what can we women know except kitchen philosophy? Lupercio Leonardo aptly said: "It is possible to philosophize while preparing dinner." And I often say, observing these trifles: "If Aristotle had been a cook, he would have written much more." . . .

Although I had no need of examples, I have nevertheless been aided by the many that I have read about, in both divine and profane writings. For I have seen a Deborah giving laws, both military and political, and governing a people in which there were so many learned men. I read of that sage Queen of Sheba, so learned that she dared to test with enigmas the wisdom of the wisest of men, and suffered no reproof for it but instead was made the judge of unbelievers. I observe so many illustrious women—some adorned with the gift of prophecy, like Abigail; others, with that of persuasion, like Esther; others with piety, like Rahab; others with perseverance, like Anna, mother of Samuel; and an infinite number of others, endowed with still other kinds of graces and virtues.

If I turn my gaze to the pagans, I first encounter the Sibyls, chosen by God to prophesy the principal mysteries of our faith, in verses so learned and elegant that they arouse our wonder. I see the Greeks adore as goddess of learning a woman like Minerva, daughter of the first Jupiter and teacher of all the wisdom of Athens. I see a Bola Argentaria, who aided her husband Lucan to write the great "Battle of Pharsalia." I see a Zenobia, Queen of Palmyra, as wise as she was brave. An Aretea, the most learned daughter of Aristippus. A Nicostrata, inventor of Latin letters and most learned in Greek. . . . A Jucia, a Corinna, a Cornelia, and finally all that multitude of women who won renown under the names of Greeks, Muses, Pythonesses and in the end were nothing more than learned women, regarded and venerated as such by the ancients. Not to mention an infinite number of others of whom the books tell, such as the Egyptian Catherine, who not only read but overcame in debate the wisest sages of Egypt. I see a Gertrude study, write, and teach. And there is no need to wander far afield, for I see a holy mother of my own order, Paula, learned in Hebrew, Greek, and Latin, and most skillful in interpreting the Scriptures—so much so, in fact, that her biographer, the great and saintly Jerome, declared himself unequal to his task. . . .

BRAZILIAN SLAVERS RAID A MISSION

". . . they took . . . four thousand Indians . . . destroyed the . . . village . . . plundering the church and the Father's house, . . ."

Mixed-bloods among the Portuguese, living along Brazil's southeast coast near present-day São Paulo, made continual search-and-seize raids, entradas, into the interior. The owners of the plantations were a ready market for slaves, and royal decrees prohibiting slavery were widely ig-

nored. In the document below, two Jesuits whose missions suffered such a raid in 1629 expressed their grievances to the governor.[34]

✠ For forty years the inhabitants of São Paulo have flouted the laws of the King Our Lord with no regard for them, nor for their great offense against God, nor for the punishment they deserve. In their raids they continually capture and carry off by force of arms free and emancipated Indians, whom they keep for their own slaves or sell. Lately their boldness has been even greater than in years past, and for two principal reasons: first, this time they have gone out in greater numbers than ever, emboldened by the little or no punishment inflicted on them for their continual and unjust entradas in the past; second, they have assaulted the reductions of the Fathers of the Company of Jesus of the Province of Paraguay and taken all the people whom we were instructing.

With regard to the first point: In the beginning of the month of August 1628, some nine hundred Portuguese left the town of São Paulo with muskets, swords, cotton armor, bucklers, machetes, and much ammunition of shot and powder, and other arms. They were accompanied by two thousand two hundred Indians, unjustly taken captive on previous occasions, and also among them were the two judges of the same town of São Paulo, Sebastão Fernandes Camacho and Francisco de Paiva; two aldermen, Mauricio de Castilho and Diogo Barbosa; the Procurator of the Town Council, Cristóvão Mendes; and the son, son-in-law, and brother of Amador Bueno, the senior judge of the town. . . .

With regard to the second point: The men of the company of Antônio Rapôso Tavares, who committed these injuries which we are recording here, had said many times before setting out from São Paulo that they had decided to plunder and destroy our settlements, and thus they purposely took the route to the Plains of the Iguaçu. Here, far removed from the towns of the Spaniards and isolated in these lonely regions, where twelve reductions or Indian settlements have already been built and others, for lack of priests, merely planned, we were settling and instructing the Indians in their own lands with infinite toil and lack of necessities, being content to carry on for the love of God and for the salvation of those heathen. We suffered the poverty of the land in food and dress, planting vineyards and sowing wheat so as to have the host and wine for saying Mass.

When these bandits, then, had crossed the River Tibajiva on the eighth of September of that same year 1628, they built their palisade or fort of wooden stakes close by our villages. And—to show clearly the intention they had from the beginning—Antônio Pedroso, Captain of the advance guard of this Company, as soon as he arrived in these parts chanced upon some seventeen Christian Indians from our settlement of Encarnación on the Ñatingui, who had left their wives and children in the village under the protection of the Fathers and gone to the woods to collect mate, which they drink with warm or cold water after grinding it into powder. Pedroso seized them and carried them all off. . . .

On the thirtieth of January, 1629, they came to take by force not only Tatabrana but also all the others whom the Father was instructing in the village of San Antonio. Thus, as they themselves admit, they took from it four thousand Indians or burden bearers along with a crowd of others, and they destroyed the entire village burning many houses, plundering the church and the Father's house, and desecrating an image of Our Lady. With great violence they removed the Indian men and women who had taken refuge in the Father's house, and they killed an Indian at the very door of the house, as well as another ten or twelve persons in the same village. They took most of the Father's meager belongings, including a few shirts, two blankets, shoes, hats, napkins, tablecloths, spoons, knives, ten or twelve iron wedges, and six or seven chickens that he had. They killed one of three cows they found, and took other small things. . . .

What is of gravest concern in this whole affair is that the Holy Gospel is now so disesteemed and its Preachers so discredited that—with the door now completely closed to the preaching of the Gospel among all those heathen—the Indians imagine and repeat that we did not gather them to teach them the law of God, as we told them, but to deliver them by this subterfuge to the Portuguese. They also say that we tricked them by telling them so often that they were safe with us and that the Portuguese, being Christians and vassals of the same king, would not touch nor harm those who were with the Fathers, for they were then Christians and children of God. Therefore, since an action so atrocious goes unpunished and with no effective remedy, it seems to me that we shall be forced to abandon all these heathen, whom year after year we have been gathering together and instructing by order of His Holiness and His Majesty with so much labor and hardship. . . .

But let us return to the Portuguese and consider the wiles they employ to deceive the courts and avoid the punishment which they deserve. This does not require much effort, for they have as companions in crime not only all the people of São Paulo but also the very judges and administrator of the council of this same town. However, so that they might have a way of deceiving the higher magistrates of the state (if it can be called deceit, against persons who witness enough cases of the constant entradas, carried out with so many wrongs and cruelties, to have no illusions about such clear and open deceits) they requested I know not what sort of legal writs. . . .

What we aspire to and came to seek on such long and wearying journeys by land and sea, with such toil and hardship, is some effective remedy for the past and for what is to come. For the past, we feel that there can be no proper satisfaction unless all the captured Indians are given their freedom, and unless all or most of them are returned to their lands and the reductions. In this way they can bear witness to those of their lands that we are innocent, that we did not deliver them to the Portuguese, and that we took measures here to try to secure their freedom. And moreover they can remove the bad opinion which the infidels not yet in reductions have already formed of us of the Company, that we are traitors and deceivers, and thus we would regain the credit which we enjoyed with them and without which it seems impossible to convert them to Our Holy Faith. . . .

It is said that simply the band of Antônio Rapôso Tavares, which plundered our villages, carried away as many as twenty thousand souls, and it is therefore certain that if a very genuine remedy is not supplied in the briefest time, they will soon destroy everything and depopulate these populous lands as they have done in most of the state of Brazil. . . .

In this City of Salvador Bahia de Todos os Santos, October 10, 1629.

PROPOSED AMELIORATION OF SLAVERY

"Whoever is . . . discontent with this proposal . . . is not a Christian or has no understanding."

A question of concern was how to abolish Indian slavery for conscience's sake and still have a labor force to sustain the plantation economy and remit profits to Lisbon. Brazil seemed addicted to slavery; even the plantations belonging to the dioceses and religious orders depended on the system. To resolve this issue and other urgent problems, King John IV sent to Brazil Antônio Vieira (1608–1697), an eloquent and trusted friend. In Maranhão on the northeast coast below the Amazon River, Vieira preached to the colonists a sermon that revealed his morality and his pragmatism. His courage and shrewd leadership accomplished some reforms, but eight years later the colonists revolted against them and expelled him to Portugal. These selections from his Lenten sermon in 1653 give insights into the labor system and the growing tension resulting from slavery. [35]

✠ Christians, nobles, and people of Maranhão, do you know what God wants of you during this Lent? That you break the chains of injustice and let free those whom you have captive and oppressed. These are the sins of Maranhão; these are what God commanded me to denounce to you. Christians, God commanded me to clarify these matters to you and so I do it. All of you are in mortal sin; all of you live in a state of condemnation; and all of you are going directly to Hell. Indeed, many are there now and you will soon join them if you do not change your life.

Is it possible that an entire people live in sin, that an entire people will go to hell? Who questions thus does not understand the evil of unjust captivity. The sons of Israel went down into Egypt, and after the death of Joseph, the Pharaoh seized them and made slaves of them. God wanted to liberate those miserable people, and He sent Moses there with no other escort than a rod. . . . When Pharaoh refused to free the captives, the plagues rained down upon him. . . . Who brought to Maranhão the plague of the Dutch? Who brought the smallpox? Who brought hunger and drought? These captives. Moses insisted and pressed the Pharaoh to free the people, and what did Pharaoh respond? . . . Do you know why you do not give freedom to your illicitly gotten slaves? Because you do not know God. Lack of Faith is the cause of everything. If you possessed true faith, if you believed that there was an eternal Hell, then you would not take so lightly the captivity of a single Tapuya. . . .

I know what you are going to tell me . . . our people, our country, our government cannot be sustained without Indians. Who will fetch a pail of water for us or carry a load of wood? Who will grind our manioc [cassava]? Will our wives have to do it? Will our sons? In the first place, this is not the state into which I am placing you as you soon will see. But when necessity and conscience require such a thing, I answer yes and repeat again yes. You, your wives, your sons, all of us are able to sustain ourselves with our own labor. It is better to live from your own sweat than from the blood of others! . . .

I have studied the matter carefully, and in accordance with the most lenient and favorable opinions have come to a conclusion by which, with only minor worldly losses, all the inhabitants of this state can ease their consciences and build for a better future. Give me your attention.

All the Indians of this State are either those who serve as slaves or those who live as free inhabitants in the King's villages, or those who live in the hinterlands in their natural or free condition. These latter are the ones you go upriver to buy or "to rescue" (as they say), giving the pious verb "to rescue" to a sale so involuntary and violent that at times it is made at pistol point. These are held, owned, and bequeathed in bad faith: therefore they will be doing no small task if they forgive you for their past treatment. However, if after you have set them free, they, particularly those domestics whom you raised in your house and treated as your children, spontaneously and voluntarily wish to continue to serve you and remain in your home, no one will or can separate them from your service. And what will happen to those who do not wish to remain in your service? These will be obliged to live in the King's villages where they also will serve you in the manner which I shall mention. Each year you will be able to make your expeditions into the interior during which time you can really rescue those who are prisoners ready to be eaten. Those justly saved from death will remain your slaves. Also, all those captured in just wars will be made slaves. Upon this matter the proper judges will be the Governor of the State, the Chief Justice of the State, the Vicars of Maranhão or of Pará, and the Prelates of the four orders: Carmelite, Franciscan, Mercedarian, and the Company of Jesus. All of these who after judgment are qualified to be true captives, will be returned to the inhabitants. And what will happen to those captured in a war not classified as just? All of them will be placed in new villages or divided among the villages which exist today. There, along with the other village Indians they will be hired out to the inhabitants of this State to work for them for six months of every year alternating two months of hired work with two months devoted to their own labors and families. Thus, in this manner, all the Indians of this State will serve the Portuguese either as legitimate slaves, that is those rescued from death or captured in a just war, or those former slaves who freely and voluntarily wish to serve their old masters, or those from the King's villages who will work half the year for the good and growth of the State. It only remains to set the wages of those village Indians for their labor and service. It is a subject which would make any other nation of the world laugh and only in this land is not appreciated. The money of this land is cloth and cotton, and the ordinary price for which the Indians work and will work each month is seven feet of this cloth which has a market value of about twenty cents. An Indian will work for less than a penny a day. It is an insignificant amount and it is unworthy of a man of reason and of Christian faith not to pay such a slight price to save his soul and to avoid Hell.

Could there be anything more moderate? Could there be anything more reasonable than this? Whoever is dissatisfied or discontent with this proposal either is not a Christian or has no understanding.

PRIESTS ON THE SUGAR PLANTATIONS

"...a chaplain...teaching...all that pertains to the Christian way of life."

The basic economic units in colonial Brazil were the plantations. Each one of them centered around the "Big House" and constituted a patriarchal community that included the owner and his family, his chaplain and overseers, his slaves, and his retainers — free adults of low social status who, in return for the landowner's protection, assisted him in a variety of ways. A Jesuit priest, João António Andreoni (1650–1715) went to Brazil in 1667 and later wrote a valuable account of its farming and mining industries. In his description of the world of the sugar plantations at the end of the seventeenth century, we note the role of the resident priest.[36]

✠ If the plantation owner must display his capacity in one thing more than another, it is in the proper choice of persons to administer his estate....

The first choice that he must make with care, on the basis of secret information concerning the conduct and knowledge of the person in question, is that of a chaplain to whom he must entrust the teaching of all that pertains to the Christian way of life. For the principal obligation of the planter is to teach, or have taught, his family and slaves. This should be done not by some slave born in Brazil, or by some overseer who at best can only teach them their prayers and the laws of God and the Church by word of mouth, but by one who can explain to them what they should believe and what they must do, and how they must do it, and how they are to ask God for what they need. And for this reason, if he must pay the chaplain a little more than is customary, the planter should understand that he could not put the money to better use. . . .

The chaplain should live outside the planter's house; this is best for both, because he is a priest and not a servant, a familiar of God and not of men. He should not have any woman slave in his house, unless she be of advanced years, nor should he trade in anything, either human or divine, for all this is opposed to his clerical state and is prohibited by various Papal orders.

It is customary to pay a chaplain, when he is free to say masses during weekdays, forty or fifty thousand *reis* a year, and with what he gains from the saying of masses during the week he can earn a respectable salary — and well earned too, if he does all the things described above. If he is expected to teach the children of the plantation owner, he should receive a just additional compensation. . . .

On the day that the cane is brought to be ground, if the plantation owner does not invite the Vicar, the chaplain blesses the mill and asks God to grant a good yield and to guard those who work in it from all misfortune. When the mill stops grinding at the end of the harvest, he sees to it that all give thanks to God in the chapel. . . .

BAHÍA PREPARES A RELIGIOUS PROCESSION

"The dyers, the hatters, the harness-makers, the tinkers . . . will provide a banner."

Religious processions on the days of the saints involved much preparation and much of the town's work force. In the document below, the town council of Bahía, the colonial capital of Brazil, distributes responsibilities for the Feast of Corpus Christi, 1673. It reveals some of the religious duties of the city government and also the government's secularizing influence. The final marginal entry suggests that the same arrangements persisted for generations.[37]

✠ On the 22 day of November of the year 1673 in the council chamber of this City of Salvador Bahia de Todos os Santos, . . . the said aldermen moved and proposed that forasmuch as there were badly wanting in the processions the time-honoured insignia of the past, such as the dragon, hobbyhorses, and other old-time curiosities, which greatly enhanced the splendour and festivity which Christian piety renders to God and to his Saints, and that whereas this city had grown greatly in all the arts and crafts, some of which made no contribution of any sort or kind to the said processions—in view of all this, the said officers of the municipality resolved and agreed that the carpenters would supply the banner as they usually do, and likewise the wooden frame for the dragon, sharing this responsibility with the joiners and the turners. And the tailors would be obliged to supply their usual banner, and the cloth which covers the serpent, painted and fitted, it being their responsibility to keep and look after it always; and the carpenters would provide the wood whenever this was necessary, and all these various corporations would provide Negroes who would carry it in the processions. And the cobblers would provide their usual banner, and the dragon as they always have done. And the stone-masons will supply a banner which they will make forthwith at their own cost. The dyers, the hatters, the harness-makers, the tinkers, and the coopers will provide a banner and four hobbyhorses [*cavalinhos fuscos*]. And the male and female bakers and the pastry-cooks will provide two giants and a giantess, and a dwarf which the common people call "Father of the Giants." And the blacksmiths, the locksmiths, the barbers, the sword-cutlers, and the saddlers, who all belong to the religious brotherhood of São Jorge will be obliged to provide a banner or a pennant, as they usually do, and the statue of the Saint on his bier, and likewise the statue of the same Saint seated and arrayed on horseback, together with a Page and an Ensign, a trumpet, and drummers, and six sergeants of the guard, all properly dressed and equipped. And the itinerant women who sell from door to door, and the male and female tavern-keepers will contribute with four dances, including that of the rope-makers—And thus the said aldermen decided that this regulation concerning the form of the insignia in the said processions would be mandatory from this day forward, and that the corporations whose representatives were present should be notified forthwith that a fine of 6,000 reis paid from prison for the public works of this municipality and the new prison, would be inflicted on any which failed entirely to fulfill the obligations hereby imposed on them. And the officers further ordered that all this should be entered in these minutes. . . .

[A marginal entry reads as follows:] And the officers of the municipal council further decided that the cattle-traders will provide three little barren cows. João Peixoto Viegas wrote it on the same day and it was signed by . . .

[Another marginal entry, in a later hand, reads:] At a council meeting on the 20 October 1713 we have to declare that the button-makers shall be added to the banner of the coopers.

5 ✠ Church Affluence and Traditions versus Regalism and the Enlightenment

1700–1808

The eighteenth-century Latin American church life began with the ascendancy of the first Bourbon king on the Spanish throne, Philip V in 1700, and ended with 1808, the year when King John VI of Portugal, fleeing from Napoleon's invasion, moved to Brazil. When he set up in Rio the new capital of the Portuguese Empire, the event marked the beginning of the end of the colonial era.

During the century, missions to the native peoples continued on the frontiers. Those that were organized by the Jesuits among the Guaraní (Indians in Paraguay) around present-day Paraguay were the most elaborate and best known. The bishops often asserted their authority over such missions, but the missionaries belonged to the religious orders and jealously guarded their independence. Monasteries for men and women seemed ubiquitous. Alexander von Humboldt in the 1790s observed that Mexico City, with a population of 100,000, had 23 monasteries, 15 nunneries, and 3,300 people in them.[38] He also reported that four-fifths of the lands in some provinces of Mexico were held permanently by the church.[39] Likewise, in Lima, in the early years of the 1800s, approximately half of the houses in the city were found to belong to the church in some way.[40] The Bourbon kings guarded their own powers and especially resented the ultramontane sympathies and wealth of the religious orders and placed restrictions and taxes on them. In 1767, Charles III followed the example of France and Portugal and expelled the Society of Jesus from all the Spanish colonies. The reasons seemed to be his fears of its political and financial influence. The expulsion dealt a crippling blow to the missions and to higher education.

By the end of the century, loyalty to the king was widespread. Though it prevented anarchy in the colonies, it did not quiet hostility among the races and classes. The top posts in society continued to go to the Spanish-born whites, with the Creoles receiving secondary positions. In the church, the hardship parishes generally went to the Mestizo priests, even though their race numbered nearly a third of the population. Last of all, though they represented over forty-four percent of the population, the few Indian

Viceroy Matías de Galvez (1717-84) of Mexico. He supported the School for Fine Arts and other ideas of the Enlightenment.

priests found themselves appointed to the parishes that held the least prestige. Such inequalities in the church reflected the reality elsewhere, and bitterness smoldered. In the 1790s, various groups discussed a revolt against Spain. One of them was led by Francisco de Miranda, a Creole of Venezuela, who attempted a rebellion in 1806; though it failed, it foreshadowed what was to follow.

In Brazil, the population was about one and a half million by mid-eighteenth century, with over half the people living along the coast and in the river valleys of the sugar-producing captaincies of the Northeast. After the rush for gold to the area of Minas Gerais, about two hundred miles inland from Rio, much of the population shifted to the south and west. Lisbon then moved the colonial capital from Bahía south to Rio.

The religious orders for both men and women prospered in Brazil over the first half of the century, and their houses could be found in nearly all the major centers of population. The most influential ones were those of the Jesuits and Franciscans. Almost all convents for men and women now had schools attached for boys and girls.

By mid-century, enlightenment reforms began to influence the Portuguese crown and its colonial policies. The forceful secretary of war and foreign affairs in Lisbon, the Marquês de Pombal, injected reforms in regard to trade policies, Indian slavery, anti-Semitism, racial prejudice, education, and the accumulating wealth of the church. He developed a particular suspicion of the Jesuits and in 1759 they were expelled from the Portuguese empire.

Throughout most of the eighteenth century, the Brazilian church, just as the Spanish, excluded Indians and mixed-bloods from ordination and from membership in the religious orders. Though no native priesthood was formed, local people were usually quite religious. They expressed devotion through the brotherhoods (irmandades), the Third Orders, and pilgrimages to visit saintly hermits, who emerged to prominence in various places.

Under the patronage system, the local parish priest continued as a virtual equivalent to a government official. He was responsible for the civil registry of births, deaths, and marriages, and had much involvement in overseeing the tax system and the properties and welfare institutions of the church. As Brazilian historian Eduardo Hoornaert put it, the parishes became virtual "control posts" of the government, with the vicar as a paid representative not of the local people but of a distant hierarchy. By the end of the century, some priests were reading the literature of the enlightenment from France and Britain, and some had joined the Freemasons and worked for independence. In spite of new ideas from Europe, most of the slaveholding society remained intellectually demoralized. According to C. R. Boxer, about a third of the population in 1800 were black slaves, and a large proportion of the rest were said to have been unemployed vagrants.[41] There was no university, few books, and no printing press was allowed until 1808.[42] Nevertheless, Brazilian Catholic Christianity still remained the principal cohesive element in the colonial society and the main provider of its art, architecture, education, and public welfare.

CONTRASTING CHURCH RESOURCES IN QUITO

"In the parish churches, . . . poverty is conspicuous, . . ."

Churches, convents, and church-related welfare institutions were frequent in the urban centers and not uniformly endowed. King Philip V sent two young Spanish naval officers along on a French scientific expedition to Quito, Ecuador. The two lieutenants were trained in mathematics, astronomy, and navigation. One of them, António de Ulloa (1716–1795), wrote an extensive travelogue. The following excerpt describes his observations of church life in Quito in the years 1736–1740.[43]

✠ The city is divided into seven parishes, the Sagrario, St. Sebastian, St. Barbaria, St. Roque, St. Mark, St. Prisca, and St. Blaize. The cathedral, besides the richness of its furniture, is splendidly adorned with tapestry hangings and other costly decorations; but in this respect the other parish-churches are so mean as to have scarce necessaries for performing divine worship. Some of them are without pavement, and with every other mark of poverty. The chapel del Sagrario is very large, wholly of stone, and its architecture executed in an elegant taste; nor is the disposition of the inside inferior to the beauty of its external appearance.

The convents of monks in Quito are those of the Augustines, Dominicans, and the Fathers of Mercy, which are the heads of provinces; but besides these, there is another of Franciscan Recollects, another of Dominicans, and another of the Fathers of Mercy. In this city is also a college of Jesuits; two colleges for seculars, one called St. Lewis, of which the Jesuits have the direction; and the other St. Ferdinand, and is under the care of the Dominicans. In the first are twelve royal exhibitions for the sons of auditors and other officers of the crown. It has also an university under the patronage of St. Gregory. That of the second is a royal foundation, and dedicated to St. Thomas; the salaries of the professors are paid by the crown. . . .

Quito has also several nunneries, as that of the Conception, the orders of St. Clare, St. Catharine, and two of bare-footed Theresians. Of these one was originally founded in the town of Latacunga; but having, together with the place itself, been destroyed by an earthquake, the nuns removed to Quito, where they have ever since continued.

The college of Jesuits, as well as all the convents of monks, are very large, well built, and very splendid. The churches also, though the architecture of some is not modern, are spacious, and magnificently decorated, especially on solemn festivals, when it is amazing to behold the vast quantities of wrought plate, rich hangings, and costly ornaments, which heighten the solemnity of worship, and increase the reputation of these churches for magnificence. If those of the nunneries do not, on those occasions, exhibit such an amazing quantity of riches, they exceed them in elegance and delicacy. It is quite otherwise in the parish-churches, where poverty is conspicuous, even on the most solemn occasions; though this is partly imputed to those who have the care of them.

Here is also an hospital, with separate wards for men and women; and though its revenues are not large, yet by a proper economy they are made to answer all the necessary expenses. It was formerly under the direction of particular persons of the city, who, to the great detriment of the poor, neglected their duty, and some even embezzled part of the money received: but it is now under the care of the order of our Lady of Bethlehem, and by the attention of these fathers, every thing has put on a different aspect, the whole convent and infirmary having been rebuilt, and a church erected, which, though small, is very beautiful and finely decorated.

ACCEPTABLE CONDUCT IN THE MISSIONS

" . . . I forbade it on pain of severe punishment."

The isolated missionary among the Indians had to become a practical anthropologist and was obliged to make quick judgments about those types of behavior which were acceptable. Here Joséph Och, a German Jesuit in northwest Mexico, just south of present-day Arizona, describes his reactions to traditional tribal customs being practiced by the people under his care in the mission in the 1750s and 1760s.[44]

✠ In their customs the Indians are secretive toward the missionaries. Even among those who otherwise are good Christians there always clings something of the former odor of impiety. . . . Here were observed always some of the customs inherited from their forebears, some of them amusing and some of them superstitious, which were kept by the obdurate old ones and passed on from them orally to their descendants. . . .

The children are well built. They are born very large and strong, with hair as long as their arms, are quite chubby throughout, and of reddish color, one might well say *a matre rubet*. At baptism I might have taken them to be children of mulattoes, and the latter as Indian children, because the mulatto children were much browner and less well formed. . . .

At the tender age of six to twelve months these children must endure a cruel torture. All the hair is pulled from the child's eyebrows and the little holes or pores are enlarged with a thorn. Coal dust is then sprinkled on these bloody openings and rubbed in. The upper and lower lips are turned out as far as possible and pierced with sharp thorns as much as a hundred times. These wounds, too, are sprinkled with coal dust, or with a preparation from a pod, like our kidney bean, which is used instead of nutgall for the best ink. From this treatment the lips become swollen and blue-black, as though the child had eaten large quantities of whortleberries, and they remain this way for life.

... For performing this ugly ceremony there are, besides the one who does the pricking, a godfather and godmother who must hold the squirming, crying, and bleeding child during this torture. This devilish custom, which completely transforms a person and costs many children their lives, displeased me to the extent that I forbade it on pain of severe punishment. The first one who refused to obey and permitted his child to be so diabolically marked was disclosed to me by a faithful Indian. I had the father given twenty-five stripes, well laid-on with a braided leather whip by a powerful Indian; the mother received twelve, the godfather twenty-five, and the master of the ceremony twenty-five....

Women far advanced in pregnancy are driven from the house and absolutely forbidden to give birth within it, for such women are looked upon as being poisoned. The Indians believe that a birth deprives arrows of their power so that they will never be able to hit a mark. More than once have I encountered a miserable woman in birth pangs hanging under a tree in the forest where some other old women had tied her with ropes passed under her arms so as to torment her until she delivered. This savage midwifery and banishment I corrected with whiplashes, and brought it to pass that the women had to stay in their huts. They did this reluctantly, and the men fled elsewhere with their weapons....

They also burned a house whenever anyone died in it. At first I did not understand what caused so many fire-damaged villages. But I learned the cause, for they explained to me they no longer desired to live in a certain place because the dead one had returned to it.... Since I forbade the burning of individual huts, and forced them to live in their old dwellings, they managed piece by piece to make over a house, even to the extent of digging out the floor deeply, to give it a different appearance and so to prevent the deceased from recognizing it....

When once they were instructed in the Catholic religion, they showed zeal and became quite different persons. They went happily to church and listened patiently to a sermon or exhortation, even if it lasted several hours. They had a particular liking for church services. Everything that pertained to external ceremonies, processions, and singing was most agreeable to them. Their innocent devotion often made me laugh, for particularly in towns they sometimes dragged around figures or paintings of the saints. These they decorated with flowers and provided with many large candles to light in their honor.

They like pictures excessively and hang them one next to the other, all around in a house. Saints accompanied by an animal, such as St. James on horseback, and St. Martin, St. George, St. Luke, were dearest to them. They enjoyed very much bringing their children to be baptized, and even better to stand as godfathers.

I noticed a particular whim among them; namely, that for the sake of flattery they wished always to bestow the name of the missionary on all of their children. For this reason there were in one village none but Franciscos (which they pronounce *Parancisco*, because they have no *F* in their language). . . .

EXPELLING THE JESUITS

"God be with you, dearest fathers!"

After careful preparation, Charles III of Spain acted in June of 1767 to eliminate from his colonies the influence of the Society of Jesus. They had sizable missions and plantations among the Indians, numerous convents and churches, and extensive educational enterprises. Their leadership and paternal care for thousands of Indians, students, and parishioners had won respect and affection. At the same time, their commercial and political influence and their primary loyalty to the pope had given rise to opposition in high places. For many reasons, the crowns of Spain and Portugal expelled the fathers from their realms. About 2,200 priests from across Latin America were packed off. It was a delicate operation with many consequences. The German Jesuit missionary Joseph Och was in northern Mexico at the time of the expulsion. He described the arrest and some of the public reaction.[45]

✠ It was the twenty-fourth of June in the year 1767, the day of St. John the Baptist, when our fortunes changed. . . .

The Jesuits were all in their houses and up to no mischief. Most of them were in the house garden about three in the afternoon, and were partaking very quietly of their vesper drink, . . . when behold! there strode suddenly into their midst a Captain who was at other times cordially known to the community. His expression was serious. He looked about him with sharp eyes, spoke no word, and withdrew. Before this he had searched through all the passages of the large college which counted about ninety to one hundred Jesuits. The gist of his orders was to spy out how many men we had garrisoned in the garden as soldiers, how many bulwarks had been thrown up behind the garden walls, with how many pieces these were equipped, whether the expected number of hundreds of powder kegs, weapons, and other war equipment could be determined, and so on. . . . He regretted that on pain of death he had not been permitted a single word of explanation.

At nightfall all of us retired without any cares or worries, nay without even the slightest thought or suspicion of imminent misfortune. . . .

The men marched at eleven o'clock, being deployed to all streets where there were churches or cloisters. Men's cloisters in Mexico numbered thirty; women's cloisters, twenty. All these communities were invested with twenty or more troops. The five Jesuit establishments were, however, completely surrounded with soldiers. Cavalry drew up before the palace of the Viceroy where also forty small field pieces were aimed down all streets. . . .

The other officers and royal commissioners stood by until early morning at about four o'clock. At the stroke of four on the twenty-fifth of June, a loud shout was heard at the door of the great college. When the porter asked through a little window who was there and what was wanted, he got the reply that he should open immediately, that on superior orders certain evildoers who were in the college were to be sought out. Señor Don José de Gálvez, Royal Visitor of the entire Mexican empire, used this sharp duplicity to avoid telling as big a lie as the other officer. Truly, all Jesuits were considered impious delinquents to be seized by this gentleman who had been sent out from Spain a half year earlier for this purpose. . . .

The porter became very frightened when he heard the murmuring of so many armed men and ran hurriedly to get the portal keys from the Father Rector, to whom every night they had to be given, and to ask how he should behave in this situation. He was ordered to open the gate without hesitation or resistance, which he then did. It was still quite dark (for in Mexico day and night are almost equally long). Amid much noise three hundred men entered the college with fixed bayonets and heavily loaded muskets, each man being provided with twenty-five cartridges. They took control of the belfry and, for fear that the alarm would be rung, immediately cut the bell ropes. Two hundred men remained in the court and at the portal, the others occupied the large halls and staircases of the extensive college. Almost every room had a guard. The Señor Visitor came to the room of the Father Rector with the command that he assemble all Jesuits without exception to hear a royal decree. The Rector was not permitted to leave his room. Most of us were up, and when we wished to go through the hallways to the choir, as was our custom, to visit the Blessed Sacrament in the church, we were everywhere stopped by soldiers and ordered to gather in the great house chapel. We Jesuits did not know whether all this was fact or fancy.

. . . When all were assembled they were ordered to surrender their keys, which was immediately done. Next, a briefly worded royal decree was read by a quivering and weeping secretary. "Because of weighty considerations which His Majesty keeps hidden in his heart, the entire Society of Jesus and all Jesuits must leave the country, and their establishments and properties must be turned over to the Royal Treasurer."

What manner of emotional manifestations now occurred can more easily

be imagined than described. Some stood there quite dumfounded and im-
mobile; tears streamed from the eyes of others. Some lifted their hands
and eyes passively to heaven while others sobbed. One became insane on
the spot, and another had a fit of apoplexy. Most, however, stood there
with well-controlled feelings and expressions. . . .

That which happened to us occurred also in other colleges in the city,
and all within an hour. Elsewhere soldiers forced their way into cloisters
with orders that none be permitted to leave or enter for half a day. They
seized all bell towers so that in the event of a possible general alarm they
could control the movements of the multitude. Also on this day not a bell
was tolled, all churches remained locked, and it is not known whether a
single Mass was said by any of the total of approximately two thousand
priests distributed among all the orders in Mexico.

Then came the first question: "Where is the treasure?" for these gentlemen imagined and had noised it about that we possessed many kegs of
gold, and that many millions would fall to the royal exchequer. However,
they were astonished when they examined the books of receipts and ex-
penditures which were placed before them in the procuratory. . . .

When day broke and the townspeople opened doors and windows, they
were astonished and dumfounded to see soldiers everywhere. Those who
had planned to go out turned right around at their doors and went back
in. Others, however, who for reasons of business were already in the streets
and were talking with each other were separated by nudges in the ribs and
were told not to walk along the streets except singly. . . .

In the meantime, the greatest and first concern was to have books collected from all rooms and brought to the library. On this occasion I lost all
the books I had brought with me to the Indies from Germany, Italy, and
Spain, contrary to all laws and contrary to the intent of the royal decree
wherein it was ordered that none be deprived of his personal property.
They left us only our breviaries and the little book of Thomas à Kempis. . . .

Meanwhile, it had become apparent to the city that everything was being
directed against the Jesuits. The lamentations, weeping, and wailing were
general. Some of the most noble and wealthiest people who had sons,
brothers, or friends in the Society were beside themselves, and I know of
three who grieved to death in eight days. No one was master of himself.
At seven o'clock after trumpet call there was publicly read the royal decree,
already read to us, telling of the confiscation of our properties and about
our banishment. . . .

On the twenty-sixth of June everything went along as the day before. . . . In the afternoon still another decree was issued with [sic] forbade
each and everyone to wear Jesuit clothes (many clergymen, children and
others wore such) under pain of punishment for high treason. . . .

Our Señor Visitor was not very talkative because of the rebuffs he had
received from all and sundry in the city. He wished very much as soon as
possible to remove the Jesuits from their haunts, take them elsewhere, and

lock them up in a narrow cell; all this to happen *bello motu*. To effect this he requested many fine carriages from wealthy merchants who refused his request.... Such loyalty greatly incensed the Visitor. He issued a new decree threatening any who would decline to surrender carriages needed to convey the Jesuits.... Coachmen were seized, coaches were brought out of their stalls, and all available mules were taken to be used either as draft or pack animals....

As the first four Jesuits stepped into their carriages a general wailing, crying, and lamentation filled the air. The grief displayed by the womenfolk was most extraordinary. Countesses and marquises, some recognizable, others disguised in poor clothing, fell in crowds upon the reins and harness of the six mules and held the wheels of the coaches, thus to be able to say a few words of farewell. The soldiers noted that it was inadvisable to use much force, for had they done so all would have been buried beneath a hail of stones from the roofs. As it was, several soldiers had to make a bloody withdrawal because of a few well-aimed stones. All persons who had been confounded yesterday and the day before were now aroused and angry. An uprising would indubitably have occurred had not we Jesuits called out from the carriages and prayed that in the name of God they retire and not oppose the King's orders. These words accomplished more than did muskets, bayonets, and sabers.

The procession finally started. The lamentations were renewed and many ran alongside and followed the carriages for a distance of two hours....

On the twenty-eighth of June things were better managed. About three in the morning the other half of the Casa Profesa, as well as those of San Ildefonso College, the few from San Hieronymo College, and ten from our College of San Pedro y San Pablo were made ready. I wished to be one of the first, but was told that I would have to remain here under arrest because I was bedridden, crippled and lame, and would suffer much misery if permitted to travel a great distance either on land or sea....

On the thirtieth of June things went according to plan in our college. We were now only eighty in number; forty had to leave this day at three in the morning....

It was in the dark of night. All the rest were provided with carriages, and two accompanying horsemen with bared sabers and torches. A coach was not allowed to follow until the one preceding it had gone a distance of six or seven musket shots. Also the most complete silence had to be maintained; the coaches had to proceed very cautiously. It took us two hours to reach the first village called Guadalupe (about which I will speak elsewhere). The entire trip seemed like a funeral procession of mourning coaches.

Many of the most aristocratic ladies walked to Guadalupe dressed in Indian costumes, and disguised gentlemen rode at a gallop from coach to coach until they found the right opportunity to throw into each twenty-four pesos (convention-coins) wrapped in paper. The womenfolk removed precious rings and even their ear pendants and threw them into some of the coaches with the cries: "God be with you, dearest fathers!" It is certain that had we been permitted to talk with anyone and to take leave, we would have received astonishing sums of money for alms. These condolences moved us greatly. . . .

EDUCATIONAL REFORMS IN NEW GRANADA

"They had formerly monopolized education in their cloisters. . . "

From the Enlightenment, ideas about reason and scientific inquiry filtered into Spanish America in a variety of ways. Some of the viceroys, who were sent by the Bourbon kings of Spain, brought these "French" ideas with them. Such things as public universities, public libraries, printing presses, theaters, and educational reforms were threatening to the old Aristotelian pedagogy and to the clerical control of culture. Manuel de Guirior of New Granada, present-day Venezuela, Colombia, and Ecuador, was viceroy during the years 1773–1776. He described in the document below his efforts to make educational changes and the opposition he encountered from the Dominican clergy.[46]

✠ The instruction of youth and the encouragement of the sciences and arts are among the fundamental principles of good government and are the source of the happiness and prosperity of a state. . . . Conscious of this fact, and of the zeal with which our prudent king and his government have worked to establish sound methods of instruction, I determined to make my contribution to the worthy project begun by his Excellency, my predecessor, of founding a public university. . . . By this means, at a small cost, the kingdom could make happy its young men, who at present are denied instruction in the useful sciences and the sound methods and good taste introduced by Europe in the study of belles-lettres, and are occupied in futile debate of the abstract questions posed by Aristotle.

Knowing that His Majesty had been informed of this project, and that a decision had been delayed by the opposition of the Dominican convent in this city, which at present enjoys the sole right of granting degrees, and wishing to put an end to this unhappy state of affairs before its evil effects become incurable, I determined in consultation with the illustrious prelate and the ministers who composed the *junta superior de aplicaciones* to commission the attorney of the *audiencia*, Don Francisco Antonio Moreno y Escandón, a man of sound training and one who had all the necessary qualifications for the task, to prepare a plan of study, adapted to local conditions, that might serve as a model for other educational establishments, and help to eliminate existing abuses. After he had drawn up this plan, very intelligently and in entire conformity to the royal intentions, it was examined by the same *junta superior* and approved with universal acclaim and expressions of gratitude to Don Francisco for his zeal. It was also ordered that the plan should be carried out without delay, with the said Moreno acting as royal director of education, until such time as His Majesty . . . should make known his sovereign will.

Despite the opposition of some persons educated in the ancient fashion—notably that of the regular clergy (who were aggrieved because they had formerly monopolized education in their cloisters and were conscious of their inability to teach certain subjects which they would have to learn anew), a beginning was made with the new method in the two *colegios* of this city. . . . This had had such happy results that one year sufficed to demonstrate the progress made by the students in arithmetic, algebra, geometry, and trigonometry, and in jurisprudence and theology, whose true principles they found in the Church Councils, the ancient canons, Sacred Scripture, and the Church Fathers. . . . I am confident that your Excellency, moved by zeal in this cause, will not heed the appeals and clamors of the abovementioned convent, supported by the regular clergy, but will firmly insist that this reform be carried forward, demonstrating to His Majesty and the Royal Council of the Indies the advantages to the kingdom and monarchy of continuing this method and the urgent need for a university, a workshop in which could be formed heroes capable of making this nation happy. . . .

To this end, I have proposed to His Majesty that a beginning, at least, should be made of the university establishment, with the well-founded hope that time and circumstances will bring it to a state of greater perfection, meantime endowing it with many of the revenues of the Jesuit temporalities. . . . I have also informed His Majesty that all the books found in the *colegios* of the defunct Jesuit Society have been taken to form a public library in this capital, to which persons of literary tastes may come to obtain instruction in all subjects. A spacious room has been set apart for this worthy purpose. . . . In times to come this library can be enriched with new books, and with machines or instruments of which men of science will make profitable use.

JESUIT MISSIONS IN PARAGUAY — A FEW YEARS LATER

"The curates, . . . were masters of all."

One of history's most amazing missionary experiments was by the Jesuits in eastern Paraguay, among the Guaraní Indians near the border of southern Brazil. Beginning in the early 1600s, over the next 150 years they founded more than thirty missions, or "reductions." The missionaries

*exercised a benevolent control over thousands of Indians, and their or-
ganizational success became fabled. However, they imposed an isolation
on their enterprises, and few outsiders were able to observe and write
descriptions. A Spanish soldier and scientist, Félix de Azara (1742–1808),
was in Paraguay on an official assignment in 1781, fourteen years after
the expulsion of the "Company." He described the life of the missions
and their collapse after the Jesuits left.*[47]

✠ Having spoken of the towns founded by the Jesuit fathers, and of the
manner in which they were founded, I shall discuss the government which
they established in them. . . .

In the town of Candelaria there was a father, a kind of provincial, named
Superior of the Missions, who had authority from the Pope to confirm the
Indians and was the chief of all the curacies or towns. In each one resided
two priests, a curate and a sub-curate, who had certain assigned functions.
The sub-curate was charged with all the spiritual tasks, and the curate with
every kind of temporal responsibility. Since the latter required much knowledge and experience, the curates were always priests of notable gravity,
who had earlier been provincials or rectors of their colleges; whether or
not they knew the language of the Indians was not considered important.
Their predecessors in office left them copious diaries, with directions for
the management of labor, workshops, and so forth. The curates, in sum,
were masters of all. Although each town had its Indian *corregidor, alcaldes*,
and *regidores*, who comprised a municipal council like that of a Spanish
town, they had no jurisdiction, and were in effect nothing more than the
executors of the orders of the curate, who invariably handed down mild
judgments in all cases, civil and criminal, but did not permit an appeal to
other Spanish judges or *audiencias*.

The curate allowed no one to work for personal gain; he compelled
everyone, without distinction of age or sex, to work for the community, and
he himself saw to it that all were equally fed and dressed. For this purpose
the curates placed in storehouses all the fruits of agriculture and the prod-
ucts of industry, selling in the Spanish towns their surplus of cotton, cloth,
tobacco, vegetables, skins, yerba mate, and wood, transporting them in their
own boats down the nearest rivers, and returning with implements and
whatever else was required.

From the foregoing one may infer that the curates disposed of the surplus funds of the Indian towns, and that no Indian could aspire to own
private property. This deprived them of any incentive to use reason or
talent, since the most industrious, able, and worthy person had the same
food, clothing, and pleasures as the most wicked, dull, and indolent. It also
follows that although this form of government was well designed to enrich
the communities it also caused the Indian to work at a languid pace, since
the wealth of his community was of no concern to him. . . .

It must be said that although the fathers were supreme in all respects, they employed their authority with a mildness and restraint that command admiration. They supplied everyone with abundant food and clothing. They compelled the men to work only half a day, and did not drive them to produce more. Even their labor was given a festive air, for they went in procession to the fields, to the sound of music and carrying a little image in a litter, for which they always constructed a bower; and the music did not cease until they had returned in the same way they had set out. They gave them many holidays, dances, and tournaments, dressing the actors and the members of the municipal councils in gold or silver tissue and the most costly European garments, but they permitted the women to act only as spectators.

They likewise forbade the women to sew; this occupation was restricted to the musicians, sacristans, and acolytes. But they made them spin cotton; and the cloth that the Indians wove, after satisfying their own needs, they sold together with the surplus cotton in the Spanish towns, as they did with the tobacco, vegetables, yerba mate, wood, and skins. The curate and his companion, or sub-curate, had their own plain dwellings, and they never left them except to take the air in the great enclosed yard of their college. They never walked through the streets of the town or entered the house of any Indian or let themselves be seen by any woman — or, indeed, by any man, except for those indispensable few through whom they issued their orders. If some ailing person required spiritual aid, they brought him from his miserable dwelling to a clean room near the college that was set apart for that purpose, and the sub-curate, carried in a sedan with great pomp, administered the holy sacraments to him there.

When they appeared in the church, although it was only to say mass, it was with the greatest ceremony, wearing costly garments, surrounded and assisted by about a hundred sacristans, acolytes, and musicians. All their churches were the largest and most magnificent in that part of the world, filled with great altars, pictures, and gilding; the ornaments could not be better or more costly in Madrid or Toledo. All this is convincing evidence that the Jesuits spent on churches and their accessories, and in attiring the actors and municipal officers on festival days, the vast sums that they could have appropriated for themselves if they had been ambitious.

The streets of their towns were five paces wide. The buildings were one-story structures, each consisting of a long hall that originally housed all the subjects of a chieftain; they were later divided into little rooms, each seven *varas* long, one to each family. These rooms had no window, chimney, or kitchen, and their entire furnishings consisted of a cotton hammock, for the master of the house; the others slept on skins on the floor, without any partitions between them. The food of the Indians cost the priests little or nothing, since they had a surplus of meat from the increase of the herds on their estates. For clothing they gave each man a cap, a shirt, stockings, and a poncho, all made of cotton cloth, a thick, coarse, light-colored material. They made them shave their hair, and did not permit them to wear anything on their feet. The women also went barefooted, and their only garment was a *tipos* or sleeveless shirt of the same material as was described above, girdled at the waist. . . .

From what I could learn, in visiting all the towns, none of the Indians understood Spanish, nor could they read or write, except for a few who were taught to read and write in Guarani in order to keep accounts of what was taken into and out of the storehouses and so forth. They had no scientific knowledge and only a few crafts, since they only wove cloth for their own garments and for slaves or very poor people; but some were taught the trades of ironsmith and silversmith and painting, sculpture, music, dancing, and so forth, in which they were instructed by Jesuits brought especially for this purpose.

All were baptized and knew how to say their prayers, which all the boys and unmarried girls had to recite in a chorus under the portico of the church at dawn. Yet those who have replaced the Jesuits assert that there was little true religion among the Indians. This is not strange, in view of the fact that the Indians themselves say that there were few Jesuit curates capable of preaching the gospel in Guarani. . . . As a partial remedy for this deficiency, the Jesuits had certain clever Indians learn a few sermons, which they preached in the town square after some festival or tournament; I have heard some of these, and they contained a good deal of nonsense which the orator drew out of his head. . . .

In the year 1769, the Jesuits turned their towns over to an equal number of friars, but theirs was only the spiritual power, while the temporal power formerly enjoyed by the Jesuit curate was entrusted to a secular administrator. There was also established a military governor of all the missions of the Parana and Uruguay rivers. It could be said that these towns only changed hands, but the Jesuits were more able, moderate, and frugal, and regarded their towns as their own handiwork and private possession, and so loved them and worked for their good. The secular governors, on the other hand, and the administrators whom they appointed, not only lacked the intelligence of the Jesuits but regarded the wealth of the community as a mine which was theirs to exploit for a short time. It is not strange, therefore, that the towns have grown poor, and that the Indians are compelled to work harder and are more poorly fed and clothed.

CALIFORNIA MISSION

". . . 1783 . . . the happiest year of the mission. . . "

The founder of the Franciscan missions in California was Junípero Serra (1713–1784). His parents had been farmers in Spain, and this early training on the farm was put to good use in his missionary career in northwest

Mexico. He founded nine missions, some of which are now the cities of San Diego, San Francisco, and others, and he made his headquarters in San Carlos de Monterey. Excerpts from his final report on July 1, 1784, reveal some of the spiritual and agricultural dimensions of San Carlos.[48]

✠ Hail Jesus, Mary, Joseph!

On the most solemn feast of the Holy Spirit, Pentecost Sunday, June 3, 1770, this mission of San Carlos de Monterey was founded to the joy of the sea and land expeditions. In a short time the rejoicing was shared by the entire kingdom and eagerly celebrated in both Spains. . . .

Year 1783

We can consider this the happiest year of the mission because the number of baptisms was one hundred seventy-five and of marriages thirty-six.

The sowing of all grains amounted to eighty-four bushels, eight pecks. This included one bushel and a half of wheat, half a bushel of corn, and two pecks of beans, which were sown for the [Lower] California Indians, who had moved here and were married in this mission.

And the harvest, less the amount of forty-seven bushels which belonged to these Indians and other concessions made to the people such as a portion of the barley which they might reap and some twenty bushels of wheat from the chaff of the threshing, which was stored in the mission granaries amounted to twenty-six hundred fourteen and a half bushels, . . .

Today the new Christians of this mission number six hundred fourteen living persons, even though some of them take a leave of absence from time to time. They have been maintained and are maintained without any scarcity and we supplied the quartermaster of the presidio of San Carlos with one hundred thirty bushels of Indian corn; because they did not ask for more, also with thirty bushels of beans. The escort of this mission, at the request of the ensign quartermaster, received rations in these two kinds of grain. . . .

We do not get clothing now from the soldiers, as we did formerly, not even from those who have debts to us no matter how small. The wool, which in some of the missions is enough to cover Indian nakedness, here has not been any help to us so far, because the thefts of sheep are so numerous that already for more than three years, we can not exceed two hundred head between goats and sheep, and from shearing the few that we have we get nothing worthwhile.

The condition, then, of the Mission in things spiritual is that up to this day in this Mission:

Baptisms 1,006
Confirmations 936

And since those of the other missions belong in some

way to this it is noted in passing that their number

is 5,307

Marriages in this mission 259

Burials .... 356 ...

The number of Christian families living at the mission and eating jointly, as well as widowers, single men, and children of both sexes, is evident from the enclosed census lists. . . .

They pray twice daily with the priest in the church. More than one hundred twenty of them confess in Spanish and many who have died used to do it as well. The others confess as best they can. They work at all kinds of mission labor, such as farm hands, herdsmen, cowboys, shepherds, milkers, diggers, gardeners, carpenters, farmers, irrigators, reapers, blacksmiths, sacristans, and they do everything else that comes along for their corporal and spiritual welfare.

The work of clearing the fields once, sometimes twice, or even three times a year, is considerable because the land is very fertile. When we clear new land great hardship is required. Altogether there is sufficient land cleared for sowing more than one hundred bushels of wheat, and it is sowed in that grain, barley, vegetables, and corn. Every year we clear a little more.

To the seven months' work required to take water from the river for irrigation, as mentioned above, we must add the labor of bringing it to the lagoon near the mission residence. In some years, this lagoon used to be dry. Now it is always full, making it a great convenience and a delight to the mission. Some salmon have been placed in the pool and so we have it handy.

The timber palisade was inadequate to protect the seed grain because they [some of the Indians] steal the paling for firewood. So we dug a circular trench many thousands of varas long. This was a two years' labor and withal nothing sufficed to prevent losses every year.

Some of the land which we cleared for farming was not only covered with long tough green grasses and thickets but also with great trees, willows, elders, and so forth, and it has been hard work, as we have already noted, but we hope that it will pay off at a profit. We also have a sizable walled garden [which produces] abundant vegetables and some fruit.

Mission Buildings

In the first few years we worked hard and well on the church and the rest of the buildings. [They were made] of paling with flat earthen roofs to minimize fire danger, but no matter what we did they always leaked like a sieve and between that and the humidity everything would rot. So we decided to build of adobe and thus today all buildings are [of that material]. . . .

CLERICAL SALARIES

"... immense wealth ... in the hands of a few individuals ..."

On the eve of Mexico's war for liberation from Spain, the lower clergy were supporters of independence. The hierarchy generally remained loyal to Spain. Behind that contrast of allegiances, one factor was the sharply differing levels of salary. When Alexander von Humboldt, the German scientist, visited Mexico during his five years in Latin America, 1799–1804, he took note of this disparity. He published the findings of his trip in French and therefore reported financial amounts in French francs. [49]

✠ To complete the view of the immense wealth centered in the hands of a few individuals in New Spain, which may compete with any thing in Great Britain, or the European possessions in Hindostan, I shall add several exact statements both of the revenues of the Mexican clergy and the pecuniary sacrifices annually made by the body of miners (*cuerpo de mineria*) for the improvement of mining. This last body, formed by a union of the proprietors of mines, and represented by deputies who sit in the *Tribunal de Minera*, advanced in three years, between 1784 and 1787, a sum of four millions of francs to individuals who were in want of the necessary funds to carry on great works. It is believed in the country that this money has not been very usefully employed; ... but its distribution proves the generosity and opulence of those who are able to make such considerable largesses. ...

This inequality of fortune is still more conspicuous among the clergy, of whom a number suffer extreme poverty, while others possess revenues which surpass those of many of the sovereign princes of Germany. The Mexican clergy, less numerous than is believed in Europe, is only composed of ten thousand individuals, the half of whom are regulars who wear the cowl. If we include lay brothers and sisters, or servants, (*legos, donados y criados de los conventos,*) all those who are not in orders, we may estimate the clergy at 13 or 14,000 individuals. Now the annual revenues of the eight Mexican bishops in the following list, amounts to a total sum of 2,695,000 francs.

Revenues of the Archbishop of	Double piastres
Mexico	130,000
Bishop of la Puebla	110,000
Valladolid	100,000
Guadalaxara	90,000
Durango	35,000
Monterey	30,000

Yucatan	20,000
Oaxaca	18,000
Sonora	6,000
	539,000

The bishop of Sonora, the poorest of them all, does not draw tithes. He is paid like the bishop of Panama immediately by the king (de Caxas reales.) His income amounts only to the 20th part of that of the bishops of Valladolid and Mechoacan; and, what is truly distressing in the diocese of an archbishop whose revenue amounts to the sum of 650,000 francs, there are clergymen of Indian villages whose yearly income does not exceed five or six hundred francs [approx. US $100]. The bishop and chapter of Valladolid sent, at different times, to the king as a voluntary contribution, particularly during the last war against France, the sum of 810,000 francs. The lands of the Mexican clergy (bienes raices) do not exceed the value of 12 or 15 millions of francs; but the clergy possess immense capitals hypothecated on the property of individuals. The whole of these capitals, (capitales de Capellanias y obras pias, fondos totales de Communidades religiosas,) of which we shall give a detail in the sequel, amounts to the sum of 44 millions and a half of double piastres, or 233,625,000 francs. Cortez, from the very commencement of the conquest, dreaded the opulence of the clergy in a country where ecclesiastical discipline is difficult to maintain. He says very frankly in a letter to Charles the Fifth, "that he beseeches his majesty to send out to the Indies religieux and not canons, because the latter display an extravagant luxury, leave great wealth to their natural children, and give great scandal to the newly converted Indians." This advice, dictated by the frankness of an old soldier, was not followed at Madrid. We have transcribed this curious passage from a work published several years ago by a cardinal. It is not for us to accuse the conqueror of New Spain of predilection for the regular clergy, or antipathy towards the canons.

MISSIONS NEAR THE ORINOCO OF VENEZUELA

" . . . they have been rendered stupid by the effort to render them obedient."

Missionaries of the Capuchin order, a strict, reformed branch of Franciscans, established in the late seventeenth century numerous missions among the Chayma people in the Orinoco River basin of southern Venezuela. Alexander von Humboldt (1769–1859), the German botanist, meteorologist, and early ecologist, visited Venezuela around 1800. These excerpts from his journals reveal his perception of the Capuchin missionary work at the time.[50]

✠ The effects of this insulated system have been such that the Indians have remained in a state little different from that in which they existed whilst yet their scattered dwellings were not collected round the habitation of a missionary. Their number has considerably augmented, but the sphere of their ideas is not enlarged. They have progressively lost that vigour of character and that natural vivacity which in every state of society are the noble fruits of independence. By subjecting to invariable rules even the slightest actions of their domestic life, they have been rendered stupid by the effort to render them obedient. Their subsistence is in general more certain, and their habits more pacific, but subject to the constraint and the dull monotony of the government of the Missions, they show by their gloomy and reserved looks that they have not sacrificed their liberty to their repose without regret.

On the 4th of September, at five in the morning, we began our journey to the Missions of the Chayma Indians and the group of lofty mountains which traverse New Andalusia. On account of the extreme difficulties of the road, we had been advised to reduce our baggage to a very small bulk. . . .

The road skirted with the bamboos . . . led us to the small village of San Fernando, situated in a narrow plain, surrounded by very steep calcareous rocks. This was the first Mission we saw in America. The houses, or rather the huts of the Chayma Indians, though separate from each other, are not surrounded by gardens. The streets, which are wide and very strait, cross each other at right angles. The walls of the huts are made of clay, strengthened by lianas. The uniformity of these huts, the grave and taciturn air of their inhabitants, and the extreme neatness of the dwellings, reminded us of the establishments of the Moravian Brethren. Besides their own gardens, every Indian family helps to cultivate the garden of the community, or, as it is called, the *conuco de la communidad*, which is situated at some distance from the village. In this conuco the adults of each sex work one hour in the morning and one in the evening. In the missions nearest the coast the garden of the community is generally a sugar or indigo plantation, under the direction of the missionary; and its produce, if the law were strictly observed, could be employed only for the support of the church and the purchase of sacerdotal ornaments. The great square of San Fernando, in the centre of the village, contains the church, the dwelling of the missionary, and a very humble-looking edifice pompously called the king's house (Casa del Rey). This is a caravanserai, destined for lodging travellers; and, as we often experienced, infinitely valuable in a country where the name of an inn is still unknown. . . .

The missionary of San Fernando was a Capuchin, a native of Aragon, far advanced in years, but strong and healthy. His extreme corpulency, his hilarity, the interest he took in battles and sieges, ill accorded with the ideas we form in northern countries of the melancholy reveries and the contemplative life of missionaries. Though extremely busy about a cow which was to be killed next day, the old monk received us with kindness, and permitted us to hang up our hammocks in a gallery of his house. Seated, without doing anything, the greater part of the day, in an armchair of red wood, he bitterly complained of what he called the indolence and ignorance of his countrymen. Our missionary, however, seemed well satisfied with his situation. He treated the Indians with mildness; he beheld his Mission prosper, and he praised with enthusiasm the waters, the bananas, and the dairy-produce of the district. . . .

Towards evening we reached the Mission of Guanaguana, the site of which is almost on a level with the village of San Antonio. The missionary greeted us cordially; he was an old man, and he seemed to govern his Indians with great intelligence. The village has existed only thirty years on the spot it now occupies. Before that time it was more to the south, and was backed by a hill. It is astonishing with what facility the Indians are induced to remove their dwellings. There are villages in South America which in less than half a century have thrice changed their situation. The native finds himself attached by ties so feeble to the soil he inhabits, that he receives with indifference the order to take down his house and to rebuild it elsewhere. A village changes its situation like a camp. Wherever clay, reeds, and the leaves of the palm or heliconia are found, a house is built in a few days. These compulsory changes have often no other motive than the caprice of a missionary, who, having recently arrived from Spain, fancies that the situation of the Mission is feverish, or that it is not sufficiently exposed to the winds. Whole villages have been transported several leagues, merely because the monk did not find the prospect from his house sufficiently beautiful or extensive.

Guanaguana has as yet no church. The old monk, who during thirty years had lived in the forests of America, observed to us that the money of the community, or the produce of the labour of the Indians, was employed first in the construction of the missionary's house, next in that of the church, and lastly in the clothing of the Indians. He gravely assured us that this order of things could not be changed on any pretence, and that the Indians, who prefer a state of nudity to the slightest clothing, are in no hurry for their turn in the destination of the funds. . . .

We were received with great hospitality by the monks of Caripe. The building has an inner court, surrounded by an arcade, like the convents in Spain. This enclosed place was highly convenient for setting up our instruments and making observations. We found a numerous society in the convent. Young monks, recently arrived from Spain, were just about to settle in the Missions, while old infirm missionaries sought for health in the fresh and salubrious air of the mountains of Caripe. I was lodged in the cell of the superior, which contained a pretty good collection of books. I found there, to my surprise, the *Teatro Critico* of Feijoo, the *Lettres Edifiantes*, and the *Traité d'Electricité* by abbé Nollet. It seemed as if the progress of knowledge advanced even in the forests of America. The youngest of the capuchin monks of the last Mission had brought with him a Spanish translation of Chaptal's *Treatise on Chemistry*, and he intended to study this work in the solitude where he was destined to pass the remainder of his days. During our long abode in the Missions of South America we never perceived any sign of intolerance. The monks of Caripe were not ignorant that I was born in the protestant part of Germany. Furnished as I was with orders from the court of Spain, I had no motives to conceal from them this fact; nevertheless, no mark of distrust, no indiscreet question, no attempt at controversy, ever diminished the value of the hospitality they exercised with so much liberality and frankness. . . .

The religious orders have founded their establishments between the domain of the colonists and the territory of the free Indians. The Missions may be considered as intermediary states. They have doubtless encroached on the liberty of the natives; but they have almost everywhere tended to the increase of population, which is incompatible with the restless life of the independent Indians. As the missionaries advance towards the forests, and gain on the natives, the white colonists in their turn seek to invade in the opposite direction the territory of the Missions. In this protracted struggle, the secular arm continually tends to withdraw the reduced Indian from the monastic hierarchy, and the missionaries are gradually superseded by vicars. The whites, and the castes of mixed blood, favoured by the corregidors, establish themselves among the Indians. The Missions become Spanish villages, and the natives lose even the rememmbrance [sic] of their natural language. Such is the progress of civilization from the coasts toward the interior; a slow progress, retarded by the passions of man, but nevertheless sure and steady.

A BAROQUE INTERIOR AND A PAIR OF DICE

". . . silver bird cages, whose inmates, in thrilling notes, join . . . the organ and . . . divine worship."

Some churches attached to well-endowed convents in the late colonial period had sumptuous baroque interiors. A witty Englishman, who was a government servant in Peru in various capacities from 1804 to 1824, described the Church of Santo Domingo that belonged to the Dominican convent in Lima.[51]

✠ The parish churches of Lima have nothing to recommend them particularly to the notice of a stranger. . . .

Of the conventual churches, only those belonging to the principal houses are remarkably rich. St. Dominic, Santo Domingo, about a hundred yards from the plasa major, is truly magnificent; the tower is the loftiest in the city, being sixty-one yards high, built chiefly of bajareque; the bells are good, especially the great one, which was cast in 1807: none of the large bells are rung as in England; having no swing wheels, the clappers are merely dragged backwards and forwards till they strike the sides of the bells. The roof of the church is supported by a double row of light pillars, painted and gilt; the ceiling is divided into pannels by gilt mouldings, and the large central pannels exhibit some good scriptural paintings in fresco. The high altar, as usual, is on an elevated presbytery: it is of modern architecture, of the Ionic order; the columns are varnished in imitation of marble, with gilt mouldings, cornices, and capitals. At the foot of the presbytery, on the right, stands the beautifully rich chased and embossed silver cased altar of our Lady of the Rosary. This altar exceeds any other in Lima both in richness and effect; it is entirely covered with pure silver; its elegant fluted columns, highly finished embossed pedestals, capitals, cornices, &c., some of which are doubly gilt, are magnificently superb. In the centre of the altar is the niche of the Madonna, of exquisite workmanship, the interior contains a transparent painting of a temple, the light being admitted to it by a window at the back of the altar. The effigy is gorgeously dressed—the crown is a cluster of diamonds and other precious gems; and the drapery of the richest brocades, laces and embroidery; the rosary is a string of large pearls of the finest orient. Such is the abundance, or rather profusion, of drapery, that the same dress is never continued two days together, throughout the year. Before the niche fifteen large wax tapers are continually burning in silver sockets; and in a semicircle before the altar are suspended, by massy silver chains, curiously wrought, fourteen large heavy silver lamps, kept constantly lighted with olive oil. Besides these are, similarly suspended, eight fancifully wrought silver bird cages, whose inmates, in thrilling notes, join the pealing tones of the organ and the sacred chaunt of divine worship. Four splendid silver chandeliers hang opposite the altar, each containing fifteen wax tapers; below are ranged six heavy silver candelabra, six feet high, and six tables cased in silver, each supporting a large silver branch with seven tapers; also four urns of the same precious metal, filled with perfumed spirits, which are always burning on festivals, and emit scents from the most costly drugs and spices; the whole being surrounded by fuming pastillas, held by silver cherubim. On those days when the festivals of the Virgin Mary are celebrated, and particularly at the feast of the rosary and octavo, the sumptuous appearance of this altar exceeds all description; at that time, during nine days, more than a thousand tapers blaze, and the chaunting and music of the choir are uninterrupted. . . .

The rents of this convent amount to about eighty thousand dollars annually, and the number of friars belonging to the order is one hundred and forty. The provincial prelates are elected by the chapter every year, being a Spaniard and a Creole alternately, and the contests run so high, that a military force has sometimes been found necessary to prevent bloodshed.

Belonging to this order is the sanctuary of Saint Rose, she having been a *beata*, a devotee of the order, wearing the Dominican habit. In the small chapel are several relics or remains of the saint, as bones, hair, &c., but more particularly a pair of dice, with which, it is pretended, when Rose was exhausted by prayers and penance, Christ often entertained her with a game. Shame having become paramount to deceit, the pious brethren have lately been loath to expose these dice, which, however, were shewn to me in 1805, and I kissed them with as much pious devotion as I would have done any other pair.

WOMEN, SLAVES, AND RELIGION IN BAHÍA

" . . . the Portuguese . . . make a great outward show of religion, . . ."

The continued importation of slaves from Africa was a major phenomenon in colonial Brazil. Their presence in Bahía, the capital, plus the signs of religious faith among the citizens, are described in these paragraphs by Amedée François Frezier, a French military engineer who spent the years 1712–1714 visiting the west coast of South America and ports of Brazil.[52]

✠ The city of Bahia, as is well known, is the capital and metropolis of Brazil, and the usual seat of a viceroy. However, the governor has not always that title; witness he that was in our time.

The inhabitants have an outside good enough as to politeness, neatness, and the manner of giving themselves a good air, much like the French. I mean the men only, for there are so few women to be seen that but a very imperfect account can be given of them. The Portuguese are so jealous that they scarce allow them to go to mass on Sundays and holidays. Nevertheless, in spite of all their precautions, they are almost all of them libertines, and find means to impose upon the watchfulness of their fathers and husbands, exposing themselves to the cruelty of the latter, who kill them without fear of punishment when they discover their intrigues. Instances hereof are so frequent, that they reckoned above thirty women murdered by their husbands within a year. Fathers show more humanity toward their daughters; when they cannot hide their shame by marrying them off, they turn them out of doors, and then they are at liberty to be common. A fine expedient!

 . . . For nineteen in twenty of the people we see there are blacks, men, and women, all naked, except those parts which modesty obliges to cover; so that the city looks like a new Guinea. In short, the streets are full of none but hideous figures of black men and women slaves, whom delicacy and avarice, rather than necessity, have transplanted from the coast of Africa, to make up the state of the rich and contribute toward the sloth of the poor, who ease themselves of their labor on them, so that there are always about twenty blacks to one white. Who would believe it? There are shops full of those poor wretches, who are exposed there stark naked, and bought like cattle, over whom the buyers have the same power; so that upon slight disgusts, they may kill them almost without fear of punishment, or at least treat them as cruelly as they please. I know not how such barbarity can be reconciled to the maxims of religion, which makes them members of the same body with the whites when they have been baptized, and raises them to the dignity of sons of God, *all sons of the most High*. Doubtless they will not suffer themselves to be unconvinced of that truth; for those poor slaves are too much abused by their brethren, who scorn that relation.

I here make this comparison, because the Portuguese are Christians who make a great outward show of religion, even more than the Spaniards. For most of them walk along the streets with their heads in their hands, a figure of St. Anthony on their breasts, or hanging about their necks, and with an extravagant furniture of a long Spanish sword on their left, and a dagger almost as long as a short French sword on their right; to the end that when occasion shall offer, neither arm may be useless toward destroying of their enemies. In reality, those outward tokens of religion are very deceitful among them, not only in regard to true probity but even to Christian sentiments; they often serve to conceal from the eyes of the world a great number of Jews; an amazing instance has been seen in that town. A curate, after having for several years behaved himself outwardly to edification, at last made his escape with the sacred ornaments into Holland, to live there as a Jew; for which reason, to be admitted to the clergy, a man must prove himself an old Christian, as they call it, that is, of ancient Christian descent.

Part II

The Agony of Colonial Christendom and the Protestant Presence

1808–1962

Over the 150 years, between 1808 and 1962, the Catholic church had to face a series of challenges that finally removed the foundations of the old Christendom. After the final break with Spain and Portugal in the 1820s, the governments of the new countries insisted on keeping the "patronage" formerly exercised by the kings and queens. This meant continued government support for the church and the attendant privileges, but it also meant continued government control. Since the Inquisition was gone, questions about the church and the role of the clergy could be debated in the legislatures, cafes, and publications. Adding fuel to these discussions were the growing numbers of foreign residents and immigrants, many of whom were Protestants.

With the passing decades, the wish of the Liberal parties among other things to curtail clerical powers finally won the day. Traditional ecclesiastical functions, such as registrations of births and control over marriages and cemeteries passed to civil authorities. Similar legislation gradually restricted the church's property and wealth, diminished its influence in the public schools, and removed its spiritual monopoly, granting freedom to other churches and religions.

Losing its traditional status in this way, the church was forced to stand on its own feet. The hierarchy had opposed the secularization process and labored creatively in the 1930–1960 period to forge a neo-Christendom. Nevertheless, by the third quarter of the twentieth century, their successors were becoming grateful to be relieved of the old ties with government; though dethroned, they found themselves free for the inner renewal that was to come.

The first sustained Protestant presence in Latin America was seen in the representatives of the Bible societies and in congregations that developed among the foreign business residents and immigrants. When the legislatures finally allowed native citizens to become Protestants, mission societies in Europe and North America began to send missionaries, and within a few generations, a wide variety of churches appeared. They attracted people on the basis of the Bible, congregational life, innovative educational institutions, and their distinctiveness from nominal Catholicism. Early prejudice against Protestants lasted long into the twentieth century and made understandable their anti-Catholic sentiments. Yet wherever these feelings became exaggerated or became a substitute for their positive message, Protestants were left unprepared for the changes that were to come among the Catholics, changes to which their own Protestant presence had contributed so much.

6 ✠ Crisis of the Wars for Independence

1808–1825

The church was now conspicuously present throughout Spanish America. In Mexico, in 1808, a traveler could count ten dioceses with over a thousand parishes and three hundred convents. Visible also were the schools, hospitals, orphanages, and even some prisons that the church managed and financed. Yet one could also see weaknesses. Too many of the priests were foreigners, and hardly any were native Americans. Spaniards born in Europe still controlled the hierarchy, and their salaries were shockingly high. The Inquisition continued to intimidate innovative thinking, and the church's financial power posed a problem. Through bequests and invested capital, the church in Mexico came to own or control something like half of the total value of the real estate of the country. In the viceroyalty of Peru, its condition was similar.[1] When the wars for independence ignited in 1810, the church *per se* was not a target, but the hierarchy and most of the lower clergy identified with the wealthy citizens. They remained loyal to Spain, and rejoiced when the early revolts were put down. When Spain took a liberal turn in 1820 and began social reforms of its own, church leaders in the colonies and most of the colonial elite quickly saw the threat to their positions and contrived to support independence in time to avoid any genuine reforms.

The colonies declared themselves republics in the early 1820s, and the lawmakers secured the official position of the church in the new constitutions. Yet resentment had clearly emerged against its wealth and power. Amid the conflicts, the governments expelled the Spanish-born bishops and priests. A few years earlier, the offices of the Inquisition had been shut down. Now the frontier Indian missions in numerous areas had to close. The break with Spain thus meant radical surgery, cutting off the foreign leadership and forcing a significant step toward rooting the church in American soil.

In contrast to what happened in the Spanish colonies, Brazil's break with Portugal was accomplished with relative ease. The transition brought little threat to the Catholic Church. In the last years of the eighteenth century, some revolts against Portugal had been attempted, but the major step towards independence came from Portugal itself. When Napoleon

Father Miguel Hidalgo y Costilla (1753-1811), priest of the parish of Dolores, near Mexico City. An educator and much influenced by the Enlightenment, he gave first impetus to Mexican independence from Spain.

invaded the Iberian Peninsula in 1807, King John VI in Lisbon rounded up the royalty, the government ministers, and church hierarchy, and in 1808 fled to Rio. He soon gave his colony the status of a kingdom, and made it equal to Portugal. When he returned to Lisbon in 1820, he left his son Pedro as prince, and instructed him that if pressure for independence emerged, he should lead it. Two years later, in 1822, Pedro declared Brazil an independent empire with a National Assembly, and himself as emperor.

Almost all the clergy supported the emperor, and the first constitution, in 1824, recognized the Catholic Church to be the official religion of the state. The church retained its privileges in education, and patronage over it passed into the hands of the emperor. This endorsement was not extended to the religious orders, because their wealth and their loyalties to the Vatican and European traditions had angered the National Assemblymen, lay and clergy alike. Indeed, the Assembly passed various laws to curtail the convents.

One innovation in the 1824 constitution was the permission granted to other religions to exist in Brazil as long as they kept to private homes or places of worship that did not have the appearance of churches. In short, the Catholic Church in Brazil emerged from the independence period without the disruption it felt in the Spanish colonies and also with less resistance to heterodox ideas.

END OF THE INQUISITION

". . . that dread tribunal; and . . . its abolition . . ."

It was the Liberal Party and the Cortes, the parliament of Spain, that finally decreed an end to the Inquisition. When they did, there was much rejoicing. A British citizen who worked for over twenty years in various capacities in Ecuador, Peru, and Chile used his ready wit to describe being arraigned by a much-weakened Tribunal in Lima in 1806. Later, he was present in 1812 when the Tribunal was closed, and accompanied the crowd of curious and vengeful citizens into the dreaded premises.[2]

✠ Having one day engaged in a dispute with Father Bustamante, a Dominican friar, respecting the image of the Madonna of the Rosary, he finished abruptly, but assuring me that I should hear of it again. On the same evening I went to a billiard-room, where the Count de Montes de Oro was playing. I observed him look at me, and then speak to some friends on the opposite side of the table. I immediately recollected the threat of Father Bustamante — I knew, too, that the count was alguazil mayor [bailiff or constable] of the inquisition. I passed him and nodded, when he immediately followed me into the street. I told him that I supposed he had some message for me; he asked my name, and then said that he had. I said I was aware of it, and ready to attend at any moment. Considering for a short time, he observed, "This is a matter of too serious a nature to be spoken of in the street," and he went with me to my rooms. After some hesitation, his lordship informed me that I must accompany him on the next morning to the holy tribunal of the Faith. I answered that I was ready at any moment; and I would have told him the whole affair, but, clapping his hands to his ears, he exclaimed "No! for the love of God, not a word; I am not an inquisitor; it does not become me to know the secrets of the holy house," adding the old adage, " *del Rey y la inquisicion, chiton,* — of the King and the inquisition, hush." ... At the appointed hour, an under alguazil came to my room and told me that the alguazil mayor waited for me at the corner of the next street. On meeting him there, he ordered me not to speak to him, but to accompany him to the inquisition. I did so, and saw the messenger and another person following us at a distance. I appeared unconcerned until I had entered the porch after the count, and the two followers had passed. The count now spoke to me, and asked me if I were prepared; I told him I was: he then knocked at the inner door, which was opened by the porter. Not a word was uttered. We sat down on a bench for a few minutes, till the domiciliary returned with the answer, that I must wait. The old count now retired, and looked, as he thought, a long adieu; but said nothing. In a few minutes a beadle beckoned me to follow him. I passed the first and second folding doors, and arrived at the tribunal: it was small, but lofty, a scanty light forcing its way through the grated windows near the roof. As I entered, five Franciscan friars left the hall by the same door — their hoods were hung over their faces — their arms folded — their hands hid in their sleeves — and their cords round their necks. They appeared by their gait to be young, and marched solemnly after their conductor, a grave old friar, who had his hood over his face, but his cord round his waist, indicating that he was not doing penance. I felt I know not how — I looked upon them with pity, but could not help smiling, as the idea rushed across my mind, that such a procession at midnight would have disturbed a whole town in England, and raised the posse comitatus to lay them. I turned my eyes to the dire triumvirate, seated on an elevated part of the hall under a canopy of green velvet edged with pale blue, a crucifix of a natural size hanging behind them; a large table was placed before them, covered and trimmed to match the canopy, and bearing two green burning tapers; an inkstand, some books, and papers. Jovellanna described the inquisition by saying it was composed of *un Santo Cristo, dos candileros, y tres majderos* — one crucifix, two candlesticks, and three blockheads. I knew the inquisitors — but how changed from what at other times I had seen them! The puny, swarthy Abarca, in the centre, scarcely half filling his chair of state — the fat monster Zalduegui on his left, his corpulent paunch being oppressed by the arms of his chair, and blowing through his nostrils like an over-fed porpoise — the fiscal, Sobrino, on his right, knitting his black eyebrows, and striving to produce in his unmeaning face a semblance of wisdom. A secretary stood at each end of the table; one of them bad me to approach, which I did, by ascending three steps, which brought me on a level with the above-described trinity of harpies. A small wooden stool was placed for me, and they nodded to me to sit down; I nodded in return, and complied.

The fiscal now asked me, in a solemn tone, if I knew why I had been summoned to attend at this holy tribunal? I answered that I did, and was going to proceed, when he hissed for me to be silent. He informed me, that I must swear to the truth of what I should relate. I told him that I would *not* swear; for, as I was a foreigner, he was not sure that I was a catholic; it was therefore unnecessary for me to take that oath which, perhaps, would not bind me to speak the truth. At this time a few mysterious nods passed between the fiscal and the chief inquisitor, and I was again asked, whether I would speak the truth: I answered, yes. The matter at last was broached; I was asked if I knew the reverend father Bustamante? I replied, "I know *friar* Bustamante, I have often met him in coffee houses; but I suppose the reverend father you mean is some grave personage, who would not enter such places." "Had you any conversation with father Bustamante, touching matters of religion?" "No, but touching matters of superstition, I had." "Such things are not to be spoken of in coffee houses," said Zalduegui. "No," I rejoined, "I told father Bustamante the same thing." "But you ought to have been silent," replied he. "Yes," said I, "and be barked at by a *friar*." Zalduegui coloured, and asked me what I meant by laying such a stress on the word friar. "Any thing," said I, "just as you choose to take it." After questions and answers of this kind, for more than an hour, Abarca rang a small bell; the beadle entered, and I was ordered to retire. In a short time I was again called in, and directed to wait on Sobrino the following morning at eight o'clock, at his house: I did so, and breakfasted with him. He advised me in future to avoid all religious disputes, and particularly with persons I did not know, adding, "I requested an interview, because on the seat of judgment I could not speak in this manner. You must know," said he, "that you are here subject to the tribunal of the Faith, you, as well as all men who live in the dominions of his Catholic Majesty; you must, therefore, shape your course accordingly." Saying this he retired, and left me alone to find my way out of the house, which I immediately did. In the evening I went to a coffee house, where I saw my friend, friar Bustamante; he blushed, but with double civility nodded, and pointed to a seat at the table at which he was sitting. I shrugged my shoulders, and nodded significantly, perhaps sneeringly; he took the hint, and left the room. Soon afterwards I met the old Count de Montes de Oro, who looked, hesitated, and in a short time passed me, caught my hand, which he squeezed, but spoke not a word.

The act of the Cortes of Spain which abolished the inquisition, and which, during its discussion, produced many excellent though overheated

speeches, was published in Lima just after the above occurrence. The Señora Doña Gregoria Gainsa, lady of Colonel Gainsa, informed me that she
and some friends had obtained permission of the Viceroy Abascal to visit
the ex-tribunal; and she invited me to accompany them on the following
day, after dinner. I attended, and we went to visit the monster, as they now
dared to call it. The doors of the hall being opened, many entered who
were not invited, and seeing nothing in a posture of defence, the first victims
to our fury were the table and chairs; these were soon demolished; after
which some persons laid hold of the velvet curtains of the canopy, and
dragged them so forcibly, that canopy and crucifix came down with a horrid
crash. The crucifix was rescued from the ruins of inquisitorial state, and its
head discovered to be moveable. A ladder was found to have been secreted
behind the canopy, and thus the whole mystery of this miraculous image
became explainable and explained: — a man was concealed on the ladder,
by the curtains of the canopy, and by introducing his hand through a hole,
he moved the head, so as to make it nod consent, or shake dissent. In how
many instances may appeal to this imposture have caused an innocent man
to own himself guilty of crimes he never dreamt of! Overawed by fear, and
condemned, as was believed, by a miracle, falsehood would supply the place
of truth, and innocence, if timid, confess itself sinful. Every one was now
exasperated with rage, and "there are yet victims in the cells," was universally murmured. "A search! a search!" was the cry, and the door leading
to the interior was quickly broken through. The next we found was called
del secreto; the word secret stimulated curiosity, and the door was instantly
burst open. It led to the archives. Here were heaped upon shelves, papers,
containing the written cases of those who had been accused or tried; and
here I read the name of many a friend, who little imagined that his conduct
had been scrutinized by the holy tribunal, or that his name had been re-
corded in so awful a place. Some who were present discovered their own
names on the rack, and pocketed the papers. I put aside fifteen cases, and
took them home with me, but they were not of great importance. Four for
blasphemy bore a sentence, which was three months' seclusion in a convent,
a general confession, and different penances — all secret. The others were
accusations of friars, *solicitantes in confesione*, two of whom I knew, and
though some danger attended the disclosure, I told them afterwards what
I had seen. Prohibited books in abundance were in the room, and many
found future owners. To our great surprise we here met with a quantity of
printed cotton handkerchiefs. These alas! had incurred the displeasure of
the inquisition, because a figure of religion, holding a chalice in one hand
and a cross in the other was stamped in the centre: placed there perhaps
by some unwary manufacturer, who thought such devout insignia would
insure purchasers, but who forgot the heinousness of blowing the nose or
spitting upon the cross. . . . Leaving this room we forced our way into another, which to our astonishment and indignation was that of torture! In
the centre stood a strong table, about eight feet long and seven feet broad;

at one end of which was an iron collar, opening in the middle horizontally, for the reception of the neck of the victim; on each side of the collar were also thick straps with buckles, for enclosing the arms near to the body; and on the sides of the table were leather straps with buckles for the wrists, connected with cords under the table, made fast to the axle of an horizontal wheel; at the other end were two more straps for the ancles, with ropes similarly fixed to the wheel. Thus it was obvious, that a human being might be extended on the table, and, by turning the wheel, might be stretched in both directions at the same time, without any risk of hanging, for that effect was prevented by the two straps under his arms, close to the body; but almost every joint might be dislocated. After we had discovered the diabolical use of this piece of machinery, every one shuddered, and involuntarily looked towards the door, as if apprehensive that it would close upon him. At first curses were muttered, but they were soon changed into loud imprecations against the inventors and practisers of such torments; . . . The rack and the pillory were soon demolished; for such was the fury of more than a hundred persons who had gained admittance; that had they been constructed of iron they could not have resisted the violence and determination of their assailants. . . . We proceeded to the cells, but found them all open and empty; they were small, but not uncomfortable as places of confinement. Some had a small yard attached; others, more solitary, had none. . . .

Having examined every corner of this mysterious prison-house, we retired in the evening, taking with us books, papers, scourges, tormentors, &c., many of which were distributed at the door, particularly several pieces of the irreligious handkerchiefs.

MISSIONS DECLINE IN THE PROVINCE OF TEXAS

". . . this province has six missions, . . ."

The expulsion of the Jesuits and the lowering of missionary vocations in the late eighteenth century resulted in a weakening of the missions in the northern provinces of Mexico. A spirited and pragmatic young governor of Texas, Manuel Maria de Salcedo y Quiroga, arrived in his province in November of 1808. He had traveled from Spain by way of Philadelphia and overland to his headquarters at Fernando de Béxar. In August of 1809, he sent a report to the king. His references to the native people and the missions give a brief account of their reduced situation on the eve of independence.[3]

✠ The handling of the Indian nations that inhabit this province is also of the greatest importance. All of them at present are peaceful and the worst they are wont to do is to steal mules and horses. But, nonetheless, it would be advantageous for the King (which would be best) or for rich private individuals to establish trading posts or commercial houses to supply the Indians and to trade with them better or at least equally in kind and more abundantly than the Anglo-Americans do. Then we would be able to get out of them anything we proposed to, because the Indians develop and behave like those who trade with them according to the degree of recognized utility, convenience and advantages that are presented to them. New establishment of presidios among some of the Indian nations that desire it would be very useful.

At present this province has six missions, two of them without a missionary; and in all of them combined is the extremely small number of three hundred and forty-three souls. This system seems useful and good; but in my opinion it is much too slow and perhaps of little value. The Indians who come to the mission are not attracted because faith has entered through their ears but through their mouths by dint of gifts and food to eat. Those who are there hardly understand Spanish. They repeat the doctrine like automatons. It, therefore, would be better to bring them into missions with considerable population and with frequent friendly intercourse, for if one works only with the parents it is absolutely impossible to make them accomplished in our language and in the understanding of religious principles. Remedy is needed.

ANNUAL BLESSING OF THE SUGAR MILL

"Two lighted candles . . . close to the rollers, . . ."

Religious traditions were often present on the sugar plantations of Brazil. Before the mills started up at harvest time, the priest was called for a blessing. Henry Koster, an Englishman born in Portugal, spent the years 1809–1820 in northeast Brazil; some of that time, he served as manager of a plantation. He left a memorable description of the traditional opening of a mill, around 1812.[4]

✠ I had had some intention of leaving Jaguaribe, owing to the turbulence of the neighbourhood, to my ill-health, and to some disagreeable occurrences which had taken place between my landlord and myself. However, as this would have been very inconvenient, I resolved to stay, notwithstanding all these and other disadvantages.

Preparations were made in the month of August for setting the mill to work; the cane had not attained this year its accustomed growth, in most parts of the country, and that which I possessed was particularly stinted in size, for I had not commenced planting until it was almost too late. Every thing being ready towards the end of the month, I sent for a priest to bless the works. Unless this ceremony is performed, every person who is to be employed about the mill, both freeman and slave, would be afraid to proceed to his destined labour, and if any accident happened it would be ascribed to the wrath of heaven, for this breach of religious observance. The priest arrived and said mass, after which we breakfasted and then proceeded to the mill. The manager and several other freemen and the negroes stood around the works; a quantity of cane was placed ready to be thrust in between the rollers, and the four negroes whose part it was to feed the mill stood at their posts. Two lighted candles were placed close to the rollers, upon the platform which sustains the cane, and a small image of our Saviour upon the cross stood between them; the priest took his breviary and read several prayers, and at stated places, with a small bunch of weeds prepared for the occasion, which he dipped in a jug of holy water, he sprinkled the mill and the persons present. Some of the negroes sprang forwards to receive a good quantum of this sanctified water; and then the master of the sugar boiling-house led the way to the portion of the works of which he had the direction; and here there was another sprinkling. When we returned to the part of the mill in which the rollers stood, the priest took a large cane, and I did the same; then the signal being given the floodgate was opened and the works were soon in motion, and according to rule the two canes which the priest and I held in our hands were the first to be ground. I had heard much of this ceremony from persons of the country, and I cannot avoid saying, that although something of the ridiculous may by many persons be attached to it, still I could not help feeling much respect for it. The excitement of devout feelings among the slaves, even of those feelings which are produced by the Roman Catholic religion, cannot fail to be serviceable, and if men are to exist as slaves this is doubtless the religion which is the best adapted to persons in a state of subjection.

PRIEST RESPECTED FOR HIS MINISTRIES

"... zeal ... for the improvement of the districts ... is unremitted, ..."

Though complaints were made about many local priests, some padres were widely appreciated by their parishioners. The Englishman Henry Koster wrote of the broad interests of the vicar of his parish in northeastern Brazil around 1812–1815.[5]

✠ The parish of Itamaraca has now for some years enjoyed the blessings which proceeded from the appointment of the present vicar, Pedro de Souza Tenorio. His merit was discovered by the governor, whom he served as chaplain, and by whose application to the Prince Regent was obtained for him his present situation. The zeal of the vicar, for the improvement of the districts over which he has control is unremitted; he takes pains to explain to the planters the utility of the introduction of new modes of agriculture, new machinery for their sugar-mills, and many alterations of the same description which are known to be practised with success in the colonies of other nations; but it is not every novelty which meets with his approbation. It is no easy task to loosen the deep-rooted prejudices of many of the planters. He is affable to the lower ranks of people, and I have had many opportunities of hearing persuasion and entreaty made use of to many of his parishioners, that they would reform their habits, if any impropriety of behaviour in the person to whom he was speaking had come to his knowledge. His occasional extempore discourses on subjects of morality when seated within the railings of the principal chapel, delivered in a distinct and deep-toned voice, by a man of commanding person, habited in the black gown which is usually worn by men of his profession, were very impressive. He has exerted himself greatly to increase the civilization of the higher orders of people in his parish; to prevent feuds among them, — to persuade them to give up those notions of the connection between the patron and the dependant, which are yet too general; he urges them to educate their children, to have their dwellings in a state of neatness, to dress well themselves, their wives, and their children. He is a good man; one who reflects upon his duties, and who studies to perform them in the best manner possible. He has had the necessity of displaying likewise the intrepidity of his character; his firmness as a priest, his courage as a man, and he has not been found wanting. He is a native of Pernambuco, and has not degenerated from the high character of his provincial countrymen; he was educated at the university of Coimbra in Portugal.

BAPTISM AND MARRIAGE OF SLAVES

". . . slaves in Brazil follow the religion of their masters; . . ."

How were the African slaves evangelized, baptized, and nurtured in the Christian faith? The keen observer of the sugar plantations in the northeast of Brazil, Henry Koster, described the traditions between 1809 and 1815.[6]

✠ All slaves in Brazil follow the religion of their masters; and notwithstanding the impure state in which the Christian church exists in that country, still such are the beneficent effects of the Christian religion, that these, its adopted children, are improved by it to an infinite degree; and the slave who attends to the strict observance of religious ceremonies invariably proves to be a good servant. The Africans who are imported from Angola are baptized in lots before they leave their own shores, and on their arrival in Brazil they are to learn the doctrines of the church, and the duties of the religion into which they have entered. These bear the mark of the royal crown upon their breasts, which denotes that they have undergone the ceremony of baptism, and likewise that the king's duty has been paid upon them. The slaves which are imported from other parts of the coast of Africa, arrive in Brazil unbaptized, and before the ceremony of making them Christians can be performed upon them, they must be taught certain prayers, for the acquirement of which one year is allowed to the master, before he is obliged to present the slave at the parish church. This law is not always strictly adhered to as to time, but it is never evaded altogether. The religion of the master teaches him that it would be extremely sinful to allow his slave to remain a heathen; and indeed the Portugueze and Brazilians have too much religious feeling to let them neglect any of the ordinances of their church. The slave himself likewise wishes to be made a Christian, for his fellow-bondmen will in every squabble or trifling disagreement with him, close their string of opprobrious epithets with the name of *pagam* (pagan). The unbaptized negro feels that he is considered as an inferior being, and although he may not be aware of the value which the whites place upon baptism, still he knows that the stigma for which he is upbraided will be removed by it; and therefore he is desirous of being made equal to his companions. The Africans who have been long imported, imbibe a Catholic feeling, and appear to forget that they were once in the same situation themselves. The slaves are not asked whether they will be baptized or not; their entrance into the Catholic church is treated as a thing of course; and indeed they are not considered as members of society, but rather as brute animals, until they can lawfully go to mass, confess their sins, and receive the sacrament.

The slaves have their religious brotherhoods as well as the free persons; and the ambition of a slave very generally aims at being admitted into one of these, and at being made one of the officers and directors of the concerns of the brotherhood; even some of the money which the industrious slave is collecting for the purpose of purchasing his freedom will oftentimes be brought out of its concealment for the decoration of a saint, that the donor may become of importance in the society to which he belongs. The negroes have one invocation of the Virgin, (or I might almost say one virgin) which is peculiarly their own. Our Lady of the Rosary is even sometimes painted with a black face and hands. It is in this manner that the slaves are led to place their attention upon an object in which they soon take an interest, but from which no injury can proceed towards themselves, nor can any through its means be by them inflicted upon their masters. . . . I doubt not that the system of baptizing the newly-imported negroes, proceeded rather from the bigotry of the Portugueze in former times than from any political plan; but it has had the most beneficial effects. The slaves are rendered more tractable; besides being better men and women, they become more obedient servants; they are brought under the controul of the priesthood, and even if this was the only additional hold which was gained by their entrance into the church, it is a great engine of power which is thus brought into action.

But in no circumstance has the introduction of the Christian religion among the slaves been of more service than in the change which it has wrought in the men regarding the treatment of their women, and in the conduct of the females themselves. . . .

The slaves of Brazil are regularly married according to the forms of the Catholic church; the banns are published in the same manner as those of free persons; and I have seen many happy couples (as happy at least as slaves can be) with large families of children rising around them. The masters encourage marriages among their slaves, for it is from these lawful connections that they can expect to increase the number of their creoles. A slave cannot marry without the consent of his master, for the vicar will not publish the banns of marriage without this sanction. It is likewise permitted that slaves should marry free persons; if the woman is in bondage, the children remain in the same state, but if the man is a slave, and she is free, their offspring is also free. A slave cannot be married until the requisite prayers have been learnt, the nature of confession be understood, and the Sacrament can be received. Upon the estates the master or manager is soon made acquainted with the predilections of the slaves for each other, and these being discovered, marriage is forthwith determined upon, and the irregular proceedings are made lawful. . . .

SERMON FOR THE EMPEROR

". . . the royal family attended Mass . . ."

In 1822, after two years as prince of the Kingdom of Brazil, Pedro declared the country to be an independent empire with a national assembly and himself as emperor. Maria Graham (1785–1842) traveled in Brazil with her father, an admiral in the British navy. At a small church in Rio in August of 1823, she attended a special service for the Virgin Mary, which Dom Pedro I and the royal family also attended. She described the occasion.[7]

✠ 15th. — The feast of Our Lady of the Assumption, called here Nossa Senhora da Gloria, the patroness of the Emperor's eldest child, is celebrated today, and of course the whole of the royal family attended Mass in the morning and evening. I was spending the day with Mrs. May, at her pleasant house on the Gloria Hill, and we agreed to go in the afternoon to see the ceremony. The church is situated on a platform, rather more than half way up a steep eminence overlooking the bay. The body is an octagon of thirty-two feet diameter; and the choir, of the same shape, is twenty-one feet in diameter. We entered among a great crowd of persons, and placed ourselves within the choir; and shortly afterwards the Imperial party entered, and I was not disagreeably surprised at being most pleasantly recognised. The salutation, as this evening's service is called, was well performed as to music, and very short: after it, for the first time, I heard a Portuguese sermon. It was of course occasional. The text, 1 Kings, chap. ii. ver. 19.— "And "the king rose up to meet his mother, and bowed himself unto her, "and sat down on his throne, and caused a seat to be set for the king's mother, and she sat on his right hand." The application of this text to the legend of the Assumption is obvious, and occupied the first division of the discourse. The second part consisted in an application of the history of the early part of Solomon's reign to the present circumstances of Brazil; the restoration of the kingdom, the triumph over faction, and the institution of laws, forming the grounds of comparison. The whole people of Brazil were called upon to join in thanksgiving and prayers to the Virgin of Glory: thanksgiving that she had given to her people, as rulers, the descendants of the Emanuels, the Johns, and the Henrys of Portugal, and of the Maria Theresas of Austria; and prayers that she would continue her gracious protection, and that most especially to the eldest hope of Brazil, named after her and dedicated to her. The whole was gravely and properly done, with as little of the appearance of flattery to the illustrious persons present as possible, and did not last above fifteen minutes. On this occasion, the veadors, and other persons attendant on the Imperial family, wore white silk surplices, and bore torches in their hands.

7 ✠ Catholics: The Crisis Deepens

1825–1850

When the white colonists broke from Spain and Portugal, the major motivation was to keep control of church and society in their own hands. This they did, but one thing they could not preserve was political unity. The liberators, like Simón Bolívar, had hoped and planned for it in the 1820s, but regional difficulties broke up the traditional viceroyalties. Only Brazil hung together; the rest broke apart, so that by 1830 the political map of Latin America became more or less as we know it today.

The old economic system continued, but it came under British influence. The new republics exported minerals, cotton, wood, leather, sugar, and other raw materials to Europe, and in return bought manufactured goods. Also, the daily life of most of the people remained just as it always had been — impoverished. In the Spanish-speaking republics, no social revolution occurred. The church continued to be the principal landholder and preserved much of its past. In spite of these continuities, things were not the same. Church leadership had been crippled in numbers; by 1829, practically the entire Spanish-born hierarchy was gone, reducing the number of priests and religious by nearly fifty percent. Hardest hit were the missions to the Indians.

Another change was reflected in the opportunity to criticize clerical power. Liberal parties and Freemasonry sprang up in almost every country to carry forward the ideas of the eighteenth-century Enlightenment. One of their principal targets was the power exerted over society by the clergy. The liberal parties of the various republics differed in many ways, but in one respect they were unified; they wished to reduce clerical influence in all sectors of society. Opposing them were the conservative parties, which claimed that the anticlerical laws advocated by the liberals were really anti-Christian.

In Brazil, the elites found a unity in their emperors, Pedro I and Pedro II, and in their common fear of slave uprisings. Amid this political unity, the church had preserved its former status, yet there were weaknesses here also. Parish churches were in bad repair; clergy and religious were poorly educated and morally lax, and vocations to the priesthood were scarce.[8]

Fanny Calderón de la Barca, the Scottish wife of the first Spanish ambassador to Mexico after independence, 1839-42. Her letters and descriptions of those years were published and widely read. She illustrates the foreign element resident for the first time in the cities of Latin America.

A WEAKENED ECCLESIASTICAL ESTABLISHMENT

"... son mui buenos Catolicos, pero mui malos Christianos ..."

After the break with Spain, the first governments in the republic tended to be liberal. They gave voice to long-felt dissatisfactions over the Spanish control of the church, and over the hierarchy's opposition to the revolution. The expulsion of most of the Spanish bishops caused disarray in the organization of the church. The British Charge d'Affaires, Henry G. Ward, described the weak condition of the church in Mexico as he saw it during the years 1825–1827.[9]

✠ The six years which have elapsed since the declaration of Independence, have rendered the concurrence of His Holiness no longer of such vital importance. The country has been prepared, gradually, for a change, which cannot now be much longer deferred; ...

A short view of the present state of the Ecclesiastical establishments of New Spain will place this point in a clearer light.

The Republic is divided into one Archbishopric, (that of Mexico,) and the nine Bishoprics of La Puebla, Guadalajara, Valladolid, Durango, Monterey, Oajaca, Yucatan, Chiapa, and Sonora....

Seven of the Bishoprics, and *Seventy-nine* of the benefices attached to the Cathedrals, are now vacant. Some of the Chapters are reduced to two or three individuals; many of whom are old, and unable to execute the duties of their situations. Of the three remaining Bishops, (those of La Puebla, Yucatan, and Oaxaca,) One (the Bishop of Yucatan), is absolutely in his dotage; and the other two, from their position in the Southern part of the Republic, are unable to ordain those who wish to enter into orders in the North, without compelling them to undertake a journey of three or four hundred leagues, in order to undergo the necessary examinations.... The Parochial Clergy distributed amongst the 1194 parishes, into which the country is divided, are those who suffer most severely from the present disorganization of the Church. They are not only deprived by it of the preferment to which their services entitle them, but many, who accepted in 1821, living in *Tierra Caliente*, or other unhealthy districts, upon an understanding that they were to be held (as before the Revolution), for a short term of years, are compelled still to retain their situations, until the exercise of the right of Patronage enables the Government to relieve them.

Under these circumstances, it is not extraordinary that the inconveniences of a dependent existence should be so strongly felt, as to create a very general desire for emancipation; and should the Pope neglect the present opportunity, or insist upon onerous conditions in the Concordat, which the Government is still desirous to frame, he will find, when too late, that he has no longer any hold upon the country, and that the *Colonial*

Policy of Rome will not be more patiently endured, than the Colonial Policy of the Court of Madrid. . . .

In 1826, the number of the secular clergy was estimated at 3473, and in 1827 at 3677. The number of those who took orders during each of these years is not supposed to have amounted to one-fourth of those who were ordained in 1808.

The Regular Clergy is divided into fourteen Provinces, possessing 150 Convents which contained in all 1918 Friars; so that the whole of the Secular and Regular Clergy of the present day does not much exceed *one-half* of the number known to exist in 1803. . . .

Of the Tithes, nothing certain is yet known; they vary, of course, every year, as the agriculture of the country revives; but they do not yet produce any thing like their former amount; nor is it probable that they will. In the Bishoprics, upon the Western coast, (Durango, Guadalajara, and Valladolid,) I found a general falling off in the amount of the Tithes complained of; and this not proceeding from the ruin of the great Haciendas alone, but from the dissemination of ideas unfavourable to the rights of the Church. . . .

Throughout the Bishopric of Valladolid the marriage fees vary from seventeen, to twenty-two dollars; in La Puebla, Durango, and Mexico, they are from fourteen to eighteen dollars, according to the supposed means of the parties; and these enormous sums are extorted from the meanest parishioners.

The fees on baptisms, and burials, are likewise very high. In the Mining districts, each miner pays *weekly* to the Church, half a real (a medio), in order to provide for the expenses of his funeral; and on the day of the *Raya* (the weekly payment), an agent of the *Cura* is always present to receive it. Thus twenty-six reals, or three dollars and two reals (thirteen shillings English money), are paid annually, by each mining labourer, in full health and employment, in order to secure the privilege of a mass being read over his body upon his decease. An Indian, who lives ten years under such a system, would pay six pounds ten shillings for the honour of a funeral; and yet would not be exempt from continuing his contributions, although the amount paid in one year, ought more than to cover any fees that could reasonably be claimed by the Church.

I do not fear being accused of an uncharitable spirit in these remarks, for I have heard many of the most enlightened of the Mexican Clergy deplore the existence of such a state of things, and admit, that the want of a moral feeling amongst the lower classes, is the natural fruit of a system, under which such abuses have been suffered to prevail.

One of the most distinguished members of a Cathedral Chapter, while lamenting, in a conversation with me, the debased state of the people of his diocese, used this remarkable phrase: "*Son mui buenos Catolicos, pero mui malos Christianos*"; (They are very good Catholics, but very bad Christians) meaning, (as he afterwards stated,) that it had been but too much the interest of the lower orders of the Clergy, to direct the attention of their flocks, rather to a scrupulous observance of the *forms* of the Catholic Church, than to its moral or spirit, from which their revenues derived but little advantage.

CALIFORNIA MISSIONS

". . . in some of the missions much misery prevails, . . . in others . . . a degree of cheerfulness . . ."

> *When the Spanish missionaries were expelled, it usually meant the collapse of their missions and the scattering of the Indians. In Mexico, this happened in 1833–1834, when the government secularized the California missions. For some years, even before the missionaries were deported, the government had substantially reduced their financial support. In the following document, we see a glimpse of the missions during 1825–1828. While a ship of the British Royal Navy was assessing commercial possibilities on the west coast of North America, its captain, Frederick W. Beechy, explored the region around San Francisco Bay and visited the Franciscan missions. His report describes the beginning of the end for the friars.*[10]

✠ The same feeling of discontent that was experienced by the garrison, pervaded the missions, in consequence of some new regulations of the republican government, the first and most grievous of which was the discontinuance of a salary of 400 dollars per annum, heretofore allowed to each of the padres: the support the former government had given to the missions amounted, according to Langsdorff, to a million piastres a year. Another grievance was, the requisition of an oath of allegiance to the reigning authorities, which these holy men considered so egregious a violation of their former pledge to the king of Spain, that, until he renounced his sovereignty over the country, they could not conscientiously take it; . . . A third grievance, and one which, when duly considered, was of some importance, not only to the missions but to the country in general, was an order to liberate all those converted Indians from the missions who bore good characters, and had been taught the art of agriculture, or were masters of a trade, and were capable of supporting themselves, giving them portions of land to cultivate. . . .

This philanthropic system at first sight appeared to be a very excellent one, and every friend to the rights of man would naturally join in a wish for its prosperity; but the Mexican government could not have sufficiently considered the state of California, and the disposition of the Indians. . . .

The Indians whom this law emancipated were essential to the support of the missions, not only for conducting their agricultural concerns, but for keeping in subordination by force and example those whom disobedience and ignorance would exempt from the privilege; and as a necessary consequence of this indulgence the missions would be ruined before the system could be brought into effect, even supposing the Indians capable of conducting their own affairs. So far from this being the case, however, they were known to possess neither the will, the steadiness, nor the patience to provide for themselves. . . .

The object of the mission is to convert as many of the wild Indians as possible, and to train them up within the walls of the establishment in the exercise of a good life, and of some trade, so that they may in time be able to provide for themselves and become useful members of civilized society. . . .

Having become Christians they are put to trades, or if they have good voices they are taught music, and form part of the choir of the church. Thus there are in almost every mission weavers, tanners, shoemakers, bricklayers, carpenters, blacksmiths, and other artificers. Others again are taught husbandry, to rear cattle and horses; and some to cook for the mission: while the females card, clean, and spin wool, weave, and sew; and those who are married attend to their domestic concerns.

In requital of these benefits, the services of the Indians, for life, belong to the mission, and if any neophyte should repent of his apostacy from the religion of his ancestors and desert, an armed force is sent in pursuit of him, and drags him back to punishment apportioned to the degree of aggravation attached to his crime. It does not often happen that a voluntary convert succeeds in his attempt to escape, as the wild Indians have a great contempt and dislike for those who have entered the missions, and they will frequently not only refuse to readmit them to their tribe, but will sometimes even discover their retreat to their pursuers. This animosity between the wild and converted Indians is of great importance to the missions, as it checks desertion, and is at the same time a powerful defense against the wild tribes, who consider their territory invaded and have other just causes of complaint. The Indians, besides, from political motives, are, I fear, frequently encouraged in a contemptuous feeling towards their unconverted countrymen, by hearing them constantly held up to them in the degrading light of *béstias*! and in hearing the Spaniards distinguished by the appellation of *génte de razón*. . . .

In some of the missions much misery prevails, while in others there is a degree of cheerfulness and cleanliness which shows that many of the Indians require only care and proper management to make them as happy as their dull senses will admit of under a life of constraint.

The two missions of Sán Francisco and Sán José are examples of the contrast alluded to. The former in 1817 contained a thousand converts, who were housed in small huts around the mission; but at present only two hundred and sixty remain—some have been sent, it is true, to the new mission of Sán Francisco Solano, but sickness and death have dealt with an unsparing hand among the others. The huts of the absentees, at the time of our visit, had all fallen to decay, and presented heaps of filth and rubbish; while the remaining inmates of the mission were in as miserable a condition as was possible to conceive, and were entirely regardless of their own comfort. Their hovels afforded scarcely any protection against the weather, and were black with smoke; some of the Indians were sleeping on the greasy floor; others were grinding baked acorns to make into cakes, which constitute a large portion of their food. So little attention indeed had been paid even to health that in one hut there was a quarter of beef suspended opposite a window, in a very offensive and unwholesome state, but its owners were too indolent to throw it out. Sán José, on the other hand, was all neatness, cleanliness, and comfort; the Indians were amusing themselves between the hours of labour at their games; and the children, uniformly dressed in white bodices and scarlet petticoats, were playing at bat and ball. Part of this difference may arise from the habits of the people, who are of different tribes. . . .

The children and adults of both sexes, in all the missions, are carefully locked up every night in separate apartments, and the keys are delivered into the possession of the padre; and as, in the daytime, their occupations lead to distinct places, unless they form a matrimonial alliance, they enjoy very little of each other's society. It, however, sometimes happens that they endeavor to evade the vigilance of their keepers, and are locked up with the opposite sex; but severe corporeal punishment, inflicted in the same manner as is practised in our schools, but with a whip instead of a rod, is sure to ensue if they are discovered. Though there may be occasional acts of tyranny, yet the general character of the padres is kind and benevolent, and in some of the missions, the converts are so much attached to them that I have heard them declare they would go with them, if they were obliged to quit the country. It is greatly to be regretted that, with the influence these men have over their pupils, and with the regard those pupils seem to have for their masters, the priests do not interest themselves a little more in the education of their converts, the first step to which would be in making themselves acquainted with the Indian language. Many of the Indians surpass their pastors in this respect, and can speak the Spanish language, while scarcely one of the padres can make themselves understood by the Indians. They have besides, in general, a lamentable contempt for the intellect of these simple people, and think them incapable of improvement beyond a certain point. Notwithstanding this, the Indians are, in general, well clothed and fed; they have houses of their own, and if they are not comfortable, it is, in a great measure, their own fault; their meals are given to them three times a day, and consist of thick gruel made of wheat, Indian corn, and sometimes acorns, to which at noon is generally added meat.

RELIGIOUS REPRESSION IN RURAL ARGENTINA

"... a procession ... with soldiers on either side ... to strike down all who are not kneeling ..."

In the cosmopolitan port cities, the authority of the priests had diminished. In isolated, rural areas, however, the medieval synthesis of church and government hung on. This is illustrated by an account written by an American, John A. King, who in 1817, as a boy of fourteen, ran away from New York and spent the next twenty-four years in Argentina. He spent much of his career as an officer in the army of the Republic in the days of Juan Manuel de Rosas, governor of Buenos Aires. In the late 1830s, King visited the town of Jujuy in the extreme northwest of the country, an old mule-train stop on the road to Bolivia. While there, he had a brush with a local friar which landed him in jail and revealed something of the continuing religious and political influence of the church in the area.[11]

✠ I set out one fine morning, with an attendant on horseback, leading a mule, which bore my valisés strapped across his back. As a measure of precaution, in case the mule should at any time get from his fastening, and stray into the woods, a small bell was attached by a strap to his neck, by which his whereabout might be known; or at every step the bell responded with a continuous "tinkle, tinkle, tinkle." We proceeded first to Oran, where I learned that the Doña Cacinta was at that time on a visit at Jujuy, and I felt gratified that I should thus have the privilege of her society during my few days of leisure. I proceeded immediately on my journey, stopping at Ladesma and San Pedro, ... and at length arrived at Jujuy. My attendant with the mule had not yet arrived; and as he often travelled slower than myself, I knew not how far behind he might be; so I gave my horse in charge, and with a friend started as far as the market-place, in which direction I knew my servant would pass. Here I waited, expecting every moment to hear the "tinkle" of his bell.

It is proper here to remind the reader, that I was in what is very significantly termed a Catholic country; or, to be more explanatory, a country governed by the Catholic religion; for although the civil authority of the country is stern, and the military sway almost boundless, the ecclesiastical is *supreme*; and woe to the luckless wight who falls into its grasp. All must own submission and pay obeisance to the church; and the governor, the general, or the judge, whatever may be his own private tenets, must hail the passing *host* with bended knee, or suffer the severest punishment of an offended priesthood for his temerity. The *holy host*, as it is termed, is borne by a procession of friars, headed with one bearing an image of the Saviour. At his side is another, carrying a small bell, which, by a continual tinkle, gives notice of their approach. These are preceded, at a distance of forty or fifty yards, by priests, with soldiers on either side, ready to strike down all who are not kneeling at their approach.

I was at the market-place, as before stated, in conversation with my friend, awaiting the arrival of my servant, and expecting every moment to hear the tinkle of the bell attached to his mule. The sound of a bell at length reached my ear, but I was in earnest conversation and gave it no heed, when suddenly I received a blow from behind, which threw me a little forward, and knocked my *garro* into the dirt. I turned to resent the insult, and met the frown of an exasperated friar. He was preceding the *host*, accompanied by his guard, from the musket of one of whom I had received the blow. But, as I always scrupulously conformed, outwardly at least, to the customs of the country, I instantly fell upon my knees, by the side of my friend, who had discovered the cause of our interruption in time to escape the holy displeasure of the advanced guard of the host.

The procession passed on. I felt that I had committed a crime sufficient to draw a watchful eye towards me, yet trusted that no further note would be taken of the circumstance. It was a vain trust, however; for, in the space of eight hours, I was arrested for contumely towards the holy church, and, without trial or examination of any kind, cast into a loathsome cell. The Doña Cacinta had no sooner learned of my arrival and imprisonment, than she wrote to Governor Civilia, urging him to demand my release; but that officer, after various vain attempts, was forced to declare, in a letter (which was clandestinely conveyed to me) that his intercessions were totally disregarded, and that it was impossible to effect my liberation. He also deplored my detention from the regiment; and stated that nearly all the provinces were in seditious commotion. Nothing, therefore, remained to me, but to submit to my miserable imprisonment and abide the result. My offence had, of course, been magnified a thousandfold. The friar who caused my imprisonment, very naturally, in making his complaint, made it strong enough to accomplish his object; and from that grew a mountain of offence in the public mind. The friend who was near me at the time of the occurrence, very wisely remained silent; well knowing, as I did, that to attempt to excuse an offender against the church, was but to become an abettor and share his punishment.

For three months I had been in this horrible confinement, which had almost deprived me of reason, when one night I was awakened from a feverish slumber, by the drawing of bolts at my prison door. Lifting my head, I saw, indistinctly, the form of a friar, with his cowl closely drawn, and holding in his hand a lamp, whose flickering flame served only to make more dreary the desolation of my prison. As he entered, the door was closed and bolted behind him. Resting on my elbow, I looked upon him from the dark corner where I lay, without speaking a word; but, as I gazed, the thought, "Is this an angel of light, or an angel of darkness?" crossed my mind. Throwing back his cowl, and shading with his hand the light from his eyes, he looked for a moment, with a straining effort, into the dark recess; then, without moving further, pronounced my name. I at once recognized the man whom I had encountered at the marketplace, and on whose complaint I had been thrown into this gloomy dungeon; and I replied, in a bitter tone—

"Well, *holy* father, what would you have of me now?"

"My son," said he, "this is no hour for irreverent blasphemy: but I forgive you. The punishment of your crime has already exceeded my intent; yet I fear the worst has not arrived."

"Well, I can bear it all, be it what it may. My life and these walls have become wedded: if I should part with them at the same time, it would not go hard with me."

"My son!" said he, in an exclamation of reproof. "Look at me," I continued, "and answer to my bones, which speak to you through the parched skin, whether it is possible for you to make a punishment of *death*. The poor machinery of my body, worn as it is by sickness and distress, hangs together but by a single thread, which barely keeps the soul within its tenement. 'Twould not cause one pang to sever it."

"Still I would save you, though I fear it is too late. The people are greatly excited towards you, and whether you shall die or suffer banishment to Casas Matar, is not yet determined."

"If I die on this issue, you may account yourself my murderer," I replied, in a calm but decided tone.

"I can prevent such a catastrophe," said he, "on one condition, which is in your power to meet."

"And what is that condition, holy father?"

"Remember, my son, that your life is dear to those who love you in a distant land. Think of them, my son, and for their sake strive to preserve it."

"But the condition, holy father; what is the condition?"

"That you become a Catholic."

"Friar, you do not know me. My life is scarce worth the holding at any price; surely, I will not buy it so dearly as that. Will nothing but apostasy serve me in my extremity?"

"Nothing but that can save you."

"Then let me die!"

"At least you will *say* you are a Catholic, that I may tell it to the holy fathers, and thus subdue your enemies; say that, and your prison doors are open."

"Father, I will not even lie to save a wretched life. While I have sojourned in your country, I have observed all the requirements of your public customs and ceremonies. I have fought for your country, I have bled for it, I have suffered for it, and now I am ready to die, if it please ye; but, if it must be so, I will die as I have lived—a man of honour!"

"You will not say it?"

"No!"

Crossing himself devoutly, he said—

"Then *I will*"; and with these words he left the cell.

What course he pursued, I know not; but for seventeen days longer I remained in all the horror of suspense, when at length a person, whom I had not seen before, entered the prison, bearing in his hand an open letter, which he handed to me. On looking at the letter, I found it to be an order for my release, with directions to leave the town in twenty-four hours; upon which I was immediately conducted to the street, and set at liberty.

I proceeded directly to the house where I had left the little all that I possessed, in hopes of obtaining a change of apparel, and a little money to assist me on my return to Oran, but I found nothing. My valises, with their contents, horse, mule, every thing had been swept away by the confiscating power of the church, and I stood once more penniless.

I determined to hasten direct to Oran, weak and emaciated as I was, in hopes of there finding leisure and means for the restoration of my health, before taking command of my regiment.

NUNNERY OF ENCARNACIÓN

"This convent is in fact a palace."

After twenty years of political independence, life for the upper classes and for the church's hierarchy was exceedingly comfortable and light years removed from the situation of the average citizen. The diary of Fanny Calderón de la Barca, Scottish wife of the first Spanish ambassador to Mexico, gives a rare view of the inside of a highly endowed nunnery, as she saw it in April of 1840. [12]

✠ Accordingly, on Sunday afternoon, we drove to the Encarnación, the most splendid and richest convent in Mexico, excepting perhaps La Concepción. If it were in any other country I might mention the surpassing beauty of the evening, but as—except in the rainy season, which has not yet begun—the evenings are always beautiful, the weather leaves no room for description. The sky always blue, the air always soft, the flowers always blossoming, the birds always singing . . .

We descended at the convent gate, were admitted by the portress, and were received by several nuns, their faces closely covered with a double crape veil. We were then led into a spacious hall, hung with handsome lustres, and adorned with various Virgins and saints magnificently dressed. Here the eldest, a very dignified old lady, lifted her veil—the others following her example—and introduced herself as the *madre vicaria*, bringing us many excuses from the old abbess who, having an inflammation in her eyes, was confined to her cell. She and another reverend mother, and a group of elderly dames—tall, thin, and stately—then proceeded to inform us that the Archbishop had, in person, given orders for our reception and that they were prepared to show us the whole establishment.

The dress is a long robe of very fine white cassimere, a thick black crape veil, and long rosary. The dress of the novices is the same, only that the veil is white. For the first half-hour or so, I fancied that along with their politeness was mingled a good deal of restraint, caused perhaps by the presence of a foreigner, and especially of an Englishwoman. My companions they knew well, the Señorita [Escandón] having even passed some months there. However this may have been, the feeling seemed gradually to wear away. Kindness or curiosity triumphed; their questions became unceasing; and before the visit was concluded I was addressed as *"mi vida, my life"* by the whole establishment.

Where was I born? Where had I lived? What convents had I seen? Which did I prefer, the convents in France or those in Mexico? Which were largest? Which had the best garden? &c., &c. Fortunately I could, with truth, give the preference to their convent, as to spaciousness and magnificence, over any I ever saw.

The Mexican style of building is peculiarly advantageous for recluses, the great galleries and courts affording them a constant supply of fresh air—while the fountains sound so cheerfully, and the garden in this climate of perpetual spring affords them such a constant source of enjoyment all the year round, that one pities their secluded state much less here than in any other country.

This convent is in fact a palace. The garden, into which they led us first, is kept in good order, with its stone walks, stone benches, and an ever-playing and sparkling fountain. The trees were bending with fruit, and they pulled quantities of the most beautiful flowers for us; sweet peas and roses, with which all gardens here abound, carnations, jasmine, and heliotrope. It was a pretty picture to see them wandering about, or standing in groups in this high-walled garden, while the sun was setting behind the hills, and the noise of the city was completely excluded, everything breathing repose and contentment. Most of the halls in the convent are noble rooms. We visited the whole, from the refectory to the *botica* [pharmacy], and admired the extreme cleanliness of everything, especially of the immense kitchen, which seems hallowed from the approach even of a particle of dust. This circumstance is partly accounted for by the fact that each nun has a servant, and some have two; for this is not one of the strictest orders. The convent is rich; each novice at her entrance pays five thousand dollars into the common stock. There are about thirty nuns and ten novices.

The prevailing sin in a convent generally seems to be pride, the

Pride that apes humility;

and it is perhaps nearly inseparable from the conventual state. Set apart from the rest of the world they, from their little world, are too apt to look down with contempt which may be mingled with envy, or modified by pity, but must be unsuited to a true Christian spirit.

The novices were presented to us—poor little entrapped things! who really believe they will be let out at the end of the year if they should grow tired, as if they would ever be permitted to grow tired! The two eldest and most reverend ladies are sisters—thin, tall, and stately, with high noses, and remains of beauty. They have been in the convent since they were eight years old (which is remarkable, as sisters are rarely allowed to profess in the same establishment), and consider La Encarnación as a small piece of heaven upon earth. There were some handsome faces amongst them, and one whose expression and eyes were singularly lovely, but truth to say these were rather exceptions to the general rule.

Having visited the whole building, and admired one virgin's blue satin and pearls, and another's black velvet and diamonds, sleeping holy infants, saints, paintings, shrines, and confessionals—having even climbed up to the *azotea* [flat roof], which commands a magnificent view—we came at length to a large hall decorated with paintings and furnished with antique high-backed armchairs, where a very elegant supper, lighted up and ornamented, greeted our astonished eyes: cakes, chocolate, ices, creams, custards, tarts, jellies, blancmangers, orange and lemonade, and other profane dainties, ornamented with gilt paper cut into little flags, &c. I was placed under a holy family, in a chair that might have served for a pope; the Señora Adalid and the Señorita Escandón on either side. The elder nuns, in stately array, occupied the other armchairs, and looked like statues carved in stone. A young girl, a sort of *pensionnaire*, brought in a little harp without pedals and, while we discussed cakes and ices, sung different ballads with a good deal of taste. The elder nuns helped us to everything, but tasted nothing themselves. The younger nuns and the novices were grouped upon a mat *à la Turque*, and a more picturesque scene altogether one could scarcely see: the young novices with their white robes, white veils and black eyes; the severe and dignified *madres* with their long dresses and mournful-look-ing black veils and rosaries; the veiled figures occasionally flitting along the corridor; ourselves in contrast, with our *worldly* dresses and coloured rib-bons; and the great hall lighted by one immense lamp that hung from the ceiling. I felt transported three centuries back, and half afraid that the whole would flit away and prove a mere vision, a waking dream.

A gossiping old nun, who hospitably filled my plate with everything, gave me the enclosed *flag* cut in gilt paper, which, together with her custards and jellies, looked less unreal. They asked many questions in regard to Spanish affairs, and were not to be consoled for the defeat of Don Carlos, which they feared would be an end of the true religion in Spain.

After supper, to try the organ we proceeded upstairs to the choir where the nuns attend public worship, and which looks down upon the handsome convent church. I was set down to a sonata of Mozart's, the servants blowing the bellows. It seems to me that I made more noise than music, for the organ is very old, perhaps as old as the convent, which dates three centuries back. However, the nuns were pleased and, after they had sung a hymn, we returned below. I was rather sorry to leave them, and felt as if I could have passed some time there very contentedly; but it was near nine o'clock, and we were obliged to take our departure; so, having been embraced very cordially by the whole community, we left the hospitable walls of the Encarnación.

TAKING THE VEIL

"In the middle . . . knelt the novice . . . arrayed in . . . white lace, veil, and jewels, . . ."

When young girls entered the novitiate, the family and parish church prepared a veritable wedding feast for friends and dignitaries. In her famous diary, Life in Mexico, *Fanny Calderón de la Barca described one of these events in June of 1840.*[13]

✠ Some days ago, having received a message from *my nun* that a girl was about to take the veil in her convent, I went there about six o'clock. Knowing that the church on these occasions is apt to be crowded to suffocation, I proceeded to the *reja* [grille], and—speaking to an invisible within—requested to know in what part of the church I could have a place. Upon which a voice replied:

"*Hermanita* (my sister), I am rejoiced to see you. You shall have a place beside the godmother."

"Many thanks, *hermanita*. Which way shall I go?"

Voice: "You shall go through the sacristy. José María!"

José María, a thin, pale, lank individual with hollow cheeks, who was standing near like a page in waiting, sprang forward: "*Madrecita*, I am here!"

Voice: "José María—that lady is the Señora de Calderón. You will conduct Her Excellency to the front of the grating, and give her a chair."

After I had thanked the *voice* for her kindness in attending to me on a day when she was so much occupied with other affairs, the obsequious José María led the way, and I followed him through the sacristy into the church where were already a few kneeling figures, and thence into the railed-off enclosure—destined for the relatives of the future nun—where I was permitted to sit down in a comfortable velvet chair. I had been there but a little while when the aforesaid José María reappeared, picking his steps as if he were walking upon eggs in a sickroom. He brought me a message from the Madre Adalid that the nun had arrived, and that the *madrecita* wished to know if I should like to give her an embrace before the ceremony began. I therefore followed my guide back into the sacristy, where the future nun was seated beside her godmother, and in the midst of her friends and relations, about thirty in all.

She was arrayed in pale blue satin, with diamonds, pearls, and a crown of flowers. She was literally smothered in blonde and jewels; and her face was flushed as well it might be, for she had passed the day in taking leave of her friends at a fête they had given her, and had then, according to custom, been paraded through the town in all her finery. And now her last hour was at hand.

When I came in she rose and embraced me with as much cordiality as if we had known each other for years. Beside her sat the *madrina*, also in white satin and jewels; all the relations being likewise decked out in their finest array. The nun kept laughing every now and then in the most unnatural and hysterical manner, as I thought—apparently to impress us with the conviction of her perfect happiness—for it is a great point of honour amongst girls similarly situated to look as cheerful and gay as possible: the same feeling, though in a different degree, which induces the gallant highwayman to jest in the presence of the multitude when the hangman's cord is within an inch of his neck; the same which makes a gallant general, whose life is forfeited, command his men to fire on him; the same which makes the Hindu widow mount the funeral pyre without a tear in her eye, or a sigh on her lips. If the robber were to be strangled in a corner of his dungeon; if the general were to be put to death privately in his own apartment; if the widow were to be burnt quietly on her own hearth; if the nun were to be secretly smuggled in at the convent gate like a bale of contraband goods—we might hear another tale.

This girl was very young, but by no means pretty—on the contrary, rather *disgraciée par la nature*—and perhaps a knowledge of her own want of attractions may have caused the world to have few charms for her.

But José María cut short my train of reflections by requesting me to return to my seat before the crowd arrived, which I did forthwith. Shortly after, the church doors were thrown open, and a crowd burst in, everyone struggling to obtain the best seat. Musicians entered, carrying desks and music books, and placed themselves in two rows, on either side of the enclosure where I was. Then the organ struck up its solemn psalmody, and was followed by the gay music of the band. Rockets were let off outside the church, and, at the same time, the *madrina* and all the relations entered and knelt down in front of the grating which looks into the convent, but before which hung a dismal black curtain. I left my chair and knelt down beside the godmother.

Suddenly the curtain was withdrawn, and the picturesque beauty of the scene within baffles all description. Beside the altar, which was in a blaze of light, was a perfect mass of crimson and gold drapery—the walls, the antique chairs, the table before which the priests sat, all hung with the same splended material. The bishop wore his superb mitre and robes of crimson and gold, the attendant priests also glittering in crimson and gold embroidery.

In contrast to these, five-and-twenty figures, entirely robed in black from head to foot, were ranged on each side of the room prostrate, their faces touching the ground, and in their hands immense lighted tapers. On the foreground was spread a purple carpet bordered round with a garland of freshly gathered flowers, roses and carnations and heliotrope, the only things that looked real and living in the whole scene. In the middle of this knelt the novice, still arrayed in her blue satin, white lace veil and jewels, and also with a great lighted taper in her hand.

The black nuns then rose and sang a hymn, every now and then falling on their faces and touching the floor with their foreheads. The whole looked like an incantation, or a scene in *Robert le Diable*. The novice was then raised from the ground and led to the feet of the bishop, who examined her as to her vocation, and gave her his blessing — and once more the black curtain fell between us and them.

In the *second act*, she was lying prostrate on the floor, disrobed of her profane dress and covered over with a black cloth, while the black figures kneeling round her chanted a hymn. She was now dead to the world. The sunbeams had faded away, as if they would not look upon the scene, and all the light was concentrated in one great mass upon the convent group.

Again she was raised. All the blood has rushed into her face, and her attempt at a smile was truly painful. She then knelt before the bishop and received the benediction, with the sign of the cross, from a white hand with the pastoral ring. She then went round alone to embrace all the dark phantoms as they stood motionless, and, as each dark shadow clasped her in its arms, it seemed like the dead welcoming a new arrival to the shades.

But I forgot the sermon, which was delivered by a fat priest who elbowed his way with some difficulty through the crowd to the grating, panting and in a prodigious heat, and esconced himself in a great arm chair close beside us. He assured her that she "had chosen the good part, which could not be taken away from her"; that she was now one of the elect, "chosen from amongst the wickedness and dangers of the world" (picked out like a plum from a pie). He mentioned with pity and contempt those who were "yet struggling in the great Babylon"; and compared their miserable fate with hers, the Bride of Christ, who, after suffering a few privations here during a short term of years, should be received at once into a kingdom of glory. The whole discourse was well calculated to rally her fainting spirits, if fainting they were, and to inspire us with a great disgust for ourselves.

When the sermon was concluded, the music again struck up. The heroine of the day came forward, and stood before the grating to take her last look at this wicked world. Down fell the black curtain. Up rose the relations, and I accompanied them into the sacristy. Here they coolly lighted their cigars, and very philosophically discoursed upon the exceeding good fortune of the new-made nun, and on her evident delight and satisfaction with her own situation. As we did not follow her behind the scenes, I could not give my opinion on this point. Shortly after, one of the gentlemen civilly led me to my carriage, and *so it was*.

As we were returning home, some soldiers rode up and stopped the carriage, desiring the coachman to take the other side of the aqueduct, to avoid the body of a man who had just been murdered within a few doors of our house.

GOOD FRIDAY IN GUATEMALA

"...a silver hammer and a...silver spike;...blood trickled down..."

The days before Easter were occasions for numerous public expressions of worship. At such times, the local parishes of Guatemala often combined several heritages—Christian, Moorish, and local traditional religion. Typical also was the fact that the week's activities took place amid the twin scourges of poverty and civil strife. John L. Stephens, an American diplomat in Central America in 1840, described scenes from Holy Week in Quezaltenango. [14]

✠ To return to the cura [parish priest]: he was about forty-five, tall, stout, and remarkably fine-looking; he had several curacies under his charge, and next to a canonigo's, his position was the highest in the country; but it had its labours. He was at that time engrossed with the ceremonies of the Holy Week, and in the evening we accompanied him to the church. At the door the *coup d'oeil* of the interior was most striking. The church was two hundred and fifty feet in length, spacious and lofty, richly decorated with pictures and sculptured ornaments, blazing with lights, and crowded with Indians. On each side of the door was a grating, behind which stood an Indian to receive offerings. The floor was strewed with pine-leaves. On the left was the figure of a dead Christ on a bier, upon which every woman who entered threw a handful of roses, and near it stood an Indian to receive money. Opposite, behind an iron grating, was the figure of Christ bearing the cross, the eyes bandaged, and large silver chains attached to the arms and other parts of the body, and fastened to the iron bars. Here, too, stood an Indian to receive contributions. The altar was beautiful in design and decorations, consisting of two rows of Ionic columns, one above another, gilded, surmounted by a golden glory, and lighted by candles ten feet high. Under the pulpit was a piano. After a stroll around the church, the cura led us to seats under the pulpit. He asked us to give them some of the airs of our country, and then himself sat down at the piano. On Mr. C.'s suggesting that the tune was from one of Rossini's operas, he said that this was hardly proper for the occasion, and changed it.

At about ten o'clock the crowd in the church formed into a procession, and Mr. C. and I went out and took a position at the corner of a street to see it pass. It was headed by Indians, two abreast, each carrying in his hand a long lighted wax candle; and then, borne aloft on the shoulders of four men, came the figure of Judith, with a bloody sword in one hand, and in the other the gory head of Holofernes. Next, also on the shoulders of four men, the archangel Gabriel, dressed in red silk, with large wings puffed out. The next were men in grotesque armour, made of black and silver paper, to resemble Moors, with shield and spear like ancient cavaliers; and then four little girls, dressed in white silk and gauze, and looking like little spiritualities, with men on each side bearing lighted candles. Then came a large figure of Christ bearing the cross, supported by four Indians; on each side were young Indian lads, carrying long poles horizontally, to keep the crowd from pressing upon it, and followed by a procession of townsmen. In turning the corner of the street at which we stood, a dark Mestitzo, with a scowl of fanaticism on his face, said to Mr. Catherwood, "Take off your spectacles and follow the cross." Next followed a procession of women with children in their arms, half of them asleep, fancifully dressed with silver caps and headdresses, and finally a large statue of the Virgin, in a sitting posture, magnificantly attired, with Indian lads on each side, as before, supporting poles with candles. The whole was accompanied with the music of drums and violins; and, as the long train of light passed down the street, we returned to the convent.

The night was very cold, and the next morning was like one in December at home. It was the morning of Good Friday; and throughout Guatimala, in every village, preparations were making to celebrate, with the most solemn ceremonies of the Church, the resurrection of the Saviour. In Quezaltenango, at that early hour, the plaza was thronged with Indians from the country around; but the whites, terrified and grieving at the murder of their best men, avoided, to a great extent, taking part in the celebration.

At nine o'clock the corregidor called for us, and we accompanied him to the opening ceremony. On one side of the nave of the church, near the grand altar, and opposite the pulpit, were high cushioned chairs for the corregidor and members of the municipality, and we had seats with them. The church was thronged with Indians, estimated at more than three thousand. Formerly, at this ceremony no women or children were admitted; but now the floor of the church was filled with Indian women on their knees, with red cords plaited in their hair, and perhaps one third of them had children on their backs, their heads and arms only visible. Except ourselves and the padre, there were no white people in the church; and, with all eyes turned upon us, and a lively recollection of the fate of those who but a few days before had occupied our seats, we felt that the post of honour was a private station.

At the steps of the grand altar stood a huge cross, apparently of solid silver, richly carved and ornamented, and over it a high arbour of pine and cypress branches. At the foot of the cross stood a figure of Mary Magdalen weeping, with her hair in a profusion of ringlets, her frock low in the neck, and altogether rather immodest. On the right was the figure of the Virgin gorgeously dressed, and in the nave of the church stood John the Baptist, placed there, as it seemed, only because they had the figure on hand. Very soon strains of wild Indian music rose from the other end of the church, and a procession advanced, headed by Indians with broad-brimmed felt hats, dark cloaks, and lighted wax candles, preceding the body of the Saviour on a bier borne by the cura and attendant padres, and followed by Indians with long wax candles. The bier advanced to the foot of the cross; ladders were placed behind against it; the gobernador, with his long black cloak and broad-brimmed felt hat, mounted on the right, and leaned over, holding in his hands a silver hammer and a long silver spike; another Indian dignitary mounted on the other side, while the priests raised the figure up in front; the face was ghastly, blood trickled down the cheeks, the arms and legs were moveable, and in the side was a gaping wound, with a stream of blood oozing from it. The back was affixed to the cross, the arms extended, spikes driven through the hands and feet, the ladders taken away, and thus the figure of Christ was nailed to the cross.

This over, we left the church, and passed two or three hours in visiting. The white population was small, but equal in character to any in the republic; and there was hardly a respectable family that was not afflicted by the outrage of Carrera. We knew nothing of the effect of this enormity until we entered domestic circles. The distress of women whose nearest connexions had been murdered or obliged to fly for their lives, and then wandering they knew not where, those only can realize who can appreciate woman's affection.

I was urged to visit the widow of Molina. Her husband was but thirty-five, and his death under any circumstances would have been lamented, even by political enemies. I felt a painful interest in one who had lived through such a scene, but at the door of her house I stopped. I felt that a visit from a stranger must be an intrusion upon her sorrows.

In the afternoon we were again seated with the municipality in the church, to behold the descent from the cross. The spacious building was thronged to suffocation, and the floor was covered by a dense mass of kneeling women, with turbaned headdresses, and crying children on their backs, their imaginations excited by gazing at the bleeding figure on the cross; but among them all I did not see a single interesting face. A priest ascended the pulpit, thin and ghastly pale, who, in a voice that rang through every part of the building, preached emphatically a passion sermon. Few of the Indians understood even the language, and at times the cries of children made his words inaudible; but the thrilling tones of his voice played upon every chord in their hearts; and mothers, regardless of their infants' cries, sat motionless, their countenances fixed in high and stern enthusiasm.

It was the same church, and we could imagine them to be the same women who, in a phrensy and fury of fanaticism, had dragged the unhappy vice-president by the hair, and murdered him with their hands. Every moment the excitement grew stronger. The priest tore off his black cap, and leaning over the pulpit, stretched forward both his arms, and poured out a frantic apostrophe to the bleeding figure on the cross. A dreadful groan, almost curdling the blood, ran through the church. At this moment, at a signal from the cura, the Indians sprang upon the arbour of pine branches, tore it asunder, and with a noise like the crackling of a great conflagration, struggling and scuffling around the altar, broke into bits the consecrated branches to save as holy relics. Two Indians in broad-brimmed hats mounted the ladders on each side of the cross, and with embroidered cloth over their hands, and large silver pincers, drew out the spikes from the hands. The feelings of the women burst forth in tears, sobs, groans, and shrieks of lamentation, so loud and deep, that, coming upon us unexpectedly, our feelings were disturbed, and even with sane men the empire of reason tottered. Such screams of anguish I never heard called out by mortal suffering; and as the body, smeared with blood, was held aloft under the pulpit, while the priest leaned down and apostrophized it with frantic fervour, and the mass of women, wild with excitement, heaved to and fro like the surges of a troubled sea, the whole scene was so thrilling, so dreadfully mournful, that, without knowing why, tears started from our eyes.

PUBLIC OPPOSITION TO THE RELIGIOUS ORDERS

"... the wealthy orders are just now in imminent danger; ..."

In contrast to those in the Spanish-speaking republics, many priests in Brazil were nationalistic and liberal. For example, they supported an effort in the National Assembly to petition the pope for priests to be free to marry. Furthermore, many diocesan priests resented the privileges and corruption of the religious orders. Some of the positive contributions of the Brazilian friars and also complaints against them were described below by Robert Walsh, an Anglican clergyman who visited Brazil in 1828 and 1829.[15]

✠ The regular clergy in Brazil are not numerous. They are Benedictines, Carmelites, Franciscans, ancient and reformed, with Capuchin missionaries. Of these orders the richest are the Benedictines and the ancient Carmelites. The others make vows of poverty, and neither do nor can possess any property. But the wealthy orders are just now in imminent danger; from the very reputation of their wealth, the present feeling of the country is not in their favor, and they seem to be held in the same estimation as they

were in France at the commencement of the revolution. It is therefore
generally spoken of, as a thing just and necessary, that their property should
be applied to the necessities of the state. The chamber of deputies have
already passed a vote to that effect, and it is imagined, that many persons
about the throne are equally disposed to the measure, in the hope of an-
nexing some of the confiscated lands to their own estates, as is notoriously
the case in every reformation, particularly in our own. The people of Brazil
have always been hostile to monastic institutions in the country, either male
or female, and for the same reason—the impediment it throws in the way
of population; and this feeling extends even to the secular clergy. On the
24th of October, 1827, Senhor Fiego, a member of the ecclesiastical committee, and himself a priest, I believe, moved in the chamber, "that it would
be proper to apply to the pope, to relieve the clergy from the penalty
annexed to marrying," and at the same time to notify to his holiness "that
the assembly could not avoid repealing the law of celibacy." The motion
did not then pass, but it is expected to be brought on again with success.
In the mean time, the regular clergy, the Benedictines and Carmelites, have
been prohibited from taking novices, an interdict which is believed to be
preparatory to their total extinction.

It is supposed, however, that their loss, at least for a time, will be very
severely felt, not only by the poor, but by many respectable families of
decent appearance, but very scanty income. The whole mendacity of Rio
is supported at their convents. A beggar is rarely or ever seen in the streets;
and at first I supposed no such class of persons existed in the country, till
I saw the steps and platform of the convent of S. Antonio crowded with
the lame, the halt, and the blind, and all receiving their daily portions of
meat and soup. With respect to persons of a better class, great numbers
are tenants to those convents, who with considerate humanity take very low
rents, and exact them with great indulgence and forbearance. The Benedictines alone are proprietors of seven hundred houses in Rio. They are, I
am told, exceedingly kind landlords to their tenants, who are generally of
the humble, but respectable class I have mentioned.

RELIGIOUS BROTHERHOODS IN BRAZILIAN LIFE

". . . every member is entitled to support in sickness or in poverty . . ."

The roots of lay activism in Brazilian church life go deep into history.
They can be seen in the community services rendered by the lay fellow-
ships. An English Protestant, Robert Walsh, in Rio de Janeiro in 1828
and 1829, described the ministries of these organizations.[16]

✠ Besides these regular societies, there are various *irmandades*, or brotherhoods, which seem to be on the plan of our benefit societies, but on a

more extended scale. They take the name of Carmelites, Franciscans, Minims, and are called "Third Orders," though they consist entirely of the laity, and are composed of trades-people, and such of a higher class as may be disposed, from a spirit of devotion, to become members. About fifteen dollars are paid at entrance, and an annual contribution of one dollar to the general fund. For this, every member is entitled to support in sickness or in poverty, and to a funeral free of expense, and other advantages conferred by our societies. But besides this, a considerable part of the expense of public worship is borne by them. These *irmandades*, under one denomination or another, build and repair churches, pay for masses for the souls of the departed, found hospitals for the sick, bury the dead, and indeed, I am told, it is quite inconceivable to an Englishman, what immense sums of money these lay-brothers annually expend, in what they conceive to be pious and charitable uses. The large edifice of S. Francisco de Paula, with its magnificent church and fine hospital, was built and is supported by their voluntary contributions; and their utility is so felt and acknowledged, that many people at their death bequeath them their property for the same uses, and in this way they also are proprietors of many houses in Rio, and distinguished for their kindness and indulgence to their tenants.

BRAZILIAN CLERGY — NO STATUS, NO RACIAL BARRIERS

" . . . none but persons in the lowest ranks of life devote their children to it . . ."

A Protestant observer from England, Robert Walsh, visiting in southeast Brazil in 1828–1829, described some weaknesses and a commendable strength among the Catholic clergy.[17]

✠ The native clergy are not, generally speaking, learned men, for they have not the means of being so. The poverty of the bishops, is an impediment to the establishment of ecclesiastical seminaries, on a scale sufficiently extensive or liberal to give the candidates the means or opportunities of a learned education. The inducements to enter the church also are so small, and its stipend so limited, that men of opulent families or brilliant abilities always prefer some more attractive or profitable avocation; and none but persons in the lowest ranks of life devote their children to it; the resources which it affords in other countries, to the younger members of respectable families, not being thought of in this. The candidate, therefore, is a person whose parents are unacquainted with liberal education, who has no knowledge of, nor desire for it himself, and who, even if he had, does not find the means of acquiring it, in the seminary to which he is sent.

To this cause perhaps may be attributed, in some measure, the admission of negroes to holy orders, who officiate in churches indiscriminately with whites. I have seen myself three clergymen in the same church at the same time; one of whom was a white, another a mulatto, and the third a black. The admission of the poor despised race, to the highest functions that a human being can perform, strongly marks the consideration in which it is held in different places. In the West Indies a clergyman has been severely censured by his flock, for presuming to administer the sacrament to a poor negro at the same table with themselves. In Brazil a black is seen as the officiating minister, and whites receiving it from his hands.

FUNERALS AND BURIALS

". . . the spectacle is very revolting . . . the odor dangerously offensive . . ."

Death, the inevitable visitor, placed all people on an equal footing. Nevertheless, funerals and burials revealed glaring social distinctions. An Anglican chaplain, visiting Brazil with a business group in the late 1820s, observed several funerals and described what he saw. [18]

✠ Funerals are among the most pompous and gaudy displays of the people. Those of the better class are always conducted by night, by the light of large wax tapers, the size of flambeaux. These are borne not only by the friends of the deceased, but by any passing stranger of respectable appearance. For this purpose, one of the conductors generally stands at the door of the house in which the corpse lies, and invites the passenger to come in and take a taper. Every week, at least, I have been in this way arrested as I passed by, and as it is deemed not good manners to refuse, I latterly learned to pass over to the other side, to avoid the necessity of either complying or declining.

The coffin is carried before, and the taper-bearers follow in a long procession behind to the church, where the funeral service is read. It is there laid on a catafalk, or pedestal, which stands for that purpose in the middle of every aisle: priests attend, who chant the funeral service, accompanied by the organ; and when this is concluded, either the flooring of the church is raised and the body deposited beneath, or it is brought to the cloisters, where a small receptacle, like an oven, is opened to receive it. Before it is so deposited, the lid of the coffin is raised, and a quantity of quick-lime thrown in; and when it is decomposed by this process, the bones are shut in with a lock and key. Notwithstanding their preservation of the bones of the dead, the people are remarkably careless of the remains of their deceased friends. Their only concern is, that they shall receive the last rites of their church, which they consider indispensable to the welfare of their souls. Few or no relations are present at the interment; and there

is a great indifference, amounting to levity, not only among the acquaintance who attend the funeral, but among the clergy themselves.

On some occasions of the funerals of infants, the coffin is an elegant
embroidered trunk, in which the child lies enveloped in artificial flowers;
and when placed on the catafalk, it looks like a work-box on a lady's dressing table. The cloisters where they are deposited are remarkably dry and
neat, kept always fresh with paint and whitewash, and generally in a pretty
garden embellished with parterres and aromatic flowering shrubs; so that
the charnel-house is divested of everything offensive or even dismal, and
redolent with incense and perfumes.

The gaiety of this is strongly contrasted with the funerals of negroes.
Their naked bodies are met every day, thrown into an old mat suspended
on a pole between two others, their arms and legs often hanging down and
trailing on the ground. They are brought in this way to the large cemetery
attached to the Misericordia Hospital; and here they are thrown into a long
trench, where I have seen ten or twelve bodies lying in a heap without any
covering of earth yet thrown on them.

When the person is deposited under the flooring of the church, a very
offensive spectacle is often exhibited. The ground is so crammed that it is
impossible to find room, and the aperture made is not sufficient to contain
it; so that when the naked corpse is laid down, part of it is often seen rising
above the ground. A man then takes a rammer, like a pavior's, and deliberately pounds the body into a flat mass, till it is accommodated to its
situation; while all the people look on with the most perfect indifference.
It is true that it is divested of all feeling, as a Brazilian sensibly remarked
to me when I mentioned the circumstance, and deserves to be held in no
more estimation than the clay with which it is about to incorporate. But
certainly the spectacle is very revolting, and the odor dangerously offensive;
and many people are compelled to leave the church from a sense of sickness.

ORAL EXAMINATION AT A CARMELITE CONVENT

"... the padres defendentes appeared to be tolerably clever lads..."

*Traditions in theological education were brought to Brazil from Europe
and usually preserved the pedagogy of pre-Enlightenment scholasticism.
Nevertheless, in the oral examinations of graduands, notes of pride and
apprehension were visible, which students and teachers of all times and
places can understand and smile about. In his widely-read reports, Daniel
Kidder, a Methodist missionary from North America, was visiting in Bahía
in 1840 and attended the public examination of two Carmelite candidates
for the priesthood.*[19]

✠ On the 12th of December I attended an examination in logic, at the convent of the Slippered Carmelites, to which the public had been invited by a pompous announcement in the newspapers. The hour appointed was nine o'clock A.M., but I did not reach the place until later, when the exercises had already been opened by an introductory address. When I reached the front of the edifice, no one was to be seen who could direct me to the room of the assembly; wherefore I undertook to find it myself, and followed a line of green leaves scattered over a stairway, and then through a veranda, until I came to the place, a large salon in the rear of the building, where I found a good seat apparently in reserve for my use. The ornaments of the room were the usual gilt and crimson hangings, together with some twenty paintings, portraits of distinguished Carmelites. Among these was a head of pope Dionysius. A part of the floor was spread with a carpet, and over the whole leaves and flowers had been scattered in profusion.

In the middle of the room, opposite the door, sat the padre-mestre, the presiding officer of the occasion, whom I supposed to be the prior of the convent. At one end, upon a sort of throne arranged for that purpose, sat the archbishop, in his usual woman-like dress, not of black like that of the other priests, but of red and yellow, surmounted by a lace jacket, or garment of some name, resembling an old lady's short-gown, and very suitable to be worn with petticoats.

Immediately in front of this most reverend prelate, was an open space extending to the middle of the room, and flanked on either side by benches full of friars, with their heads newly shaved, and dressed out as primly as possible. I counted about thirty Carmelites, all distinguished by a white silk scarf or mantilla, hung about their neck and shoulders in the style of a *poncho*. At the foot of the pulpit or box in which the presiding officer was stationed, sat two noviciates styled padres defendentes, towards whom, as will afterwards appear, was directed the entire brunt of the battle. In front of and facing them, sat six examiners, a part clergy and others laymen. At the other end of the room was stationed a band of musical performers, and before them was ranged the miscellaneous spectators, a part of whom were also priests, and a larger part colored persons. The band was playing when I entered. On its ceasing, the prior addressed himself to his excellency the archbishop, as much with nods and obsequious grimaces as with words, requesting him to commence the examinations of the day. The said prelate took the word and answered, still sitting in his chair. He expressed his excessive satisfaction in being permitted to take part in the brilliant scene before his eyes. He felt this some reward for the efforts he had made for the promotion of education and religion. He especially congratulated the rising prospects of the glorious order of the Carmelites (whereupon all the members thereof rose on their feet and made a gracious obeisance). Moreover, he lamented his own weakness and incapacity to perform the momentous duties at this moment before him, &c. &c.

After a speech of moderate length, most of which was very sensible, he opened a book of themes, with which most present were furnished, and addressed some questions to one of the *defendentes*. After having sufficiently discussed the proposition he had selected, he surrendered the floor, and the band played an air.

The presiding officer then called upon another examiner, who immediately rose and made some half a dozen bows successively to the archbishop, to the chair, to the friars on one side, to the friars on the other side, to his brother examiners, and to the audience in general. He then sat down and commenced his harangue. This etiquette was observed by all the examiners in turn. Each one had a studied exordium, abounding with the most fulsome compliments (*do costume*), aimed at others but meant for himself, after which he proceeded to some one of the themes. The object seemed not so much to ascertain what the pupils knew, as to display what they knew themselves. Consequently the spaces between their questions were so abundantly interlarded with explanatory words of learned length and thundering sound, that in the course of half an hour they would scarcely suffer the neophytes to respond more than a few meagre monosyllables. I could have conceived the gentlemen examiners to be rival candidates for the office of chief wrangler in the convent. When any one succeeded in confusing the respondents, which seemed to be the special ambition of each examiner, the good prior was disposed to help his students out of the fog, and thus there were sometimes three or four persons speaking at once. The propositions chosen were more worthy of the days of the schoolmen than of the "*seculo das luzes*," our own enlightened age. The padres defendentes appeared to be tolerably clever lads, and I thought did remarkably well, considering the circumstances in which they were placed. The scene on the whole was truly novel and interesting. The music was no small addition, as it served to banish the drowsiness brought on from time to time by the hair-splitting discussions to which the attention was directed. The exercises continued nearly four hours, and were to be renewed again at three p.m. But I had no motive to return.

HOLY WEEK PROCESSION IN RIO

"I wish her mamma had kept her large earrings, bracelets, . . . and necklace at home."

The religious processions through the street during Holy Week provided an illiterate population with an audio-visual presentation of the passion narrative of the Gospels. It also provided color, movement, community participation, and a clear civic endorsement of the position and message of the church. Thomas Ewbank, a Protestant North American and tourist in Rio in 1845 described a procession which he witnessed.[20]

✠ As the procession of the Carmelites today will equal any thing of the kind during the rest of my stay in Rio, I was in Dereita Street by 4 p.m. The balconies were filled by ladies in full dress, and the side-walks occupied by waiting spectators. A finer evening could not have been selected for the spectacle. Soldiers fell into ranks, the crowd thickened, and soon the first image of the series was seen emerging from the Carmo Temple. The brotherhood extended from the church, some three hundred feet, to where I stood. In their uniform of cream-colored albs, and armed with waxen staffs, they presented a fine sample of the Church's troops. Here and there one hurried to and fro, giving orders, and wielding his candle as a marshal's baton. Others clutched winged cherubs by the hand, and dragged them onward, as if they had just captured or brought them down with their truncheons to ornament the fête.

The particulars were briefly these: Infantry troops formed two walls between which the procession was to pass. It was headed by horse soldiers with drawn swords, three abreast; then a banner, inscribed S.P.Q.R.; next, brothers and candles; a crimson bag on a silver pole, with a mourning candle on either hand, the wax being painted with black spiral stripes. Brothers and candles; three angels abreast—the middle one, with a banner, personated St. Michael the Archangel. She wore a shining helmet, a silver breastplate, nankeen pantalettes, and scarlet boots. Her wings were spotted prettily, and the cloud behind her was bordered with (paper) lace. Her arms were naked. I wished her mamma had kept her large earrings, bracelets, fingerrings, and necklace at home.

1. As the first image now was drawing near, the soldiers fixed bayonets and shouldered muskets to do it honor. It represented *The Passion*. A large statue of Christ in a kneeling posture, with the hands clasped as in prayer. Drops of blood rolled down the pallid cheeks. An angel, between three and four feet high, stoops and presents the cup. Three silver lanterns were borne on each side, and a file of soldiers, with drawn swords, attends.

2. A long line of brothers follow, who are followed by the second stage, on which stands *Christ before Pilate*, pale, emaciated, and submissive.

Brothers and angels three abreast.

3. *Christ scourged*. This image is naked, except a fillet round the loins. It is tied by ropes to a pillar, and the face, breast, back, thighs, arms, and legs are painted streaming with gore—vividly horrible.

Crowd of brothers and angels.

4. *Christ mocked*. Seated, a reed in his hand, and a short purple robe thrown over his lacerated shoulders. He is bruised and bleeding all over.

Brothers and angels.

5. On this stage Christ appears standing, and holds a stalk of Indian-corn or sugar-cane in one hand. A similar spare robe to the last covers a

small part of the naked body. (The incident represented I did not perceive; perhaps the scene *before Herod* is intended.)

Brothers and angels.

6. *Bearing the Cross.* The figure is similar to, or the same as the one noticed in the procession of 27th ult [of previous month]. Great numbers of devout Brazilians, and the blacks generally, knelt as it passed them. The attending angels were quite numerous. Of the symbols, one had the sponge of vinegar on a rod, another the spear that pierced him.

7. *Christ on the Cross.* The top of the latter is, I should think, nearly twenty feet from the ground. The shaft rises from a green hillock on the stage, and springs considerably. As it drew nigh, the cause of this was apparent. The cross is of plank, and the weight of the image causes it to bend to and fro, for it has no support except at the foot. I surmised that the large image might be of papier-mache, but I subsequently learned that it is of hard, heavy wood, and nearly 200 years old. A crimson stream flowing from the wound in the side contrasted strongly with the chalk-like hue of the face and body.

Brothers and angels followed, and behind the latter two negroes with boxes of bon-bons, to refresh them during pauses in the procession.

8. The managers under a long canopy. Of the sea of heads in sight, theirs only are covered (by skull-caps, rochets, and mitres), besides being screened by the golden drapery over them. Every spectator in front falls at their feet, not excepting the soldiers. Among the young smirking monks is my confessor friend of the Lapa. They are passed, and how the drums, bugles, and French horns burst forth and do their best. The air is not Yankee Doodle, but it is quite as lively. The foot-soldiers wheel in, a guard of honor to the fathers, and sway their bodies as in ecstasy. Finally, the national banner brings up the rear, and closes the Pomp.

I afterward met it in Quitanda Street, through whose entire length people were waiting. As the image bearing the cross came up, many knelt and most stooped, but some young fellows got into a squabble and fight with three or four blacks for looking over their shoulders.

8. ✠ Protestant Beginnings

1630-1850

When the Reformation began in Europe in 1517, only a few decades passed before Protestants began to trickle into Latin America. Some English sailors, occasional merchants, and buccaneers landed on the coast of Mexico, and ran afoul of the Inquisition. Some French Protestants made attempts to colonize in the 1550s and 1560s, one group on the central coast of Brazil and the other on the northeast coast of Florida. Opposition to these quickly arose from the Portuguese and Spanish. Hurt by internal weaknesses among the Protestants themselves, the settlements soon came to an end.

The seventeenth and eighteenth centuries were quite different. After the British routed the Spanish armada in 1588, hardly a dozen years passed before the Protestant powers of Britain, Holland, and Denmark organized trading companies. These soon took from the Spanish various Caribbean islands and enclaves on the continent. When they came to settle, they brought their churches with them. For example, in northeast Brazil around present-day Recife, the Dutch West India company founded a thriving colony that lasted from 1630 to 1654. The Calvinist pastors cared for their Dutch flock, and at least one of them worked as an evangelist among the neighboring Indians. When the British took Jamaica, the Barbados, and other islands, the Anglican church came with the conquerors and established congregations for the planters and their slaves. In the 1730s, Moravian missionaries began work among the African slaves on the Danish island of St. Thomas and among the Africans and indigenous people in the Dutch territory on the South American continent, present-day Surinam. Soon British Methodists and black North American Baptists were starting churches in the area.

In the first half of the nineteenth century, the wars for independence broke up the last of Iberia's attempted monopoly on trade. One important result was that the port towns were opened to foreign residents. As business people, government officials, and their families from North America and from Protestant areas of Europe moved in, government authorities began to close their eyes to local laws or so interpret them as to allow foreign

Lutheran Church, St. Thomas, Virgin Islands. The building dates from 1793, though it was restored in the nineteenth century after substantial damage by a fire and a hurricane.

churches to exist. The first such congregation to gain permission to erect a building was of a group of Anglicans in Rio de Janeiro in 1810. Others followed in Valparaíso, Buenos Aires, Vera Cruz, and other port cities. The largest group of foreign Protestants outside the Caribbean were the German Lutherans, who immigrated into southern Brazil. By 1830, there were said to be 4,800 of them.

Permission for wealthy foreign Protestants to worship in public was one thing. Allowing the local Spanish and Portuguese people to form such congregations was quite another. Indeed, this was not permitted until the second half of the century. An exception was in Haiti, a nominally Catholic and former French territory, where in 1816-20, the government actually invited Protestant missionaries to come from Britain and America.

ANGLICAN CONGREGATIONS IN THE CARIBBEAN

". . . as complete a Coxcomb as ever I met with in a pulpit . . ."

The first continuing Protestant churches were on the Caribbean islands. Just before the North American revolution, a vivacious woman, Janet Schaw, from an upper-class family in Edinburgh, Scotland, accompanied one of her brothers to his new home in the West Indies, then visited another brother in North Carolina. With their servants and a few family friends, they sailed down to Portugal, then across to the Caribbean to the British islands of Antigua and St. Kitts. In each place, Schaw visited prosperous Scottish friends, and every day wrote letters home, describing her experiences and observations. In some of these we get a glimpse of the Anglican congregations as she saw them in 1774 and early 1775. [21]

✠ My brother has gone to make the tour of the Islands without us. Every body was so desirous of our staying here [Antigua], and we were so happy, that we easily agreed to their obliging request, nor have we reason to repent our compliance, as every hour is rendered agreeable by new marks of civility, kindness, and hospitality. Miss Rutherford has found several of her boarding school-friends here; they have many friends to talk of, many scenes to recollect. . . .

I was yesterday at church, and found they had not said more of it than it deserved; for tho' the outside is a plain building, its inside is magnificent. It has a very fine organ, a spacious altar, and every thing necessary to a church which performs the English Service. You know I am no bigoted Presbyterian, and as the tenets are the same, I was resolved to conform to the ceremonies, but am sorry to find in myself the force of habit too strong, I fear, to be removed. The church was very full, the Audience most devout. I looked at them with pleasure, but found I was a mere Spectator, . . . if one considers that the last Clergyman I heard in Scotland was Mr Webster, and that the last service I heard him perform was that of a prayer for myself and friends, who were bidding adieu to their native land, in which were exerted all those powers, which he possesses in so eminent a degree, his own heart affected by the subject, and mine deeply, deeply interested. It was no wonder that those now read from a book by a Clerk, who only did it, because he was paid for doing it, appeared cold and unapropos. The musick tho' fine added as little to my devotion as the sniveling of a sincere-hearted country precentor, perhaps less; but the beauty, the neatness and elegance of the Church pleased me much, and in this I own, we are very defective in Scotland. The seat for the Governor General is noble and magnificent, covered with Crimson velvet; the drapery round it edged with deep gold fringe; the Crown Cyphers and emblems of his office embossed and very rich. Below this is the seat for the Counselors equally fine and ornamented, but what pleased me more than all I saw, was a great number of Negroes who occupied the Area, and went thro' the Service with seriousness and devotion. I must not forget one thing that really diverted me; the parson who has a fine income is as complete a Coxcomb as I ever met with in a pulpit. He no sooner cast his eyes to where we were than he seemed to forget the rest of the Audience, and on running over his sermon, which he held in his hand, he appeared dissatisfied, and without more ado dismounted from the pulpit, leaving the Service unfinished, and went home for another; which to do it justice was a very good one.

We found Mr Martin at the Church door with our carriages, into which we mounted, and were soon at Mr Halliday's Plantation, where [w]e this day dined; for he has no less than five, all of which have houses on them. This house is extremely pleasant, and so cool that one might forget they were under the Tropick. We had a family dinner, which in England might figure away in a newspaper, had it been given by a Lord Mayor, or the first Duke in the kingdom. Why should we blame these people for their luxury? since nature holds out her lap, filled with every thing that is in her power to bestow, it were sinful in them not to be luxurious. . . .

I have paid several visits both in town and country [St. Kitts], and have been at church in the town, which tho' not so large nor indeed so magnificently fitted up as that at St John's, has an excellent organ and every thing necessary for the most solemn parts of the church of England-service. We had prayers decently and properly read and an excellent sermon from a Scottish Clergyman. Miss Milliken and her lovely friend were particularly devout, to which the state of health they are both in no doubt contributed, nor did they fail to have an effect on those within whose observation they were placed, even I myself found I could join with this church as a member, and was not to be present as a mere Spectator when my heart was warmed. And I will venture to tell you, tho' you may laugh at me, that I was much pleased with the discovery I made of myself. For tho' the whole Island is divided into regular parishes, and each has a handsome church, yet there is not the semblance of presbytery, and much as I approve of it myself, 'tis not my talent to make proselytes.

DISTRIBUTING THE BIBLE

". . . introducing the Scriptures as it were by stealth."

After independence from Spain and Portugal, many Latin American citizens were eager for educational reforms, even if these brought Protestant connections. Also many, including clergy, welcomed the Bible. Illustrative of both was the experience of James Thomson, a Baptist from Scotland, who was employed by the British and Foreign Bible Society and the Lancasterian Educational Society. At the request of the new governments of Argentina, Chile, Peru, and others, Thomson spent several years in the early 1820s organizing hundreds of primary schools on the Lancasterian plan in which students help in the teaching. The schools provided an opening for him to sell Bibles. Excerpts from his letters describe the earliest organized Protestant witness among Catholics in South America.[22]

✠ *Santiago de Chile, 8th October,* 1821
I wrote you a few lines on the 26th February, and then mentioned that it was my intention to visit Chile. . . .

[No] interruption to the circulation of the Spanish New Testament has yet been experienced. Soon after my arrival, I gave to an Englishman, who has a shop here, some copies to sell. This man is a Roman Catholic, and I am happy to say, he recommends the Scriptures to the natives of this country, who are of his own religion. He has already sold about twenty. He is very anxious for the arrival of the Spanish Bibles, which I told him I expected, as he thinks he could sell many of them. . . .

I shall now mention some things not formerly noticed, regarding the circulation of the Scriptures in Buenos Aires, and in the surrounding country. — A military officer, commanding on a station a short distance from the city, has been greatly delighted with the New Testament, and in consequence, very anxious to make others acquainted with it. . . .

In my letter of 26th February, I requested the Society to send me 200 of Scio's translation to Buenos Aires, and 300 to Valparaiso. I hope these will respectively arrive in due time. I then noticed to you the advantage that would arise from lettering them on the back, and varying them in the binding. I particularly request your attention to this, as I am sure it will contribute greatly to their sale. Let the binding be in many cases elegant. . . . I shall, as I have said above, most readily act as your agent in distributing the Scriptures in Buenos Aires, and in Chile. The most judicious and effectual way of doing this is through the booksellers in these places. . . .

Lima, 11th July, 1822

Through the unceasing goodness of God towards me, I have now arrived safely in this city. On the 18th of last month I sailed from Valparaiso, and after a pleasant passage of ten days we cast anchor in Callao Bay. Callao is an excellent harbour, the best I have yet seen. . . .

On the day on which I arrived in this city, I called on San Martin, and delivered him the letters of introduction which I had brought from Chile. He opened one of the letters, and observing its purport, said "Mr. Thomson! I am extremely glad to see you;" and he rose up, and gave me a very hearty embrace. . . . We conversed about our schools, and other similar objects for some time; and in going away he desired me to call on him next morning, and said he would introduce me to the Marquis of Truxillo, who is at present what is called the Supreme Deputy or Regent. I called on him accordingly next morning; and he took me with him and introduced me to the Marquis, and to each of the ministers.

From all the members of the government I have received great encouragement. On the 6th current an order was issued relative to our schools, and published in the Lima Gazette of the same date. . . . By this order one of the convents is appropriated to the schools, and is now in our possession. I believe the convents here will decrease in number as the schools multiply. There is no contest or balancing of powers between the civil and ecclesiastical powers in this place. The former has the latter entirely at their nod. The case in regard to this convent is a proof of what I have said. The order for the friars to remove was given on Saturday, on Monday they began to remove, and on Tuesday the keys were delivered up. . . .

Lima, 1st March, 1824

I stated to you, some time ago, my expectation of being able to introduce the New Testament undisguised into our school. Blessed be God, that object is now accomplished. I have sold several copies to the children publicly in the school. In the usual course of our lessons, we have occasion to speak of several incidents in the Gospel history. On these occasions, I desire our pupils, particularly on Saturdays, to find out in their New Testaments where such a thing is spoken of, giving them certain limits. On the Monday following, a number are well prepared with their New Testaments marked with slips of paper at the places in question, and often through their pretty impatience to communicate their discoveries, they tell me before we get into the school, that they have found out the parable of the sower, the conversion of Paul, &c. You may easily imagine that these circumstances are great sources of enjoyment to me, and make up for many disadvantages. I have said that we have got the New Testament introduced into our school *undisguised*. You probably perceive what I mean by using the word undisguised. The truth is, the New Testament, in one sense, has all along been used in our schools in South America, not however in the open manner we now use it in Lima, but, as I may say, disguised; that is, we have used for lessons extracts from it, printed on large sheets, and in little books, thus introducing the Scriptures as it were by stealth. Each part of these lessons I cause to be read repeatedly in the classes, until the children can read them readily. By the time they can do so, the substance of what they have read, and the instruction contained in it, is tolerably imprinted on the memory. Children, you know, have a habit of repeating to themselves what they have been saying or reading frequently. In consequence of this, what portions of Scripture they have read in the school, they repeat in this way at home. My excellent friend and companion, the clergyman, already well known to you, informs me that several of the parents of our scholars tell him that their children are talking about the Gospel at home all the day long.

MISSION SOCIETIES RECONNOITER

"We must wait patiently a little longer . . ."

> *Though a liberal spirit was influential in the early years after independence, Protestant mission societies in Europe and North America saw little opportunity to evangelize. An influential Congregationalist agency in Boston, the American Board of Commissioners for Foreign Missions, sent two seminarians, Theophilous Parvin and John C. Brigham, to explore the feasibility of such work in Argentina, Chile, Peru, and Mexico. The trip lasted from 1823 to 1826. A report by Brigham to the board in October of 1826 describes the prospects for Protestants as he saw them.* [23]

✠ Having completed my exploring tour in South America and Mexico, it will of course be expected, that I inform the Board, under whose direction I travelled, of the course pursued, and present them the result of my inquiries. . . .

In placing their religious condition before you, it will be well, perhaps, that I first give a concise view of the state of the church, and its connexion with government, in each of the Republics separately; and afterwards describe some of the religious practices and ceremonies common to their churches generally.

Taking the places in the order, in which I visited them, the first to be noticed is *Buenos Aires . . . Chile . . . Peru . . . Colombia . . . Mexico . . .*

Entering a Catholic country, the first object which strikes you in their religion, next to their numerous churches, is the *cross*, which every where meets the eye. It is seen on the top of every high hill, on all the steeples and towers, in every dwelling—house and shop, in their prisons, custom-houses, mints, halls of legislation . . . .

Entering their houses, if you hear any thing said of religious duties, it is of their attendance at *mass* (church service) said by a priest or friar in Latin. . . .

This service generally continues for fifteen or twenty minutes, during which time the congregation kneel before the great altar where the mass is read and incense burned. It must be understood, that their churches, immense as they are, are wholly without pews or slips, often without seats of any kind, or any objects through the centre, except long rows of hewn pillars, connected by arches, and hung with paintings.

I will add, too, in this place, as illustrating the interior of their churches and forms of worship, that along the sides of these spacious buildings are a series of deep alcoves and niches, where images of different saints, richly dressed, are placed, before which are small altars, where deluded beings, at all hours of the day, may be seen invoking aid.

Go into one of those dark temples at the time of vespers; see a few feeble lamps on the far distant altar, throwing their pale rays on the image of a bleeding Saviour, and the long rows of apostles and martyrs; see the numerous paintings of saints and angels staring from every column, and looking down from the high arches above; hear the deep slow tones of an unseen organ, mingled with the mournful prayers of an aged monk, in a tongue long since dead;—and you have at once the feelings, which they mistake for the purest devotion.

When the mass is ended, the congregation retire, each dipping his hand in the vase of holy water at the door, and crossing himself. On reaching their dwellings, which, on feast days, is generally before the hour of break-fast, the black dress of the church is exchanged for one the most showy and extravagant, and they are prepared for visiting the coffee house, the promenade, the cockpit, the bull fights, or for a drive in the country, as fancy may suggest, and in the evening they go to the theatre. Thus passes the Sabbath throughout Spanish America, both with the priest and the people. . . .

One, who watches the signs of the times, may see, too, that causes are beginning to operate, which must make the secular clergy truly tolerant, or deprive them both of their influence and their living. The government in all those places are themselves disposed to be liberal. I do not believe that one man in ten, in civil authority, would now oppose a perfect toleration of religion, if the common people were thought prepared for such an event. The uniform language of political men was, so far as I saw them, "Sir, I am no more in favor of that intolerant article of our constitution than you are, and I hope the time is near, when the bigotry, which old Spain has left us, will be so diminished, that we can with safety expunge that article."

With this spirit in the governments, and most other leading individuals, particularly the young men, we can see what must eventually be the conduct of the clergy, whose all depends on their favor. . . .

Think, for a moment, how their character has already been changed, since the Revolution, not so much in their little religious ceremonies, as in the great principles of action.

Their inquisitions are now changed into school houses, and the peaceful halls of legislation; the number of feast days is diminished; the practice of selling indulgences stopped; the wealth and power of the priesthood lessened; in one country there is already a free religious toleration, and in all, protestants live and die undisturbed; the Scriptures too are now freely circulated; and in some instances their children are instructed by protestant teachers.

Protestant Preachers Not Yet Admissible

The question might be suggested, for it is often asked, whether protestant preachers could not now be usefully sent to those countries.

The answer is, that they could not at present. Such a measure, in most places, would be opposed, as yet, to articles of their constitution, and would create such excitement among the lower orders, that the most liberal enlightened statesmen would discourage it.

Although there are many individuals in South America, who have noble and expanded views on all subjects, men who are up with the spirit of the age, still there is in that field a putrid mass of superstition, on which the sun of liberty must shine still longer before we can safely enter in and labor.

In a few places, a protestant preacher could labor profitably among foreigners collected there, and by private intercourse, if judicious, be widely useful to those of the country. But these places are yet few; as are those where one could be successful in procuring a school; and those are mostly occupied.

We must wait patiently a little longer, till the Ruler of nations, who has wrought such wonders in those countries the last ten years, shall open still wider the way, and bid us go forward.

A CHURCH FOR FOREIGN TRADERS IN RIO

" 'The English,' said he, 'have really no religion . . .' "

Long before Protestant churches were allowed among the local inhabitants, exceptions were made for the foreign Protestants living in the port cities. Here Robert Walsh, an Anglican clergyman who visited Brazil in 1828-29, described an Anglican chapel in Rio and its condition when he saw it.[24]

✠ The Sunday following our arrival, was the baptismal day of the emperor, and one of those festivals observed with great ceremony. Early in the morning, the Brazilian ships of war hoisted their flags and ensigns, and all the stays and yard-arms were covered with them. . . . Towards mid-day, a discharge of sky-rockets, and other fire-works, was seen over different parts of the town, and then a general salute of artillery commenced. . . .

After this display of pomp, I returned to the quiet and simplicity of our English church service, as more according with the feelings which our sabbath excites. The edifice stands on the Rua des Barbonos, and is distinguished as being the first ever erected in South America. Before it was built, divine service was only performed occasionally on board any king's or merchant's ship, in the bay, of which the English on shore used to avail themselves. But in the year 1810, by one of the articles of the treaty then made by Lord Strangford, with the Brazilian government, it was stipulated, that the British should be permitted to build a church for divine service, provided it was erected, not as a public edifice, but as a private house, and did not use bells to assemble the congregation. . . .

The bishop of Rio . . . was a strenuous advocate for the measure. He is not only a tolerant and liberal man, but a man of excellent good sense and knowledge of the world. He advocated the cause, in a characteristic manner, with the prejudiced few who opposed it. "The English," said he, "have really no religion; but they are a proud and obstinate people. If you oppose them, they will persist, and make it an affair of infinite importance; but if you concede to their wishes, the chapel will be built, and nobody will ever go near it." . . .

I was concerned to find that this chapel was never entirely finished; and at present it exhibits marks not only of neglect, but decay. The portico at the entrance was not leaded, and the rain having penetrated, has rotted the roof, which is continually falling on the heads of the scanty congregation who attend it; the windows, which were broken so long ago by the outrage I mentioned, have not since been repaired; the blinds inside are all stained and soiled; and instead of the neatness and propriety which always distinguished the house of God in England, it had an air of dirt and neglect, quite painful to contemplate; and the congregation, as if to confirm the prediction of the bishop of Rio, wanted to take no interest in it when it was built, notwithstanding their zeal to have it established. It is capable of containing six or seven hundred persons, and there is that number of the reformed church at Rio to fill it, yet I never counted more than thirty or forty. . . .

RELIGIOUS TOLERANCE IN BRAZIL

". . . I have never received the slightest opposition . . . from the people."

Observers in the empire of Brazil wrote that though the Catholic hierarchy tried to discourage Protestantism, the people were generally tolerant. A

North American Methodist missionary, Daniel P. Kidder, traveled widely in the country in the 1830s and 1840s. His report, written, in part, by his Presbyterian colleague, James Fletcher, became a classic description of Brazilian life toward the middle of the century. There was little Protestant activity to describe, but in the following paragraphs Kidder wrote of the welcome he experienced as a foreigner and as a missionary.[25]

✠ It is my firm conviction that there is not a Roman Catholic country on the globe where there prevails a greater degree of toleration or a greater liberality of feeling toward Protestants.

I will here state, that in all my residence and travels in Brazil in the character of a Protestant missionary, I never received the slightest opposition or indignity from the people. As might have been expected, a few of the priests made all the opposition they could; but the circumstance that these were unable to excite the people showed how little influence they possessed. On the other hand, perhaps quite as many of the clergy, and those of the most respectable in the Empire, manifested toward us and our work both favor and friendship.

From them, as well as from the intelligent laity, did we often hear the severest reprehension of abuses that were tolerated in the religious system and practices of the country, and sincere regrets that no more spirituality pervaded the public mind. . . .

Portugal has never published the Bible or countenanced its circulation save in connection with notes and comments that had been approved by inquisitorial censorship. The Bible was not enumerated among the books that might be admitted to her colonies when under the absolute dominion. Yet the Brazilians, on their political disenthralment, adopted a liberal and tolerant Constitution. Although it made the Roman Catholic apostolic religion that of the State, yet it allowed all other forms of religion to be held and practised, save in buildings "having the exterior form of a temple." It also forbade persecution on the ground of religious opinions. By degrees, enlightened views of the great subjects of toleration and religious liberty became widely disseminated among the people, and hence many were prepared to hail any movement which promised to give them what had so long been systematically withheld, — the Scriptures of truth for their own perusal. Copies exposed for sale and advertised in the newspapers found many purchasers, not only from the city, but also from the distant provinces.

At the mission-house many copies were distributed gratuitously; and on several occasions there was what might be called a rush of applicants for the sacred volume. One of these occurred soon after my arrival. It was known that a supply of books had been received, and our house was literally thronged with persons of all ages and conditions of life, — from the gray-headed man to the prattling child, — from the gentleman in high life to the poor slave. . . .

It was not to be presumed, however, that so great an amount of scriptural truth could at once be scattered among the people without exciting great jealousy and commotion among certain of the padres. Nevertheless, others of this class were among the applicants themselves. One aged priest, who called in person, and received by special request copies in Portuguese, French, and English, on retiring, said, "The like was never before done in this country." Another sent a note in French, asking for *L'Ancien et le Nouveau Testament*. In three days two hundred copies were distributed, and our stock was exhausted; but applicants continued to come, till it was estimated that four times that number had been called for. All we could respond to these persons was to inform them where Bibles were kept on sale, and that we anticipated a fresh supply at some future day.

9 ✠ The Catholic Church: Rupture of the Old Christendom

1850–1930

Over the next eighty years, most of the new Latin American republics broke their traditional ties with the church. From Britain, Germany, France, and the United States came an increasing number of traders, naval personnel, immigrants, and missionaries. Their contact was with the small urban middle class that was emerging and desiring to "modernize" their countries.

In nearly every republic, the two political parties were the "conservatives," the traditional holders of power and privilege, and the "liberals," small land-holders, lawyers, and other professionals, shopkeepers, and artisans who wanted to break up the hierarchical social structure inherited from the colonial past. Much of their discontent was aimed at clerical influence over the economy and the social institutions. As the decades passed, there was a zigzag of power between these two groups.

By the end of the period, 1930, the position of the Catholic church across most of Latin America had changed profoundly. Except in a few countries, the church was no longer in partnership with the government. Legislators had taken away its control over essential services, such as education, cemeteries, and registration of births and marriages. In addition, the church no longer held a monopoly in the field of religion, and Protestants and members of other faiths were allowed to propagate their messages. After losing traditional prestige and subsidies, the clergy, especially the bishops, looked to Rome for support. Under Pius IX, 1846–78, and Leo XIII, 1878–1903, the Vatican played a more active role in Latin America and found it much easier than under the old patronage system. By the 1920s, the Vatican's influence and local necessity had led to significant innovations in the church's life in the region.

SUNDAY ON A PLANTATION

"... the good cura, with his gown tucked up, dancing the bambuco ..."

In Colombia, the liberal party was in control from 1849 to 1880, and led the country to be the first to make the drastic rupture with the church.

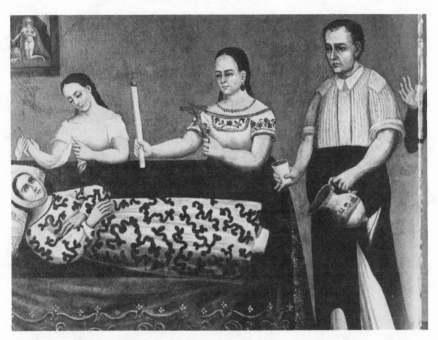

Religion in a home where a family grieves over the dying mother.

They expelled the Jesuits, legalized divorce, annulled the tithes, curtailed other clerical privileges, and went on to separate by law church from state. Later in the 1880s, the conservatives regained power, and most of the church's privileges were restored. The reforms of the 1850s were not the kind that were noticeable in the Sunday routine of a parish priest. In the Valley of the Cauca on the western side of the country, Isaac F. Holton, a North American botanist and Presbyterian, was on a scientific expedition. In the middle 1850s, while a guest on a hacienda in the region, he took note of "the actual events of a single Sabbath." [26]

✠ On Saturday night the bells of the chapel rung a little—just enough to say that there would be mass in the morning. The good Cura leaves San Vicente occasionally for a day, and comes and spends the Sabbath with us; and well he might, for more than half his salary comes from this hacienda. I went to church in the morning, as I always do when I have the opportunity. Well, in the first place, we had one baptism and two fractions: that is, two of the babes had received just enough baptism to save them from hell had they died before this time, but not enough for decency.

The priest met the unbaptized at the door of mercy, or side door of the church. One assistant held a little plain wooden cross, and another a lighted candle. After the prayers he put salt in the babe's mouth, and went to the font, an excavated stone, on a pedestal, with a hole for the water to run off. Here awaited the other two babes. One was held on the *left* arm. "Put the head *there*," said the priest. The woman turned herself, so as to bring the head to the required spot; the feet of the babe were more out of their place than ever. An exclamation of impatience from the fasting Cura led an assistant to aid in placing the babe on the right arm. First he put spittle on the ears and nostrils of each; then he completed them one by one. He took from his portable baptism-box a silver vial, with a rod passed through the silver-capped cork, and some cotton. With the rod he made a cross on the breast of each, and another between the shoulders, and wiped the oil off again with the cotton. The dress of one tried the Cura's patience again. He exclaimed, amid his prayers, "Better bring your babe naked than with a dress tight at the neck." I held it away with two fingers as well as I could. Then the babe's head was held over the font, face downward, and holy water was poured from the little silver *teapot* on the crown of the head. Another cross was made on the crown of the head with the oily rod, the head covered for a moment with a white cloth, and the task was done. These prayers would occupy a Protestant clergyman about two hours, but our curate dispatched them very soon. If he skipped a word, or pronounced it wrong, he left it for next time.

He went back to the vestry, put on different robes, and, again accompanied by the cross and candle, met a marriage party at the door of mercy. These were more awkward than the mothers. First, the groomsman, who happened to be the husband of the bridesmaid, placed himself next the bride. Then the bridegroom tried to insinuate himself between the bride and bridesmaid, apparently intending to be married to one of them at least. When the parties were placed aright, the priest read them a long address, telling them, among other things, that it was their duty to endeavor to raise up heirs, not so much to their goods as to their religion, their faith, and their virtue. The bride, though never married before, need not excite his anxiety on that point. Not only were two of her children witnesses of the ceremony, but, besides, she was visibly in a state which is here designated by the word *embarazada*. I am aware that this detracts materially from the poetry of my picture, but I can not help it; the sole merit of my sketch is its fidelity. I must add, then, that the older of her two children appeared to be three fourths black, and the younger three fourths white. The mother was a mulata, the other three adults of pure African blood. All were barefoot; the females wore that plain dress which alone is permitted to rich or poor in church — the head covered with a shawl, the body with a dark-colored skirt (saya).

The address through, the priest directed them to join their right hands. This was accomplished after much delay. When the priest asked the bride if she was willing to have this man for her husband, she made no answer. He repeated the question; no answer. "Say yes or no," exclaimed the priest; she said "yes." Two rings were taken from the small silver tray used in the mass. The priest put one on the finger of the bridegroom, and the latter put the other on the little finger of the bride. It was large enough for her thumb, and she instantly removed it to another finger. Then the priest took eight or ten reals, half francs, and dimes, from the tray, put them in the hands of the bridegroom, and he in those of the bride. In the course of the subsequent prayers the fasting priest fairly lost his patience at their awkwardness, as might be seen by the angry tones and snappish accent he gave his Latin. Then he stopped short off, and administered a rebuke in plain Castilian.

These prayers over, their hands still joined, the priest passed the band — estola — of his robe round the man's waist, and led the pair, followed by the other pair, to the altar. They knelt, and mass commenced. Two golden chains, united by a ribbon, were put on their necks. Two yards of white cloth, with a fringe, was spread over her head and his shoulders. Regularly, they ought to have partaken of the Eucharist. I afterward asked the priest why they did not; he informed me that the bride's situation did not admit of the delay and fasting that were necessary to prepare them for that sacrament.

Mass over, every one is at liberty to amuse himself as he pleases, for Sunday is a holiday, and it is a sin to work more than two hours, but no sin to play. At night I found that an extraordinary activity had prevailed in the kitchen; fresh pork and chicken appeared on the dinner-table, and a bottle of aguardiente. At the head sat the Cura, and a vacant space opposite me was at length filled by the four who had figured so conspicuously in the morning. I was not prepared for this. If I must eat with negroes, I will do it with a good grace, but I could well have spared the company of an *"embarazada"* bride. During the dinner we had the music of two octave flutes and a drum.

This was ominous of the evening; in short, bad as was the weather, we had a ball. When I went for my chocolate, I found the good Cura, with his gown tucked up, dancing the bambuco with unusual grace with one of the nymphs of the pastures. As I was making my retreat, young Carlos, about 16, was waltzing with an aged manumitted slave that had been his nurse, and that of all his brothers and sisters before him. Later in the night was a scene yet more curious, as I am told. The pretty little Mercedes, of 17, the white man's daughter, waltzed with the negro blacksmith, Miguel. He appears over 70, is very tall, very grim, and is the most pious man on the plantation.

RELIGIOUS FESTIVALS

". . . Holy Ghosts of tin, . . . seventy-five cents per hundred."

At the annual religious festivals celebrated for the local patron saints, there were occasions for worship, eating, drinking, camaraderie, and even for doing business. To increase attendance, the sponsors advertised in the local papers. James C. Fletcher, a Presbyterian sent to Brazil by the American Bible Society during the years 1854–1856, recalls some of the interesting announcements.[27]

✠ It is particularly observable that all the religious celebrations are deemed interesting and important in proportion to the pomp and splendor which they display. The desirableness of having all possible show and parade is generally the crowning argument urged in all applications for Government patronage, and in all appeals designed to secure the attendance and liberality of the people.

The daily press of Rio de Janeiro must annually reap enormous sums for religious advertisements, of which I give one or two specimens.

The announcement of a festival in the Church of Santa Rita is thus concluded: —

"This *festa* is to be celebrated with high mass and a sermon, at the expense of the devotees of the said Virgin, the Most Holy Mother of Grief, who are all invited by the Board to add to the *splendor* of the occasion by their presence, since they will receive from the above-named Lady due reward."

The following is the advertisement of a *festa* up the bay, at Estrella, and is as clumsily put together in Portuguese as it appears in the literal English translation which I have given: —

"The Judge and some devout persons of the Church of Our Lady of Estrella, erected in the village of the same name, intend to hold a festival there, with a chanted mass, sermon, procession in the afternoon, and a *Te Deum*, — all with the greatest pomp possible, — all on the 23d instant; and at night there will be a beautiful display of fireworks. The managers of the feast have asked the Director of the Inhomerim Steamboat Company to put on an extra steamer that will leave the Praia dos Mineiros at eight o'clock in the morning and return after the fireworks.

"It is requested that all the devotees will deign to attend this solemn act, to render it of the most brilliant description.

> Francisco Pereira Ramos, *Secretary*
> "Estrella, Sept. 17, 1855"

The following will be to Northern Christians as novel as it is irreverent: —

"The Brotherhood of the Divine Holy Ghost of San Gonçalo (a small village across the bay) will hold the feast of the Holy Ghost, on the 31st instant, with all possible splendor. Devout persons are invited to attend, to give greater pomp to this act of religion. On the 1st proximo there will be the feast of the Most Holy Sacrament, with a procession in the evening, a *Te Deum*, and a sermon. On the 2d, — the feast of the patron of San Gonçalo, — at three p.m. there will be *brilliant horse-racing* [!]; after which, a *Te Deum* and magnificent fireworks."

But it is not the Church alone which advertises the *festas*. The tradesmen, having an eye to business, freely make known their ecclesiastic wares through the agency of public journals. The following is a specimen: —

"Notice to the Illustrious Preparers of the Festival of the Holy Spirit. — In the *Rua dos Ourives*, No. 78, may be found a beautiful assortment of Holy Ghosts, in gold, with glories, at eighty cents each; smaller sizes, without glories, at forty cents; silver Holy Ghosts, with glories, at six dollars and a half per hundred; ditto, without glories, three dollars and a half; Holy Ghosts of tin, resembling silver, seventy-five cents per hundred."

In some particulars the festivals of all the saints are alike. They are universally announced, on the day previous, by a discharge of skyrockets at noon and by the ringing of bells at evening. During the *festa*, also, — whether it continues one day or nine, — the frequent discharge of rockets is kept up. These missiles are so constructed as to explode high up in the air, with a crackling sound, after which they descend in beautiful curves of white smoke if in the daytime, or like meteoric showers if at night.

VESPERS ON A BRAZILIAN PLANTATION

"All . . . folded their hands . . . evening prayer to the Virgin."

The religious faith as practiced on the slaveholding plantations of Brazil could be questioned as to quality, but its extensiveness was not debatable.

A North American Protestant, who was a guest on a sugar plantation in the southeast in the middle 1850s, described a pastoral evening and the ritual that he saw.[28]

✠ I cannot enter into the details of my journey in Minas-Geraes, but I am reluctant to pass over a visit to one of the finest plantations in the province. The proprietor was a Brazilian, and the whole fazenda [plantation], in its minutest details, was carried on in the manner peculiar to the country, without any admixture of foreign modes of government and culture.

Twelve miles beyond the Parahibuna (an affluent of the Parahiba), we turned aside from the highway, and, after riding through a belt of enclosed forest-land, we saw before us the large plantation-house of Soldade, belonging to Senhor Commendador Silva Pinto. The approach to the mansion was between two rows of palm-trees, around whose trunks a beautiful *bignonia* ... entwined itself, and then threw its climbing branches over the feathery leaves of the *palms*, thus forming a magnificent arch of flowers and foliage. The buildings, in the form of a hollow square, occupied an acre of ground. On two sides of the square was the residence of the Commendador and his family, while the remaining sides consisted of the sugar-establishment and the dwellings of the slaves. . . .

At dinner we were served in a large dining-room. The Commendador sat at the head of the table, while his guests and the various free members of his family sat upon forms, the *feitors* (overseers) and shepherds being at the lower end. He lives in true baronial style, and I was reminded of the description by Mr. J. G. Kohl of castle-life among the noblemen of Courland and Livonia. A pleasant conversation was kept up during the long repast, and at its close three servants came — one bearing a massive silver bowl a foot and a half in diameter, another a pitcher of the same material containing warm water, while a third carried towels. The newly-arrived guests were thus served in lieu of finger-basins, which are rarely seen outside the capital.

The Commendador had a chapel in his mansion, and each morning mass was performed by an amiable young Portuguese priest, who knew much more about music than the gospel. The padre had many questions to ask concerning the peculiar doctrines of Protestants, and I was surprised to find that he possessed no Bible. I presented him with a New Testament, and before my departure we had many most earnest and serious conversations in regard to vital piety and the solemn responsibility that was upon him to teach the truth as it is in Christ Jesus. With the approval of the Commendador (which was heartily given) explanations of the Scriptures were hereafter to constitute a portion of the chapel-service on Sundays. . . .

On those interior plantations there is a beautiful custom at vespers of offering a short prayer and wishing each other a good-night; not that they then retire, but *boa noite* is the form of a blessing. We were all sitting on the veranda as the last rays of the sun were gilding the hill and the distant forest. The chapel-bell struck the vesper-hour. The conversation was arrested; we all arose to our feet. The hum of the sugar-mill ceased; the shout of the children died away; the slaves that were crossing the courtyard stopped and uncovered the head. All devoutly folded their hands and breathed the evening prayer to the Virgin. I too joined in devotion to the blessed Saviour, the sole Mediator, and when the padre and others wished me the blessing in the name of *Nossa Senhora*, I returned the benediction *en nome de Nosso Senhor Jesus Christo*. The noise of merry voices again rang through the courtyard; the day's labor was finished; and soon night, with its darkness, silence, and repose, reigned over Soldado.

WORSHIP AND NURSES IN HAVANA

". . . the Sisters . . . are all from abroad, . . . and . . . with . . . yellow fever . . . many . . . die . . ."

In Cuba, the break with Spain was delayed until the end of the nineteenth century. One of the reasons was that its clergy had been thoroughly Spanish and emotionally tied to Spain. This foreign loyalty also made it difficult to recruit native Cubans for the priesthood and for the religious orders. An American from Boston, vacationing on the island in 1859, described his observations during a mass in a Jesuit church and during a visit the next day to a government welfare institution, which was served by foreign nuns.[29]

✠ At break of day, I am in the delightful seabaths again, not ill-named Recreo and Elíseo. But the forlorn chain-gang are mustered before the Presidio. It is Sunday, but there is no day of rest for them.

At eight o'clock I present myself at the Belen. A lady, who was passing through the cloister, with head and face covered by the usual black veil, turned and came to me. It was Mrs. _____ , whom I had seen last evening. She kindly took me to the sacristy, and asked some one to tell Father _____ that I was there, and then went to her place in church. . . .

Father _____ appears, is unrobed, and takes me to the gallery of the church, near the organ. From this, I looked down upon a sea of rich costumes of women, veiled heads, and kneeling figures, literally covering the floor of the church. On the marble pavement, the little carpets are spread, and on these, as close as they can sit or kneel, are the ladies of rank and wealth of Havana. A new comer glides in among them, seeking room for her carpet, or room of charity or friendship on a carpet already spread; and the kneelers or sitters move and gather in their wide skirts to let her pass. Here and there a servant in livery winds his way behind his mistress, bearing her carpet, and returns to the porch when it has been spread. The whole floor is left to women. The men gather about the walls and doorways, or sit in the gallery, which is reserved for them. But among the women, though chiefly of rank and wealth, are some who are negroes, usually distinguished by the plain shawl, instead of the veil over the head. The Countess Villanueva, immensely rich, of high rank, and of a name great in the annals of Cuba, but childless, and blind, and a widow, is led in by the hand by her negro servant. The service of the altar is performed with dignity and reverence, and the singing, which is by the Jesuit Brothers themselves, is admirable. In the choir I recognized my new friends, the Rector and young Father Cabre, the professor of physics. The "Tantum ergo Sacramentum," which was sung kneeling, brought tears into my eyes, and kept them there. . . .

The Casa de Beneficencia is a large institution, for orphan and destitute children, for infirm old persons, and for the insane. It is admirably situated, bordering on the open sea, with fresh air and very good attention to ventilation in the rooms. It is a government institution, but is placed under charge of the Sisters of Charity, one of whom accompanied us about the building. Though called a government institution, it must not be supposed that it is a charity from the crown. On the contrary, it is supported by a specific appropriation of certain of the taxes and revenues of the island. In the building, is a church not yet finished, large enough for all the inmates, and a quiet little private chapel for the Sisters' devotions, where a burning lamp indicated the presence of the Sacrament on the small altar. I am sorry to have forgotten the number of children. It was large, and included both sexes, with a separate department for each. In a third department, are the insane. They are kindly treated and not confined, except when violent; but the Sister told us they had no medical treatment unless in case of sickness. (Dr. Howe told me that he was also so informed.) The last department is for aged and indigent women.

One of the little orphans clung to the Sister who accompanied us, holding her hand, and nestling in her coarse but clean blue gown; and when we took our leave, and I put a small coin into her little soft hand, her eyes brightened up into a pretty smile.

The number of the Sisters is not full. As none have joined the order from Cuba, (I am told literally none,) they are all from abroad, chiefly from France and Spain; and having acclimation to go through, with exposure to yellow fever and cholera, many of those that come here die in the first or second summer. And yet they still come, in simple, religious fidelity, under the shadow of death.

The Casa de Beneficencia must be pronounced by all, even by those accustomed to the system and order of the best charitable institutions in the world, a credit to the island of Cuba. The charity is large and liberal, and the order and neatness of its administration are beyond praise.

BRAZILIAN PRIESTS – OBSTACLES TO PROGRESS

". . . there is no laborious, cultivated class of priests, . . ."

Corruption and moral laxity cost the clergy in Brazil much respect in the community. Various attempts to remedy the situation met with limited success. A Harvard zoologist and his wife, Louis and Elizabeth Agassiz, visited the country on a scientific expedition in 1865 and 1866. In the published report of their findings are observations about the quality of religious leadership. [30]

✠ My scientific life has brought me into relations with a world wholly unknown to me before; under conditions more favorable than were possible for my predecessors in the same region, I have studied this tropical nature, so rich, so grandiose, so instructive; I have seen a great Empire founded in the midst of unlimited material resources, and advancing to higher civilization under the inspiration of a sovereign as enlightened as he is humane. . . .

There is much that is discouraging in the aspect of Brazil, even for those who hope and believe as I do, that she has before her an honorable and powerful career. There is much also that is very cheering, that leads me to believe that her life as a nation will not belie her great gifts as a country. Should her moral and intellectual endowments grow into harmony with her wonderful natural beauty and wealth, the world will not have seen a fairer land. At present there are several obstacles to this progress; obstacles which act like a moral disease upon the people. Slavery still exists among them. It is true that it is on the wane; true that it has received a mortal blow; but the natural death of slavery is a lingering illness, wasting and destroying the body it has attacked. Next to this I would name, among the influences unfavorable to progress, the character of the clergy. In saying this I disclaim any reference to the national religion. It is of the character of the clergy I speak, not of the church they represent. Whatever be the church organization in a country where instruction is still so intimately linked with a state religion as it is in Brazil, it is of infinite importance that the clergy themselves should not only be men of high moral character, but of studious, thoughtful lives. They are the teachers of the people, and as long as they believe that the mind can be fed with tawdry street processions, with lighted candles, and cheap bouquets; and as long as the people accept this kind of instruction, they will be debased and enfeebled by it. Shows of this kind are of almost daily occurrence in all the large cities of Brazil. They interfere with the ordinary occupations, and make working days the exception rather than the rule. It must be remembered that in Brazil there is no laborious, cultivated class of priests, such as have been an honor to ecclesiastical

literature in the Old World; there are no fine institutions of learning connected with the Church. As a general thing, the ignorance of the clergy is
universal, their immorality patent, their influence very extensive and deep-
rooted. There are honorable exceptions, but they are not numerous enough
to elevate the class to which they belong. But if their private life is open to
blame, the Brazilian priests are distinguished for their patriotism. At all times
they have occupied high public stations, serving in the Legislative Assembly,
in the Senate, and even nearer to the throne; yet their power has never been
exerted in favor of Ultramontane tendencies. Independent religious thought
seems, however, rare in Brazil. There may perhaps be scepticism; but I think
this is not likely to be extensively the case, for the Brazilians are instinctively
a believing people, tending rather to superstition, than to doubt. Oppression
in matters of faith is contrary to the spirit of their institutions. Protestant
clergymen are allowed to preach freely; but, as a general thing, Protestantism
does not attract the Southern nations, and it may be doubted whether its
advocates will have a very wide-spread success. However this may be, every
friend to Brazil must wish to see its present priesthood replaced by a more
vigorous, intelligent, and laborious clergy.

A FORMER SLAVE VIEWS RELIGION IN CUBA

"Poor people, . . . were married . . . at the back of the church."

*Toward the end of the century, the plantation economy in Cuba was still
based on the labor of African slaves. North American economic influence
was growing, and so was the desire for independence from Spain. In this
respect, the church dragged its feet, since the clergy were royalist and
conservative. An interested observer of religious life was an African slave
who was on the island in the 1870s and 1880s. He was Esteban Montejo,
a runaway, who, after his escape, wrote about his experiences. His critique
of the church foreshadowed its separation from the state in 1901.*[31]

✠ The Congolese used the dead and snakes for their religious rites. They
called the dead *nkise* and the snakes *emboba*. They prepared big pots called
ngangas which would walk about and all, and that was where the secret of
their spells lay. . . .

The other religion was the Catholic one. This was introduced by the
priests, but nothing in the world would induce them to enter the slaves'
quarters. They were fastidious people, with a solemn air which did not fit
the barracoons [slave quarters] — so solemn that there were Negroes who
took everything they said literally. This had a bad effect on them. They
read the catechism and read it to the others with all the words and prayers.
Those Negroes who were household slaves came as messengers of the

priests and got together with the others, the field slaves, in the sugar-mill towns. The fact is I never learned that doctrine because I did not understand a thing about it. I don't think the household slaves did either, although, being so refined and well-treated, they all made out they were Christian. The household slaves were given rewards by the masters, and I never saw one of them badly punished. When they were ordered to go to the fields to cut cane or tend the pigs, they would pretend to be ill so they needn't work. For this reason the field slaves could not stand the sight of them. The household slaves sometimes came to the barracoons to visit relations and used to take back fruit and vegetables for the master's house; I don't know whether the slaves made them presents from their plots of land or whether they just took them. They caused a lot of trouble in the barracoons. The men came and tried to take liberties with the women. That was the source of the worst tensions. I was about twelve then, and I saw the whole rumpus.

There were other tensions. For instance, there was no love lost between the Congolese magic-men and the Congolese Christians, each of whom thought they were good and the other wicked. This still goes on in Cuba. The Lucumi and Congolese did not get on either; it went back to the difference between saints and witchcraft. The only ones who had no problems were the old men born in Africa. They were special people and had to be treated differently because they knew all religious matters. . . .

The plantation was of medium size, owned by a man called Ariosa, a pure-blooded Spaniard. It was one of the first plantations to become a mill, and a large-gauge line ran through it, bringing the cane direct from the fields to the boiler-house. It was much the same there as anywhere else. There were the usual yes-men and toadies to masters and overseers alike. They always questioned new workers to discover their views. This was on account of the hatred which has always existed between the groups of slaves, because of ignorance. This is the only reason for it. The freed slaves were generally very ignorant and would lend themselves to anything. It even happened that if some fellow became a nuisance, his own brothers would undertake to kill him for a few centenes.

The priests interfered in everything. If they said a Negro was troublesome, he had to watch out, otherwise he would find someone ready to dispose of him at the first suitable opportunity.

Religion was strong at Ariosa. There was a church nearby, but I never went because I knew the priests were the real supporters of the inquisition in Cuba; I say this because the priests were known to do certain things. They were devils with women. They turned the sacristy into a brothel. Anyone who has lived in Ariosa knows the stories, they even got to the barracoons. I know quite a few, and some things I saw myself.

The priests put women in dungeons, in holes where they had torturers ready to murder them. Other dungeons were full of water and the poor wretches drowned. This has been told me many times.

I saw priests with loose women who slept with them and afterwards said, 'Father, a blessing.' They also talked at Ariosa of what life was like in the churches and monasteries. The priests were like other men, but they had all the gold, and they didn't spend it. I never saw a priest enjoying himself in a tavern. They shut themselves up in their churches and there they wasted away. They made collections every year for the church, for the saints' vestments and flowers.

I don't believe the question of the sugar-mills ever interested them. They never went as far as the machines. They were afraid of suffocating or being deafened. They were the most delicate people imaginable. . . .

One of the funny things about those days was courting. When a young man had his eye on a girl he would use thousands of tricks. They didn't set about these things the way they do now, quite openly. There was more mystery; and tricks, all sorts of tricks. If I wanted to make a respectable woman fall for me, I dressed myself in white and walked right by her without looking at her. I did this several days running until the time came when I decided to ask her something. The women liked seeing men dressed in white. A black man like me in white was something which caught the eye. A hat was an essential piece of equipment, because you could do a thousand and one things with it; put it on, take it off, raise it to a woman and ask, 'Well, how are you, then?' . . .

The custom was for the girl's parents and the couple's godparents to give the groom half a dozen chickens, a large sow, a young heifer, a milch cow and the wedding dress, which had to have a train because she was not allowed to show her ankles. Any woman who did was not religious or respectable. The man provided for the home; he was the head of the household. She carried out his orders and to begin with did no outside work except perhaps a little washing for some family or other. Once they were settled in their routine they began receiving visitors, and they would talk about the wedding reception and the beer and food they had served there. Every morning the girl's mother or her old man would come round and pay a duty-call.

The priest might call round too, although they were more concerned about visiting the rich people. All those saintly types were after was cash. When people were married they had to pay six or seven pesos, rich and poor alike. Poor people, plantation workers, were married in the chapel, which was at the back of the church. Rich people were married right in the middle, in front of the main altar, and they had benches with cushions on them, whereas the poor sat on wooden stools in the chapel or sacristy, as it was sometimes called.

A YOUNG GIRL AND HER FAITH

"Everybody knows that I am no saint, . . ."

Within three eventful years in Brazil, 1888–1890, slavery was abolished, the country was declared a republic, and the church was separated from

*the state. That meant changes in traditional clerical control over public
education, marriage, and cemeteries. The church could keep its own properties and institutions, but received no further subsidies.*

*In the weekly routine of family and parish life, the average church
member probably noticed little change. For example, the writings of a
young girl in the town of Diamantina in Minas Gerais reveal much continuity. Helena Morley kept a diary during the years 1893–1895, when she
was six and seven years old. Her grandfather had been an Englishman
and a Protestant, and had been the beloved town physician. Granddaughter Helena was a Catholic, and these extracts from her lively diary tell
something of religious life in the family.*[32]

✠ *Holy Thursday, March 30*
During Holy Week my family takes advantage of the children's not having
to go to school to get together at the *chácara* [country house].

Yesterday, Ash Wednesday, Iaia Henriqueta read the Passion of Christ
out loud while we all listened. Because it was a codfish day, grandma had
three bottles of port wine opened for dinner. We all ate and drank until
we were full; Aunt Carlota drank more than all the rest of us and her eyes
got very tiny and her nose as red as sealing-wax. After dinner we all went
to confession at the Bishop's Palace.

We children are never allowed to confess to Senhor Bishop because he
asks lots of questions that we can't understand and my father says it's silly
of mama to let us confess to a man already in his dotage. He's very old.
Since there are lots of priests at the Palace, mama picked out Father Flo-
rencio for us. He is very nice and gives very small penances, but we leave
the confessional worn out with all the stories of the lives of the saints that
he takes the opportunity of telling, and advises us to imitate. As if it were
up to us. I decide for myself; I admire good and holy people but I can't
possibly stop being the way I am.

Aunt Carlota went to the Bishop to confess. He won't let anyone tell his
own sins, he likes to ask them himself. Aunt Carlota said that she was
feeling very dizzy and she would like to have the Senhor Bishop ask her so
she'd only have to reply. He began:

"Do you ever speak evil of others?"
She answered, "Often, Senhor Bishop."
"Do you miss Mass on Sundays?"
"Often, Senhor Bishop."
"Do you wish harm to others?"
"Often."
"Do you steal?"
"Often."
Then he said, "You are very drunk. Go home and sober up and then
come back again."

We were all helpless with laughter when Aunt Carlota told us the story
of her confession.

Easter Sunday, April 2nd

Ever since Chininha came to spend her vacation at the *chácara*, pretending to be a saint all the time just to please grandma, my life has been a hell. At evening prayers I get so mad at her and hate her so much that I always have to confess it as a sin when I go to confession. When our mothers call us to come and pray, even if we're at the most exciting moment in a game, she's the first to run and fall on her knees at the *oratório*. She rolls up her eyes at Our Lady, folds her hands, and puts on such a sanctimonious expression that anyone could tell she's just pretending. I'm getting pretty sick of her.

When she came from Montes Claros to enter the convent school, she was so badly brought up that mama wouldn't let me play with her alone. But with one year of school she's turned into such a saint that the aunts talk about nothing but the change in her and when anyone praises her she gets more hateful than ever.

At school she's got used to kneeling a great deal, and now evening prayers are a torture for all of us cousins. After we've said the rosary and a lot of prayers, she always has the idea of going on praying for the souls of relatives who were dead long ago. I told her I didn't believe that prayers were really of any use in getting souls out of purgatory and that she only did it to make up to grandma. She went and told on me and grandma said she was surprised at my saying such things. Then I said, "Grandma, grandpa and my uncles and those people have been dead so long! If they've been in purgatory all this time they must be used to it, and we aren't going to help by praying on our knees all that time, the way Chininha wants to." Grandma said that no one ever gets used to purgatory; that Chininha was learning to be a saint with the nuns, and that I only want to run around and play.

I never spent such a disgusting day in my life as Good Friday. Chininha pretended she was sad about the death of Jesus Christ and she went to read the Passion of Christ out loud to grandma, the way they do at school, and we all had to sit and listen to her. Everybody knows that I am no saint, but when I'm in a group with others just like me, nobody notices. And now comes all this horrible pretending so the aunts will notice her. But grandma, thank God, doesn't let anyone speak against me to her very much.

Good Friday was a fast day for everyone in the house. I'm very unhappy about making sacrifices. I don't like to make sacrifices. But when I know I have to, I can fast. In the morning, at seven o'clock we take a cup of weak coffee which amounts to nothing at all. At ten o'clock we have lunch: codfish with pumpkin, black beans and mush; things we only eat to make us hungrier. During the day we have the same very weak coffee. Dinner at four o'clock and nothing more.

If Dindinha hadn't had a big kettle of green corn cooked for dinner, I think I could have fasted until the end. But the devil got into the kettle of corn and tempted me. I immediately planned to do something wicked. I thought, "I'm going to eat one ear, secretly, and afterwards I'll confess it to the priest." I took out the ear and went to eat it behind the Church of the Rosário. Chininha missed me and followed me, and then she went running to tell grandma that I'd lost my indulgences. She told her tales, but she got disappointed because grandma said, "Poor child, she was hungry. It doesn't matter Chininha, she'll earn the indulgences some other time."

When I learned about it I had my revenge because I ate two more ears while she watched me, dying with envy. Hurray! . . .

Sunday, December 29th

Today, Sunday, it's raining in Boa Vista, and I am thinking nostalgically of my First Communion. When all the little girls had studied the catechism a year, Father Neves told us that we were ready for our First Communion, which would take place in a month.

I was in raptures at this news and I told mama to begin to get everything ready immediately: the long white dress, the veil, the wreath, and the decorated wax candle.

On the evening of the great day, Father Neves brought all the pupils together in the church, and he went behind the grating of the screen to hear our confessions. The little girls knelt outside, confessing and then going away. My turn came and I knelt down with my list of sins all memorized: Gluttony, Envy, Luxury (the desire for pretty dresses), stealing fruit from my grandmother, gossiping. I told everything and made my act of contrition, but I left the confessional with a small nail in my conscience.

There were lots of ex-slaves at grandma's who told nursery tales, tales of the spirits of the other world and the sins that had carried them off to purgatory and hell. If one stole an egg, for example, then the egg would turn into a hen, and one would have to spend as many years in purgatory as the hen had feathers. They also believed that it was an unpardonable sin to think that a priest was homely.

I listened to everything attentively and I couldn't have stolen an egg under any circumstances. But the sin of finding a priest homely haunted me all year long. Every time Father Neves came into church I thought to myself, "Am I really committing a sin? I do think he's so homely!" I kept trying to put this wicked thought out of my head but it kept coming back again, and even at the end of the catechism class it hadn't left me.

When I went to confess that day, I reasoned, "No, I haven't committed a sin because I've never told anyone I think Father Neves is homely. It's better not to think about it any more."

I left the confessional very penitent but not quite as peaceful and relieved as one should be. I made a retreat all that day with as much contrition as a seven year old girl is capable of.

On the next day, the great day, mama woke me up early and helped me get dressed, giving me some last bits of advice on how to make a good communion. When I got to church I found all my playmates already in their places, just waiting for me for the priest to begin the sermon.

To give this sermon, Father Neves had asked an Italian priest, rather fat and red, who knew how to shout and make a big impression on little girls. The priest began:

"My children, this day is the happiest and most important of your lives. You are going to receive the body, blood, and soul of Jesus into your hearts. It is an amazing grace, my dears, that God grants you! But to receive it you must be prepared, and contrite, and you mustn't have concealed any sin whatsoever in the confessional. To hide a sin and then to receive communion is an abomination! I know of many horrible cases, but I am going to tell you just one as an example.

"Once a group of little girls were making their first communion just the way you are making it today. They received the host and went solemnly back to their places, and at that very moment one of them fell down and died. The priest said to the little girl's mother, 'God has taken her to Glory!' And all the others were envious of their playmate who had died in the grace of God. And then, what do you suppose they saw? The devil dragging the body of the miserable little girl behind the altar. Do you know why? Because she had concealed a sin in the confessional."

When I heard this I amazed everyone by bursting out howling. Father Neves ran to find out what was wrong. I said, "I concealed a sin in the confessional." Father Neves tried to comfort me very gently, "Don't be so upset, daughter; come and tell the sin and God will forgive you and you can take communion." I told him, "I want to tell the sin to the other priest, not to you, Senhor." He took hold of my hands, still very gently, and said, "You can't do that, little one; you confessed to me so you have to tell me the sin. Don't be afraid; the priest is here to listen to everything. Come on, I'll look the other way; you can tell me and go away in just a minute."

He took me to a corner of the sacristy and was very nice and insisted that I confess. Sobbing and horrified at what I was going to say I hung my head and whispered, "I confess to having thought that a priest was very homely." Father Neves said, "That isn't a sin, my child. What's wrong with thinking that a priest is homely?" I took courage and said, "But the priest is you, Father!"

Father Neves let go of my hands and got up, exclaiming, "I really *am* homely! And what of it? I can't stand such silly little girls! Here I spend the whole year struggling to get them ready for communion and at the end they come to me to confess that I'm homely. It's too much!"

REVOLUTIONARIES TARGET ABUSIVE CLERGY

"General Villa, you are a very sinful man; . . ."

The Reform Laws of 1857–1876 in Mexico sought to curb the church's power, but during the rule of the dictator Porfirio Díaz, 1876–1910, the church was able to recoup much of its former position. Díaz brought prosperity for a few, but for the mass of Indian citizens there was continued poverty and unrest. The church's siding with the wealthy was again resented. A widespread desire for reforms was revealed in 1910 by the election of the liberal Francisco Madero. Out of fear of him, the church backed a bloody revolt led by Victoriano Huerta, and that precipitated in 1913 an eruption of pent-up emotions. Much of their fury was aimed at the priests and the large land-holders. Some of the feelings toward the clergy are described by Pancho Villa, one of the leaders of this outbreak. The following are excerpts from his memoirs of conversations around 1914. Villa's feelings provide the background for the severe restrictions on the clergy in the 1917 constitution.[33]

✠ I made the trip to Santa Isabel, Bustillos, Guerrero, and other towns in the district, where my sister Martina lived. She wanted me to be present for a baptism, and the priest who, as I said before, was performing the bishop's duties in Chihuahua, went with me. That priest was a man who had his own ideas, though he was also my friend. And knowing that I followed no religion, and was especially opposed to the ways of the Jesuits, he discussed the protective doctrines and teachings of the Church with the intention of influencing me.

"Sr. General, as you have consented to contract the duties of god-father, you do recognize the laws of our Catholic Church, as God disposes; you live under the mantle of our Holy Religion, and you are therefore obligated to follow its decrees and practices and to obey it insofar as it commands us to live and die as its good sons."

"Señor, to contract the duties of godfather does not imply recognizing any laws in this world or any other. Men are compadres by virtue of the bonds of friendship and custom. That is, if a man consents to take on himself the tutelage of the child of another in case the other man fails or dies, this is not because of religious doctrine but because the duties that unite us with our fellowmen require it, and this is true although the believers believe something else, seeing that the Church intervenes in these deeds to sanctify them. However, I do not deny belief in God. I affirm it and certify to it since it has comforted me and all men in many of life's crises. But I do not consider everything sacred that is covered by the name of religion. Most so-called religious men use religion to promote their own interests, not the things they preach, and so there are good priests and bad priests, and we must accept some and help them and prosecute and annihilate others. The bad priests, Señor, like the Jesuits, are the worst men in the world because it is their duty to teach what is good by means of sacrifice but instead they dedicate themselves to the fulfilment of their passions in ways that are evil. I think they deserve greater punishment than the worst bandits in the world, for the bandits do not deceive others in their conduct or pretend to be what they are not, while the Jesuits do, and by this deception they work very great hardships on the people."

The priest said, "Sr. General, the bad priests will be punished in their time, but while they walk on earth they deserve our respect. God puts them here among us, and if He does it, He knows why."

"No, Señor. If I, as a Revolutionary, arise to punish rulers who fail to fulfil their duty to the people, I must extend the punishment to religious men who betray the cause of the poor. And our punishment is beneficial to the churches in warning the clergy to be charitable and useful, not greedy and destructive, just as the punishment of a bad soldier is beneficial to the military. I understand your reasons, Señor, for thinking God has good and bad priests in the world. He knows why, and He will reward them afterward or punish them according to the conduct of each. But you can be sure, Sr. Priest, that God has many ways, as you religious men preach in your sermons, and that one of the punishments He can impose upon bad priests is the punishment we mete out. God has us, too, the Revolutionaries, and if He permits us to struggle for our love of the people in the way we do, He knows why."

The priest replied, "Yes, Sr. General, Revolutionaries are also sons of God. For that I bless them, as I do all creatures. Those men who die or suffer for their fellowman are not untouched or abandoned by the hand of God. But He has His ministers here to prevent these men from exceeding the limits in their passionate impulses, and the law of God does not entitle the Revolution to deny sacred ministers and annoy and persecute them instead of listening to what they preach."

"Remember, Sr. Priest, that our Revolution is the struggle of the poor against the rich, who thrive on the poverty of the poor. And if in this struggle we discover that the so-called priests of religion, or most of them, are on the side of the rich and not of the poor, what faith, Señor, can the people have in their advice? In my opinion, our justice involves such holiness that the priests and the churches who deny us their help have forfeited their claim to be men of God."

On the trip we went to the Hacienda Bustillos, which belonged to one of the richest families in Chihuahua. The owner was a lady by the name of Doña Luz, who was married to an uncle of Sr. Madero's. As a friend of mine in former times, she welcomed us and treated us cordially. She asked us to stay in her house, which was grand and elegant as a palace. The meals prepared for us were excellent. She did her best to make us comfortable. And, in truth, we had a happy time there.

She too spoke for religion, giving me advice on my duties to God. She did it every time she spoke with me, and I consented to it because she was agreeable, and really very kind, and closely related to Sr. Madero, but principally because she was a woman of great beauty. I enjoyed looking at her while she was speaking about God, and I answered yes to everything or argued only to get her to say more, and did everything she recommended unless it conflicted with my own sacred duty.

With a smile or a reproach she passed judgment on my conduct. Each time we saw each other, she said, "General Villa, you are a very sinful man; your hands are stained with much blood; in thought and act you have committed many other crimes. Put yourself in God's graces and He will pardon your sins."

I said, "Sra. Doña Luz, I have never killed anybody without reason."

She answered, "I believe you, Sr. General. But God says, 'Thou shalt not kill,' and He does not say with or without reason."

I said, "Señora, to kill is a cruel necessity for men who are at war. If we do not kill, how can we conquer? And if we do not conquer what future is there for the cause of the people? Death is an accident in the course of our struggle, and we all either kill or die."

She replied, "Not all your deaths have occurred in war, Sr. General."

I said, "Sra. Doña Luz, for me the war began when I was born. I am a man whom God brought into the world to battle with I do not know how many enemies."

She answered, "Moreover you have committed many robberies, Sr. General Villa, and God says, 'Thou shalt not steal.'"

I replied, "I have never stolen, Sra. Doña Luz. I have taken from those who had much in order to give to those who had little, or nothing. For myself, I have never taken anything belonging to another except in a situation of the most urgent necessity. And he who takes food when he is hungry does not steal, Sra. Doña Luz. He only complies with his duty to sustain himself. It is the rich who steal because, having everything they need, they still deprive the poor of their miserable bread." . . .

A group of religious men and women came to see me; they said, "Sr. General Villa, we know nothing of war or politics or revolution, although we would like to know about these things in order to pray for the triumph of the armies that fight for justice. But, Sr. General, while we do no harm to anyone with our prayers, which are words of love for our fellowmen, as the God who illumines us commands, General Diéguez ordered our churches closed. For that reason, Sr. General Villa, we come to ask you: what harm can the candles on our altars and our sacred images do the cause of the people?"

I answered, "Señores, I agree in general with your reasoning. The relief that the sad implore cannot harm the the people. But behind the altars that the poor erect you must admit that bad priests are often hidden. It was wrong for Diéguez to close your churches and I am going to open them, although he closed them to appear a great Revolutionary and by opening them I will appear to be an instrument of reaction. But if I find the clergy exploiting and deceiving the people under the protection of the churches, especially if they are Jesuits, I will not pardon them; I will punish them as I have punished them in other cities, because the church that shelters the poor under its mantle is one thing and the church that shelters itself under the mantle of the poor is another."

RELIGIOUS INDIFFERENCE

". . . my anxiety about this problem of the soul, . . ."

Argentina's constitution of 1853 assured that the "government supports the Roman Catholic religion." As the decades passed, however, some of the public supports of that religion were removed. In 1888, education was secularized, and marriage became a civil contract. When waves of immigrants came from Europe, they brought other kinds of churches and philosophies. Intellectual life stirred, and much of it was critical of traditional Christianity. By World War I, it was observed that most males never went to mass. Reflecting on the religious situation, Ricardo Rojas, a prominent Argentine educator and rector of the University of Buenos Aires, published in 1928 a series of dialogues that took place between himself and a Catholic bishop. Extracts from these conversations reveal the writer's concern about the lack of a genuine religious commitment in his country.[34]

✠ GUEST: I understand that the Church clings to its strict traditional principles to save itself as a historical institution; but it ought to save mankind also, although this may mean a change in its polity, as it has changed on other occasions.

BISHOP: There have been changes, not essential. The schisms cleansed the Church of heresy. External modifications, including those made in the mass, did not affect dogma. And for this reason the Church of Christ considers itself unchanged through twenty centuries, both in the name of its founder and in its system of faith. This is what I mean when I say that Christian tradition endures among our people.

GUEST: Perhaps, but the fetishism of the common people and the pretense of piety on the part of the upper classes are not Christian. It is true that worship is practiced, but without understanding its significance. Charity among us is nothing more than an egoistic instinct or a worldly vanity. The reconciliation realized by Saint Augustine, between obedience to ecclesiastical discipline and the necessity of understanding God as the highest expression of truth, searching for him in one's own heart — *interiu intimo meo* — is something which in our country is neither practiced nor understood. If I should write a book for the purpose of setting forth my anxiety about this problem of the soul, I would be looked on with suspicion or hostility.

BISHOP: That would depend on what you might say in the book. If it were written for the purpose of saying what we have so far said, there would be nothing scandalous in it. Some Argentine Catholics would consider your attitude with alarm, others benevolently.

GUEST: That is doubtful! Catholics would believe that I had turned Protestant, or would dub me atheist. As for freethinkers, who are even more superficial in their thinking, they would consider me a fanatic and would call me reactionary. In all Spanish America there is no serious study of these problems, no taste for them, no understanding of them. It is possible that in some countries, as in our own, for example, there has never been a real religious anxiety.

BISHOP: In our country, as in others of the continent, the ancient faith has suffered from the coming of international commerce and materialistic education. But the old ember still glows beneath the ashes.

GUEST: I do not know whether the fire on the hearth can be rekindled, but the ashes are without light and heat. Furthermore, I am not referring to the indifferent or lukewarm, but to ordinary believers and the emancipated thinking classes, when I state that there has never been real uneasiness in Argentina in regard to the religious problem. This is serious for a young civilization, because metaphysical transcendence widens and deepens thought, without taking into account that this process might develop a moral content in politics. . . .

BISHOP: I suppose that you will not deduce from all this that secularism, or atheistic materialism, as you should rightly call it, is more powerful in our country than Christianity.

GUEST: I believe that both are equally superficial, with the exception of the powerful individualities which you have mentioned, and others that I might cite who fought on the other side, since I maintain that a calm Christian sentiment inspired the democratic attitude of San Martin, Belgrano, and Mitre, leaders of the people, or the liberal doctrine of Echeverria, Sarmiento, and Gonzalez, educators of the people.

BISHOP: You incur in a contradiction.

GUEST: Not at all: I ignore the various political devices simply to emphasize the importance of lives. It would be easy to show that democracy, liberalism, and public instruction are remote consequences of the Christian spirit in modern society. Sarmiento was educated by Oro, a clergyman, in the reading of the gospels, and wrote Christian catechisms for the children of the public schools.

BISHOP: Therefore the Spirit of Christ is that which triumphs.

GUEST: Liberalism and romanticism, which constitute the generous background of Argentine civil tradition, spring from Christianity as a sentiment. Those who have been estranged from Christ in our modern epoch belong to a certain group which read the scientific materialism of Comte, and another with atheistic and anti-clerical tendencies which read Renan; but both forgot that Comte founded the religion of humanity, including the saints in his worship, and that Renan, in his *Life of Jesus*, says: "No revolution shall hinder us from following, in religious matters, the intellectual line, at whose front shines the name of Jesus, and, in this sense, we are Christians." All this is definite and proves what I told you: the superficiality of Argentine consciousness is all that refers to the religious problem.

BISHOP: In spite of it all, the Church which the evangelists of the sixteenth century founded here still subsists in its entirety, and we distrust all those who, in the name of Christ, have weakened Catholic sentiment, whether they were violent like Luther or skillful like Renan. For that reason Latin America remains Catholic.

10 ✠ Protestants: The Missionary Societies Arrive, Churches Organize and Grow

1850–1930

The Protestant pattern of growth was first a Bible, then a Protestant immigrant, then a church. In the early part of the period, 1850–1890, the largest group of Protestants lived on the Caribbean islands of the British, Dutch, and Danes. Likewise on the mainland, the first permanent congregations came by way of immigrants and the foreign business communities: Lutherans in Brazil, Italian Waldensians in the Rio Plata area, and after the North American Civil War, some Baptists, Methodists, and Presbyterians from the Confederacy came to Brazil and elsewhere. The immigrants were usually not active in evangelizing their Hispanic neighbors, but their presence and the later prominence of many of their children helped open the doors for local citizens to become Protestants. As the first barriers against Protestants began to fall, mission societies sponsored the first trickle of missionaries.

In the second half of the period, 1890–1930, legal obstacles and social prejudice loosened further, and more Protestant missionaries came. By the turn of the century, the ideas of Manifest Destiny, the Spanish-American War, the opening of the Panama Canal, the growing investments, and a new missionary enthusiasm among students made mission to Latin America seem to be a special call from God.

The mission boards and societies sent personnel, literature, and funds, and in response, churches emerged. By 1900, the Protestant community was small but growing, the largest proportion living in the Caribbean. In Brazil, Protestants reported 11,376, and in the rest of South America, only 5,246.[35] Growth was rapid, but relative to the whole population, Protestants were hardly visible. In 1930, they numbered about half a million, 575,000, less than one percent of the population.

Protestant leaders in the 1890–1930 period described the Catholic scene in different ways. Some spoke polemically; others in irenic terms. All emphasized the Bible, preaching, organizing congregations, and establishing networks of schools and centers for leadership training. Other types of

North American Presbyterian missionaries, "The Colombia Mission," Barran-quilla, Colombia, 1923.

Protestant witness could be seen in medical services, YMCAs, and Protestant newspapers. Amid the diverse currents of Protestantism were also efforts of ecumenism. In 1893, the North American mission boards began annual consultations. By 1910, in Edinburgh, Scotland, they began meeting with mission colleagues from western Europe. In Latin America, this pattern of consultation began in 1916 in Panama and continued in 1925 in Montevideo. Both were region-wide convocations for joint study and planning.

OBSTACLES TO PROTESTANT WORSHIP

"To permit . . . a new religion . . . is to sow the seed of discord . . ."

When Spanish-speaking groups began to organize for Protestant teaching and worship, local authorities considered such efforts to be quite different from the congregations of foreign Protestants. For example, when Peruvian Protestants in Callao announced the inauguration of buildings for a church and school, the local vicar wrote to the archbishop in Lima, who in turn wrote to the Minister of Justice and Worship, on September 29, 1864. Some paragraphs of that letter are given below.[36]

✠ I transmit to you the letter (of the 12th inst.) which the vicar of Callao has addressed to me informing me of the building of a Protestant Temple and School which are soon to be opened in that city.

The work appears sufficiently advanced, and its originators doubtless pretend to ridicule our worship and show the want of respect which they have to our Constitution and the laws of our country.

I will not stop to offer any remarks on the fundamental principles of which the 4th Article of our Constitution is a corollary. God alone can prescribe the worship with which He seeks to be adored, to Him alone it is directed, and He alone can command it. Since we recognize the Catholic faith as the only true one, it is deduced by legitimate consequences that the exercise of the Catholic worship is that alone which can be offered to the Divinity. Our legislators had considered these principles well, and established in all our political constitutions, that the religion of the Peruvian nation was the Catholic, Apostolic, Roman, without permitting the public exercise of any other. . . . The people, without exception, is Catholic. There does not exist the lamentable germ of religious discord. Perhaps all are not members of the Church, as they ought to be; perhaps there are men who have scarcely the smallest tincture of religion; there may be others in whom the corruption of manners has blotted out the religious feeling which is innate in man, which grows and becomes strengthened by education. But the existence of such persons is not a sufficient reason why our laws should be infringed, or our Constitution changed. Those persons, if not good Catholics, will not be Protestants. Their tendency is to have no religion, to renounce all forms of worship, and in short to forget the Divinity. For those toleration is an absurdity, and any worship is an act of fanaticism. With their manners and theories they undermine the fundamental laws of society, of the family, and the individual, and, consequently, for such as these we should not infringe the laws which we obey in this matter.

To permit, then that the public exercise of a new religion be established in a land which has preserved the benefit of its unity, is to sow the seed of discord in our country, and reap, at a future period, too bitter fruits.

Peru is tolerant to excess, as far as true charity, religious feeling and national honour demand. She persecutes no one because he may hold a different belief, and in return for that toleration, demands, with right and justice, that her religion be publicly respected and honoured.

But now they do not desire to observe this just measure. They seek to dogmatize in public, to place in open contest the faith and religion of the Peruvians with the beliefs of other nations. They ask for the public exercise of the Protestant worship, in order that Protestantism may be propagated, its errors preached, published and communicated to the ignorant, to the curious, to the friends of novelties, to the weak in the faith, and to the poor who may be under the protection or influence of dissidents. Protestantism seeks public exercise of its worship, in order, with that pretext, to propagate its doctrines, and diffuse its erroneous instruction among the masses, not only by means of preaching, but also by education in Schools and Colleges. . . .

As Catholic Bishop, I am obliged to preserve from irreligious and heretical contagion the souls redeemed with the blood of the Saviour, and forming part of the flock of our Lord Jesus Christ, which have been confided to my charge. It is my duty, then, to give the cry of alarm against those attacks which are so imprudently made against the purity of the holy religion which we possess; and to demand the fulfillment of the laws of our Fatherland.

FIRST PROTESTANT MISSION IN MEXICO

". . . I went to Monterey, and found the way prepared . . ."

When the Reform Laws of 1857 in Mexico began to be enacted, the door partially opened for Protestant missionaries to go to the local people. The first sustained mission effort was organized by a North American, Melinda Rankin, who was supported by the American Foreign Christian Union. She began in Brownsville, Texas, and in 1865 moved into Mexico. To arrange stronger support for her work, she appealed in 1873 to the Amer-

ican Board of Commissioners for Foreign Missions, a Congregationalist agency located in Boston. The paragraphs about her work, which follow, are extracted from what she wrote to the ABCFM.[37]

✠ In 1854, through aid received from friends in the United States, I built a Protestant seminary for Mexican girls, at Brownsville. I found Mexican youth susceptible of moral and mental improvement, and presented my labors in this department with much encouragement. In 1860, after a strife of some four or five years, the Mexican Government proclaimed religious freedom. The 'gates of brass and the bars of iron were cut in sunder,' and eight millions of enslaved souls emerged into the light and liberty of the Christianity of the Bible. It was a time of general rejoicing throughout the country. Persons came over to me from Matamoras for any amount of Bibles, Testaments, and tracts, which I could furnish. I sent on to New York and obtained a full supply, and the work of circulation, in that hitherto Papal land, went briskly forward. After a few months, I felt the work demanded an agent from the Bible Society. Accordingly I procured a suitable man, Rev. Mr. Thompson, of the Methodist Episcopal Church South, and wrote to the Bible Society; and he received an appointment in November, 1860.

Mr. Thompson went into Mexico as far as Monterey, and everywhere was most cordially received. The authorities gave him leave to plant Protestant institutions, circulate the Bible, and do anything which might conduce to the benefit of the people. He continued the work until the commencement of our civil war in the United States, when, on account of the blockade of the Southern ports, all communication was cut off with New York, and after our supply of Bibles was exhausted, we could procure no more. After waiting some time, he felt obliged to suspend his labors, and returned to Texas.

At a later period a port was opened on the Mexican side of the Rio Grande, and we were again in communication with New York. About the same time, Rev. Mr. Hickey, colporter [traveling seller of Bibles] of the American Tract Society for Texas, was obliged to flee the South on account of being a Union man, and came to Matamoras. He saw what a good work was commenced in Mexico, and being an earnest Christian man, he entered upon it with true zeal. I furnished him with Bibles, and he not only distributed them, but preached the Word to all who would listen. He expressed a willingness to accept an agency. I wrote to the Bible Society, and he received an appointment in 1863, and went to Monterey. He collected a congregation, and after a little time administered baptism to a dozen Mexicans, who gave evidence of genuine conversion. At Cadareita, a place some thirty miles from Monterey, believers were found who evidently had received the truth in the love of it before ever seeing the living teacher. I was not surprised at this, because, when the Word of God found its way into that dark land, I believed that the same Spirit which indicted that Word could carry the truths it contained to the hearts of those poor enslaved people, to their salvation. Mr. Hickey's duties compelled him to leave Monterey, and he selected a suitable man from the converts to continue religious services, and carry forward the work.

In 1865 I went to Monterey, and found the way prepared for establishing a permanent Protestant mission there. This city contained a population of forty thousand, and was really the most important city of that portion of the country. It was regarded as an important center, and I decided to build a mission house, which might answer the purpose of chapel and schools, and also for a residence. To obtain the means to do this, I was obliged to come again to the United States and ask aid of friends, which I did in the fall of 1865. In a few months I obtained $15,000; $10,000 of which was given by one individual, E. D. Goodrich, Esq., Cambridgeport, Mass.

I returned in 1866, and early in 1868 my edifice was completed, and we commenced religious services in it, and also schools for both sexes. Converts increased, and among them were men well calculated to do good among their countrymen. The first impulse of the spiritual life of these new-born souls was to preach the gospel to their people. I consulted several of them in regard to their going out as colporters and Bible-readers. They were delighted with the idea, and said they would rejoice to work without compensation, but their families were dependent upon them for their daily support, and in abandoning their business they would require the necessary amount, which was about a dollar per day. I applied to the A[merican] and F[oreign] Christian Union for aid, but it could not be granted, and rather than see such an important work neglected, I resolved to appeal to the Christian ladies of the United States.

During the interval in which my building was being completed, 1867, I came to New York, laid my purpose before the Society, received their approval, and commenced the work of obtaining funds for the support of Mexican colporters. I visited Hartford, Conn., and was very kindly received, the ladies of the different evangelical churches pledging $1,000, yearly. I then went to New Haven, and the ladies there pledged the same. (This liberal contribution from Hartford and New Haven has been continued ever since.) I visited other places, and obtained sufficient funds to employ seven native workers; so that when I returned, in 1868, and commenced work in my new building, I had the operatives to go forth scattering precious seed broadcast over the land. In looking back, it seems that an important position had been obtained in Mexican evangelization, but at that time — so much work appeared necessary to be done — I scarcely stopped to congratulate myself, but pushed forward to the things which were before. The workers sent out proved efficient, and wherever they went, gracious influences seemed to follow. Although comparatively illiterate, some intelligent Mexicans received a saving knowledge of the gospel through their teachings.

Two of these men went to the State of Zacatecas, in company with two of the Bible Society's agents, and labored there some five or six weeks. A work commenced which resulted in the conversion of thirty persons, among whom were two highly educated men, who took up the work after the departure of the colporters, and carried it forward with great success. The number of converts increased, and an evangelical paper has been published, which has done much good in Mexico. Two years ago, the number of converts amounted to more than one hundred.

The mission at Zacatecas was transferred last year, by the A. and F. Christian Union, to the Board of the Presbyterian Church, and they have now some two or three missionaries on the ground. The Monterey mission has, at the present time, six regularly organized churches, and two more, we expect, will soon be formed.

HARASSMENT OF PROTESTANTS

". . . she could not rent her house to us; . . ."

Though the Protestants had the legal right to present their message, they often met opposition from local Catholic leaders. Protestant chapels were occasionally destroyed, and their organs and Bibles burned in the public squares. Most opposition, however, was not violent; rather, it usually involved indirect harassments such as that experienced in 1888 by a missionary of the Presbyterian Church in the United States, Anthony Graybill, when he tried to rent a house in northern Mexico.[38]

✠ After much delay and difficulty I succeeded in effecting an entrance with my family into Linares on the 30th ultimo, last Thursday. The first delay was one week at Monterey, on account of impracticable roads caused by excessive rains. We arrived in Montemorelos in our hired hack, drawn by four mules, on the 23d, where we were cordially received and entertained by Rev. Leandro Garza y Mora and his amiable wife. On the 25th, he and I went on horseback to Linares, thirty miles, to secure a house, before taking my family to the place, which turned out to be a more prudent precaution than we had suspected. On the night of our arrival, two houses were offered us, and the owners were anxious to rent. Next morning they informed us very unexpectedly that they were not ready to rent.

We were taken by a friend to another house. The owner, a polite old lady of one of the first families, showed me a very suitable house for fifteen dollars per month. I agreed to the price. She handed me the key, and told me to return at 3 p.m. for the written contract. I did so, but she shook her head, and said she had learned we were Protestants, and she could not rent her house to us; whereupon Leandro preached her a good sermon. But she pointed to an image of the Virgin, and said, "We are all under her care here." I returned the key. A friend told us that the priest had been there after our departure in the morning.

Another house was offered to us the same day. We told the owner we were Protestants, and we had learned that that was a difficulty to proprietors of houses in Linares. He replied that it was none with him; but in an hour he was visited by a commission of senoras, and repented. The priest was now fully aroused, and determined to keep us out of the city. Another house was offered for twenty-five dollars per month by a physician. . . .

On Monday a telegram announced that we could not get the house.

I immediately accepted, by telegram, three lower rooms of a house belonging to the city, which was the only resort. And we arrived here on last Wednesday. The house has no windows or fireplace. There is a big family over head; several families use the same yard, as also horses, mules and hogs, all with rights and privileges that we have no power to dispute. But it is the best we can do, and the priest is beaten, so far as his effort to keep us out of the city is concerned.

But on Sunday (yesterday) we were greatly cheered by the spiritual outlook. In the first place, we had no sort of insult offered us as we went to the hired room on the edge of the city, in which Leandro has been holding services monthly for a year—the only permanent Gospel work ever done in Linares. A believer, who had helped us to hunt a house, had the room opened and in order, and about fifty persons assembled and listened attentively to the Word. Mrs. Graybill organized a Sunday-school of ten children. At night we had about fifty again, including those that stood at the doors. We have not benches to seat more than thirty. I announced regular preaching four times a week—Sunday morning and night, Tuesday and Thursday nights. The people are of the poorer class, and many seemed to hear the word gladly, whereat our hearts rejoiced. We feel that the Lord has a people here, and we desire the prayers of His people at home for His blessing on the work.

My furniture and books reached here, by a good providence, the same day we arrived. The mud was so deep that two yoke of oxen had to be hired, for most of the way, to supplement the horses.

SELLING BIBLES

". . . I sold a Bible to an old grayhaired man."

The key element in the Protestant phenomenon was the Bible. The colporteurs, that is, the people who traveled about, selling Bibles, found a ready market, and occasionally a critic. One agent of the American Bible Society, Hugh C. Tucker, who was in Brazil from 1886 to 1900, describes his method of sales and his reception in southern Brazil.[39]

✠ We next stopped at the small town of Sumidouro; and, following what I thought to be a wise plan, I first called on the priest and offered him a Bible. He had but little to say, and seemed quite satisfied with his surroundings and the condition of the people. He said the only difference between our Bible and his was that his had notes and explanations while ours had none. As we canvassed the town I met a soldier of the great Italian General, Garibaldi, who had heard the Gospel in Italy. He had wandered off to Brazil and settled in this town among the hills. He gave us a warm welcome into his humble home and there we had very delightful conversation about things pertaining to the Christian warfare and the Captain of our Salvation. In the afternoon I went along a country road leading from the village and by the roadside I sold a Bible to an old grayhaired man. When I was returning to the town about sundown I saw him sitting outside his cabin door with his family and two or three neighbours all gathered around listening as he read aloud the wonderful Words of Life. I did not dare to disturb them, but prayed that the Spirit might help them to understand the truth. At night I preached to a number of attentive listeners in a room hired for the purpose. Among the auditors were the members of this household and at the close of the sermon, I had an interesting conversation with the old gentleman and others. A negro boy came up and asked what I charged for confessing a person. I asked him what he wanted to confess. He said that about fifteen days before he had confessed to the priest all the bad things he had done; but since then he had done a number of evil things, and if it would not cost him too much money he would like to confess them all to me that I might obtain pardon for him. I tried to point him to Christ, but he seemed so ignorant and so fixed in his idea of confessing only to a priest, and thus with money buy absolution, that he could not grasp the truth. We left in that town more than a score of Bibles, talked with many persons of Jesus and his salvation, preached to them the Gospel and prayed for them. As we journeyed by train the following day we sold more than twenty copies of the Scriptures, and had several interesting conversations with fellow passengers. . . .

I was impressed on my first arrival that the community furnished a rich field for Bible distribution, and while I was awaiting the arrival of a delayed colporteur I improved the opportunity of making an effort in that direction. My custom was to go, early in the morning, into the streets with as many Bibles, Testaments and Gospels as I could carry. I usually sold out by nine or ten o'clock: then returned for breakfast, a rest and some reading. In the afternoon I would go again loaded down with Scriptures, which I generally disposed of by five o'clock in the afternoon, when I returned for dinner. Occasionally a second supply had to be sought, and some times I made large sales in the market. I was much encouraged by the wide-open door for the entrance of the truth and found the people ready to listen to words of explanation and commendation of the Bible. In passing a house one day I saw a number of army officials at the window. When I offered them the

Bible they began to make fun of religion. I made no reply till they had said their say, and then entered into conversation with them, which resulted in the sale of sixteen copies before I moved from the window. Incidents of like character occurred almost daily while I was in the city.

The entries in my note book show each time I went into the streets for work such as the following: sold twelve copies of the Scriptures, sold twenty-six copies, sold eight copies, sold twenty-two copies; one day the sales reached forty-six copies. I left the colporteur to carry on the work, which he did very successfully for a time. From this central point thousands of copies have gone out into all directions through the State, and the reading of them has stirred up much interest. Both the Methodist and Episcopal Missionaries and their helpers are following up the colporteurs, establishing regular services in many places and gathering in the fruits. On my second visit to the State I made a trip on horseback one hundred and twenty miles to get an insight into the needs of the Italian and German colonists north from the city of Porto Alegre and was gratified to find that the work done by our colporteur in these colonies some years ago had developed into regularly organized churches.

IMMIGRANT LUTHERANS IN BRAZIL

"The work is . . . confined to the Germans . . ."

The German immigrants of the nineteenth century were the forerunners of Protestant churches among the Brazilian citizens. Hugh C. Tucker, a Protestant Bible salesman in Brazil, described the German Protestants in the three most southern states during the final years of the century.[40]

✠ In the German colonies and in a few towns there are twenty-seven German Lutheran pastors, most of whom are engaged during the week in teaching German schools, many of which are subsidized by the German emperor. A number of them serve several churches, and rarely minister to any one congregation more than a month. Much of their strength is consumed in these day schools. They are formed into a synod, and are now connected with the State Church of Prussia, a union which I am persuaded has very great political significance. The work of the pastors is confined to the Germans, but few of them have learned Portuguese and perhaps none have a sufficient command of the language to preach with facility to the Brazilians, had they the time and the disposition. They are not even following up that German element which is constantly passing out of the colonies and becoming absorbed in the Brazilian population. Their very presence exerts an enlightening and liberalizing influence in the State, but they are by no means a direct, aggressive force among the natives. A few years ago their Synod in session resolved to buy the Scriptures needed for their work from the American Bible Society and they have purchased from us considerable quantities of German Scriptures during the last two or three years.

There can be no doubt that the large and increasing German population in the States of Rio Grande do Sul, Santa Catharina, and Paraná is becoming a predominant element in the agricultural, commercial, political, social and religious life of that important section of Brazil. My observation is that they are pretty generally contented with their surroundings, and that there is no thought among them of creating any political disturbance or rebelling against the Brazilian government. They are law-abiding, prosperous, and happy and seem quite willing that civil affairs should continue as they are. Of course I cannot say what Germany's designs may be with reference to these colonists and the desirable territory over which they are spread. It is a well known fact, however, that all the native born Germans among them, and a large majority, if not all, of the Brazilian born Germans are thoroughly loyal to Germany, and should the issue ever arise the German Emperor may depend upon their sympathy and support. It is of the highest importance that the Bible Society should see that they are kept well supplied with the Holy Scriptures. The agent endeavours to keep at work among them at most one German colporteur. Protestant Mission enterprise should do everything possible to encourage their thorough evangelization. The younger generations spreading out and mingling with the native Brazilians form an important element to be looked after and utilised in building up an evangelical Protestant Church.

MISSION TO THE INDIANS

"But these savages are capable of improving."

If Protestant missions to the Hispanic peoples in the nineteenth century were small, their missions among the Native Americans were even weaker. In 1900, D. B. Grubb, who had worked eleven years with the South American Mission Society among Indians in the Chaco of western Paraguay, gave a report of his pioneering work. The following are extracts from that report.[41]

✠ I have been laboring since 1889 in the Republic of Paraguay. The western portion of the Republic of Paraguay is called the Chaco. It is a region rather larger than the whole of France, and it is populated, as far as I can tell, by nearly a quarter of a million of heathen Indians. These Indians have maintained a virtual independence of the neighboring republics ever since the first Spanish conquerors landed in that country; and there are no civilized residents among them except the mission party.

The people we are working among at present comprise three nations, among whom we find some tens of thousands of a very fine class of savage, men who are brave, who are skilled in pottery, and in weaving wool and cotton, and who have a certain knowledge of agriculture. These people have a most interesting religion. They believe in a creator, in the immortality of the soul, in ghosts, and devils.

The country which they inhabit is a great, level plain, stretching for hundreds of miles in two directions; in some places covered by dense forests, abounding in huge swamps, and jungle lands covered with tall grass. When we landed there in 1889, almost nothing was known about the country; we had to explore that whole region for ourselves. Not a single word was known of the language. We had no interpreter; we had to begin by going among the people, living with them, and learning their language by means of signs, step by step. In the Chaco you live, if possible, in rough huts. The huts are infested day and night by insects of all kinds. At night goats and sheep continually prance about, and lucky you are if you do not have the wind knocked out of you two or three times during one night. . . .

The people live in constant dread of devils. They are afraid to go at night to the swamp, because they say these swamps are the homes of devils. They live in constant dread of their lives, on account of the witch doctors. . . .

But these savages are capable of improving. We have a good school among them. Some of them have learned to read and write, some are making progress in the Scriptures, and some of them are truly converted. The natives themselves have built a little church, and we have native teachers there, men and women, who are doing good work among their countrymen. Through the instrumentality of these native teachers we hope to reach 300 heathen tribes in the interior of the land.

PENTECOSTAL BEGINNINGS

". . . the baptism of the Spirit . . ."

The historic Protestant churches, such as the Presbyterian, Baptist, Methodist, and Lutheran, were the first to organize in Brazil. When some of their congregations began to experience "the baptism of the Spirit," the Pentecostal churches began to appear. The movement began with two Swedes, Daniel Berg and Gunnar Vingren, members of a Swedish immigrant community in Chicago, who felt called by God to go as missionaries to Brazil. When they arrived in 1911, they joined a Baptist congregation in the northeast at Belém, where the pastor accepted them as his assistants. Later, when the pastor traveled to other congregations and left his home church in their care, they led it into a Pentecostal experience. Upon the pastor's return, he felt betrayed; his reactions were described by one of the Swedes, Daniel Berg, in the document below. This incident marked the beginning of the Assemblies of God, a large Pentecostal movement in Brazil.[42]

✠ One evening the local preacher appeared in our simple premises. When he opened the door, a wave of song and prayers struck him. We got up and invited him to take part in our improvised service. He refused and declared that it was now time to make a decision. He said that a short time before he had discovered that people had dared to engage in a discussion of doctrine, something that had never happened before. He accused us of sowing doubt and unrest and of being separatists.

Gunnar Vingren got up and declared that we did not desire any division. On the contrary, we wanted unity among everyone. If only everyone had the experience of the baptism of the Spirit, we would never be divided. On the contrary, we would then be more than brothers, like a family.

The local preacher spoke again. The discussion was open. He said that the Bible did indeed speak about the baptism of the Spirit and also said that Jesus healed the sick. But that was in *those* days. He said that it would be absurd if educated people of our time believed that such things could happen today. We had to be realistic—he continued—and not waste time with dreams and false prophecies. Nowadays we had knowledge to know what to do with it. 'If you do not mend your ways and recognize your error, it is my duty to inform all the Baptist congregations and to warn them about your false doctrine.'

Vingren listened to these words very quietly and then replied: 'Brothers, we should not allow themes as important as those we have discussed to be lost in a personal dispute. We are both servants of God and so we both want to stand in the truth, for he to whom we pray is the truth. In my view we are colleagues and not competitors. *Who* brings souls to God is a matter of secondary importance. What is important is the fact that more and more souls are saved. I would not want to say that the brother does not stand in the truth but that he has not found the whole truth. [He does not have] the truth of the baptism of the Spirit and the healing of the sick by Jesus, as we can experience them today.'

When Vingren had finished, the preacher looked round at all those present in the hope that someone would support him. But no one did so. Then he looked pointedly at a deacon and waited for his judgment on the question. This deacon, one of the oldest pillars in the church, stood up after he had been looked at in this way and remarked in the name of all those present: 'I can understand your feelings very well, pastor. You say that you have come into a group of traitors who have departed from your teaching. You think that we are not following the way you have shown us. But that is not true. We have never been so certain our of [sic] cause as we are now. We have never had as much faith as we have now. We have found even more: faith and power of the Holy Spirit.

'We do not hold it against you that you did not say these things to us, for you did not know them yourself and so you could not teach them. But we very much want you also to receive these blessings from God. Then we shall understand each other better and feel the same unity with the brothers who have come to us from abroad.

'All the members of the church, pastor, are now on "higher ground" and nearer to heaven. You yourself said that you wanted to be a realist. Very good. I will give you some instances of realities of the healing power of Jesus in our days: these sisters, who have belonged to our congregation for years, used to have to walk on crutches (perhaps you never even noticed). Now they no longer need them. The crutches hang on the wall of their house, visible to everyone, so that all can see the wonderful way in which Jesus has healed them. And Jesus has healed not only them, but also a tumour on the throat.

'Dear preacher,' the deacon continued, 'we cannot and will not accuse you. You have worked to win souls for Jesus. You have asked Jesus for strength to stand fast in sickness. But you have not prayed for healing from sickness, because you did not believe in that. Now you have seen with your own eyes the instances which I have mentioned.'

Hoping for an expression in his support, the preacher let his eyes sweep round the room. In vain. He turned to me and brother Vingren and said, 'I have come to a decision. From now on you may not meet here any longer. Look for another place. After what has happened here we no longer want you.' Then he turned to the small group of people and asked, 'How many of you are in agreement with the false teaching?' Eighteen people resolutely raised their hands. They knew that that meant their expulsion from the church.

We thanked the preacher for the common life (that lay behind us) and hoped that he would soon receive the blessing of the baptism of the Spirit. He did not reply, but turned his back on us and walked out. . . .

MISSION SCHOOL FOR GIRLS

". . . a Christian education for the daughters . . ."

Though Protestants began with Bibles, immigrants, and preaching, their schools were not far behind. Indeed, emphasis on the Bible required literacy and education. By 1913 they had established 3 colleges, 18 theological and teacher-training schools, and 156 primary day schools.[43] For a region the size of Latin America, it was only a beginning. In the midst of the Mexican revolution, Carrie Carnaham, of the Women's Board of

Mission of the Methodist Episcopal Church U.S.A. described the Methodist schools for girls in Mexico in 1912.[44]

✠ In Mexico our Woman's Board has four boarding schools and a number of village day schools. It is really surprising how the interest and attendance of these schools have kept up during the past two or three years of political unrest. There have been long, weary months when those in charge have dreaded what each day might bring forth, but aside from the disquiet caused by many flurries and one serious riot in Pachuca, our work has gone on effectively until the frightful outbreak of war in Mexico City. This seriously interfered with the work of our two schools there, but we hope normal conditions are sufficiently restored to permit them to resume.

Of our four schools, the strongest is the Normal Institute in the City of Puebla which has a faculty of twenty-seven members and a curriculum which includes all grades from kindergarten through a full normal course. There is a department for the training of kindergarten teachers and a large graded English school which reaches the better class of Mexicans, who without it would send their children to the States or Europe for an English education. This department has been a success almost from the beginning. The teachers are normal and college trained Christian women from the United States and the course of study is kept up to that of the best schools in the country.

Owing to the illness of the missionary principal, the Institute during 1912 had as acting principal Miss Juana Palacios, a brilliant Mexican woman, a graduate of Boston University. In spite of the unrest throughout the country the matriculation reached 595, an increase of 130 over any previous year, and the self-support income was more than $29,000.00 Mexican currency — nearly $15,000.00 gold. Considering the financial depression prevailing through the Republic, we think this a remarkable showing for a Protestant school. But better than all this is the fact that the constant aim has been to raise the students' standard of religious, moral and intellectual things. Many girls have been truly converted and have gone out as teachers and home makers, whose influence is bound to tell mightily for the cause of Christ.

In Mexico City we have two schools — the Sarah L. Keen School, located in one of the best residential parts of the city and founded to provide a Christian education for the daughters of the well-to-do classes; and an Industrial School which has been opened to give poor girls training in household economics and domestic science. There had been a great demand for a school of this sort because of the many girls in the city who were unable — for financial or other reasons — to obtain a higher education, but who needed to become self-supporting. The school was almost immediately full to its utmost capacity and the popularity of the domestic science course has been surprising among a people who have always been taught that manual labor is degrading. Two young women from the better class have taken the course this year and they beg for an extension of the work in the city where their friends may have the opportunity of attending. The plan is to conduct domestic science classes in the S. L. Keen School this year.

The large grounds of the Industrial School have been made a source of income—vegetables are grown to supply the college table, flowers are cultivated and a certain variety of carnation has become very popular in the flower market of the city. Even rabbits and pigs are being raised and sold to the city restaurants.

In Pachuca we have a school with an enrollment of 500. It is in great need of enlarged quarters, and children desiring to attend have frequently to be turned away.

Our school at Guanajuato was honored last July by a visit from fifty Government school teachers accompanied by the Superintendent of Public Schools and the President of the State College. They came to inspect our building and our methods. They were very much pleased with the work being done, and were especially interested in the kindergarten which was at that time the only one in the city.

Later in the summer upon the request of our missionaries that our school be incorporated with the Government schools, an examiner was sent to look into our methods of work more carefully. He spent two days going thoroughly into things and his final report was that the school was the best in the city. Of course incorporation speedily followed. Government officials are very friendly toward our schools and it is no uncommon thing for the governor of the state to attend the commencement exercises and to present the diplomas to the graduates.

HOW LONG FOREIGN TUTELAGE?

". . . we are able to govern ourselves. . . ."

Establishing congregations, linking them into denominations, and raising up indigenous leaders were primary goals of Protestant missionaries. To attain these goals, the Presbyterians in Brazil formed a synod in 1888, and the Baptists formed an association in 1894 and a national convention in 1907. Though formal organization was accomplished, the contextualization of church life and the transition of authority from the missionaries to Latin American church leaders was often delayed. A controversy among the Baptists in the Recife area illustrated an early rebellion against North American tutelage. In 1923, a dissenting congregation and pastors presented to the Brazilian Baptist Convention a manifesto from which the following is an extract.[45]

✠ We do not believe that the Gospel extirpates from the Brazilian heart the love of his fatherland and its concerns, the vital interest in national problems, something which this same Gospel does not do in other lands. We believe even less that the Gospel must always come under the cover of the particular dispositions of this or that race. We have come to think that exactly the same Gospel which in England is adapted to the British and assumes Saxonic characteristics, can do the same in Brazil by imparting purely Brazilian approaches and characteristics to our work. Even here in Brazil, the methods adopted in Rio de Janeiro are not always appropriate in Recife or Bahia and vice-versa. Let us live then within the liberty which the Gospel establishes. On the other hand, everything or almost everything here differs from the United States, and the religious conditions of the Brazilian people ... demand that we change our ecclesiastical policy. The ultramontanes spread the rumor that we "sold" ourselves to the United States. We know how silly, illogical, and unfair that campaign is, but unfortunately some workers act as if the United States were our Holy Apostolic See.

Is it not a shame that after forty years of missionary work in Brazil, the denomination should not have succeeded in producing a man able enough to be the editor of the *Jornal Batista*? In so many years these prodigious workers (the missionaries) have not yet discovered a Brazilian able to use his own language better than a foreigner? ... And thus many other positions in the economic system of the denomination are held by foreigners. ... Why were the property rights of institutions which supposedly belong to the Brazilian Baptist Convention, *colégios*, seminaries, a publishing house and even the temples, transfered to the Commission in Richmond [Virginia] or to its representative? The Brazilian denomination as represented by the Convention, does not even own a single tile. ...

The missionaries demonstrated that they do not know how to work without assuming control of everything. They deny us the right to direct our work by withdrawing spiritual and financial support which they could lend to this Convention at the precise moment when it decides to assume control over the work of evangelization. They only pay in order to control, for according to one of them, the one who pays gives the orders!

Our beloved brethren, the missionaries, are not convinced that we are able to govern ourselves. ... This is the idea of the American Government with regard to the Cubans, the Filipinos, and, in part, to almost all the peoples of Central and South America. ... Is the Brazilian Baptist people inferior to other peoples? ... For how long do the missionaries want to have us under their tutelage as if we were children? ... Their mission here consists of helping us to develop the work, but not to direct it perpetually as if they did not intend intelligently and sincerely to develop the national forces by providing opportunity to direct and to serve.

11 ✠ Catholics: The Renaissance of the Elites and the Model of a "New Christendom"

1930–1962

The world economic crisis of 1929 left a deep mark on the Catholic Church. The Depression nearly wrecked economies that were dependent on cash crops and markets in North America and Europe. When these markets collapsed, the prices of raw materials and foodstuffs that the Latin economies exported fell more sharply than those of the manufactured goods they imported. People were angry over the failures of the capitalist system, and many wanted reforms, modernization, and more attention to national self-interest. People may have differed in policies and degree, but from across the region voices called for democracy, land reform, secular education, trade unions, and economic independence from the United States. Along with these often went anti-clericalism and religious doubts or indifference.

Pope Leo XIII, in his social encyclical *Rerum Novarum*, had long before recognized the need for reforms such as these. That was in 1891, but his ideas had been slow to percolate into Latin America. By the 1930s, however, some bishops were recognizing the social needs and the spiritual crisis. They also recognized that in most of their countries the church had lost its former means of influencing society. How was it now to guide and educate the people? How might the indifferent and the hostile be re-evangelized?

Some bishops read the writings of European philosopher Jacques Maritain and dreamed of a new Christendom, a Christian democracy. The way to build it seemed to be on the foundation of groups of laity that would be guided by the clergy and the religious and that would carry the church's message and moral guidance into the public arena. Pursuant to this ideal in the 1930s, "Catholic Action" was organized in most countries. Through study clubs, night schools, and regional and national conventions, it motivated and equipped thousands to help re-Christianize their nation. Likewise, the church encouraged Catholic student associations and trade unions; it organized a number of Catholic universities, eucharistic congresses, associations of "Opus Dei" for spiritual renewal, and even political

Departure of the funeral cortege of dictator Raphael Trujillo, San Cristobal Church, Santo Domingo, Dominican Republic, 1961.

parties that stressed their ties to the church. These movements stirred a wide renewal. Yet, for the most part, their activities were restricted to the small middle and upper classes, and this mainly in the countries that were already most open to new ideas, countries where the traditional church faced the most serious challenges—Mexico, Chile, Argentina, and Brazil.

In later decades, Catholic leaders reflected on the period and saw elements of genuine renewal and also major inadequacies. In a culture that had become divided between the mass of poor and a small population of elites, the means chosen for reaching the whole population, for constructing a "neo-Christendom," had been focused almost exclusively on that small middle class, or the elite element in society. The renewal had not filtered down to the poor, nor was it appropriate for them. When leaders of Catholic Action from across Latin America met in conference in 1953 in Chimbote, Peru, they honestly concluded that "the vast majority of the Catholics are *solo de nombre*, that is, nominal Catholics. . . ."[46] Some new form of renewal would have to emerge.

RELIGIOUS AMALGAM IN GUATEMALA

". . . a historical merging of two religions."

Under Guatemala's dictator Jorge Ubico (1931–1944), the Catholic Church was able to keep many of its traditional privileges. Even with his help, however, the church found it difficult to provide adequate instruction and nurture for its members. In 1937, a North American anthropologist, Charles Wagley, studied a village of Mam-speaking Indians in the northwest, called Santiago Chilmaltenango. His findings revealed an advanced degree of religious syncretism.[47]

✠ Ostensibly Chimaltecos are Catholic and they are recognized as such by the Roman Catholic Church. Obviously, their religion is not Catholicism as we think of it. Their entire culture is a fusion of Maya and European cultures and this fusion is perhaps most striking in their religion. In prayers, for example, Christ, a Catholic saint, an aboriginal day deity, and a Guardian of the Mountain may be appealed to in that order. Their concept of any one of these deities, whether it be of Catholic or aboriginal origin, is a blend of European and Maya beliefs. One cannot say that the Chimalteco concept of Christ is Catholic nor that the Guardian of the Mountain is a Mayan deity, for the fusion of aboriginal and foreign elements is complete in each detail. The result is not an American Indian religion with a veneer of Catholicism nor is it Catholicism with many aboriginal appendages. Chimalteco religion is a new form—a new religion—arising out of a historical merging of two religions. Their religion is different from each original ingredient and particular to Chimaltenango.

Nevertheless any Chimalteco will tell you that he (or she) is a *muy buen Católico*; to be a good Catholic is to be respectful of all religious forms whether Catholic or aboriginal in origin. In fact, Chimalteco religion does not have much contact with the Catholic Church. The Catholic Padre from Huehuetenango visits the village every year or two to baptize children and to perform mass in the church. The mass, however, is unimportant for the Chimalteco. Catholic confession is unknown, and there are no church weddings. The local religion is normally in charge of the local village functionaries. Indian men who have learned Latin chants by rote from previous *cantores*, direct burials, chanting for the wake and in the burial procession. The *sacristanes* take care of the church and the *mayordomos* arrange the celebrations for the Saints. In the sphere of individual and family religion, the native soothsayers or priests (Mam *chimanes*) are the mediators between the layman and the supernatural. In 1937, there were eleven of these, all past middle age, and the most renowned of them was the municipal priest (*Chimán del Pueblo*) who directed his activities toward public ritual.

SUNDAY IN TABASCO

". . . no secret Masses in private houses . . ."

The federal and state governments of Mexico in the early 1930s feared a rebirth of clerical power and severely reduced the numbers of priests allowed in the country. From a previous total of 4,500, they were down to 230 by 1935. The federal and state governments exiled bishops, secularized schools, nationalized church properties, and prohibited the use of the mails for religious purposes. After widespread protest, tensions began to ease by 1938. In the spring of that year, a noted Catholic novelist, Graham Greene, visited the states of Tabasco and Chiapas in the far south. He found that the anti-clerical decrees had been harshly enforced in the area. In the following paragraphs Greene described what he saw.[48]

[Villahermosa, Tabasco]

✠ The anonymity of Sunday seems peculiarly unnatural in Mexico: a man going hunting in the marshes with his dog and his gun, a young people's fiesta, shops closing after noon—nothing else to divide this day from all the other days, no bell to ring. I sat at the head of the stairs and had my shoes cleaned by a little blond bootblack—a thin tired child in tattered trousers like someone out of Dickens. Only his brown eyes were Mexican—not his transparent skin and his fine gold hair. I was afraid to ask his name, for it might have been Greene. I gave him twice what I usually gave (twenty

centavos—say, five cents) and he returned me ten centavos' change, going
wearily down the stairs with his heavy box into the great heat of Sunday.

Garrido has fled to Costa Rica and yet nothing is done. "We die like
dogs." There were no secret Masses in private houses such as are found in
the neighbouring state, only a dreadful lethargy as the Catholics died slowly
out—without Confession, without the Sacraments, the child unbaptized,
and the dying man unshriven. I thought of Rilke's phrase: "An empty,
horrible alley, an alley in a foreign town, in a town where nothing is forgiven."

There are, I suppose, geographical and racial excuses for the lethargy.
Tabasco is a state of river and swamp and extreme heat; in northern Chiapas there is no choice between a mule and the rare plane for a traveller,
and in Tabasco no choice between plane and boat. But a mule is a sociable
form of transport—nights spent with strangers huddling together in the
cold mountain air, talk over the beans and the embers; while in a boat you
are isolated with the mosquitoes between the banana plantations.

And then there are no Indians in Tabasco, with their wild beliefs and
their enormous if perverted veneration, to shame the Catholic into *some*
action. Too much foreign blood came into Tabasco when it was a prosperous country; the faith with the Grahams and Greenes goes back only a few
generations. They haven't the stability of the old Spanish families in Chiapas.

Nothing in a tropical town can fill the place of a church for the most
mundane use; a church is the one spot of coolness out of the vertical sun,
a place to sit, a place where the senses can rest a little while from ugliness;
it offers to the poor man what a rich man may get in a theatre—though
not in Tabasco. Now in Villahermosa, in the blinding heat and the mos-
quito-noisy air, there is no escape at all for anyone. Garrido did his job
well: he knew that the stones cry out, and he didn't leave any stones. There
is a kind of cattle-tick you catch in Chiapas, which fastens its head in the
flesh; you have to burn it out, otherwise the head remains embedded and
festers. It is an ugly metaphor to use, but an exact one: in northern Chiapas
the churches still stand, shattered and ruined and empty, but they fester—
the whole village festers away from the door; the plaza is the first to go.

So in Villahermosa there is nothing to do all the long Sundays that go
on and on but sit in Victorian rocking-chairs, swinging back and forth waiting for the sunset and the mosquitoes. . . .

[Las Casas, Chiapas]

It was a lovely town to wake to in the early-morning light, as the donkeys
went plodding round laden with bright chemical gaseosas for the saloons—
low single-story houses with brown-tiled roofs and little flowery patios, the
mountains crouched all round like large and friendly dogs; twenty-two
churches, of which five were open—but no priest allowed inside.

The finest church is the old colonial church of Santo Domingo sharing a little green square with La Caridad and the prison—once the presbytery. A long flight of steps down into the square, barley-sugar pillars up the facade—the colour of pale terra-cotta—statues headless where the troops have reached them; inside, flowers and white drapery had been set for Easter, the church was scrupulously clean, a heavy curtain hung before the altar, and Christ lay dead among flowers. The walls were crammed with dark old eighteenth-century portraits of bishops and saints set in heavy and tortuous gilt. It gave an effect of fullness—and of emptiness, like a meeting when the leader has gone. Nothing meant anything any more; it was just sentiment to spread the flowers and drapery; the Host wasn't here. There was no more reason to remove the hat than in a ruin—than in the church on the hill above the city, smashed and shady with love-initialled walls and snaky chambers. Santo Domingo, La Caridad, La Merced with a ruined cavalry barracks next door in what was once the presbytery, a broken square outside with a rotting bandstand in the middle of a rubbish dump—well, it was Easter, we were celebrating the death of God. This emptiness and desolation was right—in a way. . . .

I got up at a quarter to six. The two little boys who did all the work of the hotel lay asleep in their clothes on benches by the door with only a serape to cover them. A mass of golden clouds lay over Guadalupe. From all directions women moved towards one point in the sleeping town with shawls over their heads. There was no real concealment. The police, I suppose, were bribed; though sometimes, I was told, when money was scarce a Mass house would be raided, the congregation fined, the priest held for ransom in jail.

Mass was celebrated in a small room hung with white lace. Half the congregation was ouside on a balcony a few feet above the small flowery patio. There were about a hundred and fifty people there, but this was only one of several Mass houses in Las Casas. Most were women; there were a few small boys, a few youths, and a number of middle-aged men: a cripple wrapped up to the mouth in his serape leaned against the door.

The priest arrived in a motoring-coat and a tweed cap. His face was hideously disfigured with mauve patches and his eyes were shielded with amber-tinted glasses. Mass was said without the sanctus bell—silence was a relic of the worst penal days when discovery probably meant death; they were days which might at any time return at the whim of some police officer. . . . "I looked about and there was no helper: I fought, and there was none to aid"; "He was broken for our sins, the discipline of our peace was upon him"; the priest trod carefully between the kneeling women, bringing the Body of God out from the altar onto the balcony, handing Christ across the bowed heads. Afterwards the housewife stood at the door saying good-bye to her guests (there had been no collection: the cost of the Mass was shared among the leading Catholics in the town). You could detect a touch of pride, of condescension, because she had sheltered God in her house. One person at least would feel regret and disappointment if the Mass was ever celebrated again in the churches.

RELIGION AS USUAL IN TEPOZTLÁN

"males and . . . youths . . . tend to. . . scoff at the nuns, the Acción Católica and other 'fanatics.' "

In the absence of traditional ways to influence Mexican society in the late 1930s and 1940s, bishops organized various lay associations of laborers, students, and others. These were to express in the world the morality and message of the church. Their impact was felt more in the middle classes of the urban areas; in remote towns, the old patterns prevailed. During various periods from 1943 to 1948, Oscar Lewis, a well-known North American anthropologist, studied the town of Tepoztlán in the state of Morelos, just south of Mexico City. His description of its religious life indicates much continuity with previous generations. The following selections are a part of his findings.[49]

✠ Just as the cycle of religious fiestas in Tepoztlán follows Catholic practice, with some local modifications, so does the individual Tepoztecan. Only a few persons, mostly women, in the village fulfill all the ritual and other obligations set by the priest and church. These people are looked upon by the rest as fanatics who are "always dressing the saints." The priest does not consider his flock to be "good Catholics." The older people maintain a respectful passivity toward most church activities, while the adult males and many older youths, although not irreligious, tend to scoff at the nuns, the Acción Católica and other "fanatics." Among these recalcitrants there is much more interest in the barrio fiestas and one or two of the nearby village fiestas than in the regular daily and weekly religious acts which are required of them. On the other hand, the nuns and the religious associations tend to emphasize the latter. The school, too, so far unsuccessfully, discourages attending fiestas because of the disastrous effects upon school attendance. Regular participation in church ritual is associated with becoming "more cultured." Those who go to boarding schools or who have occasion to live in Mexico City for some time learn to attend Mass, to confess, and to take communion more often than is customary in the village.

Prayers for various occasions are memorized by Tepoztecans. The older generation learn them in Náhuatl, the younger in Spanish. The people do not know how to improvise prayers, and when their memory fails they prefer to keep silent, or merely cross themselves, or kiss a scapulary to invoke the protection of the appropriate saint. The obligatory morning prayers are seldom said with regularity. Some of the old people still say a prayer at noon when the bell of the municipal clock strikes; the men remove their hats and give thanks to God because they still have strength to work. When the evening church bell rings, the men are again supposed to take off their hats and the women to kneel to give thanks because the day has passed without mishap. We cannot estimate the number of people who fulfill the latter obligation, but in all the time we were in the village we never observed anyone kneeling in prayer outside the church. But men returning home from the fields lift their hats respectfully whenever they pass a cross, and on the bus from Tepoztlán to Cuernavaca all hats go up in unison each time a church is passed. . . .

As indicated earlier, most Tepoztecans do not feel strongly the need to attend Mass every Sunday or even on holy days. On the basis of our own observations and informants' estimates, it appears that, on the average, about two hundred, mostly women, attend church on Sundays. The 6:00 Mass is preferred; those who attend the 8:00 a.m. Mass risk being called lazy. Mass, like other public gatherings, is a welcome form of diversion. It is one of the opportunities for sweethearts to see one another; young people are said to attend not out of devotion but to flirt. Everyone puts on his best clothes for Mass. The older men wear huaraches, white *calzones* [knee-length shorts], and shirts; the youths wear trousers and modern shirts, and many wear jackets. The women use *rebozos* [shawls] to cover their heads. Upon entering the church, the women cross themselves with holy water and take seats up toward the front. The men generally do not cross themselves and remain in the rear. Some of the youths stand at one side of the nave, leaning against the pillars so as to be able to see the girls during the service. The children sit with their mothers and sisters. Five- and ten-centavo pieces are dropped into the plate passed by the sacristan.

After Mass the young men are the first to leave. They remain at the church door, talking, joking, and laughing quietly among themselves, until the girls appear. The older men are the next to leave the church, and then the women. Most of the men go off to drink, while the women go home in little groups of relatives.

Tepoztecans do not like to confess; the majority do so only once a year. Not giving much importance to sin, Tepoztecans do not regard confession as necessary. Most men consider confession important only when one is about to die but "with the pangs of death, who's going to remember to confess properly?" Women, particularly married women, are less reluctant to confess, and about fifty women are known to take communion and confess quite often. Through the Acción Católica the number of young people of both sexes who do this has increased. Perhaps the most important deterrent to confession, especially among the old people, is that the priest may exact from the confessor the recitation of certain prayers which most people cannot say accurately. Fearing a scolding from the priest, they prefer to avoid the situation. There is no such difficulty with communion. "We would all take communion more often if we didn't have to confess; that we always avoid."

In general, the Tepoztecan feels obliged to contribute to the church and does so by paying *limosnas* [alms]. There is a belief that he who refuses to give alms will find that no one receives his soul in heaven and that therefore he must go to hell. . . .

Tithes, which were obligatory and were collected by the government for the church before the Revolution, no longer exist. The local priest, however, hires a *limosnero* at harvest time to go about the fields, riding on a mule, to collect contributions from the farmers. As a rule, each farmer gives about twelve ears of corn, so that the priest collects a good amount for his stores.

RELIGION IN A SMALL BRAZILIAN TOWN

". . . I am not afraid of hell, . . . I am in it right here . . ."

The Brazilian bishops organized numerous lay Catholic associations to reassert the church's moral influence in economic and social life. However, the church lacked the leadership to address in a substantial way the religious indifference of the majority of the people. Many towns and villages remained untouched. In 1950–1951, a North American anthropologist, Marvin Harris, studied Minas Velhas, a small county seat town, population 1,427, in the mountains of Bahía along the central coast. Though he found the formal side of Catholicism to be exceedingly weak, the informal use of prayers, santos, and promessas remained active.[50]

✠ At best, the people of Minas Velhas exhibit but a mediocre concern for the formal aspects of their religion. The priest and the rituals he performs inside the church — confession, communion, mass — are regarded with emotional disinterest. On any given Sunday, the majority of adult townspeople do not attend mass. . . .

There is also a significant difference between male and female attendance. At a typical novena, the ratio is about four females to one male — about 160 to 40. In religious processions, the ratio is 400 to 200, at communion 60 to 10. Moreover, the males include a higher ratio of children than among the women. At Sunday mass, the majority of the adult males stay near the rear of the church; some are really more outside than in. . . .

In Minas Velhas the men expect to see the women in church, and the women do not expect to see the men there — much as it is the women who wash clothes and carry things on their heads and not the men. This difference in roles is perhaps rooted in the symbolic structure of Catholicism. Psychologically, Christ, the central figure in the pantheon, would appear to be of little use to the male in Minas Velhas. He represents qualities which in real behavior the culture classifies in a hundred different ways as effeminate. His ministers are denied the male function. He is the idol of the meek and the poor-groups which simply are not idolized in the urban context where the rich and the powerful and the unmodest inherit the visible earth from generation to generation. Moreover, the story of the Crucifixion, the Western world's great tradition of suffering and redemption, is meaningful to the women in a sense in which it is not equally meaningful to the men. Among the men, even among the economically marginal, a sense of oppression does not exist. As long as he has a wife and children, there is an excellent chance that the male's dominating domestic role more than compensates for whatever oppression he may experience at the hands of others. The women, however, do often exhibit a sense of oppression, and are in fact subject to greater and more frequent duress than their husbands, especially if one considers the prolific rate at which they keep bringing children into the world. . . .

The role of the priest further reduces the ability of the menfolk to see the church as the center of their religious life. Rather than invest the priest with an air of holiness, the condition of celibacy only creates an air of suspicion. The men automatically associate duplicity with this requirement, and in many instances in the past their suspicions have been justified. A former priest of Minas Velhas, for example, is widely known as the father of three children—a fact which he made no great effort to conceal. The present priest is notably free from these accusations, but the standard conception is a greater force by far than the immediate example. . . .

The priest's income derives principally from baptisms, marriages, funerals, and special masses. The fees for these services are variable and depend upon the amount of pomp involved and/or the degree of inconvenience to which the priest is subjected. . . .

In the memory of the community, however, it is unknown for a priest to confine himself to an income derived exclusively from religious functions. Some sold religious pictures, others were rich landholders, almost all of them were important financiers for the local gold miners. . . .

It is not strange, therefore, that the men of Minas Velhas do not place much importance upon having their sins absolved by the priest. They do not feel sinful and the priest is scarcely the person who can convince them that they should. The situation may be summed up by the words of Sr. Paulo whose attitude is thoroughly typical. The last time Paulo confessed was in preparation for his marriage eighteen years ago. "The *padre* asked me how many women I had slept with. I told him, 'Excuse me, I can't tell you. I've traveled a great deal.'" Asked why he had never confessed since, he replied, "Why should he know the secrets of my life. I don't know his."

In keeping with the weak role of official Catholic dogma, the concepts of heaven and hell are not vital issues to the average townsman. The threat and promise of otherworldly rewards make little impression upon the sophisticated, materialistic urbanites. Some of the perfunctory performance of church ritual is undoubtedly maintained, especially among the men, by force of this dogma. In most instances, however, the threat is too ironic, and the promise too remote, to really make an impression on anybody. Eunice, a townswoman deserted by her husband and left alone to bring up six small children by working in a leather shop, expressed the viewpoint typical of many of the inhabitants of Minas Velhas: "I am not afraid of hell," she said, "because I am in it right here and now. I don't believe there is any place where you suffer more than you do on earth." . . .

The principal agency available to the villagers and townsmen by which a religiously mediated influence may be brought to bear upon the immediate material world is individual prayer. The belief that events may so be influenced is held by most townspeople and all villagers. Miracles are accepted by the villagers as not only possible but also as relatively frequent; the townsmen regard them as possible but rare. It is this accessibility of supernatural assistance which marks the vital core of Catholicism in Minas Velhas. . . .

This devotion usually exists as a long-established relationship with a saint, i.e., the deity most likely to be appealed to is the individual's patron saint. This relationship is marked by pictures or images representing the saint which the suppliant keeps in his house; by the observance of the saint's day as a holiday, on which he does not work, has paid for a novena, and perhaps sets off some skyrockets; and possibly by the name of the saint which he has been given by his parents and which he, in turn, will pass on to his offspring: . . .

A man whose wife is sick, for example, prays to his favorite saint: "Misericordia. Hear a humble voice. Grant my wife health and I will set off a half-dozen skyrockets in front of the main door of the church on your day." If the wish is granted, the man carries out his promise. This is the basic type of *promessa* — a prayer which contains a bribe in the form of a promise to express devotion and gratitude if the prayer's wish is granted. . . .

During a thunderstorm the roof tiles crashed down into the room where a brass-smith's children were sleeping. When the debris was pulled off the bed, the children were found to be unhurt; one of them, in fact, was still sleeping. The father decided that a miracle had been performed by his patron saint, Bom Jesus. He had a photograph taken of the children in the ruined bedroom and said he was going to leave it at the shrine of Bom Jesus.

Considering the town's total cultural edifice, we can safely say that Catholicism, even in its folk aspects, is not the keystone in the arch. Far from constituting an important cohesive force, formal religion itself suffers from a series of internal tensions that result from its inability to be reconciled with the institutions which provide its setting. It is at a tangent to the whole complex of masculinity and hence is deprived of the full support of the sex whose participation would be most important in this outspokenly male-dominated culture. It is partisan to the leisure class, maintaining economically based criteria of association which tend to exclude at least one quarter of the population from active participation. Its priests have been caught in the web of political intrigue and have been forced to choose among the local political parties. Its forms of religious association are senescent and secondary to political parties and purely social clubs. The entire edifice is impregnated with a type of philosophy sufficiently materialistic to convert its holy days into occasions for making money.

SEEKING ALL CUBANS THROUGH THE ELITE

" . . . neglecting the poor and courting the rich."

The lay associations for rechristianizing society had a slow start in Cuba. In the period 1930–1962, the native Cubans volunteering to be priests were few, so the island remained dependent on foreign clergy, especially Spanish, and these outnumbered their Cuban colleagues four or five to one. Furthermore, almost all the clergy were very Spanish and traditional in their outlook. Leslie Dewart, a Canadian Catholic with many ties to Cuba, described the situation in the 1950s.[51]

✠ Immemorially, then, the Church in Cuba thought of itself, correctly, as impotent, as barely surviving under duress, as threatened by secularism, indifference, freemasonry and, in the last twenty years or so by Protestantism as well. To the Cuban high and low clergy this was especially humiliating in view of the privileged position of the Church in Spain. They knew that Cuba would never realize the Spanish ideal, yet this ideal, being a matter of Christian principle, as they thought, was never to be given up in intention. The Church, thus, was caught in a vicious circle: it was discontent with the here and now, but it saw no other solution than trying to hold on to the past. This was the sort of posture that, by its own implications, could not but confirm the stagnation from which the Church suffered.

The problem of the shortage of priests may provide an enlightening instance of how the vicious circle went. For two generations the shortage was made up, as far as it was ever made up, by the massive importation of Spanish regulars. It is relatively unimportant that the heavy dependence upon regular clergy appears to have reduced appreciably the influence of the dioceses, though this condition may have tended further to increase the reaction of involution of the hierarchy. It is more important that the Spanish as a whole have not yet become quite reconciled to the reality of having lost their Empire, and most especially Cuba. Many still entertain, and voice, thoughts of a possible reversal of history. The Spanish clergy's militant Spanishness toward the former colony, no less than their conception of what the relations between clergy and people should be, operated generally only to the disadvantage of the Church and tended to diminish the appeal that the priestly ministry might have had for Cuban Catholics.

Naturally, with few native vocations the congregations could not very well maintain seminaries and houses of study in Cuba, so Cuban candidates were sent abroad. Until recently that meant, of course, Spain: Thus, even the native clergy became hispanicized. One should not misconstrue this disadvantage of a Spanish clergy as due to xenophobia, from which Cuba is fortunately almost totally free. The difficulty was specifically Spanish. For example, Canadian priests were sufficiently liberal, and up-to-date to earn respect and admiration. And what was probably the most powerful single agency in the Catholic revival of Cuba's middle classes, namely, the Christian Brothers—who established their first Cuban foundation at the turn of the century—was until very recent times almost entirely French in composition. It should be added that, unlike the Spanish clergy, the Christian Brothers usually became Cuban nationals. In time they attracted native vocations in great numbers. They were also unique in having had a native Cuban provincial. Their contribution to the modernization of the Church in Cuba was as magnificent as it was unemulated.

Further to compound the sinuosity of the circle, since early Republican times the Church had concentrated its resources in education work for the upper-middle and upper classes, a condition that prevailed without exception until after World War II, when a few schools for the poor began to appear. The hierarchy seem to have reasoned logically, but not necessarily perspicaciously, that the faith of these classes could be built up most easily and quickly, and that once this was accomplished the middle classes would constitute a sort of elite that would help carry the Gospel to the humble and the poor. The plan was successful enough in the first respect, but certain side effects were not foreseen. They may well have been unforeseeable. For instance, the Church lay itself open to the charge that it was neglecting the poor and courting the rich. Worse, it also lay itself open to the temptation of actually doing so. It seems, indeed, that to some extent it did so: And, upon occasion it did so extravagantly and even unnecessarily. For instance, despite the traditional policy of the Cuban Church to avoid taking sides in temporal matters, "in view," as the formula went, "of the spiritual mission of the Church," Batista's last regime, after his *coup d'état* in 1952, enjoyed an unprecedented degree of episcopal benison during six and a half of its not quite seven years. Some Cubans thought that this departure from custom was not totally unrelated to the justly famous largess of Batista's second wife—a largess which was itself a departure from Cuban type. Since Batista's first wife was still living, Marta Fernandez de Batista's generosity was, justly or unjustly, suspect and was widely commented upon unfavorably.

However, the Cuban Church's consortium with the rich was never so much a compromising reality as a tempting thought to be delighted in morosely. But the Church by its own choice did depend especially upon certain classes for whatever native clergy could be recruited. Would vocations come out of this middle- and upper-class elite? This was, of course, the objective of the policy: Otherwise, the problem could not be solved.

The answer, as it turned out, was disappointing. There were many vocations, of course, but in general the distance between the Spanish clergy and the Cuban people proved too much, even under these conditions, to be bridged very rapidly. The hope of a native clergy simply did not materialize.

"CATHOLIC ACTION" TO PENETRATE SOCIETY

"I do not understand why they are being organized, these . . . Catholic laborers, Catholic lawyers, Catholic doctors, and Catholic farmers."

While Juan Domingo Perón was president of Argentina, 1946–1955, the Catholic Church regained some of its earlier privileges, such as religious instruction in the public schools. However, church attempts at social reform through lay Catholic Action groups ran counter to the president's vision of a religiously neutral state. In 1954, Perón expressed his opposition to the movement, and in the selections below he describes his position.[52]

✠ The organization "Catholic Action of Argentina," which is international in character, includes among its members certain anti-Peronists. In fact, the anti-Peronists control this organization. They act with suave hypocrisy. It is their custom to attend meetings and to talk like this: "I do not come here in the name of Catholic Action. . . ." Yet, in reality, they are operating in its name. We must subject this type of Catholic Action member to our careful scrutiny. It is often the same with the clergy. What is the clergy? An organization, like any other, where we may find good people, bad people, and very bad people. I have never heard of an organization of men in which every single one was good. This would indeed be an extraordinary case. In all organizations there are always many bad members, and in all justice this fact must be acknowledged. So, there are bad members among the clergy, and there are Peronists and anti-Peronists as well. This is no secret. All that is necessary is that we know how to distinguish between these men, and that we treat the Peronists as Peronists, and the anti-Peronists as anti-Peronists.

This has nothing to do with the Church in itself, and I want to make this point quite clear. I have talked with high dignitaries of the Church, with bishops and archbishops, who are simply men like any of the rest of us. I presented to them the problems now being encountered by those organizations that are suffering injury because of the attitudes of several Catholic groups. And I confronted the prelates in the presence of the representatives of those organizations that are being injured. I had received urgent notice that restlessness was mounting not only in the small syndicates but also in the General Confederation of Labor, in the Confederation of Professionals, in the General Confederation of Professionals, in the General Confederation of University Students, in other student organizations, and in many other groups. So, I told the prelates:

> I do not understand why they are being organized, these groups of Catholic laborers, Catholic lawyers, Catholic doctors, and Catholic farmers. We are Catholics too! But to be Peronists we do not have to proclaim that we are Catholic Peronists. We are simply Peronists, and within this context we can be Catholic, Jewish, Buddhist, Orthodox, or what have you. It is not necessary for us to ask a Peronist which God he prays to. For us, the faith that a person professes is irrelevant, so long as the person is a good human being. That is all that counts!

The prelates agreed with us, and before all those representatives of the victimized organizations who were present as witnesses, they—the bishops and archbishops—were the first to condemn those priests who were not faithful to their duties. They added that they not only condemned such men, but declared them enemies against the ecclesiastical dignity. This was said by the prelates, and certainly I ought to honor and place credence in the voice of the prelates!

IN THE SLUMS OF SÃO PAULO

". . . stop talking about resignation and rebel . . ."

> *In response to the urban poverty in the 1950s, the church promoted a number of social centers and some training for social workers. However, the massive problems were hardly touched. A widely read testimony of this came from Carolina María de Jesús, a poor Catholic woman in a shanty-town outside São Paulo. She kept a diary during the years 1955–1959 and in it described the favelas [slums] and the people around her who seemed "predestined to die of hunger." When her manuscripts were discovered by a newspaper reporter and published, they caused a national sensation. Her occasional contacts with the churches reveal something of the extent and nature of their ministry in the shanty towns.*[53]

✠ *July 18, [1955].* I got up at 7. Happy and content. Weariness would be here soon enough. I went to the junk dealer and received 60 cruzeiros. I passed by Arnaldo, bought bread, milk, paid what I owed him, and still had enough to buy Vera some chocolate. I returned to a Hell. I opened the door and threw the children outside. Dona Rosa, as soon as she saw my boy José Carlos, started to fight with him. She didn't want the boy to come near her shack. She ran out with a stick to hit him. A woman of 48 years fighting with a child! At times, after I leave, she comes to my window and throws a filled chamber pot onto the children. When I return I find the pillows dirty and the children fetid. She hates me. She says that the handsome and distinguished men prefer me and that I make more money than she does. . . .

[July 4, 1958]. When my children were smaller I used to lock them in when I went to pick up paper. One day I came home to find João crying. He told me:

"Mama, Dona Rosa threw dog shit in my face."

I made a fire, heated water and washed the children. I was terrified with the evilness of Dona Rosa. She knows that here in the favela no one is allowed to rent a shack. But she rents. She is the worst woman I've ever seen in my life. Why is it that the poor don't have pity on the other poor?

July 5. Brother Luiz visited us today in the church car. He told us he's going to teach catechism to the children so they can make their first communion. Saturday he's going to teach us the biblical texts.

July 6. I woke up at 4:30 because of Neide's cough. I knew that cough wouldn't let me sleep. I got up and gave her a little syrup because I felt sorry for her. She doesn't have any father. When the father was sick, the mother left them. There are three girls. Neide's mother has a heart of stone. She wouldn't take care of her sick husband nor raise her children, who are cared for by their grandparents.

I heated rice and the fish and fed the children. Afterward I went to pick up kindling wood. It seems that I came into the world predestined to pick things up. The only thing I don't pick up is happiness.

I spread the clothes out to dry. Beside me was the wife of the *nortista* [one from the Northeast of Brazil] who slept with Chó's woman. She was nervous and talked a lot. Seemed as if she had an electric tongue. Seemed like Carlos Lacerda when he talked about Getulio. She said she washed the clothes of Chó's woman. And her own husband paid her to do it.

It's 5:30. Brother Luiz is coming to show a film here in the favela. He's already put up the screen and the *favelados* are waiting.

The people in the brick houses near the favela say they don't know why people of culture pay attention to the people of the favela. The kids of the favela complained when the movie began showing scenes of the Bible and the Birth of Christ. Brother Luiz arrived in the church car. He is a priest who helps the *favelados*. While the movie played the Brother explained. When the three wise men came on the Brother explained they were wise because they could read the future of people from the stars. He asked if anyone knows the name of one of them. One was very well known and called Baltazar.

"And the other is called Pelé [Brazil's world famous soccer player]," shouted a little black.

Everybody laughed. A truck arrived with the soccer team at the moment the padre was praying. My kids came home from the movie and I gave them supper. . . .

July 8. I wasn't feeling well and went to bed early. I awoke because of the clamor in the street. I couldn't understand what they were saying because everyone was talking at the same time and there were many voices. All sorts of voices. I wanted to get up and ask them if they would mind letting people sleep. But I know I'd be wasting my time. All of them were drunk. Leila was giving her show. And their shouts didn't let the neighbors sleep. At 4 o'clock I began to write. When I wake up it's difficult to go back to sleep. I started thinking of this troubled life and of the words Brother Luiz gave us in his humble sermons. I thought: if Brother Luiz was married, had children, and earned the minimum wage, I would like to see if he would be so humble. He said that God blesses only those who suffer with resignation. If the Brother saw his children eating rotten food already attacked by vultures and rats, he would stop talking about resignation and rebel, because rebellion comes from bitterness. . . .

July 22. I went out to work and told my neighbors:

"If Alexandre makes trouble, let me know." I walked thinking of my wretched life. For two weeks I haven't been able to wash clothes for lack of soap. The beds are so filthy it makes me want to vomit.

I don't get upset when I see a stranger looking at my dirt. I think I'll start traveling through the streets with a sign on my back:

"If I'm dirty it's because I don't have soap."

I arrived at the slaughterhouse. The boys went inside and each one got a small sausage. While I was waiting a Spaniard came out to clean and he started shouting at me. Today I'm nervous and I'm not going to let a stranger shout at me.

There is a Spanish woman who comes to the slaughterhouse to pick meat from the garbage and when she saw the Spaniard she said:

"He isn't from my country. That's a Portuguese!"

And there was a Portuguese woman who said:

"That beast isn't from Portugal!"

And I, giving the final touch, said:

"Well, thank God, at least he's not a Brazilian!"

July 23. I left the bed at 7 o'clock. I was not well. Thank God Alexandre quieted down.

I warmed up some food for the children and started getting them ready to go to the Divine Master Center to get those free clothes. When the people saw the favela women in the streets they asked if we were on our way to the Ministry to present our manifesto.

"There has been a disagreement," I replied. And the women laughed.

At the Divine Master Center, Senhor Pinheiro received us, smiling. There was no prejudice or class distinction. I got two light jackets, one for Vera and the other for José Carlos. João got a pullover sweater. Senhor Pinheiro's words cheered me up. . . .

[July 26, 1958.] Adalberto came looking for clothes. I didn't pay any attention to him because he is becoming too familiar. Yesterday he talked dirty while Vera was near. He's annoying me.

Senhor Manuel arrived. He gave me 80 cruzeiros and I didn't want to take it. I was happy when I saw Senhor Manuel. I told him that I was going to spend all night writing. When he was leaving he said:

"It can be another day."

Our eyes met. I told him:

"See that you don't come back here. I'm an old woman. I don't want men. I only want my children."

He went away. He is very kind and educated. And pretty. Any woman would like to have a man as pretty as he is. Pleasant to talk to.

Brother Luiz came by and gave a catechism lesson to the children. Then they had a procession. I didn't go.

July 27. I heated food for the children and started to write. I looked for a place where I could write in peace. But here in the favela there aren't any such places. In the sun I feel the heat. In the shade I feel cold. I was wandering around with the notebooks in my hand when I heard angry voices. I went to see what it was. I thought it was a fight. I saw all the John Does running. A fight is a show that they don't miss. I'm so used to seeing fights that I'm not impressed. . . .

October 24. . . . I rested, made lentil soup with rice and meat. I sent João to buy half a kilo of sugar and the donkey bought rice.

He spends all day reading comic books and doesn't pay attention to anything. He lives thinking of the Invisible Man, Mandrake, and all the other trash.

October 25. The favela today is having a party. There is going to be a procession. The Fathers are sending an image of Our Lady. For those who want it, the image will stay 15 days in each shack. They are saying their rosaries in the park. The procession will go to the streetcar stop.

In Chica's shack they are dancing.

October 28. I. separated from her husband and is living with Zefa. Her husband found her with his cousin. Now I. has begun to commercialize her body, in her husband's presence. I thought: a woman who separates from her husband shouldn't prostitute herself. She should get a job. Prostitution is the moral defeat of a woman. It's like a building that fell. . . .

November 27. I am pleased with my literate children. They understand everything. José Carlos said that he is going to be a distinguished gentleman and that I'll have to treat him as Senhor José.

They have one ambition: they want to live in a house of bricks.

I went to sell paper. I got 55 cruzeiros. When I was coming back to the favela I met a woman who was complaining because she had been fired from her city job.

How horrible it is to hear the poor lament. The voice of the poor has no poetry.

In order to cheer her up I told her that I had read in the Bible that God said he was going to fix everything up in the world. She became happy and asked:

"When is this going to be, Dona Carolina? How wonderful! And just as I wanted to kill myself!"

I told her to be patient and wait for Jesus Christ to come to earth and judge the good and the bad.

"Ah! Then I *will* wait."

She smiled.

I said good-by to the woman, who was more cheerful. I stopped to fix the sack that was sliding off my head. I stared at a vacant lot. I saw the purple flowers. The color of the bitterness that is in the hearts of the starving Brazilians. . . .

December 6. I left the bed at 4 a.m. I turned on the radio to listen to the day dawn with a tango.

I was shocked when I heard the children saying that the son of Senhor Joaquim went to school drunk. The boy is 12 years old.

Today I am very sad.

December 8. In the morning the priest came to say Mass. Yesterday he came in the church car and told the *favelados* that they must have children. I thought: why is it that the poor have to have children — is it that the children of the poor have to be workers?

In my humble opinion who should have children are the rich, who could give brick houses to their children. And they could eat what they wanted.

When the church car comes to the favela, then all sorts of arguments start about religion. The women said that the priest told them that they should have children and when they needed bread they could go to the church and get some.

For Senhor Priest, the children of the poor are raised only on bread. They don't wear clothes or need shoes.

December 11. I was complaining to Dona Maria das Coelhas that what I earned wasn't enough to keep my children. That they didn't have clothes or shoes to wear. And I don't stop for a minute. I pick up everything that I can sell, and misery continues right by my side.

She told me that she is sick of life. I listened to her lament in silence. And told her:

"We are predestined to die of hunger."

PEASANT LEAGUES IN NORTHEAST BRAZIL

". . . the church . . . widened the scope of its activities, . . ."

The career of Francisco Julião, a Catholic lawyer in northeast Brazil, demonstrated the ferment for social and economic reforms. Born in the state of Pernambuco, and raised in a peasant family, he finished law school in Recife in 1939 and spent the next fifteen years as a peasants' lawyer, defending tenants and laborers against the latifundios (large landed estate) and sugar refineries. Then, in 1955, he organized the peasant league which became a large movement, uniting scores of thousands of landless farmers to campaign for agrarian reforms. With the military coup of 1964, the League was suppressed and Julião exiled. He describes the way some Catholic and Protestant leaders in 1959 and 1960 related to the movement.[54]

✠ With the church things happened in reverse. In the beginning the League met with systematic hostility from clerical authorities. Knowing the deep religious sentiments of the peasantry and the constant labours of parish priests to stifle the spirit of rebellion among the working masses, the League always avoided open conflict with the church: it would have been easily suppressed had it confronted an institution then still reactionary and insensitive towards the peasants' conditions since its ties were rather with the *latifundio* as they had earlier been with the slave-owners. . . .

It's not easy for a man who has spent ten years under the rigid discipline of a seminary to rebel against the rules when he has sworn to obey them without question; just as it is hard for a professional soldier to break out of the system of barrack-room hierarchies and support a revolt against a dictatorship maintained by force in minority interests. One can thus readily understand why Catholic workmen's circles led by weak-willed priests at first opposed the League: such circles constituted a small and lifeless organization confined to the narrow limits of the parish. The priests feared clashes with the owners who controlled local political life so that the workmen's circle was controlled by a larger, more inflexible organization—the *latifundio*.

When the peasant movement led by the League gained impetus, the cities were invaded by a mass of country people coming not to fairs, masses or burial grounds but to the judges and prefects to demand their rights, or to demonstrate in the streets with banners calling for agrarian reform. As a result the church, concerned by events in the countryside, decided to widen the scope of its activities, and the bishops and priests were split into two clearly divided groups: one reactionary, bent on suppressing the League by denouncing its activities as subversive and dangerous; the other sympathetic to the movement, adopting a courageous, intelligent and progressive attitude towards it. In between these two groups a few priests lit a candle for God and another for the Devil, talking radicalism and revolution to the peasants and secretly collaborating with the *latifundio* and the state's repressive organizations in an attempt to patch up social divisions.

But before things got to this point the League had started out on a difficult path which brought it into inevitable conflict with the *latifundio*. It is only fair to say that the League was able to count from the start on the steadfast support of a few Protestant missionaries from several sects who went about, bible in hand, delivering sermons about the land, seed, ploughs, sowing, harvesting and work, drawing on symbols and passages from the two Testaments to win followers and widen their field of action. It was only natural that a persecuted religion should seek out the persecuted, and the League welcomed the support of such preachers, but always avoided giving preference to any one sect, just as it always refused to discriminate between Catholics, Protestants or any other faith.

The League's only objective was to win the support of all groups, to attack the *latifundio*. Without doubt the Protestant preachers netted many a fish, especially in areas where the Catholic Church was directed by intolerant priests in league with the wealthy landowners: such priests were refusing to marry, baptize or confess League members, on the grounds that membership was a sign of communism. João Pedro Teixeira, for example, who was a Protestant pastor, led the Sapé League where the overwhelming majority of members was Catholic. Joaquim Camilo and José Evangelista, both Protestants, led the League at Jaboatão in Pernambuco, one of the most active in the state.

Jaboatão (the only city in Brazil to elect a communist prefect, Dr. Rodrigues Calheiros) was the scene of an episode between a Protestant peasant and member of the League and the vice-prefect of the city, a landowner, and the incident is an indication in itself of the level of politicization and acuteness of the peasantry.

Whenever a League centre was opened in a city or town it was our custom to invite the local authorities to be present at the ceremony; this was a public demonstration of the organization's legality. Some authorities would attend; others found a thousand excuses to keep away; many refused on the grounds that the League was subversive because it aimed at changing existing law and at agitating the peasantry against the landowners. When the vice-prefect of Jaboatão was invited to the inauguration of the Jaboatão League he refused on the grounds that the League was communist. Whereupon the peasant retorted: 'The League's inside the law. It's been registered. It has proper statutes. You can see them.'

The landowner, however, counter-attacked: 'The devil knows what clothes to wear. He puts on pilgrim's clothes to fool you, but the people look at his feet and can see they're goat's feet. Communism is like the Devil.'

'Excuse my ignorance, boss; but I've noticed that whenever something turns up that'll benefit the poor they tell you it's communism. That way they're stoking communism up. It'll end by winning...'

'Do you know what communism is?'

'No. My law is of another kind, Jesus Christ's, our Lord's.'

'Then I'll tell you. Communism is taking other people's goods, outraging other people's wives and daughters and attacking our religion. That is the law of communism.'

The Protestant thought for a while and gave the following reply which is still remembered in the North-East.

'Well, if that's the law of communism, we're already in it. Look: the poor man rents some land, builds a house, puts up a fence, plants some trees and makes some other improvements. One day the boss goes against him, chucks him out and doesn't give him a penny. So he's taking other people's goods. If the poor man has a pretty daughter, there'll soon be some foreman or plantation-owner or rich man to dishonour her. It's no good his complaining: rich men don't marry poor women. As for the rest, I'm a Protestant myself, and the landowner where I live is a Catholic woman. I can't worship in my own house or sing my hymns because she doesn't like them. She's attacking my religion. . . . There we are, boss. The League came to finish with this law which you call communism and make another, a fair law, to protect the poor.'

Possibly the fact that Protestants joined the League and made inroads among tenants in areas where the priests were most intolerant, put the church on the alert and helped persuade the bishops to look on the agrarian problem in a new light. The fact is that the church could not remain indifferent in the face of a conflict as tense as that which had blown up amongst the now awakening peasants and the enraged and fearful landowners. Faced with this the church could not stay silent, and compromised with the *latifundio* as it had done in the previous century during the struggle for Abolition of black slavery. The world had changed so radically in the last fifty years that a passive attitude would have been irremediably damaging to the church.

Pope Pius XI had already declared that the greatest scandal of the nineteenth century was the church's loss of the working classes. On the basis of this declaration Father Francisco Lage noted that if the church became isolated from popular movements in Latin America and was turned into an ally of the oligarchies and wealthy classes another later Pope would one day say something similar but more serious: 'The greatest scandal of the twentieth century was the church's loss of Latin America.'

12 ✠ Protestants: Systematic Expansion

1930–1961

In the social change and urbanization of the period 1930–1960, scores of thousands of families became uprooted from the rural areas and lost their traditional patterns of life. For many families in the midst of this stress, Protestant churches offered support and guidance; they became a spiritual home, a doorway to literacy and survival in the new environment, and provided a sense of self-worth.

Lingering prejudices and informal barriers against Protestants were now rapidly diminishing. An exception was the violent persecution which they suffered in Colombia from 1948 to 1958. That frightening episode kept alive traditional Protestant fears. Yet across Latin America, "believers," as the Protestants referred to themselves, were multiplying. At the end of the 1920s, they had numbered about one-half million, but by the 1950s they had grown to something approaching five million, with about half of them living in Brazil.[55] Relative to the populations as a whole, the Protestants in 1960 were still small, perhaps five percent in Chile, and in other countries more like one to three percent. This minority status often led to their feeling weak and restricted.

The largest churches were the various Pentecostal and Seventh Day Adventist congregations—not the Baptists, Presbyterians, Methodists, or other historic churches from which most of the missionaries came during this period.[56] The outreach methods of all the *evangélicos* were their strong points—preaching, gathering congregations, organizing schools and establishing Bible institutes to train leaders. Yet several weaknesses persisted; theological education was inadequate, and both fundamentalism and excessive fear of the Catholic Church were pervasive. Morality tended to be privatized and restricted to a list of prohibitions. North American missionaries, wittingly or unwittingly, often served as agents of the economic system from which they came, and remained silent about or unaware of its unhealthy grip on Latin America. The local Protestant communities often remained dependent on foreign subsidies for their schools, hospitals, and other services, and too often looked elsewhere, usually to North America, for their music, literature, and architecture.

Protestant bodies were badly fragmented, and the small ecumenical

Pentecostal youths, singing in the streets on the way to the Jotabeche church, Santiago, Chile, in the 1960s.

movement only partially offset the divisions. Through the Committee on Cooperation in Latin America [Presbyterians, Methodists, etc.], based in New York, both missionary and local leaders of the "daughter" churches in Latin America consulted and occasionally acted together. Other agencies, also based in Britain or North America, such as the World Sunday School Association, the Bible and literature societies, the World Dominion Press, and the World Evangelical Alliance served to connect the separated Protestant bodies. Friendships and cooperation through these were mutually instructive, but friendly critics at the time perceived across the region an inadequate ecclesiology and a truncated sense of mission in the world. In the subsequent period, 1960–1985, these would become central issues.

AMERICAN MISSIONARIES REPORT HOME

". . . aggressive evangelism characterizes the work . . ."

Protestant missions grew rapidly in the 1930s. Typical was the West Brazil Mission of the Presbyterians in the western sector of Minas Gerais. Their annual report "from the field" to the sponsoring body in the United States contained the following paragraphs about their work in the year 1932.[57]

☨ In all her long and turbulent history Brazil has perhaps never passed a more agitated year than the one that has just closed. A civil war involving the largest armed forces ever assembled in South America dominated the life and thought of the nation during the closing trimester of the Mission year. The collapse of the coffee market has given Brazil her share in the world-wide depression. Profound social, economic and political changes are taking place. For more than two years the nation has been governed by a dictatorship. No one can forecast what form the future government will take.

In the midst of it all the pure Gospel of Jesus Christ has never had a greater opportunity than it has today in Brazil; and never has the responsibility for giving a true witness to Jesus been greater than at the present moment. In spite of war, depression, cuts, etc., the annual meeting of the Mission held in Barretos was one of the happiest in years. This year marked the close of the Seven Year Progressive Program of the Mission. Seven years ago the Mission established certain goals to be attained during this period. Practically every goal has been reached. Organized congregations have increased from 11 to 32; preaching points from 42 to 65; communicants from 1,053 to 1,977; Sunday Schools from 15 to 41; Sunday School pupils from 717 to 2,274; Woman's Societies from 1 to 18; native contributions from $7,375 to $11,375. In 1924 Sao Sebastiao do Paraiso was the farthest interior Station, while today it is the nearest to civilization. Our Mission today presents a solid front advancing to the great interior of Brazil.

An aggressive evangelism characterizes the work of our West Brazil Mission. It is encouraging, too, to see the extent to which the work is becoming self-sustaining. The church at Sao Sebastiao do Paraiso, not satisfied merely with self-support, has manifested a fine missionary spirit by contributing most of the support of a native worker in one of the points in the field, and by maintaining a ministerial candidate in the Presbyterian Seminary at Campinas. Throughout this field there has been encouraging progress, and the program of the Mission calls for the organization of a Presbytery in the field, and the turning over of this section to the native church within four years.

Seven years' work in the Barretos field has produced two organized churches, five organized congregations, eight Sunday Schools, about 300 church members, more than 500 Sunday School members, six Woman's Societies, two Christian Endeavor Societies, and other splendid results. The field already has four church buildings, and will have two more within this year. Extending out from these points there is a vast region that has never been touched by the Gospel. Our present missionary personnel is wholly inadequate for overtaking this wider responsibility. As this report is being written, Rev. and Mrs. J. R. Woodson are alone in all this vast missionary field except for one native worker. . . .

One of the most significant developments in the work of the Mission for the year has been the beginning of the training school for lay workers at Patrocinio under the direction of Miss Frances Hesser and Dr. Lane. As we can never hope to occupy the growing towns and villages of the frontier with ordained evangelists, of whom there is scarcely a sufficient number to man the established churches of the eastern seaboard, this training school for lay workers has been created for the purpose of releasing in this territory a lay force that will be able in a limited measure at least to meet the needs of these fast developing areas. The Mission expects great things for the future from this school, which marks a distinctive step forward in the methods of our work in Brazil. . . .

West Brazil Statistical Summary

	1932
Population of our field, estimated	700,000
Foreign workers	13
Children of foreign workers	14
Native workers, evangelists and teachers	16
Outstations, places of regular meeting	96
Organized congregations	32
Communicants	1,977
Additions during year	170
Sunday Schools	40

Sunday School membership.................................. 2,590
Schools.. 1
Students 56
Income from native sources................................. $10,448

ECONOMIC POSITION OF PROTESTANTS

" . . . the majority . . . come from the humbler walks of life, . . ."

What kinds of people were attracted to the Protestant churches? What were the possibilities of self-support? To find out, the International Missionary Council, an ecumenical organ through which many mission societies cooperated, sent a Protestant economist to Mexico in 1940 to survey the evangélicos. His report, based on the self-perception of the Protestants, reveals the backgrounds of many of them at the time.[58]

✠ The Evangelical Church membership represents a wide cross-section of the occupations and professions of the community in Mexico. A majority of the members, — in many cases a very large majority — come from the humblest of circles. In the rural churches, day laborers, tenant farmers and farm hands are mostly in evidence, with a sprinkling of artisans, shopkeepers, machinists, teachers and transport workers. In the semi-urban churches, the proportion of small tradesmen, factory hands and clerical workers rises, while in the urban churches, a fair cross-section of the varied activities of the city is represented in the membership, with a number of professional people and petty officials and a very few men of some financial means. Even in the city church, however, the majority of the members come from the humbler walks of life, with a comparatively low earning power.

The following table shows the proportion of 1,532 evangelical church members of 15 Churches found in various occupations. It is probable that fully 75 per cent of the members of evangelical churches in Mexico are related directly or indirectly to agriculture as an occupation.

Day laborers, including farm hands .... 22. per cent
Students .... 11.2 "   "
Agriculture (farmers) .... 10.1 "   "
Workers.. 9.3 "   "
Artisans... 9.3 "   "
Teachers.. 6.5 "   "
Servants.. 5.8 "   "
Professions... 4.1 "   "
Commerce .... 2.5 "   "
Government Employees.................................. 1.8 "   "
Transport .... 1.3 "   "

Other occupations...................................... 7.7 per cent
Unemployed.. 2.4   "   "
Unclassified... 6.   "   "

100. per cent

About 38 per cent of evangelical Christians of the churches answering the questionnaire are in debt, with an average debt of 200 *pesos*. The chief causes for indebtedness, given in their order of frequency, are:

Rising cost of living.

Poverty.

Bad management.

Low salaries.

Unemployment.

Inadequate tools and equipment.

However, the economic and social status of evangelicals as contrasted with their non-evangelical neighbors is illuminating and points to the possibility of a sound and expanding evangelical group of the future. Of the churches replying to this question, 57.1 per cent stated that their members were in better economic circumstances than non-evangelicals of the same classes and occupations, 33.3 per cent rated their members as equal to the average in economic strength, and only 9.6 per cent rated them as inferior.

AIRPLANES AND EVANGELISTIC INSTITUTES

"... rural congregations built crude airstrips."

In Mexico in 1957 the Protestants numbered about 911,000; that was less than three percent of the population. The Baptists, Presbyterians, Swedish Free Mission, Methodists, Seventh Day Adventists, and Pentecostals, in that order, were the largest churches. In part, their growth came through evangelistic campaigns. One such effort among the Presbyterians in Tabasco in the 1950s and early 1960s was described by a pilot of the Missionary Aviation Fellowship.[59]

✠ Tabasco had virtually no roads and few motor vehicles during those years of rapid growth. The myriad rivers and swamps made even horseback travel torturously slow. Motor launches plied the larger rivers, stopping at almost every house along the way. Seven days and sleepless nights, spent sandwiched between freight and animals, were needed to travel by launch the 105 air miles between Villahermosa and Tenosique. A local air company flew shuddering, wired-together, 1928-vintage airplanes between the major towns on a somewhat regular basis.

In 1947 the Presbyterian Mission, with approval from the local Presbytery, invited the Missionary Aviation Fellowship to assist with the transportation problems of the Tabasco churches. (The MAF was already serving the Wycliffe Bible Translators in nearby Chiapas.) One airplane was used on a part-time basis for three years. After 1951 a Missionary Aviation Fellowship pilot was assigned to give full time to operating an airplane purchased by the Presbyterian (U.S.A.) Mission. The Mission paid all operating expenses. Local pastors and missionaries had equal voice in authorizing flights, either for themselves or for lay workers traveling on church business.

Isolated rural congregations built crude airstrips. Cow pastures, sand bars, village streets, tops of levees, and 300-yard swaths hacked from the jungle were used as landing places. A total of 102 such airstrips were used in Tabasco, 68 of them built exclusively for the mission airplane.

With the airplane available, the Presbytery authorized Rev. Fred Tinley to mobilize all the leadership elements of the Tabasco Church, both ordained and lay, to carry out an intensive program of evangelistic and three-day training institutes. As many as 125 such institutes were held in a single year. Occasionally outstanding evangelists came to assist from other parts of Latin America, but the bulk of preaching and teaching was done by local men. The Presbyterian Mission paid transportation costs and the local congregations took care of all other expenses.

Most of these isolated congregations seldom saw an ordained minister except during the institutes. During the day, the visiting pastors and teachers would lead the local believers in Bible study. In the evening the entire community turned out for the evangelistic services, which often lasted far into the night. Baptism of both adults and children and reception of new members were usually included in the program.

Rev. and Mrs. C. H. Denman arrived to augment the missionary staff in 1954. Mr. Denman assumed responsibility for the institutes and evangelism. Rev. Fred Tinley then began to dedicate most of his time to assisting the new congregations in eastern Tabasco (Los Rios region). Mr. Denman organized the work of the institutes around a common theme for each year and printed study helps. He also held training retreats for the leaders who would teach in the institutes. Evangelistic campaigns were expanded to one week or more in strategic centers, with careful preparation and follow-up. Between 1957 and 1960 these campaigns registered about a thousand first-time decisions for Christ each year, though a much smaller number attained full church membership.

For several years virtually all travel for the institutes was by air. As roads and bus service increased, travel gradually shifted to more economical means. Increased numbers of trained leaders and other factors caused the demand for the institutes to decline. Although reduced in number, they continue to perform a vital service to the pastorless congregations in Tabasco. In most cases they have amounted to a small Evangelical *fiesta* — the social event of the year for the isolated congregations.

Between 1948 and 1965, three different MAF pilots served in Tabasco and literally wore out as many different airplanes. (The author was the last of the three pilots and served the longest period.) During those years they made almost 15,000 individual flights—slightly less than a half-million air miles—within Tabasco, plus many hundreds of additional flights in Chiapas and Yucatán. Individual flights averaged less than fifteen minutes in length.

As roads improved, airstrips in the more populated areas were abandoned. New congregations in the outlying fringes of the state built new airstrips to replace those closed. In addition to serving the program of institutes and evangelistic campaigns, the mission airplanes carried medical personnel, sick and injured, church officers traveling to committee meetings, and sometimes delivered urgent mail.

PIONEER MISSIONS IN THE AMAZON BASIN

"Marj is on the radio checking with the jungle stations . . ."

Though the Protestant community in Ecuador had grown tenfold since 1929, it was still small in 1957, numbering approximately 4,800. One way the Protestants communicated their message was by a radio station, HCJB, in Quito, begun in 1931. By the mid-1950s, it was broadcasting twenty-four hours a day in seven languages. Much more limited was their evangelism among the Indians in the jungle regions in the east of Ecuador. There, the means of transportation was the airplane. Nate Saint, a pilot in the Missionary Aviation Fellowship, kept logs of his flights; a part of one of those in 1956 is given below. Later, when Saint and four colleagues attempted to contact an isolated tribe of Aucas, they were killed.[60]

✠ It's a clear sunrise. Feels like a good day coming up.

6:30 a.m.—Gassing the plane and making inspections while Marj [wife of the writer] goes over the priority lists of missionary cargo.

7:00 a.m.—Marj is on the radio checking with the jungle stations while I am stowing away some breakfast. The plane is loaded and ready. Dos Rios reports ground fog. Pano station has no fog. I could land there in case the fog at Dos Rios doesn't clear by the time I get there. First destination: Dos Rios, 45 miles.

7:21 a.m.—Off the runway at Shell Mera.

7:44 a.m.—The fog has risen and somewhat broken. I am preparing to land at Dos Rios.

8:00 a.m.—The Dos Rios mail has been sorted and remaining cargo rearranged. Off the runway and bound for Pano station, 4 miles away.

8:03 a.m.—Preparing to land at Pano.

8:10 a.m. — Weekly food supply. Fresh vegetables and mail are unloaded and off to Shandia, 6 miles from Pano. This is the north jungle "milk run."

8:15 a.m. — On the ground at Shandia. Mail and food supplies unloaded.

8:18 a.m. — Off the runway for return to Pano. A missionary has to be flown out for dental work. The Pano strip is short so the plane had to be emptied before taking off from Pano with a passenger.

8:26 a.m. — Off Pano for Shell Mera. As I radio in the position reports I hear Marj handling the morning radio traffic for all parts of the eastern jungle as well as Quito and Guayaquil. We get word that permits have come through for the importation of the new engine we will need next month. That is cause for rejoicing. We've been trying to get the permits since the end of January.

8:33 a.m. — Report position: Ila, 4500 feet altitude.

8:45 a.m. — Landing at Shell Mera.

9:00 a.m. — Marj is still handling radio traffic. Kathy and Stevie [children of the writer] are out of their Pj's and into play clothes. They seem to have had breakfast. Ralph Stuck, a fellow missionary outbound on this next flight, has his load all ready and is securing it in the plane while I pump gas and check oil.

9:15 a.m. — Off Shell Mera for Sucua, 75 miles deep in the south jungle. Passengers are Ralph Stuck; a national worker; and a seven-year-old Jivaro boy who had been flown out a week ago with a broken arm. He returns with a cast and a barrelful of wild tales about the 'big city' to share with tribal playmates.

9:54 a.m. — Planning to land at Sucua.

10:08 a.m. — Off Sucua to Shell. Passengers: G. Christian Weiss, mission executive, who last visited the field on foot in 1946. He is thrilled with the implications of missionary aviation; Señor Carlos Malordo, Ecuadorian soldier left stranded when a military plane pulled out without him yesterday.

10:47 a.m. — Preparing to land at Shell Mera.

11:00 a.m. — While servicing the plane, we try to decide which flight should have next priority. Frank Mathis is waiting for the plane at Montalvo, 85 miles east. He's surveying for Wycliffe Bible Translators; has no radio; expects the plane today. Decide that that must come next but we can go by way of Macuma and leave a load there to economize. It is 53 miles southeast so it will be a triangle flight.

11:15 a.m. — We are about ready to leave when the military commander for the eastern jungles arrives. He explains that they dropped supplies to the military post at Montalvo but that a good share of them burst open on impact with the ground and were lost. They urgently need 200 pounds of rice and our plane is the only one in the region small enough to land on the small landing strip that the soldiers have finished recently.

11:17 a.m. — Off Shell Mera for Macuma. Miss Dorothy Walker, missionary to the Jivaro tribe, and Linda Drown, daughter of Frank Drown, are passengers.

11:48 a.m. — Out of Macuma for Montalvo with 200 pounds of rice and a good map. Area over which I will be flying is almost uninhabited and relatively unexplored except along rivers.

12:17 p.m. — Sight Bobanaza River and start letting down from 8000 feet. Finishing cheese sandwich Marj sent along. Thermos of cold milk hits the spot. The sun is clear and hot through the windshield even though the air outside is cold at this altitude.

12:30 p.m. — Planning to land at Montalvo. On the approach I spot Frank. He has made it in from his overland survey on schedule. I was a little worried about this. The strip seems clear. I go in for the landing.

12:35 p.m. — About 50 Ecuadorian soldiers have jammed around the plane. The captain explains that their radio is dead because their light plant is broken down. He has the broken parts for us to take out to be fixed. Capt. Jacome is a good friend. He used to be at Shell Mera. He consents to my giving out tracts and gospel literature to the men. I have opportunity to speak to the men a minute. Give them a word of personal testimony.

12:50 p.m. — Off Montalvo for Shell Mera. Establish radio contact with Marj. Frank is grinning behind a battered half cheese sandwich. Weather seems to be holding off okay in spite of scattered showers. We follow the Bobanaza River northwest for half an hour, then decide that we'll detour a little to be able to drop Frank off at his mission station on the way to Shell Mera. His strip is a small one but we are light on gas now and find a favorable wind blowing.

1:31 p.m. — Preparing to land at Llushin. Frank's family is tickled to have him back safe and sound. Miss Kathy Peeke, on the strength of Frank's survey findings, decides to go out to Quito to get ready for moving into Montalvo. She climbs aboard and we take off for Shell Mera where she will catch a bus for Quito. . . . [Three more stops, then]

3:46 p.m. — Landing at Shell Mera. Weather is still holding up fine, but I'm not. We call it a day.

INTERIOR LIFE OF "BELIEVERS"

"Among many ministers and laymen, a certain dissatisfaction . . ."

The Protestant community in Brazil in the late 1950s numbered about 1,775,000 (two percent or less of the population). The Pentecostals, Bap-

tists, Presbyterians, and Methodists were the largest churches. Their devotional or interior life showed some strengths and also some weaknesses. Two Presbyterian theologians in the São Paulo area, Rubem Alves, a Brazilian, and Richard Shaull, a North American missionary, described that life as they saw it in 1956.[61]

✠ When Christians of other lands visit Brazil, they are amazed, and at times somewhat confused, by the type of devotional life which they find in the Protestant churches. They are impressed by the extraordinary vitality of the simple piety of the average Christian. Here are people for whom the experience of a personal relationship with Jesus Christ is the very centre of life, people who read their Bibles and pray daily. Churches are filled, not only on Sunday morning, but also Sunday evening and at the midweek services. . . .

At the same time, the picture is somewhat confused and chaotic. No clear structure can be discerned either in private devotions or in public worship. Many of those who take their devotional life most seriously often wonder just what relevance it all has to the problems of the world in which they live. . . .

Vitality

When we attempt to examine more closely the reasons for the vitality of this devotional life, several factors deserve our attention:

1. It is the result, in the first place, of the pietism and revivalism brought to Brazil by the early missionaries and which has now been taken over and made an integral part of modern Brazilian Protestantism. . . . They produced the dynamic expanding Christian Church that we have today throughout Brazil. They have raised up several generations of Christians for whom the experience of salvation and of the new life in Christ has been a powerful transforming reality. . . .

2. It is the product of a type of Protestantism which has given a central place to the reading and study of the Bible. One hundred years ago the Bible was practically an unknown book in Brazil. Thanks to the unceasing efforts of the Protestants, it is now widely known and read. Even the Roman Catholic Church has reacted to this emphasis by organizing a Bible Correspondence Course and sponsoring Bible Weeks throughout the country. . . .

3. The Protestant churches in Brazil live on a missionary frontier, the existence of which is taken very seriously. This fact has a tremendous influence on the devotional life of Brazilian Protestantism. It means that the church is constantly being stimulated by the influx of large numbers of first-generation Christians, who bring with them the intensity of life and the awareness of the radical power of the Christian faith which is always so evident to the convert. . . .

Problems

Despite this rather amazing vitality, all is not well with the devotional life of Brazilian Protestantism. . . .

1. The first question has to do with the meaning and structure of worship. This problem is the almost inevitable result of the development of pietism and revivalism in a Roman Catholic environment. These Evangelical movements had no clear theology of worship. They were principally concerned about leading people to a decision for Jesus Christ through an intense emotional experience, and the church service aimed to achieve that goal. At the same time, the reaction of many converts against the sterility of Roman Catholicism often led them unconsciously to reject all liturgical and devotional practices found there. Today we are reaping the harvest of all this. We have no clear understanding of what should happen in a worship service, nor any definite idea of how such a service should be structured to express what takes place in human encounter with God. For many, a service whose primary aim is to lead those who take part in it to a certain emotional experience, can hardly offer a satisfactory type of public worship. As a result, the sermon tends to become the centre of worship, and often takes up forty to fifty minutes of the service.

The same sort of problem is evident in the devotional life of the individual Christian. Here too he has been led to feel that the criterion of his devotional life is to be found in the intensity of his emotional experience. . . .

2. A second question concerns Bible study, both for the individual and for the Christian community. Many, especially of the younger generation, do not become enthusiastic when they are simply told to read a certain number of chapters each day. And when they go to church and Sunday school and discover that Bible study means listening to someone talk about a certain chapter, often using it as a point of departure for a homily, they tend to lose interest. . . .

3. One of the most serious weaknesses of our pietist heritage is its inability to show the relevance of the believer's experience of Jesus Christ to the problems which he faces in his life in the world. . . .

4. Many are beginning to become aware of the gradual tendency of the church to become more and more an ecclesiastical institution in which the layman plays an essentially passive role. In the early days of the life of the Brazilian church, the congregation was a small community in which nearly everyone had a responsibility. . . .

This is still true on the missionary frontiers. But as the church has grown, the situation has changed. The local congregation has a trained minister and a small group of capable laymen who direct most of its activities. The great majority, however, find little opportunity to assume responsibility. . . .

The Search for Answers

This situation has given rise to several efforts towards the renovation of the devotional life of the church. One of these comes from the newer revivalistic movements and sects which are flooding in from the United States or arising spontaneously in Brazil. These groups possess tremendous spiritual vitality and missionary zeal, and place great emphasis on emotion and consecration. . . .

On the other hand, we find several small groups that are attempting to emphasize the aesthetics of worship. Special attention is given to liturgy, lighting, music and art. . . .

There is a third effort at renovation which is just beginning, but which may have more far-reaching consequences, as it is attempting to grapple seriously with fundamental problems in the development of our devotional life. It is perhaps no mere coincidence that some of the leadership at this point has come from the Student Christian Movement, . . .

1. These groups are seriously concerned with the meaning and structure of Christian worship. They have given central attention to the theological basis of worship as the expression of what takes place when God enters into living encounter with man and with the congregation through the Word and the Sacraments. They are also restudying the liturgical traditions of their churches, and are seriously preoccupied with the need to secure the greatest possible participation of all in the worship service. . . .

2. Bible study is becoming a living issue in many student and youth groups as a result of the adoption of group Bible study. Susanne de Diétrich's *Rediscovery of the Bible* has been translated and well received. Group Bible study is being used not only in many student and youth groups but also in some churches. Through it many have rediscovered the power of the Bible's message.

3. It may be, however, that the most significant development in the quest for new ways of expressing the devotional life is the discussion now going on about the nature of the Church as a witnessing community. This too began in the Student Christian Movement, as its leaders tried to discover how student groups in the universities might become responsible Christian communities. It led to serious theological study of the doctrine of the Church and of witness. . . . This has provided a new context for the devotional life.

MOTIVATIONS BEHIND CONVERSIONS

"A profound feeling of peace and *gozo* never left me."

Why the rapid growth of Protestant congregations? One reason, said sociologist Emilio Willems, was that their message was being heard by poor people dislocated by industrialization and urbanization. Many poor migrants found in the Protestant churches a warm welcome and spiritual guidance. In 1959 and 1960, Willems studied this growth in Brazil and Chile. He interviewed numerous church members; below are some testimonies from what he called "lower class culture."[62]

✠ Several interviewees affirmed that they "gained health through faith." A man confessed that before his conversion he had lived "in vice and sin." Now he was living a "much better and healthier life." A woman "accepted the Spirit" because she desperately wished "to cure her sick daughter," and conversion really solved her problem. One of our male informants told us that before his conversion "he had much sickness in his family" because he was not "living in the grace of God." The idea of a "rebirth" so often associated with religious conversion thus appears to contain a physiological component. The seat of the newly acquired moral virtues is a healthier organism, a point of no minor importance in countries where the morbidity rate continues to be very high among the underprivileged classes.

Furthermore, our life histories reveal a great deal of "unhappiness" with a life of "vice and sin," even if the person is *not* afflicted with physical maladies. The following excerpts may cast some light on this aspect of conversion.

H.A.L. MALE. AGE 78. Formerly rural laborer, now street peddler. Married. Never had any religion.

My wife attended services in the local Methodist temple and invited me to join. I refused because I was drunk almost every night. Once in a dream I saw God who invited me to go to church. I went and accepted Christ. I felt that the Lord had forgiven all my sins. When the services were over I felt relief, satisfaction and *gozo* [joy]. I gave up drinking and became a different person. Before my conversion I had a violent temper, but now I live in peace with my wife, my granddaughter and my neighbors. I have more self-confidence now, work regularly and make more money. We had a winter that was almost like summer, there was never any lack of bread. Not like before when there were days without any food at all.

Wants to learn to read and write, "to learn more about God and the Holy Scripture."

E.G.G. FEMALE. AGE 18. SINGLE. Domestic servant. She liked the Gospel since she was a child.

Grandmother used to take me to a Pentecostal temple, but I had no energy to resist temptations. Afterwards I returned to church to repent but I always fell back into sin. One day I heard the voice of the Lord who told me that all my sins had been forgiven. My heart filled with *gozo* and I was seized by the Holy Spirit. I danced and heard soft voices singing exquisite melodies. I felt carried away to another place of wondrous beauty. When I recovered I found myself kneeling and praying in front of the altar. Immediately all temptations and anxieties ceased. I gave up painting my lips and curling my hair. My only desire is to work and to go to church. Once I fell sick with paratyphoid fever. Two weeks later, still very sick, I went to church and was again seized by the Spirit. An *hermana* [sister] who did not know of my sickness, also had a *tomada del Espiritu* [seizure by the Spirit], walked over to the place where I knelt and laid hands on my head. The same day I felt completely cured. When I was fourteen years old I had ear surgery and became almost deaf. After my conversion I took part in a *cadena de oración* (continuous prayer meeting of seven days). During one of these meetings an *hermano* [brother] laid hands on my head and gradually my hearing went back to normal.

C.C.T. FEMALE. SINGLE. AGE 21. Seamstress. She was a Catholic, but found that Catholicism "lacked foundations."

When I was sixteen I began to go to a Protestant church with my uncles, but remained indifferent during the first year. Suddenly, during a church service, I felt invaded by a great sadness and understood the presence of the Lord. I repented my sins and ceased to crave the distractions of the world. Never again did I go to a dance or to the movies. I only wish to work for the Gospel.

M.H.A.A. MALE. AGE 28. MARRIED. Soldier. Was educated in Catholic school, but "hypocrisy of priests" made him lose respect for church.

I began to attend church services in Valparaiso. I gave up smoking, drinking, gambling and relations with prostitutes, but did not become emotionally involved in this new religion until three years later when suddenly, in a Methodist church in Santiago, I felt a strange impulse which carried me to the altar. I was not aware of what I was doing; I had the impression of being alone in the church and felt the presence of God, a *gozo* I had never felt before. I wished to surrender my life to the Lord to serve him. I experienced a strong desire to shout and communicate what I was feeling to everybody. I felt forgiveness of my sins and profound relief.

M. is somewhat critical of the "lack of faith" and "the professional attitude" of pastors. What keeps him in church is "his hope for a revival."

M.C.A. FEMALE. AGE 63. WIDOW. Was seamstress, lives with son. Was Catholic, but never attended mass. Conversion to Protestant faith was gradual.

Invited by friends, I attended Methodist and Baptist services, but could not bring myself to get interested. Eventually I found a Methodist church whose services I liked. Frequently I asked God to cure my arthritis. One day I knelt in front of the altar, and when the hands of the preacher touched my head I felt a shiver running through my whole body, a strange sensation I had never had before. I felt no weight, exactly as if my feet were not touching the ground, and my nerves relaxed. I thought I was another person and for the first time in twenty years I raised my arms to heaven. I prayed for forgiveness, but I cannot recollect my words. A sensation of well-being and pleasure as never before invaded me completely. I wept with joy. During the next half hour my whole body kept shaking violently. Since then my life has been peaceful and contented. Now I can use my hands again. Every day I feel better, I don't take sedatives anymore, and my arms are improving, thank God.

G.A. FEMALE. AGE 63. MARRIED. She was an agricultural laborer. Husband who was construction worker, is now street peddler. Long ago she ceased to practice the Catholic religion because it failed to assuage her anxieties. Invited by a preacher she attended church service and was converted. "I felt a great relief, an inexplicable joy. The Lord had forgiven my sins. There is now peace in my soul. Before my conversion, I had a terrible temper. I smoked a great deal, but now I don't smoke anymore. I live in peace with my husband and the neighbors. To help my husband I work with satisfaction and joy." She is illiterate, but feels a strong desire to learn to read and write in order to "learn the word of God."

G.S. MALE. AGE 51. MARRIED. Repairs and sells shoes. Never practiced any religion at all. Was alcoholic and suffered from "anxieties." Approximately thirty years ago S. killed a man and was sentenced to death for first-degree murder.

When I arrived in prison, I was in a terrible fury. Like a maniac I shouted vengeance against everybody, members of my family, neighbors, the judge, the police, just about everybody. My only wish was to escape for a couple of days to take revenge. They called me *el loco* [the crazy one]. After the first week or so, somebody gave me a Bible and I began to read. I also had some talks with another convict who had been converted in prison. Then one day I had a vision in plain daylight. Out of the corner of my cell walked a beautiful woman followed by an old man with a white beard and penetrating eyes. They walked all around the cell and disappeared in the same spot they had come from. My brother, the convict, said to me: "The angel of Jehovah is walking around. Be prepared to receive the baptism of the Lord." One day, some weeks later, when I felt desperate, I heard a voice: "All thy sins are forgiven . . . This is what the world has given thee . . . I shall pick thee up like a filthy rag and cleanse thee in my precious blood so that thou preach my Gospel in the streets." I felt a shiver and for the first time I bent my knees and prayed with all my soul. I changed completely, the prison seemed pleasant and my cell different. A profound feeling of peace and *gozo* never left me.

While G.S. was waiting to be executed, the prison was destroyed by an earthquake. Unlike most prisoners, S. made no attempt to escape but saved many inmates who had been buried under the debris. The Supreme Court commuted his sentence to 20 years, then to 15 and finally to 11 years. Since G.S. left prison he has devoted almost all of his free time to the preaching of the Gospel. He is now pastor of a Pentecostal congregation.

"EVANGELISM-IN-DEPTH" PROGRAM

"Nicaragua Shall Belong to Christ."

Though the numbers of Protestants in Central America were minuscule, they were growing. Seminaries appeared, and along with them Bible institutes, primary and secondary schools, bookstores, periodicals, and various health-care services. Church leaders planned their message to induce conversion. Nurture and social concerns were secondary and often neglected. Some of the strengths and weaknesses of their work were visible in the program called "Evangelism-in-Depth," which was widely used. R. Kenneth Strachan, general director of the Latin American Mission, wrote about the first experiment held in 1960.[63]

✠ It was a Monday afternoon in March, 1960. Hot winds were throwing up clouds of dust in the plaza of the little Nicaraguan town of Rivas. That night, evangelistic crusades were getting underway in six different cities of the republic. In spite of their small numbers, the Christian forces in Rivas, sparked by the fine leadership of some Nazarene missionaries, had courageously decided to launch their campaign with a parade through the main streets of the city—no light undertaking in Roman Catholic Latin America.

When we arrived that afternoon at the scheduled point of departure, there were only a few clusters of believers looking rather scared and subdued. Even I was feeling butterflies in my stomach. But little by little, groups from surrounding villages began coming in, carrying Nicaraguan flags, texts and slogans, and their church banners.

In a little while we started off, headed by a few cars, a small band on foot, some young flag-bearers on horseback, and followed by hundreds of believers, marching on foot with their flags and banners. We sang as we marched, past central Park and the Cathedral, by the Army Barracks, along the main streets of the city. Soldiers, police and citizens lined the sidewalks and looked on with amazement. The band in front was doing its best with "Onward Christian Soldiers," and those nearest were singing out the words in Spanish, "With the cross of Jesus, going on before."

Farther down the line, we were singing the theme chorus that had swept the country. "Nicaragua será para Cristo"—"Nicaragua Shall Belong to Christ." A block or so behind, others were singing something else, but all of us were singing, and it made an impressive sound never before heard in the streets of that city. I felt a thrill of pride to be walking beside those Nicaraguan Christians in their brave and dignified witness for Christ.

That night a great crowd was present in the plaza for the opening meeting of the campaign. What a joy to hear the Gospel hymns ring out under the leadership of Vern Van Hovel, from HCJB in Quito, Ecuador! And what a thrill to hear the simple, powerful preaching of Rubén Lores from New York City, as he held the crowd spellbound with the clear claims of the Gospel. In five other centers something similar was taking place, with more than a dozen other outstanding evangelists and Gospel singers, who had come from a number of neighboring countries to help us out.

My mind went back over the previous weeks of intensive preparation which had led up to this moment—to the untiring efforts of Juan and Elisabeth Isáis; to the enthusiastic cooperation of the local committee and especially of its president, Dr. Rodolfo Mejía, Vice-President of the National Bank of Nicaragua and an outstanding Baptist layman; to the tremendous job of training hundreds of Nicaraguans, carried out by George Sánchez, Sam Clark, and others; to the splendid campaigns of visitation sparked by John Thomas; to Bill Thompson's leadership on the Atlantic Coast; to Dorothy Andrews' help in the central office; and to all the other pastors and missionaries. I felt a sense of gratitude to them and to those of you in the homeland who with your prayers and gifts had made this possible.

I also thought of my father, Harry Strachan, who had pioneered campaigns in Rivas thirty-five years before—and I wondered whether he might be looking down on the scene that night, rejoicing with the angels in Heaven over souls that were being saved.

It was a happy experience. We were in the midst of an experiment that might result in a new strategy of evangelism for Latin America—a plan of action that would enlist the Latin American Christians themselves, working out of their local church centers, uniting their forces for all-out efforts aimed at completing the Great Commission in their own countries. We were wondering, as we carried out our evangelistic assignments in Nicaragua, whether this might not offer the key whereby the Church of Christ in these tremendous days of revolutionary opportunity might be able to meet the challenge of the exploding population without Christ and without hope in the world.

Others, too, were asking the same questions. This first experiment of Evangelism-in-Depth in Nicaragua was observed with penetrating interest from all sides. Christians throughout Latin America watched to see whether the plan might be worth trying in their own countries. Mission authorities in the United States, both of denominational and faith missions, followed it cautiously to see whether such cooperation on a national scale would help, rather than hurt their work.

Part III

The Churches and Latin American Liberation

1962–1985

"Christendom" was long gone, and even "neo-Christendom" was proving ephemeral and of limited effect. Both ways of being society's "mother and teacher" assumed that the hierarchy had the answers for human needs and needed simply to devise ways to apply them. Communication was from the informed elite down to the masses. Both the assumption and the procedure were soon to be questioned.

Over the years 1962–1985, the Catholic Church's understanding of its life and mission underwent a profound change. With the change came a renewal of worship and theology and an unprecedented participation by the laity in the church's life. Before 1962, the Latin American bishops had lived in virtual isolation from each other. It was the Second Vatican Council in Rome, 1962–1965, that gave them a corporate identity and injected new vigor into their regional council, the Latin American Episcopal Conference (CELAM). When the latter met in 1968 at Medellín, Colombia, to interpret Vatican II to their area of the world, it was a watershed event in Latin American church history. The long-standing poverty and injustices of the region had grown more acute and had impressed themselves upon the bishops. The social realities and the gospel message entrusted to them, said the bishops at Medellín, pointed them no longer in the way of elitism but toward identification with the poor and advocacy of their cause. The bishops committed themselves to a pastoral ministry that would be decentralized and in collegiality with priests and laity. The objective was the full liberation — physical, mental, political, economic, and spiritual — of the Latin American people. Such a resolve on the part of the bishops stirred hope and also opposition. It soon placed many priests, lay leaders, and religious brothers and sisters in conflict with the military regimes proliferating across the region, and many Catholics sealed their witness with their blood. Conflicts also arose within the church. Some influential bishops felt that Medellín had gone too far, and that the liberation theology which it encouraged distorted the faith. The opponents of Medellín gained control of CELAM, yet in its meeting in Puebla, Mexico, 1979, the liberationist currents seemed irrepressible.

Protestant experiences paralleled those of their Catholic neighbors. They too were caught up in an international ecumenical context of renewal, and they joined in region-wide consultative processes. Protestants of various denominations, many for the first time, discovered each other, learned the social realities of the region, and debated the church's role. Much Protestant rhetoric rejected "ecumenism"; nevertheless interchurch communication and cooperation multiplied. Protestants also experienced the relentless poverty of the region. In their analyses of causes and remedies they were divided, but the matters were being discussed and the possibility of there being social injustice and therefore systemic violence against the poor were increasingly recognized. Liberation theology was also being written by Protestants, and discussions of it divided them. Yet even the most conservative were finding it more and more difficult to avoid a wholistic mission to the world around them.

13 ✠ Catholics: A New Beginning

1962–1985

The year 1962 was the beginning of Vatican Council II in Rome, and for the 601 Latin American bishops it was a conversion experience. In previous councils, they had viewed themselves as an expatriate European church. At Vatican II, the prelates came to know each other and were encouraged to take seriously their own region and its social realities. When the bishops returned from the Council and sought to work out its implications in 1968 at Medellín, Colombia, they called attention to their region's "excessive inequalities ... willful oppression ... growing distortion of international commerce ... [and] injustice that can be called institutionalized violence, ..."[1] They called the church to "maintain ... independence in relation to the political establishment and specific regimes,"[2] to work for the "re-evangelization of the ... continent,"[3] and in the face of injustice and neo-colonialism, both local and international, to "defend the rights of the poor and oppressed, ... urging our governments and upper classes to eliminate everything which might destroy social peace: ...."[4]

Meanwhile, the various republics were experiencing military dictatorships, and economies were being managed for the benefit of powerful sectors of the population and foreign investors. Organizations working for reforms were often tagged as subversive or Communist and repressed in the name of "national security." In Brazil in the late 1960s, various clergy and religious had tried to defend the oppressed, and government forces used prison, torture, exile, and even assassinations to silence them. This prompted their bishops to a new unity and courage to lead the cause of human rights over the next decade. In other countries, the bishops were not as bold, but various mixtures of laity and priests and hierarchy were willing to join the struggle, and Commissions for Justice and Peace or Human Rights appeared in many dioceses.

Institutional violence and repression drove some leaders to despair of the political process and to join an armed revolt. An illustration was the prominent Camilo Torres Restrepo (1929–1966), a Colombian priest, educator, and political leader. A different response was that of Bishop Helder Câmara of Brazil, who called for a vigorous resistance without violence. As these positions were discussed across the region, and people sought the

"The Good Samaritan," Luke 10:25-37, by a peasant artist in Nicaragua, 1981.

church's role in unjust societies, the categories of Karl Marx (e.g., oppressor and oppressed) were used in social analysis and some form of socialism was proposed as an alternative to laissez-faire capitalism.

By the early 1970s, a Latin American theology was born. With the writings and leadership of Gustavo Gutiérrez as well as many others, the theology of liberation became a recognized discipline and widely influential. The role of the laity in the governing structures of the church was still virtually nonexistent in the 1960s, but at the local level a new phenomenon was emerging, and CELAM, the Latin American Conference of Bishops, endorsed it at Medellín. The new thing was called the "base ecclesial communities" (CEBs), or grass-roots congregations. By the 1970s, CEBs were spreading to many countries. Usually they were groups of fifteen to twenty rural peasants or urban poor, who gathered under lay leaders to read the Bible and to address problems related to their own survival and that of their neighbors. They began because other self-help groups had been repressed. Furthermore, they reflected the need for Christian community and the scarcity of priests.

When CELAM met in 1972 in Sucre, Bolivia, conservative bishops, unhappy with the directions of their session at Medellín and the rise of liberation theology, collected their forces and elected officers congenial to their sympathies. They planned for the Third General Conference of bishops (CELAM) set for Puebla, Mexico, in 1979, to neutralize the liberationist commitments by emphasizing the more spiritual tasks of the church. But Medellín's sympathies had become too pervasive. In the final Puebla documents the Medellín commitments emerged in the context of evangelization and spiritual renewal, and this gave the liberation themes an even firmer base. Nevertheless, CELAM's leadership remained in the hands of the traditionalists, and sociological analyses and political commitment were bound to receive less attention than the Church's authority, unity, and spiritual mission. A point of much interest was the role of the pope in CELAM's future directions. At mid-decade, his dialogue with the Brazilian bishops seemed to be substantial, and his support seemed to go to the traditionalists.

By the early 1980s, political democracy returned to some key countries, and in Central America guerrillas were struggling for liberation. In Nicaragua a popular revolution toppled the forty-three-year Somoza dynasty in July of 1979, but in Guatemala and El Salvador traditional oligarchies with much aid from the United States were able to hold power. The church was involved in all levels of these struggles, and in them numerous members, priests, and at least one bishop lost their lives. As the period ended, the future of the Catholic Church in Latin America could not be known, but its participation in the search for justice was vigorous. Bishops were divided, but the two decades following 1962 had brought a new beginning.

CATHOLIC AID – A CRITIQUE

"The influx of U.S. missioners coincided with the Alliance for Progress, . . . and CIA projects and looks like a baptism of these!"

> *In 1962, U.S. Catholics undertook an ambitious program of aid to the Latin American parishes, including a goal of sending 20,000 missionary priests. This effort coincided with President Kennedy's "Alliance for Progress," designed to ward off future social revolutions similar to the one in Cuba. The aid programs of the U.S. Catholics and the U.S. government intertwined in ways usually left unexamined. A provocative North American Catholic, Ivan Illich, directed for six years the training of hundreds of these missioners at his center in Cuernavaca, Mexico. In 1966, he wrote a provocative description and critique of the U.S. Catholic program. Excerpts are given below.[5]*

✠ Five years ago, U.S. Catholics undertook a peculiar alliance for the progress of the Latin American Church. By 1970, ten per cent of the more than 225,000 priests, brothers and sisters would volunteer to be shipped south of the border. In the meantime, the combined U.S. male and female "clergy" in South America has increased by only 1,622. Halfway is a good time to examine whether a program launched is still sailing on course and, more importantly, if its destination still seems worthwhile. Numerically, the program was certainly a flop. Should this be a source of disappointment or of relief? . . .

I will not focus on details. The above programs themselves continually study and revise minutiae. Rather, I dare to point out some fundamental facts and implications of the so-called papal plan – part of the many-faceted effort to keep Latin America within the ideologies of the West. Church policy makers in the United States must face up to the socio-political consequences involved in their well-intentioned missionary ventures. . . .

Men and money sent with missionary motivation carry a foreign Christian image, a foreign pastoral approach and a foreign political message. They also bear the mark of North American capitalism of the 1950s. Why not, for once, consider the shady side of charity: weigh the inevitable burdens foreign help imposes on the South American Church; taste the bitterness of the damage done by our sacrifices? If, for example, U.S. Catholics would simply turn from the dream of "ten percent," and do some honest thinking about the implications of their help, the awakened awareness of intrinsic fallacies could lead to sober, meaningful generosity.

But let me be more precise. The unquestionable joys of giving and the fruits of receiving should be treated as two distinctly separate chapters. I propose to delineate *only the negative* results that foreign money, men and ideas produce in the South American Church, in order that the future U.S. program may be tailored accordingly.

During the past five years, the cost of operating the Church in Latin America has multiplied many times. There is no precedent for a similar rate of increase in Church expenses on a continental scale. Today, one Catholic university, mission society or radio chain may cost more to operate than the whole country's Church a decade ago. Most of the funds for this kind of growth came from outside and flowed from two types of sources. The first is the Church itself, which raised its income in three ways:

1. Dollar by dollar, appealing to the generosity of the faithful, as was done in Germany and the Low Countries by Adveniat, Misereor and Oostpriesterhulp. These contributions reach more than $25 million a year.

2. Through lump sums, made by individual churchmen—such as Cardinal Cushing, the outstanding example; or by institutions—such as the NCWC, transferring $1 million from the Home missions to the Latin America Bureau.

3. By assigning priests, religious and laymen, all trained at considerable cost and often backed financially in their apostolic undertakings.

This kind of foreign generosity has enticed the Latin American Church into becoming a satellite to North Atlantic cultural phenomena and policy. Increased apostolic resources intensified the need for their continued flow and created islands of apostolic well-being, each day farther beyond the capacity of local support. The Latin American Church flowers anew by returning to what the Conquest stamped her: a colonial plant that blooms because of foreign cultivation. Instead of learning either how to get along with less money or close up shop, bishops are being trapped into needing more money now and bequeathing an institution impossible to run in the future. Education, the one type of investment that could give long-range returns, is conceived mostly as training for bureaucrats who will maintain the existing apparatus.

Recently, I saw an example of this in a large group of Latin American priests who had been sent to Europe for advanced degrees. In order to relate the Church to the world, nine-tenths of these men were studying teaching methods—catechetics, pastoral theology or canon law—and thereby not directly advancing their knowledge of either the Church or the world. Only a very few studied the Church in its history and sources, or the world as it is.

It is easy to come by big sums to build a new church in a jungle or a high school in a suburb, and then to staff the plants with new missioners. A patently irrelevant pastoral system is artificially and expensively sustained, while basic research for a new and vital one is considered an extravagant luxury. Scholarships for non-ecclesiastical humanist studies, seed money for imaginative pastoral experimentation, grants for documentation and research to make specific constructive criticism—all run the frightening risk of threatening our temporal structures, clerical plants and "good business" methods.

Even more surprising than churchly generosity for churchly concern is a second source of money. A decade ago, the Church was like an impoverished *grande dame* trying to keep up an imperial tradition of almsgiving from her reduced income. In the more than a century since Spain lost Latin America, the Church has steadily lost government grants, patron's gifts and, finally, the revenue from its former lands. According to the colonial concept of charity, the Church lost its power to help the poor. It came to be considered a historical relic, inevitably the ally of conservative politicians.

By 1966, almost the contrary seems true—at least, at first sight. The Church has become an agent trusted to run programs aimed at social change. It is committed enough to produce some results. But when it is threatened by real change, it withdraws rather than permit social awareness to spread like wildfire. The smothering of the Brazilian radio schools by a high Church authority is a good example.

Thus Church discipline assures the donor that his money does twice the job in the hands of a priest. It will not evaporate, nor will it be accepted for what it is: publicity for private enterprise and indoctrination to a way of life that the rich have chosen as suitable for the poor. The receiver inevitably gets the message: the "padre" stands on the side of W. R. Grace and Co., Esso, the Alliance for Progress, democratic government, the AFL-CIO and whatever is holy in the Western pantheon.

Opinion is divided, of course, on whether the Church went heavily into social projects because it could thus obtain funds "for the poor," or whether it went after the funds because it could thus contain Castroism and assure its institutional respectability. By becoming an "official" agency of one kind of progress, the Church ceases to speak for the underdog who is outside all agencies but who is in an ever-growing majority. By accepting the power to help, the Church necessarily must denounce a Camilo Torres, who symbolizes the power of renunciation. Money thus builds the Church a "pastoral" structure beyond its means and makes it a political power....

I know that there is no foreign priest or nun so shoddy in his work that through his stay in Latin America he has not enriched some life, and that there is no missioner so incompetent that through him Latin America has not made some small contribution to Europe and North America. But neither our admiration for conspicuous generosity, nor our fear of making bitter enemies out of lukewarm friends, must stop us from facing the facts. Missioners sent to Latin America can make 1) an alien Church more foreign, 2) an over-staffed Church priest-ridden and 3) bishops into abject beggars....

Massive, indiscriminate importation of clergy helps the ecclesiastical bureaucracy survive in its own colony, which every day becomes more foreign and comfortable. This immigration helps to transform the old-style hacienda of God (on which the people were only squatters) into the Lord's supermarket, with catechisms, liturgy and other means of grace heavily in stock. It makes contented consumers out of vegetating peasants, demanding clients out of former devotees.

SEMINARIAN AS POLITICAL PRISONER

"Now there are fifty of us in this cell, . . ."

In November of 1969 a Dominican seminarian, Carlos Alberto Libanio Christo, twenty-five-year-old son of a well-to-do family in Brazil, was arrested and charged with giving aid to "subversives" sought by the police. He spent several years in prison, and while there wrote graphic letters to his family and friends. The letters remind one of those written three decades earlier by Dietrich Bonhoeffer.[6]

To His Parents

✠ Tiradentes Prison
São Paulo
December 7, 1969

. . . The only news here is my new prison life. Since I only arrived here a week ago, everything is still new to me. It's likely that I will be in Tiradentes Prison for some time. There are about two hundred of us political prisoners here, young people of both sexes. Our cell is big, roomy, and airy. We have two bathrooms with showers, a washtub, and a kitchen with stoves. There are thirty-two people in our cell, almost all of them young. The few older men have adapted perfectly to their new style of life. We have two injured people. One was beaten up by the police when they seized him; the other threw himself out of a fourth-floor apartment window. Both are convalescing now. The group is divided into teams, which take daily turns at housekeeping. Yesterday it was my team's turn. We got up early, swept the cell, and made coffee (with milk and bread and butter). Some members of our team helped bathe the injured, while others did the cooking. I was a cook and by some miracle did not do too badly. . . .

To a Religious Community

February 22, 1970

. . . It is a rainy and gloomy Sunday here. Now there are fifty of us in this cell, and we are trying to make the best of it. Many are sleeping on mattresses on the ground because there is no room for more beds. The silence reflects the darkness of this gray day. It is not the silence of tranquility or inner peace; it is a kind of suffocation. . . .

To His Brother, Luiz Fernando

March 3, 1970

. . . Tito is back with us. He stays in bed or drags himself around, limping. He is recuperating from the terrible suffering he endured. He was tortured for three days: parrot-perch, electric shock, whippings, beatings. They even reached new heights of sadism, putting an electrode in his mouth. It was the intention of the army to interrogate all the Dominicans once again, because they felt our interrogators at DOPS [political police] had been in too much of a hurry. To escape the suffering they were inflicting on him and to make a public protest against such interrogations of political prisoners, Tito finally resolved to commit suicide. He had a razor blade, and he slashed the veins and arteries on the inside of his left elbow. He lost a lot of blood.

We have done all we can to get the church to issue a protest. It must take a stand on the grave situation in Brazil before it is too late. But the bishops are used to being on the defensive, and they prefer omission to risk. Maybe someone will have to die before the church will react . . . .

To His Cousin Maria

December 31, 1970

. . . There are three Dominicans left in prison with me: Fernando, Ivo, and Tito. Tito is included in the list of prisoners demanded in exchange for the Swiss ambassador, but the negotiations have bogged down. Roberto was freed on October 18 after he had attempted to commit suicide by slitting both wrists, It was not an act of weakness but the protest of a man who had been in prison for almost a year without any charge whatever having been lodged against him. Maurizio, who has left the order (he decided to leave even before his arrest), was freed in November. Our Christmas gift was the release of Giorgio, an Italian, on December 24. There had been no charge against him either. So the four of us are left, waiting for a trial whose date has not yet been set. We are accused of a "crime," namely, that we hid people wanted as subversives by the police and helped them to flee the country. This is an offense according to Brazilian law, but not according to church tradition. Church precedent for aiding fugitives dates from the time when Mary, Joseph, and the child Jesus fled into Egypt to escape Herod's persecution — as I told the Joint Military Council. . . .

We spend our time in prison reading, doing calisthenics, and studying theology. We are not idle. Every evening we get together for prayer. We recite the Psalms, chant hymns, and receive the body of our Lord. We have not received permission to celebrate Mass, but the chaplain of the military police comes with consecrated hosts every so often.

For me all this represents a revival of the life lived by the church during the first three centuries of its existence. It would be incredible if the church were not present somehow in prisons under a regime that oppresses human beings. Here we are in fellowship with "the wretched of the earth." We are in communion with those who have been invited to the Lord's banquet. All this is grace, as is any suffering endured in a Christian spirit.

I can assure you that prison has effected a radical transformation—a profound conversion—in us. Behind these bars many things lose the value they once had, and new discoveries turn us into new people. It is good for the church to go through prison. There it rediscovers the way that Christ had pointed out, the way of poverty and persecution. . . .

A CHRISTIAN STUDENT JOINS THE GUERRILLAS

"This is the only path that remains."

While he was a medical student at the university in La Paz, Bolivia, Nestor Paz volunteered time to improve conditions for the poor majority in the city. When he realized that the military government allowed no reforms, he joined other students in a guerrilla movement, the Teoponte Campaign, to overthrow the dictatorship. Just before his twenty-fifth birthday, eighty-seven days after joining the guerrillas, he died of starvation. His letters to his family became a diary of his thoughts and experiences. Here we have his message on leaving to join the revolt, July 17, 1970.[7]

✠ "Every sincere revolutionary must realize that armed struggle is the only path that remains" (Camilo Torres, January 7, 1966).

Following the glorious path taken by our own heroes, the guerrillas of the Peruvian highlands, and by the continental heroes, Bolívar and Sucre, and the heroic commitment of Ernesto Guevara, the Peredo brothers, Darío, and many others who lead the march of the people's liberation, we take our place in the long guerrilla file, rifle in hand, to combat the symbol and instrument of oppression—the "gorilla" army.

As long as blood flows in our veins we will make heard the cutting cry of the exploited. Our lives do not matter if we can make our Latin America, *la patria grande*, a free territory of free people who are masters of their own destiny.

I realize that my decision and that of my companions will bring upon us a deluge of accusations, from the paternalistic "poor misguided fellow," to the open charge of "demagogic criminal." But Yahweh our God, the Christ of the Gospels, has announced the "good news of the liberation of man," for which he himself acted. We cannot sit and spend long hours reading the Gospel with cardinals, bishops, and pastors, all of whom are doing fine right where they are, while the flock wanders about in hunger and solitude.

Doing this is called "non-violence," "peace," "Gospel." These persons, sadly, are today's Pharisees.

People no longer listen to the "Good News." Man is always betrayed by his "brother."

"Peace" is not something one finds by chance; it is the result of equality among people, as Isaiah says in his chapter 58. Peace is the result of love among people, the result of an end to exploitation.

"Peace" is not attained by dressing up in silk and living in a medieval palace, or by robbing the people in order to have a millionaire's salary, or by playing on the people's religious superstition in order to live at their expense.

"Greater love than this no man has than to lay down his life for his friends." This is the commandment which sums up the "Law."

For this reason we have taken up arms: to defend the unlettered and undernourished majority from the exploitation of a minority and to win back dignity for a dehumanized people.

We know that violence is painful because we feel in our own flesh the violent repression of the established disorder. But we are determined to liberate man because we consider *him a brother*. We are the people in arms. This is the only path that remains. Man comes before the "Sabbath," not vice versa.

They say violence is not evangelical; let them remember Yahweh slaying the first-born of the Egyptians to free his people from exploitation.

They say that they believe in "non-violence." Then let them stand clearly with the people. If they do, the rich and the "gorillas" will both demand their lives, just as they demanded Christ's. Let them take courage and try it; let us see if they are consistent enough to face a Good Friday. But all that is demagoguery, isn't it, you canons, generals, *cursillistas* [laity who do weekend training retreats], priests of the established disorder, you priests of the peace enforced by violence, of the massacre of San Juan, of the complicity of silence, of the 200-peso salaries, of the widespread tuberculosis, and of pie in the sky when you die. The Gospel is not mechanical moralism. It is a shell hiding a "life" which must be discovered if we are not to fall into pharisaism. The Gospel is "Jesus among us."

We have chosen this path because it is the only path left open to us, painful though it may be.

Fortunately, there are some, and their numbers are growing, who recognize the authenticity of our position and who either help us or have joined our ranks. We need only consider what the right-wing "gorilla" government of Brazil does to a committed Church: Father Pereira Neto was assassinated in a most cruel and inhuman manner. Or recall Father Ildefonso, a Tupamaro, assassinated in Uruguay. Or Father Camilo Torres, silenced by the government and the servile church. But Camilo Torres ratified with his blood what he had said about Christianity:

In Catholicism the main thing is love for one's fellow men: "... He who loves his fellow man has fulfilled the Law." For this love to be genuine, it must seek to be effective. If works of beneficence, alms-giving, the few tuition-free schools, the few housing projects — everything which is known as "charity" — do not succeed in feeding the majority of the hungry, in clothing the majority of the naked, or in teaching the majority of the ignorant, then we must seek effective means to achieve the well-being of this majority.... This is why the revolution is not only permissible but obligatory for those Christians who see it as the only effective and far-reaching way to make love for all people a reality.

I believe that the struggle for liberation is rooted in the prophetic line of Salvation History.

Enough of the languid faces of the over-pious! The whip of justice, so often betrayed by elegant gentlemen, will fall on the exploiter, that false Christian who forgets that the force of his Lord ought to drive him to liberate his neighbor from sin, that is to say, from every lack of love.

We believe in a "New Man," made free by the blood and resurrection of Jesus. We believe in a New Earth, where love will be the fundamental law. This will come about, however, only by breaking the old patterns based on selfishness. We don't want patches. New cloth can't be used to mend old garments, nor can new wine be put into old wineskins. Conversion implies first an inner violence which is then followed by violence against the exploiter. May both men and the Lord together judge the rightness of our decision. At least no one can imply that we look for profit or comfort. These are not what we find in the struggle; they are what we leave behind.

SQUATTERS AND A BISHOP

"I have learned a lot about politicians and the church."

In the state of Mato Grosso, in southwest Brazil, developers were squeezing peasants off the land. To remedy this, a Spanish-born bishop, Pedro Casaldáliga, and his priests struggled for land reform and protection for the squatters. The following are excerpts from the bishop's diary in 1972.[8]

✠ 3/19/72: Feast of St. Joseph. Brasilia. The "other" Brasilia of rectangular buildings, waiting-rooms, audiences, lies. I have been here two weeks.

On the evening of the 3rd, provoked by a new attempt at invasion and destruction, a group of *posseiros* [squatters] defended the clinic at Santa Terezinha — and their own freedom — with shots. Eight of the "jagunços" (bullies) from Codeara were wounded. And for fifteen days there has been a running exchange of "you-tell-me's-and-I'll-tell-you's" in the press, in various ministries and in trips. The repression on the part of those in power (economic, political, police, and military power) has been downright cynical. Five innocent men from Santa Terezinha have been imprisoned in Cuiabá, and thirty or forty *posseiros* have slipped into the forests. . . .

Fifteen days of real Lent, spent between anger and prayer, in the Passion of the People, beneath the hard and shining hope of Jesus, the liberator.

I have learned a lot about politics and the church.

The present government of Brazil is a Nazi terrorist scheme. The economic powers impose the law and put a muzzle on justice.

3/21: Still in Brasilia! Last night the heads of the Council of Bishops arrived. They have come here mainly on account of the business at Santa Terezinha. They are concerned and they are inclined to think that, as Dom Aloisio sadly put it, this may drag on forever, within the means at our disposal.

Friday I had an outspoken interview with Buzaid. His nauseating cynicism upset me so, that I refused the coffee he offered me, just as I refused to accept any more of his delays and mendacious mediations. Sunday he phoned the governor of Cuiabá, José Fragelli. The latter said, quite aggressively: "I will not release my grip." He added that he considered the *posseiros* of Santa Terezinha "as common criminals," and promised that "if Padre Jentel ever shows up here (in Cuiabá, the state capital of Mato Grosso), I will issue an order for his arrest, because he is the mastermind behind this crime." My response to this was that I myself, and not Padre Francisco, was the "mastermind," and that I assumed and still assume full responsibility for what happened at Santa Terezinha, both as regards the mission and as regards the *posseiros*. . . .

4/6: I spent some days in Santa Terezinha. And I visited the *posseiros* hidden in the *mata*. And, almost symbolically, I harvested rice. . . .

4/8: We have to make a decision about the five in jail in Cuiabá and about the *posseiros* hidden in the forest. This morning I awoke very early, with a start, at the thought of the situation of these men of our people. Freedom costs dearly! As I read in some review the other day: "The more the forces of money and oligarchy are shaken, the more clearly one perceives their overpowering talent for enslavement."

4/14: I've been in Santa Terezinha for a week, chopping rice, walking through roads, *mata*, and rice paddies. We have met with the *posseiros* in hiding and with their families. Last night and early this morning, I said Mass in Tapirapé. After several days of not being able to say Mass, I was hungry for eucharist.

Altair (a lay team-member who worked in Porto Alegre, almost at the

headwaters of the Tapirapé River, and also in Santa Terezinha) is imprisoned in the miserable little hole of the local jail. He's been there seven
days, now. . . . The Codeara Company persists in its campaign of nuisances:
they've closed both exits from the town. We have had no details from
Brasilia. Father Francisco is still there. Nothing will come of it all anyway,
unless it comes from the unity and hardheadedness of the people. There
is no force to equal the desperate hope of the poor!

The "Church of the *Mata*" has been born. God keep it in the hollow of
his hand!

4/17: Yesterday was *"domingo do doce"* (sweets Sunday), and we had ket-
tlesfull of papaya and calabash candy with the women and children of the
posseiros. Then Mass at the "Antonio Gross." Mass again at the *roca grande*
(the great clearing), with the men in hiding. The altar was a burnt tree-
stump, with a shotgun leaning against it, draped in a *posseiro's surroncico.*
Evening was falling, and the gospel told the story of the two men walking
along the road to Emmaus. The persecuted men attending the Mass—
rather hungry, rather anxious, suffering greatly—listened to the reading,
enthralled by it.

Sister Beatrice gave them a tetanus vaccination. Then, as we began to
relax, we all laughed a little.

Twilight cast a thick, amber light on the premonitory clouds that were
piling up behind the tall, dense forest.

Today, Psalm 84 tells us "Happy are they whose strength you are! Their
hearts are set upon pilgrimage. When they cross the parched valley, they
shall turn it into a spring." Then James tells us: "Speak and act as men
destined to be judged under the law of liberty."

LAITY AND PARISH RENEWAL

". . . could we not also give Communion . . . baptize and marry as well?"

*Amid large population growth, myriad community problems, and a short-
age of priests, the pressures for pastoral care mounted and drove some
pastors to despair. Father Alfredo Kunz, on the central coast of Brazil,
described the way some innovative parish members in 1974 brought new
hope to their padre.*[9]

✠ Our friends and those who are indifferent all agree about this, that
"there are not enough priests." In the diocese of Crateús half the priests
have left the ministry. Today we have only seven priests for a population
of 350,000 baptized. There are not enough priests for three reasons: death,

lack of vocation among the young people, and the disillusionment of priests who in all conscience find they cannot continue.

Often it is the demands of the Christian people which prevent the priest from remaining in the priesthood. On 9 September 1974 I baptized twenty-three children in the town of Joaquim, Moreira. After the baptism a woman asked me to celebrate mass on her farm, if possible on the 25th of that month, her wedding anniversary. Only one family lives there. I answered her: "The parish has forty-five chapels and communities that I must serve, as well as the neighbouring parish of Parambu where two sisters, Siebra and Alice, are responsible for the pastoral plan. Fifteen of these communities are begging insistently for my presence. Last year we baptized 2554 children and performed 280 weddings. Last week I walked ten leagues to serve the people of St. Lucia. Obviously I cannot celebrate mass in one home for just one family."

But she would not accept my answer and insisted by saying: "How much money do you want for celebrating mass in my home?" This made me very sad. The people are always after mass, baptism and weddings, forgetting that the first job of the priest is to witness by his life and word the Gospel of Christ, and to be a prophet. And the people want the priests to be only religious employees of the municipality. No priest can stand this situation for very long. We are also people.

If the priest stops being a man of God in order to become an employee, a giver of sacraments, he loses his reason for existing. It is very difficult to evangelize if one has to perform more than 100 baptisms and up to thirty-six weddings in one day. I became sad: how not to be crushed by all this? God helped me to find a solution by placing in my path the animators of the region. They said to me:

"We are celebrating the Word every Sunday, could we not also give Communion? We are preparing the three preparatory meetings for baptisms and weddings; could we not baptize and marry as well? All this will not impede us from continuing to aid the seed bank, the community vegetable garden and the little pharmacy, supporting the hopes of the people. But what we would like from the priest is the following: let us invite the animators of Marrecas, Missão and Vila to meet on the farm of this woman one or two days, to experience prayer, Bible study, the silence of the desert, a meeting with God and the brethren. We need you to help us discover the will of God in the events of our life, in order to make the connection between life and the Gospel. . . ."

This proposal was good news to me. To live every day more intensely a life of prayer and contemplation, to experience God to help sustain the faith and hope of the animators, to read and study in order to remain up to date, to be available to help my brother discover the marvels of God in his life. I could do this here in Tauá for the rest of my life! . . .

And each day will be a reason for me to praise God who called me to be a priest. To Him glory and praise forever. "Lord, grant me the grace to love my priesthood more every day, and through it to help my fellow priests scattered all over the world to be happy in their vocation."

From now on I shall make an effort to withdraw from all types of leadership in the parish of Tauá, letting the Christians of each community themselves stimulate religious life, human promotion, community projects and the administration of the church and chapel.

A BASE ECCLESIAL COMMUNITY

"... some people have lots of extra shirts, and others don't have any."

A remarkable phenomenon was the emergence of the base ecclesial communities (CEBs), or grass-roots Christian communities. These groups of peasants or urban slum-dwellers gathered around the Bible to read and discuss and to help each other amid the harsh living conditions. In the island village of Solentiname, in southern Nicaragua during the dictatorship of Anastasio Somoza, one such group formed. The local priest, Ernesto Cardenal, encouraged them and often attended their meetings. He taped and transcribed some of their Bible studies. Below is part of their discussion of a message of John the Baptist in Luke 3:1–20.[10]

✠   *Then the people asked him:*
          "What shall we do then?"
          He answered them:
          "The man that has two shirts
          must give one to the man that has no shirt;
          and the man that has food must share it
          with the man that has no food."

LAUREANO: "If he said that to them, those guys must have been rich. Because if they'd been poor there was no reason to tell them to give to others."

FELIPE: "I think he was saying that to the poor, too, creating that conscience in them, not to let their poor comrade starve to death. What I do believe is that this basic doctrine is the doctrine of socialism. John is telling us that this is the society that we have to create. That nobody ought to have one shirt more than his comrade.... We're going to be all equal. That's what we have to seek: socialism, because that way we'd all be living a just life, like God wants."

MANOLO: "If somebody who has two shirts has to give one away, there's even more reason for somebody who has several houses or estates or a million *pesos*. . . ."

WILLIAM: "I don't think this should be understood so literally—that if I have two shirts I have to give one away. . . . That's all right, but we're not going to stop there, just looking for somebody who doesn't have a shirt. What this means, it seems to me, is that we have to change the system where some people have lots of extra shirts and others don't have any. This is leveling the roads, as I said before."

I [Ernesto Cárdenal] said that this applies mainly to the rich, as Laureano said, who do not only have many shirts but also houses, lands, factories, mines, railroads. But it can also be applied to the poor, as Felipe says, for example when one has to share his lunch with a friend. . . .

ALEJANDRO: "It's easy to share your meal with a friend. It's harder to share with people you don't know, with the rest of society. . . ."

FÉLIX: "I think this applies more to the *campesino* [peasant] than to the rich, because the rich help one another, as long as they all have money. A rich person comes across another rich person and sees that he's naked and runs to give him a shirt and he doesn't have to be asked. Because it's among themselves, the one who has money helps out those who have money. But with us poor people it's different. If one of us has some little thing that God didn't give somebody else, he doesn't share it. And that's why that comparison of the two shirts is for us poor *campesinos*. And I think that us poor people are more selfish than the rich. We said that the reading of the Gospel is aimed more at the rich than at the poor, but it's not true. It's aimed almost more at us. The selfishness of the rich is that they don't look twice at the poor person because he doesn't have any money. . . ."

OLIVIA interrupts: "And how could you be any more selfish than that?"

FÉLIX: "Well, yes. But then if I'm poor I should also seek out my poor comrade. I meant that us poor are often more selfish than the rich. Among themselves they're good about money. Their selfishness is toward the poor."

WILLIAM: "But they murder each other. In business they all try to ruin the other guy."

FÉLIX: "The truth is that the nice thing would be if we were all equal. But John's word was not accepted in olden times and it's not accepted among us either."

JULIO MAIRENA: "What John says can apply to us, too, because we can all make a contribution to the struggle to take away from the guy that has a lot and so level ourselves off."

NATALIA: "There are times when we don't trust each other. If I don't have something—a dress, a meal—maybe I'll be embarrassed to tell anyone. But if you have trust then anybody can help you. Because if they're on close terms with me and they say to me, 'Look, Doña Natalia, ...' I tell them, 'Go ahead and take it....' But if they don't have that trust then there's no way I can know they need a little salt, a little sugar. But if they come to me and I have a little, I share it."

FÉLIX: "Lack of trust is because we don't have love. If I see a fellow full of love, I trust him enough to ask him a favor, to say to him, 'Look brother, I need this.' "

An elegant lady was with us who had come from the city, and she said: "Has it occurred to you that maybe some people have more than others because they've worked harder, and they've earned it through their own efforts? You know there are people that don't work and still want you to give them things."

JULIO MAIRENA: "We work all day long and we kill ourselves working with our machetes, and the rich are the ones who don't work."

TOMÁS: "You have to be careful, because if I have two shirts and I see that the other guy is a bum and won't work, well I'm not going to give him one of my shirts. But in this community we all work. Because if I don't want to work, because I'm drinking a lot, the other guy notices it and he doesn't give me anything and nobody else does either. Once in a while we've had a loafer, but they go away. It used to happen more. It's been getting better recently."

FÉLIX: "If somebody didn't work here he'd have starved to death by now. Even if you work hard you still have a lot of troubles. How about if you didn't work ...."

WOMAN DOCTOR AND CHILEAN POLICE

"Look after her, girls, she's had a hell of a time."

A thirty-four-year-old Australian Catholic woman, Sheila Cassidy, studied medicine at the University of Oxford, and later went to Chile, where she practiced plastic surgery in a Santiago public hospital. She was there during the right-wing coup of General Pinochet in 1973, and during the repression that followed. Friendship with some North American nuns who were working in the city slum stimulated her nominal faith and also led her to volunteer some hours to the Catholic mission for medical assistance in a poor district. When a wounded member of the resistance, Nelson Gutiérrez, was granted temporary sanctuary by some of the American nuns, Cassidy was called on to treat his wound. Later the political police, DINA, arrested her, accused her of revolutionary activity, and with torture tried to extract information and a confession. She spent most of October– December of 1975 in Tres Álamos prison. The following are excerpts from her account of the experience.[11]

✠ When we returned to the Casa Grimaldi I was led to an office where I was interrogated by men who judging by their manner of speaking I took to be senior officials. The fact of my earlier lies had obviously stung them for from now on they repeatedly called me *'la gringa mentirosa'* – 'the lying gringa.' I was made to tell again in detail the story of how I had been asked to treat Gutierrez and where I had attended him. They had obviously expected to find Nelson in the house where I had treated him but when I told them that he had been given asylum in the Nunciatura they were enraged. I heard one of them suggest that the Nuncio's house be raided but the other told him that there were orders from above to the contrary.

They were anxious to know the whereabouts of the baby [of Nelson and Mariella Gutierrez, in the care of an unknown peasant woman] but mercifully believed me when I said I didn't know. While I was there they spoke on the telephone to Helen's house and I was momentarily filled with terror when he said to me, 'the nuns don't know anything about Gutierrez.' Desperately I said, 'They are lying,' but he said simply, 'But a nun would not lie, *doctora*.'

In retrospect it is almost funny because so many people had been involved that it was impossible for the DINA to decide whom to arrest. The North American missionary nuns in Santiago must number over forty and though they belong to different congregations they are all friends and often visit each other's houses and, because of the difficulty of transport, spend the night there. They are nearly all in their early or middle thirties and many have short fair hair, wear jeans and anoraks and have names like Jean or Joan or Jane or Janet or Jo. Even had they all spoken the truth it would have been difficult to unravel the tale and explain why one nun who was a Holy Child nun had been spending a week with some friends of the Notre Dame community but was no longer in the same house because she had gone to spend the night with a friend who was a Sister of Mercy in the house of a Maryknoll sister because the Maryknollers were out of Santiago for the weekend at a conference being held in a retreat house run by the Society of the Sacred Heart! It is small wonder that one officer cried out in disgust, 'Nuns, priests, bishops, it's all too much!'

When my interrogators discovered that Gutierrez and his lady had eluded them they turned their attention to Andres Pascal Allende and Mary Ann. They could not believe that I did not know where they were for they had convinced themselves that I was working with the MIR [an outlawed party in revolution against Pinochet's rule]. I told them repeatedly that I had treated Nelson Gutierrez because he was badly injured and that it was not within my code of ethics to refuse to treat someone for ideological reasons. They were floored. They sat one side of a table and I stood blindfolded before them while they shouted at me that I worked with the MIR and I repeated again and again that Nelson was my patient, neither more nor less. Eventually, finding that the trail which had at first seemed so promising was now cold, they returned me to the torture squad.

For the third time I was stripped and bound to the bed [uncovered mattress springs, electrified]. I was completely desperate. They were convinced that I knew the whereabouts of the MIR leader and I had no idea. I don't know if they increased the strength of the current or if the hours of torture had lowered my resistance, but the pain seemed each time more terrible. My interrogators, too, were sexually excited and the fear of being raped was ever present for I knew that this was quite common. As it happened, I was lucky, because although a Chilean church worker (an ex-nun) was raped in this same place just a week later, I escaped.

Determined to break what they thought was my lying, they interrogated me about the events of that day. Each event was explored and I was questioned about all the people I had mentioned. Eventually they came to the encounter with Margaret and when I hesitated as to the subject matter of our conversation they realized that I had something to hide. Now there was no stopping them and piece by piece they dragged out of me the last information that I had: that a certain priest had been going to attempt to get Andres Pascal and Mary Ann into asylum the previous night.

When they found that this involved yet another church group in a completely different area of Santiago their exasperation and disbelief reached new heights; but at seven or eight o'clock in the morning they went off to look for the priest as he celebrated his first mass of the Sunday.

While one group went off to search I was again taken before the senior officers. They shouted and reasoned with me alternately. They offered to take me to the British embassy if only I would cooperate. They showed me photographs taken at church functions to see if I could point out the priests I knew. They made me listen to a recording of a telephone conversation in English to see if I could identify the voice. Perhaps the most unnerving was the man who spoke kindly and with an educated voice and said, 'Doctor, you are a sensible woman. You have seen what three sessions on the *parrilla* [grill] are like. If you do not tell us what we want we will go on, and on, ten, twelve, thirteen times, and you must see that you will get weaker and weaker and that you will tell us in the end.'

Again and again they returned to the question, 'Why did you treat Gutierrez?' and again I repeated, 'He was sick. I am a doctor.' Exasperated, one of them said, 'But if I had a wounded leg you wouldn't treat me,' to which I replied, 'Of course I would.' There was a long silence and then he said slowly, 'I do believe you would.'

I don't know how long I spent being questioned by these men; not more than half an hour, I think, because after a while one of them insisted that I be returned to the *parrilla*. Twice more during the next couple of hours I was stripped and tied to the bed but it must have been at the time they were looking for the priest because though I spent what seemed like hours cold and afraid on the bunk they did not give me any more shocks.

I think it was during this time of waiting that I was conscious of praying. I remember little except that I prayed for strength to withstand the pain and for courage to die with dignity if that was to be my fate. Most of all I remember a curious feeling of sharing in Christ's passion. Sick and numb with pain and fear, and spread-eagled so vulnerably on the bunk, it came to me that this was perhaps a little how it had been for him one Friday so many years before.

When it was quite light they untied me once again and I was led stumbling across the courtyard. As we left they joked that their friend was going to sleep with me and, bruised and bleeding, it seemed too much to bear. I heard a door being unlocked and he pushed me gently on to a bed and covered me with a blanket. It was only then that I realized that they had been joking and that we were not alone, for he said, 'Look after her, girls, she's had a hell of a time.' The door closed and a key turned in the lock and for the first time in twelve hours I found myself among friends.

MURDER OF FR. JOÃO BOSCO

"We reached the police station . . . where two aggressive soldiers were waiting for us."

The treatment of the Indians and landless peasants in Brazil's southeastern state of Mato Grosso was often brutal. The bishop of São Félix, Pedro Casaldáliga, described what happened when he and a local priest sought to intercede for two poor women in October of 1976.[12]

✠ Sao Félix, Mato Grosso
October 19, 1976

Dear Brethren

To all of you, in this one letter, I send a deeply affectionate embrace in the Lord Jesus—in his Passion—because once again the Paschal suffering is definitely with us.

On October 11th, at seven p.m., Fr Joao Bosco Penido Burnier, a Brazilian Jesuit priest, was mortally wounded at the local police station. His aggressor was a soldier of the Military Police of the State of Mato Grosso. Shot in the head, the priest died the following day in Goiania.

The repercussion has been widespread and profound. Father Joao Bosco was a missionary among the Indians in the neighbouring Prelature of Diamantino, on the other side of Xingu. Diamantino, Guirantinga and Sao Félix made up our regional unit of the Mission Indian Council (CIMI). Since Fr Joao Bosco was a regional coordinator, we invited him to attend our annual Indian Meeting held in Santa Terezinha, October 4th to 6th.

On October 11th, in Ribeirao Bonito, we were taking part in the procession on the river bank where he blessed the baptismal water for the baptisms on the following day.

A little later a boy brought me the message that two women who were prisoners in the police station were being tortured. A police contingent had come from Barra on account of the death of Corporal Félix, well-known in the region for his brutality and even murders. The two women were the sister and the daughter-in-law of Jovino, who killed Corporal Félix, practically out of self-defense. . . . With the arrival of the police, terror has again spread in Ribeirao, Cascalheira and the *sertao* (interior part of the country). The police beat, arrest and torture the people. . . . The boy said that the women could be heard from the street crying, "Don't hit me!"

I felt obligated to go to the police station to intercede on behalf of the poor women. The boy wanted to go with me, but I would not let him. He was very young, and afterwards he would be a target of the police. Fr Joao Bosco overheard our conversation and insisted on going with me.

We reached the police station yard, enclosed with wire, where two aggressive soldiers were waiting for us. They insulted us when we tried to carry on a calm dialogue. The priest said he would report their arbitrary action to their police superiors when he passed through Cuiaba. One of the soldiers, Ezy Ramalho Feitosa, then slapped him in the face, hit him with his revolver and fired the fatal shot.

Dr. Luis y Bia attended the priest in our small mobile health unit. The doctor, the priest and I, escorted by friends in another car, travelled the road to Xinga by night to find an hacienda which we knew had an air taxi. The next day, before daybreak, we flew to Goiania and took the priest to the Neurological institute. It was all of no use, as Luis y Bia had already concluded. It had been a soft-nosed bullet and had entered the brain.

The impressive thing is that Fr Joao Bosco had been able to talk for more than two hours to those of us who accompanied him. It was a truly Christian death. He repeatedly said that he was offering his life for the Indians and for the people. He called on Jesus. He remembered the CIMI. Repeating the *consummatum* of the Lord, he said to me, "Dom Pedro, we have finished our task."

He died for justice and charity. In the Amazon region. In a particularly critical hour or, if you wish, a time of martyrdom.

We buried Fr Joao Bosco in Diamantino, under the Mato Grosso sun and under the songs of victory of the people. The reporters were impressed. One of them wept.

What more? Pray that we may be faithful, that the Spirit preserve among us the gift of joy, that the Church be a witness until the end.

Do not be dismayed; help "our people" not to be dismayed. The Lord is the Resurrection and the Life, and the whole Church accompanies us in fellowship. This death and the threats are a testimony to others "outside," who are also struggling for the formation of the new man. It is not a sad hour. It is a beautiful hour of the gospel.

I embrace you all in Christ with the most fraternal communion.

Pedro Casaldáliga

CHALLENGE OF WOMEN'S LIBERATION

"From the day she is born, the female is regarded as inferior."

The low status and difficult role expected of women in El Salvador is described by Ana Audilia Moreira de Campos. She was director of the Guadalupe Center, which was established and run by Catholic nuns, in San Miguel in the eastern section of the country, in 1979, as she wrote the lines below. After working six years, she had helped to train 895 rural women "catechists, volunteer workers who are dedicated to the Christian faith."[13]

✠ Life is especially difficult for our rural women. Living conditions are extremely harsh. Health and nutrition are only as good as the quality of the water, food, and sanitary facilities, all of which range from poor to non-existent. All the good land for farming is owned and operated by a small oligarchy that is politically committed to keeping things just as they are. With so little of the land available to the small farmer, the rural people are dependent on the mercy of the landed few. Because of this, men who earn little or no income have almost nothing to be proud of except their virility. They have few ways to relieve their frustrations, so women often bear the brunt of their discontents.

There is absolutely no respect for the human dignity of women. It is common for their husbands and fathers to beat, kick and humiliate them in the most vulgar ways. They act ashamed to be seen in public with their wives, sisters or mothers, as if it would make them seem less manly among their friends. Much of the Salvadoran man's free time is spent competing with his cronies for the attentions of casual girlfriends to prove their masculinity. The tragic results are unwanted, illegitimate children.

The majority of men in our rural communities refer to women as "idiots," "pigs," "worthless," "disobedient," "deceitful," "disloyal," "lazy," "stupid," and "daughters of whores." A man most often thinks of his wife as an expensive burden because she eats and consumes food that would otherwise be his. If it suits his mood, any of the above perceived qualities serve as sufficient reason for him to mistreat his wife.

The story is as old as my country. From the day she is born, a female is regarded as inferior. The birth of a girl child is a great disappointment; the father is disappointed because his friends will think him less of a man, because now he will have another worthless "mouth" to feed and because he cannot count on a daughter to earn him income. The mother is disappointed because her husband will think less of her than he already does because she could not make him a son. The daughter is disparagingly referred to as an *"hembra,"* the word used for female animals, and she is treated accordingly from then on. No one is joyful, for there is nothing to be joyful about. No one celebrates the birth of a girl; instead, the parents consider that they are in for trouble and many headaches.

On the other hand, when a boy is born, they say they have "won the prize," or "hit the jackpot," and they celebrate for days with all their friends. If the father has a gun, he shoots for joy and gets drunk in the village. No one condemns him because *he* just had a son. If it was a girl, it was the wife's fault; if it is a son, he takes the credit. The male child is not referred to as a *"macho,"* a male animal, the counterpart of *"hembra."* Instead, he is respectfully called a *"varon,"* meaning a human being of the male sex. The midwives long ago noticed this difference and very shrewdly charge more when a boy is born than when it is a girl. . . .

The plight of rural housewives in El Salvador is especially discouraging. Caring for a house and children is hard work—especially if the house has only a dirt floor, is open to insects and rodents, has no electricity or water, and no latrine. The daily preparation of breakfast, lunch and dinner for a hungry family means long hours over a hot fire or coals. It means grinding corn and making *"tortillas"*—but, it can also mean making something out of nothing. Being a housewife in the *"campo"* [rural areas] usually requires scrounging for firewood; feeding and caring for the animals—pigs, chickens, whatever—and sometimes taking them to market; caring for the children and doing the laundry; mending the clothes; and carrying lunch in a pail each day to your husband, wherever he is working. Depending on the circumstances, this can mean several miles.

Because few rural homes have water, *"campesinas"* [peasant women] carry the family laundry to the nearest stream or river where they beat the clothes on the rocks with home-made soap to loosen the dirt. Some of the larger villages have a central well and a community sink with cold running water where the women both wash and fill huge jugs to carry home for drinking. The woman's job never ends. She has to work at least sixteen hours a day to complete her chores. She is invariably the first up in the morning and the last to go to bed at night. Only the very rich women can afford to do otherwise.

Men, however, think women's work has little value. They say you can't see women's work—that it provides no money for the family to live on; therefore, it cannot possibly be worth as much as the job of a man. As one "*campesino*" told me, "Women are able to work in the shade where it is cool and comfortable. A man must earn his living by the sweat of his brow in the heat of the sun."

Some women are now beginning to realize that this argument "doesn't hold water." Women work at least twice as long as men every day, Sundays and Holy Days included. There is no time off to drink beer, gamble, play "futbol" in the road, or meet with friends—except possibly over the laundry. Many are aware that it is mainly through their efforts that the body and soul of the family is held together. A tremendous amount of time is needed to keep the small business called "home," working—or as it is sometimes said, "make ends meet." . . .

In our society, men control almost every facet of life. From the government to the Church, from political parties and cooperatives to sports, men run things. They make the decisions about what's good and what's bad. Women have become the nation's beasts of burden, shouldering the basic responsibilities of the family and society in order that men may be free to pursue whatever work and pleasures they desire. If husbands, fathers and sons are involved in violence outside the home, which has also become a way of life, the women suffer equally. When men are wounded, bruised and lacerated as the result of the terrorism which has held our country in its grip, women faithfully patch them up and nurse them as best they can with pitifully little knowledge of first-aid and no medicine, only to see them go and involve themselves in fighting again—maybe the next time to be killed. But it is not for the woman to question why. She has no say in any of the affairs that may leave her homeless, widowed, and at the mercy of the violence which surrounds her. Every day this problem grows worse.

The participation of women in the social and economic order is restricted to serving and taking orders. They are never allowed to make decisions of any consequence. Although women now have the right to vote, it doesn't mean very much. They are told how to vote by their men. Social and political comments and opinions of women are made fun of or "put down." Any attempts by women to alter their situation is quickly censured—by government, family, and social pressure.

As a result, Salvadoran women are confused about who they are and their status in society. They are led or driven to believe that men are superior, that they are worth more. . . . Many women have even come to see men as more like God, which is contrary to all Christian tenets and makes no common sense at all.

The myth of women's inferiority continues to flourish because of traditional customs and educational biases that have conditioned both sexes to believe the male is superior, both mentally and physically. This national inferiority has been created and forced by men. Institutionally, it is maintained and reinforced by the school system, the government, the Church, the community and the family.

It is up to the women of our country to take it upon themselves to change this humiliating condition. One way we can do this is by carefully developing our aptitudes and abilities, then using them to assert ourselves. There are a number of things we can do if we make up our minds that we must have equal rights and responsibilities at the same time we share our lives. The responsibility, however, lies with us.

As director of the Guadalupe Center in San Miguel, I head a program especially designed for women. We train and sponsor groups of rural women catechists who work in their own communities to make other *"campesinas"* aware that each is an important part of the society in which she lives. We try to help them become an integral part of the community, and to understand their rights and responsibilities. As human beings and as Christians, women have to struggle for our God-given right to equality. This is the only way for *"campesinas"* in particular, to rise above the sin of ages-old oppression for which men, historically, have been responsible. Resolution of the problem must begin in the home, so we take a grassroots approach. Our *"campesina"* catechists live in their communities and are on the spot to tell others about our program and share the information they learn at the Center. Their closeness to the other village women makes it possible for them to help those who are interested to come to the Center for training, too.

The kind of training we give always revolves around improving the lives of rural women; this is the core of the program. The training is implemented in courses of fifty-one ten-hour days in which the women learn about leadership, health, reading and writing, Christian rights and responsibilities, prayer, the history of El Salvador, the family, self-awareness and community organization. We also introduce Christian ethics through studying women of the Bible, the history of liberation, the true Christian man and a general introduction to the Bible.

At the termination of each course, the women return to their communities to put in practice what they have learned. After six months, we follow up by visiting to see how they are getting along and if they need any additional help. The parish priest is also very helpful in passing along information. They hold community meetings to generate self-awareness, as well as meeting with individual women in their homes where more personal dialogue can take place. . . .

The *"campesina"* catechists, along with many others in El Salvador, are committed to the eradication of ignorance which has led to the complete oppression of women by men, and to the brutality and injustice which is sweeping over the country like a tidal wave. Our commitment will help to create a more just society of which all our people can be proud.

September, 1979.[14]

CHURCH LIBERATIONISTS CONFER

"... I suddenly felt a deep pain. I would never feel at home any more in this traditional Church, but will I ever in the Church of the *lucha*?"

For six months in 1981–1982, Henri Nouwen, a North American Catholic theologian and author, visited missionary friends whose ministry was to the poor in the Andean republics. In March of 1982, he attended a conference in Cuzco, Peru, where Catholic priests, religious, and laity discussed issues related to the full liberation of the people. In these excerpts from Nouwen's diary, he described some of his reactions to the conference and to Gustavo Gutiérrez, its leading theologian.[15]

✠ *Friday, March 12*

... I guess that my joy in knowing Rolando has something to do with my difficulties in relating to the people in the course. I find the participants tough and even harsh. They have so identified themselves with the *lucha* [struggle] that they permit little space for personal interchange. They are good and honest people, but difficult to get to know. They work diligently, not only in their parishes but also in this course. They are serious, intense, and deeply concerned men and women.

When I met Rolando and experienced his personal warmth, his kindness, and his spiritual freedom, I was suddenly able to come in touch with the feelings of oppression that I myself was experiencing in the course. Rolando invited me to come to his parish and to live with him for as long as I wanted. There I would be able to experience that it was possible to be fully involved in the struggle for the poor while at the same time remaining sensitive to the personal and interpersonal quality of life. That explains my immediate feelings of closeness to him.

Saturday, March 13

For the last few days, the course has dealt primarily with the new agricultural law. A lawyer from Lima came to explain the law, and triggered a lively debate about the way the poor *campesinos* would be affected by it. Most pastoral workers felt that this law was simply one more way in which the poor would be made poorer. The law opened the way for rich people who had lost their land during the agrarian reform to reclaim it. One of the French pastoral workers presented an alternative law that would serve the poor farmer. This law had been formulated by the *campesinos* themselves, with the help of leftist lawyers and economists.

When I reflect on these legal debates and discussions, I become strongly aware of the new style of this liberation-oriented Church. It would have taken an outsider a long time to find out that this was a group of priests, nuns, and Catholic laymen and laywomen dedicated to the preaching of the Gospel. The style of the dialogue, the fervor of the discussions, and the ideological language suggested a meeting of a political party rather than a church group. I feel that this is true not only for the formal sessions, but also for the informal relationships between the participants — during meals and coffee breaks. Yet these men and women from France, Spain, Italy, and the United States have left their countries to serve the poor of Peru in the name of the Lord Jesus Christ. Their religious dedication has led them into the lives of the poor. Therefore the sophisticated and highly critical analysis of the new agrarian law was for them not purely political but a necessary step in the struggle for freedom for the people of God.

Yet two Churches are gradually developing in Peru, and they are at the point where they are no longer able to talk to each other. On the one side is the Church that speaks primarily about God, with little reference to the daily reality in which the people live; on the other side is the Church that speaks primarily about the struggle of the people for freedom, with little reference to the Divine mysteries to which this struggle points. The distance between these Churches is growing. This morning I went to the Cathedral of Cuzco, and when I walked from altar to altar and statue to statue and listened to the monotone voice of a priest saying Mass, I suddenly felt a deep pain. I would never feel at home any more in this traditional Church, but will I ever in the church of the *lucha*? . . .

Monday, March 15

Today the last part of the course began. After three days about the political and ecclesial state of affairs in Peru, and two days about the new agrarian law and its possible alternatives, the emphasis now shifts to a spirituality of liberation. Gustavo Gutiérrez flew into Cuzco from Lima this morning, and he will be our guide in a four-day workshop. Just as in the summer course in Lima, Gustavo's presence had a vitalizing effect. Many of us showed signs of fatigue after six days of intense discussions, but Gustavo unleashed new energies and engendered new enthusiasm.

Two ideas in Gustavo's presentations impressed me deeply. The first focused on the Gospel terms, which have passed through the filter of individualism and thus have been spiritualized and sentimentalized. The word "poor" has come to mean "humble," the word "rich," "proud." Terms like "the children," "the blind," "the sinner" have lost their historical meaning and have been "translated" into ahistorical, asocial and apolitical words. Thus, "child," which in the New Testament refers to an insignificant, marginal, and oppressed human being, has become an expression for simplicity, innocence, and spontaneity. Jesus' call to become "like children" has been passed through the filter of individualism and has thus been romanticized.

This explains how the idea of a spiritual combat has lost its social, political, and economic quality and now refers only to an inner struggle. Gustavo showed us as an example of how the Magnificat is mostly read in a very individualistic way and has lost its radical, social dimensions in the minds of most contemporary Christians. In the Magnificat, Mary proclaims: "[The Lord God] has shown the strength of his arm, he has scattered the proud in their conceit. He has cast down the mighty from their thrones and has lifted up the lowly." These words have a concrete historical, socioeconomic, and political meaning; the interpretations that relate these words exclusively to the inner life of pride and humility rob them of their real power.

A second idea that touched me in Gustavo's presentation was that affection, tenderness, solitude are not to be rejected by those who struggle for the freedom of the people. There is a danger that these important realities of the Christian life are considered by the "revolutionaries" as soft and useless for the struggle. But Gustavo made it clear that love for the people is essential for a true Christian revolution. Those who do not value tenderness and gentleness will eventually lose their commitment to the struggle for liberation.

This observation was extremely important to me, especially in the context of my earlier feelings about the participants in this course. Someone mentioned to me that "new fighters" in the struggle for liberation often are tense, harsh, and unfeeling, but that those who have been in the struggle for a long time are gentle, caring, and affectionate people who have been able to integrate the most personal with the most social. Gustavo himself is certainly an "old fighter."

14. ✠ Protestants: Facing the Social Questions

1961-1985

Protestants grew in numbers and social status in the 1960s and following, but were fragmented and often divided within their respective denominations over questions about the relations of the churches to society around them. Numerically, Protestants were still growing, especially the Pentecostals and Seventh Day Adventists. Relative to the whole population, it was estimated that by 1985 their members and affiliates represented about 14.5 percent of the people.[16] The actual statistics in 1980 were higher in some countries—with Chile having 28.8 percent and Brazil 21.2 percent—and lower in others, with Mexico having 6.7 percent and Colombia 3.1 percent. Other countries were near the average, such as Nicaragua at 14.5 percent and Guatemala at 12.8 percent.[17] The Protestants also grew more Latin Americanized and self-confident. They occupied some important business and government positions across the region. For example, in Brazil and Guatemala, Protestants even served terms as presidents of the republic.

Up to the 1950s, the Protestant self-image had been that of a persecuted minority. Securing freedom to build schools and hospitals and to start publications had been their primary political concerns, and this had allied them with liberal-modernist, anti-clerical politics. As their social status rose, however, many Protestants tended to support the established order, even if it was oligarchic and autocratic. Meanwhile, other Protestants were aware of social injustices and were studying ways to address them.

Protestants in this period could be roughly clustered into three groups that often overlapped: the Mainline, the Evangelicals, and the Pentecostals.[18] The first group was characterized by their historical organizations and continuing relation to their denominational partner-churches in Europe and North America. The "Evangelical" group was marked by its ties with Evangelical Protestants in North America and their three-fold insistence on the authority of the Bible in matters of faith, conversion as a distinct experience, and evangelization as the main mission imperative. The Pentecostals held to these same three convictions but added their distinguishing experience of the baptism of the Holy Spirit and its charismatic manifestations. As social issues in the region demanded attention and many

Social worker with Matacos Indians at an Anglican mission in northern Argentina, 1985.

people urged ecumenical cooperation, the three groups tended to respond in a variety of ways.

The mainline Protestant churches were the first to address the social issues. In 1961, they met in the second Latin American Protestant Conference (CELA II), which brought together two hundred delegates from forty-two denominations. Out of that emerged three organizations that became widely influential among Protestant leaders: the Church and Society Movement in Latin America (ISAL), organized in 1961; the Latin American Commission for Christian Education (CELADEC), 1962; and the Latin American Movement for Protestant Unity (UNELAM), 1964. All three organized conferences and published materials to stimulate reflection and consultation in their areas of responsibility. All three related to the CELA churches, to their overseas partner churches, and to ecumenical bodies, such as the World Council of Churches. After Vatican II, the three were also ready to include Catholics in their studies and conferences. At the end of the decade, 1969, CELA III met in Buenos Aires. The concern for evangelism was strong, and increasingly the delegates recognized the imperative of involving themselves in the process of social, economic, and political transformation.

The World Congress on Evangelism in Berlin in 1966 spurred a similar regional convocation in Bogotá, Colombia in 1969. This was the first Latin American Congress on Evangelization (CLADE). It was an assembly of nine hundred delegates; they sought ways to make evangelism more effective, and they opposed rapprochement with Catholics and the ecumenical movement, as this was represented by the CELA conferences. The CLADE leaders and churches were much influenced by the Billy Graham Evangelistic Association in the United States. Within their number, however, was an influential group of younger theologians, led by Samuel Escobar, René Padilla, Orlando Costas, and others who in 1969 organized the Latin American Theological Fraternity to contextualize the gospel in the Latin American society, to remove the North American garments from their evangelicalism, and in the light of "biblical realism" to address the social problems of the region. Like ISAL, the Theological Fraternity also stimulated conferences and publications that influenced many Protestants.[19] Thus Evangelical Protestantism had begun a process of region-wide consultation that was to lead them toward deeper inculturation and the addressing of "church and society" issues.

Protestant leadership thus constructed several networks for cooperation. They differed over the believer's role in society, but they were not opposites. Their commitments to evangelism overlapped, and they were connected by various other bridges. For example, the four regional associations for theological education, begun in the 1960s, occasioned friendships and enlarged the areas of trust. Moreover, numerous national agencies for refugees, social service, development work, and Bible distribution all demanded practical forms of cooperation and unity. In spite of these joint efforts, differences of emphasis remained among the Protestants and were often sharp.

The mainline churches met in CELA IV in Oaxtepec, Mexico, 1978; delegates came from 110 churches that now included some Pentecostal ones. The conference revealed a variety of perspectives and tensions; nevertheless, it produced study papers on the systemic injustices of the region. The conferees also condemned violations of human rights and approved a plan for a "Latin American Council of Churches (CLAI) — In-Formation." Most of the denominations approved the plan, and in 1982 in Lima, CLAI was inaugurated with over 100 denominations and ecumenical organizations as charter members, including several large Pentecostal churches.

In the same year, 1982, in Lima, the evangelical Protestants also met in CLADE II. They reaffirmed the central task of evangelism, and, though they continued to hold strong reservations about ecumenism and liberation theology, they took large strides in contextualizing their organization through more regional funding, and through encouraging more Latin American leadership and cultural sensitivity. Furthermore, there was greater willingness to discuss the social issues.

Of interest in the early 1980s were the involvements of the churches in the civic life of El Salvador and Guatemala under traditional military rule and in Nicaragua within the Sandinista socialist revolution. In spite of earlier apolitical traditions, the Protestants in each case were now participating in community life. Like their Catholic neighbors, however, they were divided over what their part should be. Amid the onrush of events across Latin America and the burgeoning of theological reflection, the Protestants were becoming better acquainted with each other, with the gospel, and with social ethics.

A TENACIOUS DUALISM

"... the dichotomy 'church' (good) vs. 'world' (bad) ..."

In preparation for a conference on Church and Society in San Luís Potosí, Mexico 1962, two Protestant educators working in Mexico made a survey of the social and theological perspectives of the evangélicos *in their country. Their findings revealed that for most Protestants to reflect on social problems would require a change in their theology.*[20]

✠ It is undeniable that in this survey there emerges the dichotomy "church" (good) vs. "world" (bad), which tends to lead to complete rejection not only of those aspects of the old life that are harmful, and sinful, but also of those that are morally neutral or even of positive value. Instead of carrying out the admonition to "test everything; hold fast what is good," the "world" is rejected (at least in theory) *in toto,* cutting off at the same time the lines of effective communication with the very relatives and friends to whom, if the Protestants had shared their problems and concerns, it might have been possible to present with greater relevance Christ and his gospel. At the same time, insistence upon a radical break with the "world" leads to danger of an ambivalent attitude — to say nothing of schizophrenia — since in actual practice such a break can be only partial as long as the Christian is still physically present in the world and in his society. . . .

If our study has any validity, it would seem to be imperative that those responsible for Christian education and for teaching in the seminaries adopt a less naive position with regard to the sinlessness of the church, and a less extreme position with regard to the sinfulness of the world. In other words, the situation calls for a reconsideration of the sovereignty of Jesus Christ not only in the church (where it is explicitly confessed) but also in the world (where it is not explicitly confessed).

This opposition of "church" vs. "world" becomes especially complicated in view of the fact that the average Mexican Protestant equates "church" with the Protestant community, and "world" with the rest of society, which is predominantly Roman Catholic. Most Protestants make no distinction between orthodox Catholicism (with which, in spite of the basic differences, Protestantism has a great deal in common) and folk Catholicism (that "Christo-paganism" which has resulted from a syncretism of Christian concepts and elements from the Indian religions). They tend to see in every Catholic, even the best instructed, a polytheist who follows the syncretized religion of the Indians; although sometimes, after some courses in a Bible institute, they tend to interpret the gospel message to everyone, including the Indians, as though they were orthodox Catholics. One crucial consequence of all this is that most Mexican Protestants are unable to see the elements of genuineness that are present in the current renewal in the Roman Catholic Church, which is potentially one of the most hopeful developments toward the improvement of that "world" rejected as hopelessly sinful.

PENTECOSTALS AT WORSHIP

". . . violins, flutes, clarinets, horns, . . ."

As head of a large Pentecostal Protestant church, "O Brasil Para Cristo," Manoel de Melo led his community in innovative directions. A Lutheran pastor described de Melo and a typical occasion of worship at the church's immense pavilion in São Paulo about 1968.[21]

✠ From Pernambuco, where he was active as pastor of the Assembléias de Deus, his course took him to São Paulo. A few years later, he broke away from the Assembléias there and put his extraordinary gifts as an evangelist, his famous oratorical talent and his inexhaustible capacity for work at the service of the Cruzada National de Evangelização. There were gigantic attendances at his evangelization meetings in tents, in open places and in parks, which often resulted in astonishing cures of the sick. All he needed for such meetings was an easily transportable loudspeaker system and a couple of musicians, whose songs first attracted the attention of the people. It is said that meetings with an audience of 100,000 were by no means rare and he himself estimated the audience for his morning radio programme at five million. . . .

I was there when one Thursday he had to bring forward the regular service in his provisional main church in São Paulo, a former market hall, from its appointed time on Saturday to Friday evening. Despite this, the church was packed with more than five thousand believers so that there was not even standing room; people were left outside the doors and even on the streets. The two-hour service had all the marks of Brazilian Pentecostal services with their lively, joyful, even hilarious mood: there was vigorous and extremely rhythmical singing emphasized by hand-claps and accompanied by an *ad hoc* 'orchestra' of violins, flutes, clarinets, horns, etc.; all five thousand joined in loud spontaneous prayer which went on for minutes and swelled to a crescendo, suddenly dying away at a sign from the preacher. (Individuals who seemed to have lapsed into speaking with tongues were silenced with an imploring yet sharp 'silêncio!'.) The sermon — about the parable of the five foolish and five wise virgins — was very emotional and had a strongly admonitory tone, but it was an extraordinarily clear, concrete and attractive exposition of the biblical text. The attention of the congregation did not slip for a moment, and their intensive preoccupation could be seen and heard in movements, laughter, loud interjections and — above all after certain key expressions — cries of 'Glória a Deus,' 'Alleluia' or 'Louvada seja o nome do Senhor!'

Without question, this temperamental, dark Pernambucan with his squat figure and harsh voice is one of the most popular figures in Brazil and surely the best-known evangelist in the country, admired by some, attacked and criticized by others.

MINISTERS IN THE CUBAN CANEFIELDS

". . . the entire Protestant church was quite opposed to the Revolution . . ."

Eleven years after the Cuban revolution the Protestant churches were still reluctant to support the social changes taking place on the island and were critical of anyone who seemed to be collaborators with the government program. In 1969, a dozen pastors joined in the annual cutting of

*the sugar cane — the island's major export. During the following year, in
a nationwide mobilization to cut ten million tons of cane, the students
and faculty of the Protestant seminary at Matanzas joined the effort. A
journalist interviewed some of them in the fields, and their responses
provide insight into Protestant thinking at the time.*[22]

✠ One afternoon when the heat was close to 90 degrees and the noise of
the tractors made us shout to be heard, we got together in the shade of a
palm grove, stretching out on the layers of fronds to talk about volunteer
work and life in the camp. There was something special about the occasion:
a dozen Protestant leaders, enthusiastic revolutionaries, had signed up for
volunteer work in the province of Matanzas, and during three or four hours,
taking time off from their chores, we chatted away while a tape recorder
took down our conversation. . . .

Q. Why are you here? What made you decide to come to the volunteer
work?

René Castellanos, fifty years old, pastor of the church at Sagua and
professor of the Matanzas seminary, spoke up first. "I think that one of
our principal obligations as Christians is to participate in the world we live
in; in its activities, its worries, its collective dreams. I volunteered to come
here for at least four reasons. First I want to associate myself with the
people of Cuba, with that part of society that doesn't belong to the church
but is eager to reach the ten-million-ton sugar harvest. Second, here is a
chance to identify myself with members of the church who are also doing
this work. Third, I feel a serious obligation to collaborate in one way or
another in producing what can satisfy people's hunger in places where they
have no sugar — that is, when I cut cane I feel I am helping to feed children,
women and men in India, China, England, or anywhere else in the world
where they have no sugar. Finally, I don't want to stand apart from this
great campaign of the Government to reach ten million tons. We share a
common responsibility, we want Cuba to make its goal. Those are my four
basic reasons for feeling that I should do volunteer work. As you know, we
aren't liable for it. The Government doesn't require anything of the sort
from us, but we are doing it with pleasure."

Javier Naranjo, peeking out from under a floppy peasant's hat, is dressed
in work clothes like his comrades. "I'm in the voluntary work because I'm
a citizen of this island of Cuba," he tells me. "Besides, I feel that a minister
shouldn't isolate himself from reality but be plunged into the society where
he has his ministry. What witness can we give if we stay in our parish
churches preaching, or studying at the seminary? Finally, I'm here because
my conscience tells me I should be here. As you know, the country is
pledged to increase its production of sugar and other crops, since that is
our only way to get out of this underdevelopment."

Carlos Manuel Piedra, thirty years old, agrees. "At present," he says, "I
am pastor of the missionary circuit of Ecrucijada . . . and also editor of the

magazine *Su Voz*. . . . One of the great mistakes that we believers were guilty of in the Cuban process," said Pastor Piedra, "was precisely in not standing up to be counted when we should have involved ourselves and risked our necks. Even now, we are quick to criticize on any occasion. That is to say, the church will criticize today, but didn't have the courage to roll its sleeves up and make sacrifices at the crucial moments. I can never forget those words of Martí: 'Those who aren't brave enough to risk their lives should at least be modest enough to stay silent in the presence of those who are taking the risks.' Anyone who remembers how little the church did in those days of insurrection knows that it can hardly condemn anyone today." . . .

Q. What was your reaction, you believers who are now wholeheartedly with the Revolution, when it swung to the left and openly chose socialism? Did you hesitate? Did you think you might have to break with the movement?

"Not exactly," replied Piedra, "I don't think that just because the Revolution is Marxist, we who are loyal Cubans have to remain outside the mainstream of its evolution. I'm sure there were good reasons, justifications for going socialist. We're not very much up on international politics. But just seeing what was going on made us think it was inevitable."

Pastor Naranjo would go farther: "Look," he breaks in, "the only way that poor countries can get out of their underdevelopment is by a completely socialist revolution. Besides if you look at how so much of humanity is underdeveloped, that's the only practical, viable hope the people have."

In the group around me was Sergio Arce, rector of the Matanzas seminary, a doctor in philosophy and letters from the University of Havana and holder of a theological degree from Princeton. He had kept silent, listening to his comrades and apparently absorbed by the cadenced wave of workers attacking the canefield. "I look on Marxism," he said, "as basically a science, or, if you like, a scientific way to analyze reality in order to solve the problems facing society. Well, then, if it is the science of society, why not use it? Don't we turn to medical science when we are sick? In other words, Marxism is a science, so we use it as such. To get out of our underdevelopment, we have to use that science. I don't think there is any reluctance on our part to admit that."

Q. But how do you conciliate your faith with Marxist materialism? Comrade Naranjo has just told us very explicitly that Marx's socialist road is the only one for getting out of underdevelopment. Still, how is Marxist materialism compatible with the religion you profess?

"Let me put it in simple terms," Naranjo broke in. "You know that Cuban Governments prior to the Revolution were quite deferent to religion. Today, though, the Revolution we are going through is a Marxist-Leninist one. The problem is not just one of words, however, but of substance. We can't blot out the facts of history. Those old governments had no time for the people's plight, whereas the one we have now is very interested in it, and in producing a new man. As I see it, this new man"—

and here he quoted from Brunel—"is 'a life completely dedicated to one's neighbors.' I think that if we have to choose, and if we are honest, even though the Revolution is a Marxist-Leninist one with no place for religion, we still ought to choose that system, because somehow or other it seems to promote all the objectives in the social order that the church, here in Cuba, never managed to achieve."

Only Castellanos, the oldest in the group, seemed to disagree. "I wouldn't say that socialism is the only way that underdeveloped countries have of liberating themselves. I would concede, however, that experience has so far shown us no other way. But it's my fond dream that another way will be found to get all the peoples of Asia, Africa and Latin America out of their underdevelopment. Such a way may turn up; just look at what is happening in Peru these days. That is very interesting. But in the long run I suppose that, whatever the way, it will have to be violent, radical and revolutionary, on the Marxist-Leninist pattern. I am firmly convinced, though, that the contribution of Christian witness is indispensable. That's the responsibility that we who live immersed in this Revolution feel weighing on us." . . .

Q. It is common knowledge that after 1959 the Catholic and Protestant Churches both lost the great bulk of their members. Some of those members, those of the upper bourgeoisie, abandoned the country, but the majority—the former believing masses—simply gave up their Christian faith and joined the revolutionary cause. What, then, is left of the Protestant Church in Cuba? How do you feel in this new society? What is the role that, as you see it, is now yours? . . .

"In general, the entire Protestant Church," said Doctor Adolfo Ham, age thirty-nine, a Baptist and a professor at the Matanzas seminary, "was quite opposed to the Revolution from the start. We should add, of course, that there has been progress since then. Our churches have rallied to the Revolution. The number of individuals from our congregations who are joining volunteer work teams, for example, seems to be increasing all the time."

Israel Batista, twenty-eight years old, pastor of the church in Matanzas and professor at the seminary there, is less optimistic. "Though in general I agree with Doctor Ham, I am nevertheless more pessimistic. For various reasons. As I see it, the church's fundamental problem is its constitutency [sic]; the church is made up of social outcasts. That keeps the church from playing its proper role in the revolutionary process. No doubt there have been some advances in the church's attitude. But the Revolution keeps pulling farther ahead, and at top speed too, so that when the church finally changes, adapting itself to the new process, the Revolution has already moved on. I could give an example. We ministers are here taking part in the productive effort, but productive work is no longer the Government's number one priority for the simple reason that it is already accepted. Everyone is doing it now. And even then, within our churches, we are only a minority, perhaps not even an accepted one."

"I have a question, Pastor Batista," interrupted Ham. "You say—and I agree—that we are a minority. But would you say we are an influential minority?"

"Yes, we are influential because we have at least the dynamism of what is new, whereas the so-called rightists have nothing to contribute to this process, so they feel isolated. But even among those few of us who participate, not all agree on what participation means. Maybe some of the brothers here are cutting cane with a churchly motivation: to give witness, to bring their 'presence,' and so on, whereas others come out of a specifically revolutionary dedication. We are thus a minority within a church of outcasts. We are a church with an 'exile' mentality, that's the root problem. Some of us have left the country, some are about to go, and a good number of those remaining have already gone spiritually. Thus, we are people with an 'exile' mind-set: physically here, but absent from the Revolution."

"It should also be pointed out," Ham continued, "that there are a certain number of working people in the church who are fully with the Revolution. We can't say, then, that all the church's members are 'marginalized.' Wouldn't it be truer to say that its leaders are 'marginalized'?"

Pastor Batista wouldn't give in. "I still think that many of those in the church are 'marginalized.' You can say that in this congregation there is a doctor, and in another a worker, but talk to them and you'll see that they are a doctor and a worker with an outcast attitude."

"Allow me an observation about the marginalization of those in the church," interrupted Arce. "In my opinion, not all who are in the church are outcasts, but all who feel outcasts join the church." . . .

Q. Let's move on to another matter. The Revolution, and Che, have both stressed the need to create a new man. What do you think? Is there some way you people can assist the Revolution in this direction?

"We feel that Che's suggestion is a challenge for the church," replied Pastor Piedra. "But, first of all, I think we have to modify our notion of what the religious man is. As I see him, he isn't the minister or priest with a languid look and his thoughts lost in the heavens; he's the person who lives and suffers the same problems and anxieties as everyone else in our country. With that ideal, in my opinion, we can contribute in some little way by producing a rebirth, to creating a new man in our society."

"I admire Che immensely," added Castellanos. "He is one of our great heroes But I don't think you can create the new man without Jesus Christ, without the Bible ideal of man as one who lives both here and beyond here."

Pastor Batista went to the heart of the question: "I think that while our society has been calling for the new man, the church has unfortunately kept countering with its Christian man and made of him a foil, a factor of division. I believe that the church's job is to create man, to develop man. I can't see that the adjective 'Christian' adds anything. A man is expected to be a man, a new man; and all that about being a Christian man we would do well to forget. Here is what I see as the church's task. The Revolution, faced with a hundred different problems, can lose sight at times of that ultimate goal: man. But the church should keep reminding the Government that the target is the new man. Obviously, what I said before about the church's senility and its membership hardly gives me reason for being optimistic."

PENTECOSTALS: EVANGELISM AND SOCIAL ACTION

"While we convert a million, the devil de-converts ten millions through hunger, misery, militarism, dictatorship . . . "

In the early 1970s, the World Council of Churches gained a surprising new member, the Pentecostal Evangelical Church "Brazil for Christ." It was only one of many Pentecostal churches in the country, yet with over a million members it was influential. When interviewed by the editor of O Expositor Cristão *in 1970, Pastor Manoel de Melo, one of the church's leaders, described some of his thoughts on evangelism and participation in social and political change.*[23]

✠ I think that the most important task of the Church is to evangelize. This I understand in the following manner. There is a type of evangelism that produces bigots. But there is also the kind of evangelism that creates a new perspective in the individual. This second form of evangelism does not produce a Sunday Christian, but rather a believer who is able to witness in the society in which he lives. It creates a new consciousness. The Gospel of the Kingdom of God is here and now. It involves the people in concrete living. Take Bishop Helder Cámara, for example. He is winning people because his message makes men conscious. I see the Church as very complacent. The Church is greatly compromised with the power structure in the nation, and it is a structure which the people no longer accept. The Church that fails to heed this creative message of a new consciousness can prepare its own funeral within the next thirty years.

I believe that the Gospel is more than sufficient for this task of creating awareness. Actually I do not see a single preacher who is proclaiming the Gospel in all its fulness and purity, because the Gospel has a revolutionary content that is violently opposed to injustice. . . .

I was present at the Fourth Assembly of the World Council of Churches, in Uppsala. I accepted the invitation because I had heard some of the most barbarous remarks made against the World Council. Anything that is so strongly opposed becomes a star attraction, so I accepted the invitation in order to see for myself. I only accept things and talk about them after knowing them personally. I needed to know the Council which came under such attack. I arrived there and felt like an Ezekiel in the valley of dry bones. We are in the jet age and, from the religious point of view, the World Council of Churches is riding a bicycle. However, it is doing tremendous work such as we are not able to do with all our religiosity: a gigantic work of social action.

What is the use of converting a person only to send him back to the rotten Brazilian society? "Brasil para Cristo" has already called together its team of directors and advisers, and we are going to become members of the World Council of Churches. We are planning on membership, but on one condition: since, on the religious level, they are not at the level which we have already reached, we will not join to receive a religious orientation but rather a social orientation. While we convert a million, the devil de-converts ten millions through hunger, misery, militarism, dictatorship — and the churches remain complacent. Atheism is on the increase due to the conditions of injustice and misery in which the people are living. Preachers are preaching about a far distant future and forget the fact that Jesus valued and gave close attention to the time in which people lived.

The World Council of Churches concerns itself with the contemporary life of people. "Brasil para Cristo" will join the World Council of Churches because of its social mission in today's world. But, there is another reason, namely, that we must get rid of the small-mindedness that divides men into denominations. The World Council is accomplishing this. Ecumenism is another good thing the World Council of Churches offers us.

FRAGILE ECUMENISM

" . . . foremost impression . . . dyed-in-the-wool anti-Catholicism . . . the most encouraging . . . is cooperation in theological education."

The major weaknesses and incipient strengths of ecumenism among Latin American Protestants can be seen in excerpts from a report by Victor E. W. Hayward on his visits in 1970. Hayward was on the staff of the World Council of Churches, serving as secretary for Relationships with National and Regional Councils related to the WCC.[24]

✠ It is with sadness that I confess that the first and foremost impression I gained, from the viewpoint of my particular concern, was the dyed-in-the-wool anti-Catholicism of the Evangelical Churches. . . .

As regards the fragmentation of Protestantism, I was increasingly appalled at the number of evangelical Christians who seem to think they can be the Church of Jesus Christ while paying no attention to their fellow-Christians. Generally speaking, Pentecostals have few relationships with other Protestant Christians, and are at times quite separated from one another, or even subject to bitter rivalries among themselves, as in Chile. Even unity within a denomination is often quite precarious. Let me, by way of example, report the picture of the Presbyterian Church of Brazil given me by a former church leader. It has some 500 pastors, a third of whom have had no seminary training. About 40% are full-time pastors, but the trend is towards more part-time. He characterized the leadership as "fundamental messianism." Power politics are rife—Assemblies, for example, are deliberately convened in reactionary areas, air passages and first-class hotel expenses being provided for most of the Yes-men brought to the meetings. Both missionaries and pastors have been denounced to the secret police; youth have been similarly threatened. There is, not surprisingly, a hard tension between this Church and its supporting Mission Board. . . .

In Mexico less than one-tenth of Protestant Christians are in membership with the Evangelical Federation of Mexico, although its Basis is simply that it is "a fellowship of Churches and other evangelical bodies which recognize our Lord Jesus Christ as God and Saviour, as revealed to us in the Holy Scriptures." The largest Church in membership is the Methodist Church, with some 37,000 communicants. Yet neither the main body of Presbyterians nor the Baptists, each of which numbers 80,000–100,000 communicants, is in membership. Nor are the Seventh Day Adventists, who are also more numerous than the Methodists. . . .

There are fortunately some exceptions to this general picture, particularly in the River Plate region. The Argentine Federation of Evangelical Churches brings into fellowship no less than 35 affiliated denominations, including 5 Pentecostal groups—and has succeeded in providing a meeting ground for protagonists of conflicts within denominational families. A Joint Consultation of "Churches of the Reformation" has been convened in Argentina, at which the Methodist and Mennonite Churches of Uruguay have joined nine Argentinian Churches in starting processes to produce a Common Catechism and a Common Hymnal, in full recognition that such work together would easily lead to the taking of other steps towards some future Church Union. . . . "Evangelism in Depth" campaigns have been very successful in mobilizing hundreds of thousands of ordinary Christians of many different denominations in united witness to Christ (to date campaigns have been held in Nicaragua, Costa Rica, Guatemala, Honduras, Venezuela, Bolivia, the Dominican Republic, Peru, Colombia and Ecuador), although some have been critical of the ultimate results, and the co-operation engendered does not seem to last long beyond the campaigns themselves. The Pastors' Conferences organized by World Vision have probably done more to create ecumenical understanding (though no doubt that adjective is avoided!).

Many Protestant Churches in Latin America, particularly Lutheran, are largely ethnic communities. Apart from the problems of language and the desire of younger generations to be integrated into the culture of the land in which they live, these churches often preserve a certain "guest" mentality which militates against full integration with any other community, social, national, or ecclesiastical. . . .

On my first visit to Chile I had been greatly impressed by the way in which Methodist and Presbyterian church leaders spoke appreciatively of Pentecostals as representing the real national Church of their country— they were too busy evangelizing their fellow-countrymen to spend time on ecumenical travel! In this they have been but just. And if in many Latin American countries the other Protestant Churches are too much identified with the middle class (incidentally I was given the following percentages for the proportionate size of the middle class to the whole population: Bolivia 13, Brazil 15, Uruguay 31, Argentina 39.7), Pentecostals more than redress the balance, with their concern for the common people—in societies in transition from a feudalistic to a secularized, democratic state. . . .

Conciliar structures in Latin America are, generally speaking, ecumenically weak. In Brazil, internal troubles over finances and rightist repressive political influences have led to a reductionist policy as regards programme, and the Federation is now little more than an organ of public representation for the Evangelical Churches. The Evangelical Federation in Uruguay has good leadership, but lacks resources and represents only some 10,000 Christians. The Argentine Federation of Evangelical Churches affords a wide fellowship to Christian leaders, but lacks ecumenical commitment or concerted action.

In Chile, Pentecostals, having taken over the Evangelical Council and ousted the "historic" Churches, have disastrously split into two rival factions. In Mexico, the Federation represented less than one-tenth of all Mexican Protestants, and now seems moribund. In Cuba, a fine programme lacked the support of the Council's constituency, and progressive leaders have been disowned. In Puerto Rico the Evangelical Council, though strong potentially, is also rightist politically, and has failed to provide a forum for real and needed dialogue or to exercise a Christian reconciling power. These are the seven Councils affiliated to our Commission on World Mission and Evangelism. In several other countries there are Federations or Councils which have no working relationships with the World Council, for the very sufficient reason that they do not approve of the Ecumenical Movement. . . .

It must not be thought, however, that the weakness in Latin America of the Ecumenical Movement, as such, means that all ecumenical witness is lacking or feeble. On the contrary, when and where such witness is plainly made, it is the more impressive by contrast. Never before have I appreciated a single denomination anywhere as I came to appreciate the Methodist Church while travelling throughout the continent! Again and again this was the Church which I found conspicuously, and in some places solely, carrying a torch for concerns which preoccupy the Ecumenical Movement. . . .

Episcopalians often take over the ecumenical torch in the northern areas of the total region under survey. . . . Episcopalians, Methodists and Roman Catholics (as individuals) have recently inaugurated what is claimed to be "the first really ecumenical project in Costa Rica"—an organization called "Good Will Industries," to rehabilitate crippled people; 42 are being taught sewing, carpentry and radio service. This venture has the sponsorship of the Government Departments of Labour, Education and Welfare.

The same three parties have established a Permanent Emergency Committee, with help from the WCC and CWS. On an R.C. initiative, a Week for Peace was observed, starting on New Year's Day. Methodists, Episcopalians and Baptists observe the Week of Prayer for Christian Unity. Episcopalians and Baptists run Credit Co-operatives. So there are stirrings here of ecumenical co-operation—as in other places also.

By far the most encouraging ecumenical feature of the general scene is co-operation in theological education. The first item on my tour programme was, very suitably and fortunately, attendance at the first conference ever to be organized of theological professors from all Latin America. This was based on the four Associations for institutions of theological education set up with help from TEF in different areas of the continent. It was held at São Paulo from August 25 to 28, 1970. Although only Evangelical professors were invited, the 75 who came (including a few students) represented a broad spectrum of theological viewpoint, from convinced traditionalist to equally convinced radical reformist. Baptists, who frequently refuse or sit loose to membership in Evangelical Federations, were happily in evidence here. Two points struck me. The first was that, considering the great variety of theological viewpoints represented, the consultation was remarkably relaxed, genial and tolerant. The second, on the other hand, was that, whereas the panel presentations had been well-prepared and group work often produced good questions on concrete points, plenary discussion showed a remarkable propensity for escaping from the practical into the abstract (e.g. the topic "Demythologizing Theological Education" having raised seven or eight good illustrations of illusions needing to be dispelled, the conference proceeded to discuss at length the question whether the word "myth" had been correctly used, instead of the steps which might be taken to remedy the situation. . . . Anyway, this must have been one of the most ecumenical happenings to date in this continent, inasmuch as representatives of different Churches from so many countries met in real fellowship to listen to one another, in furtherance of the Church's mission.

RURAL HEALTH NURSE

". . . to work with poor rural women . . . their confidence and trust is essential, . . ."

Francisca Ramirez was born in Honduras and raised by her mother and grandmother in a poor urban area near a Four Square Gospel Mission.

After public school, some of the North American missionaries arranged for Ramirez to attend the "Bible Clinic High School" in Costa Rica and three years of nursing school. Later she directed a rural health program in Honduras that was sponsored by a coalition of Protestant churches, CEDEN (Evangelical Committee for Development and National Emergencies). Excerpts from her autobiographical essay illustrate widening social concern among Protestants in 1980.[25]

✠ I am a nurse. I have chosen to work with rural communities at this lowest level, especially the women, because this is where approximately seventy-three percent of our population is located. My goal is to help as many as possible to improve their lives, to take at least one step up. I am able to relate to these poor rural women because I have spent the majority of my years with them; I am one of them. I have found it to be a great advantage in my work with rural health clinics because there are no communication barriers between us. We speak the same language; they are comfortable with me and I with them.

The truth is that I have not always been equally as comfortable with professional people as I now am able to be, because my family was very poor. As a child, I wanted to be a nurse and was always pretending to treat my dolls, giving them injections, taking their temperature. As I grew older, I knew I had to do something constructive with my life. I am sure that this feeling was probably because my parents worked for missionaries who became my ideals. I was only able to become a nurse because they gave me a helping hand at the right time. . . .

Any successes I may have had in my work are directly due to the time I have spent and the close relationships I have developed with these poor rural families, building their confidence and trust in me, not as their nurse, but as their friend. The successful running of a rural health clinic is a very personal affair. It is imperative to convince the people who come to you that children should be loved, cared for, fed, given medicine when they are sick, and educated. You are privy to intimate family problems and expected to give advice on everything.

It is difficult to work with poor rural women with no education and very little knowledge of their own bodies. Building their confidence and trust is essential, but an approach that requires time and great patience. Little by little, their confidence in me must be reinforced by experience. When they can see that they have a healthier baby because they have more milk, and that they have more milk because they changed their eating habits at my suggestion—then they are willing to trust me to make other recommendations. It takes time to change their ways, to convince them to incorporate new ideas into their daily lives, especially when you consider that by doing so, they risk the criticism and ridicule of their families, friends and neighbors. Sometimes, the old ways are so imbedded in their customs, that it takes years to prove a point.

Motivation plus confidence and trust has been the only successful approach to ridding *"campesinas"* of old wives' tales and superstitions passed down to them from their parents and grandparents. Some of these ignorant beliefs are completely irrational and cause grave problems in their relationships with their children and other people, not to mention their eating habits, attitudes toward illnesses and family planning.

The poor *"campesina"* woman in Honduras is, without doubt, the longest-suffering element of our society. From earliest childhood, she has been forced to work. She has never had the chance to play with other children or to develop the ability to relate to other people through the kind of social contact that comes from school affairs and playground games. Almost since she was able to walk, she has been regarded by her parents as another pair of hands and feet. Because she is female, they also know she will not be able to bring in any money; therefore, she mainly represents another mouth to feed—something they don't really need. As a result, they have no hesitancy in requiring her to carry out the most menial and degrading chores, which in turn, places her in the lowest esteem of any family member. From the viewpoint of the family, she is something to be used, but not worth much in the way of attention or upkeep. She almost never gets to go to school, and even when this is possible, she seldom passes beyond the second or third grade.

The female of the very poor rural family generally passes her childhood doing small chores and insignificant work. She has not had an affectionate or close relationship with her parents because they have had to work during the day, and at night everyone goes to bed early because they are very tired and because there is no light. By the time she is an adolescent, she has retreated into herself. . . .

Sometimes when no more than thirteen or fourteen years old, this young, timid woman transfers her fear of authority to her husband. His voice alone represents power and command over her life; she must not do anything to arouse his anger. She knows she is supposed to take care of the house, the cooking and the washing; she knows she will bear the children, as did her mother before her. Beyond this, she knows little else.

Her belly becomes filled with children year after year because of fear and ignorance. She is afraid to refuse her husband his pleasure, and she does not know that she has alternatives. If she is made aware that it is possible to plan her pregnancies, fear and ignorance again work against her. . . .

My role is that of a moderator, and if I am a good communicator, a change agent, as well. I tell her, "It really isn't necessary to go against your husband—why don't you bring him to a meeting some time? I'd like to meet him."

If we are patient, she can usually persuade him to accompany her, and I listen to his objections, which may be rooted in superstitions [sic] such as "I don't believe in planning because the number of children you have is predestined." Political propaganda can be blamed for other objections like, "We have to increase the population if we want our country to be powerful," and "Family planning is a capitalist ploy to keep the poor countries weak by reducing manpower." Others are based on simple economics: "I need children to support me in my old age." ... I also suspect that men subconsciously feel their authority is being challenged by programs that are directed at women, and family planning programs almost always are. ...[26]

LETTER FROM GUATEMALA

"... the people more determined than ever to throw off the yoke of bondage ..."

The need for justice and social change was as acute in Guatemala as any place in Latin America. Nevertheless, the military regime repressed anyone whom they considered subversive. A six-member delegation from the National Council of Churches of Christ in the U.S.A., headed by its president, William Howard, visited Protestant and Catholic congregations in Guatemala during Easter Week of 1981 and found themselves inspired. Below are excerpts from a letter they wrote back to "believing communities in the United States." [27]

✠ With great joy we are pleased to greet you in the Lord from your sister congregations in Guatemala with whom we have shared in sorrow and celebration during the week of the Feast of Our Lord's Resurrection. We have been privileged to convey personally the concern you have expressed for them in their time of suffering and to share with them through fellowship, the breaking of bread and prayer, the hope we have in the Lord's victory over the forces of darkness and death. We want you to know that they appreciated this sign of your caring which our visit was able to convey. ...

During the days of our visit all of us earnestly strove to be as objective and emotionally detached as possible; yet we must confess that the things we encountered have convulsed us, churned our insides over and over, plagued us during sleepless hours and thrust us to such depths of anger and agony that we scarcely imagined possible. On the other hand these same things also aroused us, inspired us, pushed us to new levels of commitment and lifted our spirits to new heights of exhilaration. Even though we have not yet sorted out the myriad of emotions, images and impressions of these days, we want you to know that we are different people for having been in Guatemala.

By all earthly reasoning you would think that the people would have given up the struggle long ago. After the first waves of genocide against whole communities you would think that the message would have gotten across. You would think that when the people of Chimaltenango found the secret dumping ground of the bodies of those whom the soldiers had tortured and killed, that they would instantaneously have been brought to submission and resignation. When 50 farmers of the rural village Las Lomas were rounded up by the Army in February, shot and then burned in a pile as relatives watched, you'd think that fear would have paralysed the masses of poor. You would think that the murder of so many priests, evangelical pastors and lay churchworkers in the province of Quiché would have resulted in an abrupt end to the church's ministry among the Indians. When some 3,200 decision-makers among moderate political parties, farm-workers, clergy, trade-unions and newspeople were killed by government order in 1980 alone, you'd think it would have crushed the spirit of all those who seek democratic change in Guatemala.

Not so. On the contrary, the increasing waves of terror had precisely the opposite effect: they have made the people more determined than ever to throw off the yoke of bondage and to walk as free people in a free land. In the face of overwhelming evidence that the government and armed forces are presently carrying out a systematic programme to eliminate all community leaders at the grass roots of Guatemalan life, there can be no doubt that the resolve of the people to resist is becoming stronger. It is born out of sheer desperation, a pervasive feeling that all democratic options have been exhausted. After centuries of oppression by the oligarchy, the people are sensing the possibility of freedom and dignity as never before. They know that there will be great bloodshed to come and that whole villages will continue to disappear in smoke and fire. Yet they are determined to see the day of freedom come. That resolve is written deep in the eyes of those with whom we spoke; with quiet passion it surges from the depths of the soul.

When the day of liberation does come, it will be understood by many Guatemalans as a new day which God has brought us. You should know, dear friends, that the one thing that amazed us during these days was the extent to which the present struggle in Guatemala is viewed by the poor from the perspective of God's liberating acts in history. At every turn in our discussion the biblical roots were expressed in a totally easy and natural way. The present bondage bore no mere analogy to something which existed "once upon a time"; rather it was to be seen as that very same biblical drama, told by children of the same people who rose up from captivity in Egypt and followed the same God to new lands and new promises.

Even our worship together flowed in an amazingly simple and natural continuity with the events of the day and with those moments of intense sharing of struggles and hopes which nearly exhausted us. It was as if the evening songs and prayers with friends suddenly caught up all of the cares of the day and held them in God's own eternity, consecrating them and giving them back to us, transformed and renewed. When the bread of the

Eucharist was broken we were reminded that in "the body of Christ crushed for you" the bodies of those who had been crushed in the conflict were gathered, and that in the blood of Christ was mingled the blood of all those who had fallen. In that moment, as each one broke a bit of bread from the loaf and drank from the cup, it seemed as if some strange and mysterious power was grasping us and holding us, as if in that single instant all the people who were being dehumanized and debased around the world were being lifted up in God's hand. We look at our own lives of course, and the life of our own church and our own country and it fills us with a certain emptiness. Suddenly, in the mirror of the lives of these Guatemalans gathered beneath the cross of Christ we become exposed for what we really are. But in the passing of the peace, the praying of the "Our Father" and the hearing of the words of benediction, we also felt a surge of that renewing power out of which real joy is born.

You should know that throughout Guatemala there also exists a deep and pervading sense of fear. The week before we arrived a whole village of over fifty people was annihilated by the army. It is not an uncommon occurrence. No one knows which villages will be next. People are killed by burning, shooting and torturing. Most are Indians, who make up the majority in a country of over 7 million people. They are quiet, peaceable, almost naively straightforward and honest. Lists are published at the university naming those professors and students who are to be killed. Many are already dead, many more driven into exile in neighbouring countries. In the villages all local leaders, especially those who have some form of leadership in community organizations, unions, schools and churches, are destined for death. The fate is also reserved for centrist party leaders. Seventy-six leaders of the Guatemalan Christian Democratic Party have been slain in the last ten months. Even the foreign workers from the United States, Canada and European countries are told to get out of the country now or "pay the consequences." Priests and pastors are especially vulnerable because they train people to think and act together and because they have given a revolutionary book to Indians — the Holy Bible. In the villages the people hide the Bible so that the soldiers will not find it. Prayer groups are suspect.

At great risk to themselves people told us their stories. Story piled upon story until the combined weight of so many accounts of horror and violence threatened to crush our spirit. We became very nervous, questioning our own courage and integrity and the wisdom of our mission itself. Seldom had we experienced such depth of uncertainty; seldom had we had to face the harsh reality of our own fragility and vulnerability. If we now appeal to you as others have appealed to us to offer a sign of commitment to the Guatemalan people, know that this appeal is not based simply on the analysis of documents and a reading of the written record; it grows also out of the pathos of the historical moment, out of encounter with the flesh and blood and soul of the Guatemalan people; it is expressed with the groaning of the Spirit and with sighs too deep for words.

A MISSIONARY BEING EDUCATED

". . . putting aside preoccupation with being a Lutheran or a Methodist or a Roman Catholic . . ."

Facing urban poverty in the 1970s and 1980s was changing the way some Protestant missionaries were envisioning their work. During the period, a mission team from the Lutheran Church in America was in Peru and was headed by Troy Beretta, an ordained minister from Canada. Beginning in 1978, he was pastor to a small Lutheran community in Julio C. Tello (Lurin), one of the many shantytowns around Lima. In the document below, he responded to an interview with a journalist from an independent, ecumenical newspaper in Lima, in November of 1983.[28]

✠ LP: *Could you describe your work as a missionary and reflect on how you have been challenged by that experience?*

Beretta: In 1978, my family and I came to Peru in response to a request for a pastor for the Lutheran congregation in Julio C. Tello. We arrived with little awareness of what life would be like working with the poor of a Third World country. Confronted with poverty and misery of unbelievable proportions, one is soon forced to look for causes. Some 10,000 people live in our *pueblo joven*. It is one of Lima's earliest urban shantytowns and there is a tremendous mixture of people who have settled here from the mountains and from other parts of the Peruvian coast. The community hasn't been very united, and that lack of trust has worked against the community in their efforts to acquire basic services like light and water. Just to survive takes up most people's energy: they are involved in a constant struggle to find a job for a week or just for a day. The effects of the government's economic policies can be seen in their physical and psychological deterioration: malnutrition, tuberculosis, and other respiratory and intestinal diseases are rampant.

Our congregation, composed of some 80 people, has had a foreign pastor for the past 14 years. I gradually discovered that our missionary presence had caused a dependency that was stifling the development of local leadership. In the past, we have imitated styles of ministry that we imported from the United States or Canada which are totally inappropriate for work among Latin America's poor majorities. These church models are very pastor- or priest-oriented and hamper the development of a more indigenous church.

Over the years, I've had to unlearn many things. I have come to see how those of us coming out of First World experiences often distort the Gospel and use it to legitimatize the status quo. For us Lutherans, for example, the doctrine of "justification by grace," emphasizing faith over works, can lend itself to justifying complacency in the face of world poverty which is reaching astronomical proportions. If our churches do not equip their membership to ask the proper questions and spur them on to do something constructive about it, they are not proclaiming the Gospel adequately.

The Gospel sounds completely different when one reads it with the poor. For them, the good news is not just the promise of a better life in the next world. It is, rather, the achievement in this world of certain minimal rights and opportunities, access to employment and basic social services, real participation in political and economic decision making. Good news for the poor is the ultimate victory in this struggle for a dignified life. Among the poor, the Gospel can become very concrete and speak to very specific situations. For instance, last year Antonio, our 19-year-old guitarist, died of tuberculosis. In this day and age people do not die of TB at the age of 19 in First World countries. "Why does this happen in our community?" we asked ourselves. We as a believing community and I as a pastor could not just console Antonio with the promise of salvation in the next life. We are called in an ongoing, long-term way to do something about a situation that produces malnutrition, sickness, and death. We all know Antonio should not have died; his death serves as a constant challenge to us to change this situation of sin. . . .

What do you see as the tasks and challenges for the Protestant churches in Latin America?

We can fill gaps left by the Catholic Church, which, because of a shortage of priests and personnel, admittedly cannot adequately minister to all. I believe it is a real challenge to the Protestant churches not to move in and create a competitive institution, but in a genuine spirit of ecumenism, fill these gaps in the interest of the growth of a new, Christian community where none was present before.

Both the Catholic and Protestant churches must be willing to commit themselves to the search for new forms of being church as we accompany the poor on their journey. This means leaving behind those experiences of church we have learned in the United States, Canada, or Europe in favor of embracing new experiences that respond to the Latin American reality. It means putting aside preoccupation with being a Lutheran or a Methodist or a Roman Catholic and whatever that might mean in our countries of origin. It means participating in the quest for a kind of church that responds to the social, economic, and cultural realities that will make possible the coming to birth of a new model of being church — neither imposed from above or from outside — but one that is an expression of the people of God in this particular historical place and time.

Epilogue

These chapters illustrate the dimensions of the life and mission of the churches during five hundred years of history. Though the readings are not intended to support a general thesis, one can see several themes recurring. For example, the early Catholic and Protestant leaders brought to Latin America and the Caribbean the strengths and weaknesses of their churches in Europe and North America. They gave widespread support to the colonial system in both its ancient and modern forms; Catholics were reluctant to raise up local leaders for the church, and many Protestant missionaries were slow to trust their national leaders with genuine authority; and both traditions were resistant to a contextualizing of church life in the Latin American milieu. The mutual fears between Catholics and Protestants long prevented ecumenical cooperation.

At the same time, there were strengths. In each period, the church produced some prophets and demonstrated examples of genuine love. Furthermore, the message of the churches—the Gospel story, the invitation to faith, the call for morality, and the importance of worship and the sacraments—won a hearing. Many people responded in more than superficial ways; they responded to God, they established churches and communities of believers, and they went on to think critically about the church and to reform the very vehicles that had brought the witness in the first place.

Due to the weaknesses, and in spite of the strengths, by the 1970s and 1980s Protestants and Catholics found that much of the population needed to be re-evangelized or evangelized for the first time. From the Protestants this was a familiar assessment; but in 1979 the Catholic bishops, with a note of modesty, even confession, called eloquently for region-wide evangelization, for personal faith and also for a just society.[1]

The readings in this anthology illustrate that the Catholic Church long emphasized its hierarchical organization and used the authority of the civil magistrate to pass on the inherited deposit of teachings. However, from Vatican II through the middle 1980s, the bishops had recognized that they had often been co-opted by the strong and influenced by greed. Hence, to promote renewal, they were encouraging the study of the Bible, emphasizing the church's role as a servant, and recognizing the importance of the laity and of social and economic justice.

Simultaneously, though most Protestants continued to emphasize personal conversion, individual morality, and independent congregations, many were also acknowledging that the Kingdom of God extended beyond their various communities. They were also discovering ecumenicity and the need for a unity that was more than spiritual, and many were seeking to add to personal morality a sense of social responsibility.

By the mid 1980s, there had been nearly twenty years of fresh theology and hundreds of martyrs, as well as vigorous debates and amazing innovations. The words of Herbert L. Matthews, cited in the Preface, seemed to be true. Latin America was, indeed, in the midst of "one of the most dramatic and explosive movements in all history . . . comparable in its way . . . to the European Renaissance."[2] In that renewal it seemed obvious that many Christians were full participants.

Notes

Preface

1. Herbert L. Matthews, *The United States and Latin America* (New York: The American Assembly of Columbia University, 1959), p. 188, quoted by Arnold J. Toynbee, *America and the World Revolution: and other Lectures* (New York: Oxford University Press, 1962), p. 205.

Part I

1. The diary was preserved by Bartolomé de Las Casas, *História de las Índias*, quoted in Louis Bertrand and Charles Petrie, *The History of Spain: From the Musulmans to Franco*, 2d ed. (New York: Collier Books, 1971), pp. 163–64.

2. Cedular of Isabella to Ovando, Dec. 20, 1503, *Colección de documentos inéditos relativos al descrubrimento, conquista, y organización de las antiguas posesiones españolas*, ed. Joaquin F. Pacheco, Francisco de Cárdenas, and Luís Torres de Mendoza (Madrid, 1864–1889), 31:209–12, quoted in Lesley Byrd Simpson, *The Encomienda in New Spain: Forced Native Labor in the Spanish Colonies, 1492–1550*, University of California Publications in History, vol. 19 (Berkeley, CA: University of California Press, 1929), pp. 30–31. Excerpted by Benjamin Keen, ed. *Latin American Civilization*, 3d ed. (Atlanta: Houghton Mifflin, 1974), 1:169–70.

3. Bartolomé de las Casas, *History of the Indies*, trans. and ed. Andrée Collard (New York: Harper & Row, 1971), pp. 109–15.

4. Bartolomé de las Casas, *História de las Índias* (Mexico: 1951), 2:441–42. Excerpted and trans. Keen, *Latin American*, 1:170–71.

5. Quoted in Charles R. Boxer, *The Portuguese Seaborne Empire 1415–1825* (New York: Knopf, 1969), p. 85.

6. *The Broken Spears: The Aztec Account of the Conquest of Mexico*, ed. Miguel Leon Portilla, trans. Angel Maria Garibay K. and Lysander Kemp (Boston: Beacon Press, 1962), pp. 58–61.

7. Andrés de Tápia, "Relacción sobre la Conquista de México," in *Colección de Documentos*, ed. García Icazbalceta, 2:586, quoted in Charles S. Braden, *Religious Aspects of the Conquest of Mexico* (Durham, NC: Duke University Press, 1930), pp. 117–18.

8. *The Oroz Codex*, trans. and ed. Angélico Cháves, O.F.M. (Washington, DC: Academy of American Franciscan History, 1972), pp. 354–60.

9. *Letters and People of the Spanish Indies: Sixteenth Century*, trans. and ed. James Lockhart and Enrique Otte (New York: Cambridge University Press, 1976), pp. 213–14.

10. Quoted by German Arciniegas, *Latin America: A Cultural History* (New York: Knopf, 1968), pp. 149–50.

11. Francis Borgia Steck, *Motolinía's History of the Indians of New Spain* (Washington, DC: The Academy of American Franciscan History, 1951), 1:14, 148–49. Quoted by Edwin E. Sylvest, Jr., *Motifs of Franciscan Mission Theory in Sixteenth Century New Spain Province of the Holy Gospel* (Washington, DC: Academy of Franciscan History, 1975), p. 51.

12. "Christianization in Mexico," from Motolinía (Toribio de Benavente), *Motolinía's History of the Indians of New Spain*, trans. Elizabeth A. Foster (Berkeley, CA: Cortés Society, 1950), Documents and Narratives Concerning the Discovery and Conquest of Latin America, n.s., 4:124–25, 127–28, quoted by Fredrick B. Pike, ed., *Latin American History: Selected Problems — Identity, Integration, and Nationhood* (New York: Harcourt, Brace & World, 1969), pp. 76–79.

13. Fray Thomás de la Torre, *Desde Salamanca España, hasta Ciudad Real, Chiapas, Diario del viaje 1544–1545*, ed. by Frans Blom (Mexico, 1945), pp. 70–73. Excerpted and trans. Keen, *Latin American*, 1:200–202.

14. Lockhart and Otte, *Letters and People*, pp. 216–17.

15. "Carta del arzobispo al Consejo Real," *Colección de Documentos Inéditos*, 4:494–99, excerpted and trans. Charles S. Braden, *Religious Aspects of the Conquest of Mexico* (Durham, NC: Duke University Press, 1930), pp. 247–49.

16. From *Nueva Colección do Documentos*, ed. García Icazbalceta, 1:4, excerpted and trans. Braden, *Religious Aspects*, p. 249.

17. From Emma Helen Blair and James Alexander Robertson, *The Philippine Islands, 1493–1898* (Cleveland, OH: Arthur H. Clark Co., 1903–1909), 21:19–31. Quoted in N. Andrew N. Cleven, *Readings in Hispanic American History* (Boston: Ginn, 1927), pp. 250–51, 254–56, 258.

18. Miles Philips, "The Voyages of Miles Philips. . . ," in *The Principal Navigations, Voyages, Traffiques, and Discoveries of the English Nation*, ed. Richard Hakluyt (London: n.d.), 6:318–23, quoted in Keen, *Latin American*, pp. 200–202.

19. Lockhart and Otte, *Letters and People*, pp. 254–55.

20. António Vasquez de Espinosa, *Compendium and Description of the Indies, c. 1620*, trans. Charles Upson Clark (Washington, DC: Smithsonian Institution Press, 1942), pp. 157–59, 161–62.

21. Clarence Haring, "The Wealth of the Church," in *The Roman Catholic Church in Colonial Latin America*, ed. Richard E. Greenleaf (New York: Knopf, 1971), p. 178.

22. Felipe Huaman Poma de Ayala, *Letter to a King: A Peruvian Chief's Account of Life Under the Incas and Under Spanish Rule*, ed. and trans. Christopher Dilke (New York: E. P. Dutton, 1978), pp. 144–47, 149, 152, 155, 158, 160–61, 167, 169, 186.

23. Vásquez de Espinosa, *Description of the West Indies*, trans. C. V. Clark, pp. 444–46, quoted in Keen, *Latin American*, 1:306–8.

24. *A Documentary History of Brazil*, ed. E. Bradford Burns (New York: Knopf, 1966), pp. 61–64.

25. *Cartas, Informações, Fragmentos Históricos e Sermões do Padre José de Anchieta, S.J. (1554–1594)* (Rio de Janeiro, 1933), pp. 377–78, quoted in Keen, *Latin American*, 1:348–50.

26. *Thomas Gage's Travels in the New World*, ed. J. Eric S. Thompson (Norman, OK: University of Oklahoma Press, 1958), pp. 71–72.

27. *Fray Alonso de Benavides' Revised Memorial of 1643...*, trans. and ed. Frederick Webb Hodge, George P. Hammond, and Agapito Ray (Albuquerque, NM: University of New Mexico Press, 1945), pp. 100–103. Quoted by John Tracy Ellis, ed., *Documents of American Catholic History* (Milwaukee, WI: Bruce Publishing Co., 1962), 16–17.

28. In the Archivo General de las Índias (Quito 10), located in Seville, Spain. Quoted in Nicholas P. Cushner, *Farm and Factory: The Jesuits and the Development of Agrarian Capitalism in Colonial Quito, 1600–1767* (Albany: State University of New York Press, 1982), p. 185.

29. Thompson, *Thomas Gage's*, pp. 257–61.

30. Fr. Diego de Cordova Salinas, O.F.M., *Crónica Franciscana de las Provincias del Peru (1651)* (Washington, DC: Academy of American Franciscan History, 1957), pp. 949–52, quoted in Asunción Lavrin, "Women and Religion in Spanish America," *Women and Religion in America*, ed. Rosemary R. Ruether and Rosemary Skinner (New York: Harper and Row, 1983), 2:58–60.

31. *The Golden Land: An Anthology of Latin American Folklore in Literature*, trans. and ed. Harriet De Onis (New York: Knopf, 1948), pp. 72–79. I have abridged the Text of De Onis.

32. From James H. Carmichael, Jr., "Balsalobre on Idolatry in Oaxaca," *Boletin del Instituto de Estudios Oaxaqueños*, 13 (1959):1–12, quoted by James H. Carmichael, "Recurrent Idolatry and Religious Syncretism," in *The Roman Catholic Church in Colonial Latin America*, ed. Richard J. Greenleaf (New York: Knopf, 1971), pp. 140–47.

33. Sor Juana, *Carta atenagórica, Respuesta a Sor Filotea*, ed. E. Abreu Gomez (Mexico, 1934), pp. 54–58, 66–70. Trans. Keen, *Latin American*, 1:309–13.

34. From *The Bandeirantes*, trans. and ed. Richard M. Morse (New York: Knopf, 1965), 82–91, quoted in *The Borzoi Anthology of Latin American Literature: From the Time of Columbus to the Twentieth Century*, ed. Emir Rodrigues Monegal (New York: Knopf, 1977), 1:123–29.

35. *Vieira Brasileiro*, ed. Afranio Peixoto (Paris: Ailland et Bertrand, 1921), 1:203–21. Excerpted and trans. Burns, *A Documentary*, pp. 83–88.

36. Andre João Antonil (João António Andreoni), *Cultura e Opulencia do Brasil por Suas Drogas e Minas*, ed Affonso de E. Tauny (São Paulo, 1923), pp. 77–83, 91–102. Excerpted and trans. Keen, *Latin American*, 1:376–77.

37. *Atas da Câmara de Bahía*, 5 (1669–1684), pp. 114–15. Quoted in C. R. Boxer, *Portuguese Society in the Tropics: The Municipal Councils of Goa, Macao, Bahía, and Luanda, 1510–1800* (Madison, WI: University of Wisconsin Press, 1965), pp. 181–82.

38. Haring, "The Wealth of the Church," p. 179.

39. Ibid, p. 180.

40. J. Lloyd Mecham, *Church and State in Latin America: A History of Politico-Ecclesiastical Relations*, rev. ed. (Chapel Hill, NC: University of North Carolina Press, 1966), p. 38.

41. Boxer, *Portuguese Seaborne*, p. 199.

42. Hubert Herring, *A History of Latin America*, 3d. ed. (New York: Knopf, 1968), p. 231. Eduardo Hoornaert et al, *História da Igreja no Brasil: Ensaio de interpretação a partir do Povo; Primeira Época* (Petropolis, Brazil: Vozes, 1977), p. 281.

43. Jorge Juan and António de Ulloa, *A Voyage to South America*, trans. and ed.

by John Adams with introduction by Irving A. Leonard (Tempe, AZ: Center for Latin American Studies, Arizona State University, 1975), pp. 129–30.

44. Joséph Och, S.J., *Missionary in Sonora: The Travel Reports of Joséph Och, S.J., 1755–1767*, trans. and ed. Theodore E. Treutlein (San Francisco: California Historical Society, 1965), pp. 124–25, 128–30.

45. Och, *Missionary*, pp. 49–53, 57–58, 62–69.

46. "Relación del Exemo. Sr. de Guirior," in *Relaciones de los Virreyes del Nuevo Reino de Granada*, ed. José António García y García (New York, 1867). Excerpted and trans. Keen, *Latin American*, 1:314–15.

47. Felix de Azara, *Descripción y história del Paraguay y del Rio de la Plata* (Asuncion, Paraguay, 1896), 1:338–52. Excerpted and trans. Keen, *Latin American*, 1:270–73.

48. Manuscript is in archives of Academy of American Franciscan History, Washington, DC, quoted in Ellis, *Documents*, pp. 34, 43–45.

49. Alexander von Humboldt, *Political Essays on the Kingdom of New Spain*, trans. and ed. John Black (New York: I. Riley, 1811), 1:171–75.

50. Alexander von Humboldt and Aime Bonpland, *Personal Narrative of Travels to the Equinoctial Regions of America During the Years 1799–1804*, trans. and ed. Thomasina Ross (London: George Bell & Sons, 1881), 1:201–2, 218–19, 245–46, 252, 297.

51. William Bennett Stevenson, *Historical and Descriptive Narrative of Twenty Years' Residence in South America* (London: Hurst, Robinson and Co., 1825), 1:237–39, 241–42.

52. Amedée F. Frezier, *A Voyage to the South Sea . . . 1712–1713, and 1715* (London: J. Bowayer, 1717), excerpted in *Colonial Travelers in Latin America*, ed. Irving G. A. Leonard (New York: Knopf, 1972), pp. 176–79.

Part II

1. E. Bradford Burns, *Latin America: A Concise Interpretive History* (Englewood Cliffs, NJ: Prentice-Hall, 1972), p. 103. Michael P. Costeloe, *Church Wealth in Mexico* (Cambridge: Cambridge University Press, 1967), p. 2. J. Lloyd Mecham, *Church and State in Latin America* (Chapel Hill, NC: University of North Carolina Press, 1966), p. 39.

2. William Bennett Stevenson, *Historical and Descriptive Narrative of Twenty Years' Residence in South America* (London: Hurst, Robinson & Co., 1825), 1:261–74.

3. "A Governor's Report on Texas in 1890," trans. and ed. Nettie Lee Benson, *Southwestern Historical Quarterly* 71 (April 1968): p. 614.

4. Henry Koster, *Travels in Brazil* (London: Longman, Hurst, Rees, Orme and Brown, 1816), pp. 249–50.

5. Ibid., pp. 264–65.

6. Ibid., pp. 408–12.

7. Maria Dundas Graham, *Journal of a Voyage to Brazil and Residence There During Part of the Years 1821, 1822, 1823* (London: Longman, Hurst, Rees, Orme, Brown, and Green, 1824), pp. 271–72.

8. Arquivo Nacionál (Rio de Janeiro), Ministério de Império, Relatórios das Províncias, Ceará, 1839–1843, "Relatória que apresentou o Exmo. Senhor Doutor

Francisco de Sousa Martíns, Presidente desta Província, na occasião da abertura da Assembléa Legislativa Provinciál, no dia 1 de agosto de 1840," pp. 4ff., quoted by George C. A. Boeher, "The Church in the Second Reign, 1840–89, and Commentary," in *Conflict and Continuity in Brazilian Society*, ed. Henry H. Keith and S. F. Edwards (Columbia, SC: University of South Carolina Press, 1969), p. 118.

9. Henry George Ward, *Mexico in 1827* (London: H. Colburn, 1828), 1:326–28, 333–38.

10. Captain W. F. Beechy, *Narrative of a Voyage to the Pacific and Beering's Strait* (London: 1831), 2:10–23, quoted in *A Documentary History of the Mexican Americans*, ed. Wayne Moquin and Charles van Doren (New York: Praeger Publishers, 1971), pp. 131–35.

11. John Anthony King, *Twenty-four Years in the Argentine Republic* (London: Longman, Brown, Green, and Longmans, 1846), pp. 148–55.

12. Fanny Calderón de la Barca, *Life in Mexico: The Letters of Fanny Calderón de la Barca*, ed. Howard T. Fisher and Marion Hall Fisher (New York: Doubleday, 1966), pp. 205–8.

13. Ibid., pp. 260–63.

14. John L. Stephens, *Incidents of Travel in Central America, Chiapas and Yucatán* (New York: Harper and Brothers, 1841), 2:209–14.

15. Robert Walsh, *Notices of Brazil in 1828 and 1829* (Boston: Richardson, Lord, and Holbrook et al., 1831), 2:201–3.

16. Ibid, 2:203.

17. Ibid., 2:203–4.

18. Robert Walsh, *Notices of Brazil in 1828 and 1829* (London: Fredrick Westley & A. H. Davis, 1830), 1:271–73.

19. Daniel P. Kidder, *Sketches of Residence and Travel in Brazil* (London: Wiley and Putnam, 1845), 2:79–82.

20. Thomas Ewbank, *Life in Brazil, or A Journal of a Visit to the Land of the Cocoa and the Palm* (New York: Harper and Brothers, 1856), pp. 212–14.

21. Janet Schaw, *Journal of a Lady of Quality: Being the Narrative of a Journey from Scotland to the West Indies, North Carolina, and Portugal in the Years 1774–1776*, ed. Evangeline Walker Andrews and Charles McLean Andrews (New Haven: Yale University Press, 1939), pp. 92–95, 129–30.

22. James Thomson, *Letters on the Moral and Religious State of South America* (London: James Nisbitt, 1827), pp. 14, 16–18, 20–21, 33–36, 110–12.

23. John C. Brigham, "Mr. Brigham's Report Respecting the Religious State of Spanish America. To the Prudential Committee of the American Board of Commissioners for Foreign Missions," *Missionary Herald* 22 (October 1826): 297–302; (November 1826): 337–44.

24. Walsh, *Notices of Brazil*, 2:180–82, 184–85.

25. Daniel P. Kidder and James C. Fletcher, *Brazil and the Brazilians, Portrayed in Historical and Descriptive Sketches*, 7th ed., rev. (Boston: Little, Brown, 1867: repr., New York: AMS Press, 1973), pp. 255–57.

26. Isaac Farwell Holton, *New Granada: Twenty Months in the Andes* (New York: Harper and Brothers, 1857; repr., Carbondale, IL: Southern Illinois University, 1967), pp. 476–79.

27. Kidder and Fletcher, *Brazil*, pp. 146–47.

28. Ibid., pp. 438, 440–41.

29. Richard Henry Dana, Jr., *To Cuba and Back: A Vacation Voyage* (Boston: Ticknor and Fields, 1859), pp. 179–81, 183–85.

30. Louis J. R. Agassiz and Elizabeth C. Agassiz, *A Journey in Brazil* (Boston: Ticknor and Fields, 1869), pp. 495–97.

31. Esteban Montejo, *Autobiography of a Runaway Slave*, ed. Miguel Barnet, trans. Jocasta Innes (New York: Vintage Books, 1973), pp. 34, 36–37, 84–86, 100–102.

32. Alice Brant, *The Diary of "Helena Morley,"* trans. Elizabeth Bishop (New York: Farrar, Straus, and Cudahy, 1957), pp. 20–22, 278–80.

33. *Memoirs of Pancho Villa*, ed. Martin Luís Guzman, trans. Virginia H. Taylor (Austin, TX: University of Texas Press, 1965), pp. 284–86, 389.

34. Ricardo Rojas, *The Invisible Christ*, trans. Webster E. Browning (New York: Abingdon, 1931), pp. 237–39, 244–46.

35. William R. Read, Victor M. Monteroso, Harmon A. Johnson, *Latin American Church Growth* (Grand Rapids, MI: Eerdmans, 1969), p. 36.

36. *South American Missionary Magazine* 1 (1867): 97–100, quoted in Wenceslao O. Bahamonde, "The Establishment of Evangelical Christianity in Peru, 1822–1900" (Ph.D. diss., Hartford Seminary Foundation, 1952), pp. 66–68.

37. "Miss Rankin's Work in Mexico," *The Missionary Herald* 69 (1873): 140–41.

38. Anthony Graybill, "Letters from the Missions: Linares," *The Missionary* 21 (1888): 67–68.

39. Hugh C. Tucker, *The Bible in Brazil: Colporter Experiences* (New York: Fleming H. Revell, 1902), pp. 91–92, 281–82.

40. Ibid., pp. 284–86.

41. D. B. Grubb, "Indians of South America," *Ecumenical Missionary Conference, New York, 1900: Report on the Ecumenical Conference on Foreign Missions* (New York: American Tract Society, 1900), 1:480–82.

42. Quoted in Walter J. Hollenweger, *The Pentecostals: The Charismatic Movement in the Churches* (Minneapolis, MN: Augsburg, 1972), pp. 76–77.

43. Robert E. Speer, "Survey of Present Mission Work," *Conference on Missions in Latin America, 156 Fifth Avenue, New York, March 12 and 13, 1913*, ed. Committee of Reference and Counsel of the Foreign Missions Conference of North America (New York: Foreign Missions Conference of North America, 1913), pp. 15–16.

44. Carrie Carnahan, "Woman's Work in Latin Lands," *Conference on Missions*, ed. Committee of Reference, pp. 124–25.

45. Emile Leonard, "O Protestantismo Brasileiro," *Revista de História* 2 (1951): 424–28, quoted in Emilio Willems, *Followers of the New Faith: Culture Change and the Rise of Protestantism in Brazil and Chile* (Nashville, TN: Vanderbilt University Press, 1967), pp. 107–8.

46. William J. Coleman, M.M., *Latin-American Catholicism: A Self-Evaluation*, World Horizon Reports, No. 23 (Maryknoll, NY: Maryknoll Publications, 1958), pp. 20, 23.

47. Charles Wagley, "The Social and Religious Life of a Guatemalan Village," *American Anthropologist*, 51 (October 1949): 50.

48. Graham Greene, *Another Mexico* (New York: Viking Press, 1939), pp. 144–46, 211–14.

49. Oscar Lewis, *Life in a Mexican Village: Tepoztlán Restudied* (Urbana, IL: University of Illinois Press, 1951), pp. 273–75.

50. Marvin Harris, *Town and Country in Brazil* (New York: W. W. Norton, 1956), pp. 211–14, 219, 221–24, 241.

51. Leslie Dewart, *Christianity and Revolution: The Lesson of Cuba* (New York: Herder & Herder, 1964), pp. 95–98.

52. Juan Domingo Perón, "A Denunciation of Certain Argentine Churchmen," in *Conflict Between Church and State in Latin America*, ed. Fredrick B. Pike (New York: Knopf, 1964), pp. 184–85.

53. Carolina Maria de Jesus, *Child of the Dark: The Diary of Carolina Maria de Jesus*, trans. David St. Clair (New York: E. P. Dutton, 1962), pp. 3, 87–89, 92, 105–8, 131, 143–45.

54. Francisco Julião, *Cambão — The Yoke: The Hidden Face of Brazil* (Harmondsworth, England: Penguin, 1972), pp. 148–52.

55. W. Stanley Rycroft, *Religion and Faith in Latin America* (Philadelphia: Westminster Press, 1958), p. 159. Kenneth Scott Latourette, *The Twentieth Century Outside of Europe: The Americas, the Pacific, Asia, and Africa: The Emerging World Christian Community*, vol. 5, *Christianity in a Revolutionary Age: A History of Christianity in the Nineteenth and Twentieth Centuries* (New York: Harper and Row, 1962), p. 168.

56. Latourette, *Twentieth Century Outside of Europe*, p. 169.

57. "West Brazil," in "Annual Report of the Executive Committee of Foreign Missions," *Minutes of the Seventy-Third General Assembly of the Presbyterian Church in the United States with an Appendix, A.D. 1933* (Richmond, VA: Presbyterian Committee on Publication, 1933), pp. 10–11. Annual Reports are in Appendix and pagination is separate for each one.

58. J. Merle Davis, *The Economic Basis of the Evangelical Church in Mexico: A Study Made by the Department of Social and Economic Research of the International Missionary Council* (New York: International Missionary Council, 1940), pp. 45–47.

59. Charles Bennett, *Tinder in Tabasco: A Study of Church Growth in Tropical Mexico* (Grand Rapids, MI: Eerdmans, 1968), pp. 123–26.

60. Quoted by Russell T. Hitt, *Jungle Pilot: The Life and Witness of Nate Saint* (New York: Harper and Brothers, 1959), pp. 182–85.

61. Rubem Alves and Richard Shaull, "The Devotional Life of Brazilian Protestantism," *The Student World* 49 (1956): 360–66.

62. Willems, *Followers of the New Faith*, pp. 126–29.

63. R. Kenneth Strachan, "Introduction," *Evangelism-in-Depth: Experimenting with a New Type of Evangelism*, by Latin American Mission (Chicago: Moody Press, 1961), pp. 7–10.

Part III

1. "Peace," *The Church in the Present-day Transformation of Latin America in the Light of the Council*, ed. Louis Michael Colonnese (Bogotá, Colombia: United States Catholic Conference and the General Secretariat of CELAM, 1970), 2:72–78.

2. "Pastoral Concern for the Elites," Colonnese, *Church in the Present-day*, 2:135.

3. "Pastoral Concern for the Masses," Colonnese, *Church in the Present-day*, 2:124.

4. "Peace," Colonnese, *Church in the Present-day*, 2:81.

5. Ivan Illich, "The Seamy Side of Charity," *America: A Catholic Review of the Week*, 116 (21 January 1967): 88–91.

6. C. A. Libanio Christo, *Against Principalities and Powers: Letters from a Brazilian Jail*, trans. John Drury (Maryknoll, NY: Orbis Books, 1977), pp. 7, 24, 26, 135–7, 180–2.

7. Nestor Paz, *My Life for My Friends: The Guerrilla Journal of Nestor Paz, Christian*, trans. and ed. by Ed García and John Eagleson (Maryknoll, NY: Orbis Books, 1975), pp. 21–25.

8. Pedro Casaldáliga, *I Believe in Justice and Hope*, trans. Joséph C. Daries (Notre Dame, IN: Fides/Claretin, 1978), pp. 60–61, 65–67.

9. Alfredo Kunz, "A Story of the Progress of the Small Church of Marroas," *International Review of Missions* 68 (July 1979): 268–69.

10. *The Gospel in Solentiname*, ed. Ernesto Cárdenal, trans. Donald D. Walsh (Maryknoll, NY: Orbis Books, 1976), 1:106–10.

11. Sheila Cassidy, *Audacity to Believe: An Autobiography* (Cleveland, OH: William Collins and World Publishing, 1978), pp. 191–94.

12. Pedro Casaldáliga, "Letter," *International Review of Missions*, 66 (July 1977): 263–65.

13. June H. Turner, ed., "About the Author (Ana Audilia Moreira de Campos [El Salvador])", *Latin American Woman: The Meek Speak Out,* (Silver Spring, MD: International Development, Inc., 1980), p. 65, and footnote p. 71.

14. Ana Audilia Moreira de Campos, "Our National Inferiority Complex: A Cause for Violence?" in *Latin American Woman*, ed. Turner, pp. 66–72.

15. Henri J. M. Nouwen, *Gracias! A Latin American Journal* (New York: Harper and Row, 1983), pp. 169–72.

16. *World Christian Encyclopedia: A comparative study of churches and religions in the modern world: AD 1900–2000*, ed. David B. Barrett (Nairobi: Oxford, 1982), p. 783.

17. Ibid., pp. 226, 186, 487, 240, 522, and 339.

18. Orlando E. Costas, *Theology of the Crossroads in Contemporary Latin America: Missiology in Mainline Protestantism* (Amsterdam: Rodopi N.V., 1976), pp. 40–48.

19. Anthony Christopher Smith, "The Essentials of Missiology from the Evangelical Perspective of the 'Fraternidad Teológica Latinoamericana'" (Ph.D. diss., Southern Baptist Theological Seminary, 1983), pp. 3, 12–13.

20. William L. Wonderly and Jorge Lara-Braud, "Some Convictions of a Young Church," *Practical Anthropology* 14 (January-February 1967): 12–13.

21. Harding Meyer, "Die Pfingstbewegung in Brasilien," *Die Evangelishe Diaspora: Jahrbuch des Gustav-Adolf-Vereins*, 39 (1968), 43f., translated and quoted in W. J. Hollenweger, *The Pentecostals* (Minneapolis, MN: Augsburg, 1972), pp. 100–101.

22. Joaquin Andrade, "Protestant Ministers in the Canefields," trans. LADOC-U.S. Catholic Conference and quoted in Alice L. Hageman and Philip E. Wheaton, eds., *Religion in Cuba Today: A New Church in a New Society* (New York: Association Press, 1971), pp. 48–55. Reprinted from *Cuba International* (Havana), August 1970.

23. Manuel de Melo, "Participation is Everything," *International Review of Missions*, trans. World Council of Churches Translation Section 60 (April 1971): 246–48.

24. Victor E. W. Hayward, "An Ecumenical Bird's Eye View," *International Review of Missions*, 60 (April 1971): 161, 165–68, 179–84.

25. June H. Turner, ed., "About the Author (Francisca Ramirez [Honduras])", *Latin American Woman*, p. 103.

26. Francisca Ramirez, "It All Depends on the Teacher," in *Latin American Woman*, ed., Turner, pp. 105–107.

27. William Howard et al., "An Epistle to the Believing Communities in the United States," *International Review of Missions*, 71 (January 1982): 93–95.

28. Troy Beretta, "Lutheran Missionary in Peru: Option for Poor Key to Grassroots Ecumenism," interview by Latinamerica Press, *Latinamerica Press* (The English Language Publication of *Notícias Aliadas*) 15 (10 November 1983): 5–6.

Epilogue

1. *Puebla and Beyond; Documentation and Commentary*, ed. John Eagleson and Philip Sharper. Trans. John Drury (Maryknoll, NY: Orbis Books, 1979), pp. 123–285.

2. Herbert L. Matthews, *The United States and Latin America* (New York: The American Assembly of Columbia University, 1959), p. 188; quoted by Arnold J. Toynbee, *America and the World Revolution: and other Lectures* (New York: Oxford University Press, 1962), p. 205.

Index

Permissions

Grateful acknowledgement is given for permission to reprint the following:

Excerpts from *The Oroz Codex*, Angelico Chaves, trans. and ed. (1972); *Motolonia's History of the Indians of New Spain*, by Francis Borgia Steck (1951); *Motifs of Franciscan Mission Theory in Sixteenth Century New Spain Province of the Holy Gospel*, Edwin E. Sylvest, Jr. (1975); *Cronica Franciscana de las Provincias del Peru (1651)*, by Fr. Diego do Cordova Salinas (1957); and *Documents of American Catholic History*, John Tracy Ellis, ed. (1962), used by permission of the Academy of American Franciscan History.

Excerpts from "The Seamy Side of Charity," by Ivan Illich, *America* 116 (January 21, 1967). Used by permission of *America*.

Excerpts from "The Social and Religious Life of a Guatemalan Village" in "Memoirs of the American Anthropological Association" No. 71, 1949. Used by permission of the Association.

Excerpts from "Some Convictions of a Young Church," by William L. Wonderly and Jorge Lara-Braud, *Practical Anthropology* 14 (January-February 1967). Used by permission of the American Society of Missiology.

Excerpts from *A Voyage to South America*, by Jorge and Antonio de Ulloa, John Adams, ed. and trans. (Arizona State University, 1975). Used by permission of the publisher.

Excerpts from *The Broken Spears*, by Miguel Leon-Portilla, copyright © 1962 by Beacon Press. Reprinted by permission of the Beacon Press.

Excerpts from *A Documentary History of Brazil*, E. Bradford Page Burns, ed. (Alfred A. Knopf, 1966). Used by permission of the editor.

Excerpts from *Letters and People of the Spanish Indies*, James Lockhart and Enrique Otte, eds. (Cambridge University Press, 1976), copyright © 1976 by Cambridge University Press. Reprinted with the permission of the publisher.

Excerpts from *Missionary in Sonora*, by Joseph Och, S.J. (California Historical Society, 1965). Used by permission of the Society.

Excerpts from "I Believe in Justice and Hope," published by Claretian Publications (Claretian Fides Publications), 205 W. Monroe Street, Chicago, Illinois 60605, reprinted with permission of the publisher.

Excerpts from *The Philippine Islands, 1493-1898*, by Emma Helen Blair and James Alexander Robertson (Arthur H. Clark Co., 1903). Used by permission of the publisher.

mentary History of Brazil, by E. Bradford Burns (1966); *The Golden Land*, Harriet De Onis, trans. and ed. (1948); *The Roman Catholic Church in Colonial Latin America*, Richard J. Greenleaf, ed.(1971); *The Borzoi Anthology of Latin American Literature*, Emir Rodrigues Monegal, ed. (1977); and *Colonial Travelers in Latin America*, Irving G. A. Leonard, ed. (1972), all published and used by permission of Alfred A. Knopf.

Excerpts from "Lutheran Missionary in Peru," by Tony Beretta, *Latinamerica Press* 15 (November 10, 1983). Used by permission of the publisher.

Excerpts from *Life in a Mexican Village*, by Oscar Lewis (University of Illinois Press, 1951). Used by permission of Ruth M. Lewis.

Excerpts from *Against Principalities and Powers*, by Carlos Libanio Christo (Orbis Books, 1977). Used by permission of Lutterworth Press.

Excerpts from the Introduction, by R. Kenneth Strachan, to *Evangelism-in-Depth*, by Latin American Mission (Moody Press, 1961). Used by permission of Moody Press.

Excerpts from *The Bandeirantes*, Richard M. Morse, ed. and trans. (Alfred A. Knopf, 1965). Used by permission of Richard A. Morse.

Excerpts from *Conflict Between Church and State in Latin America*, Fredrick B. Pike, ed. (Alfred A.Knopf, 1964). Used by permission of the editor.

Excerpts from Captain W.F. Beechy, "Narrative of a Voyage to the Pacific and Beering's Strait" (London: 1831), 2:10-23, quoted in *A Doumentary History of the Mexican Americans*, Wayne Moquin and Charles van Doren, eds. (Praeger Publishers, NY, 1971), 130-36. Reprinted with permission of Praeger Publishers, a division of Greenwood Press, Inc.

Excerpts from "West Brazil" in the Annual Report of the Executive Committee of Foreign Missions in *Minutes of the Seventy-Third Assembly of the Presbyterian Church in the United States with Appendix, A.D. 1933*. Used by permission of the Office of the General Assembly, Presbyterian Church (USA).

Excerpts from *The Gospel in Solentiname*, Ernesto Cardenal, ed., Donald D. Walsh, trans. (Orbis Books, 1976). Used by permission of Ediciones Sigueme, Burns & Oates, Ltd., and Orbis Books.

Material reprinted by permission of the Smithsonian Institution Press from *Description of the Indies (c. 1620)*, by Antonio Vazquez de Espinosa, translated by Charles Upson Clark, Smithsonian Institution Press, 1968, pp. 157-59, 161-62.

Excerpts from *Farm and Factory* by Nicholas P. Cushner (SUNY Press, 1982) reprinted by permission of State University of New York Press.

Excerpts from "A Governor's Report on Texas in 1890," Nettie Lee Benson, ed. and trans., in *Southwestern Historical Quarterly* 71 (April 1968). Used by permission of Texas State Historical Association.

Excerpts from *Latin American Woman: The Meek Speak Out*, edited and compiled by June H. Turner, are reprinted by permission of June Haney Turner and International Educational Development, Inc., copyright © 1980.

Excerpts from "Protestant Ministers in the Canefields," by Joaquin Andrade, reprinted from *Cuba Internacional* (Havana) (August 1970), LADOC-U.S. Catholic